Microsoft®
VISUAL BASIC® 2012

for Windows® and Mobile Applications
Introductory

Corinne Hoisington

Central Virginia Community College

CENGAGE
Learning®

SHELLY
CASHMAN
SERIES®

Australia • Brazil • Japan • Korea • Mexico • Singapore • Spain • United Kingdom • United States

CENGAGE
Learning·

**Microsoft® Visual Basic® 2012 for Windows®
and Mobile Applications: Introductory**
Corinne Hoisington

Vice President, General Manager:
  Dawn Germain

Senior Product Team Manager:
  Kathleen McMahon

Senior Product Manager: Jim Gish

Senior Content Developer: Alyssa Pratt

Product Assistant: Sarah Timm

Rights Acquisition Specialist: Christine
  Myaskovsky

Manufacturing Planner: Julio Esperas

Content Project Manager:
  Jennifer Feltri-George

Development Editor: Lisa Ruffolo

Copyeditor: Michael Beckett

Proofreader: Kim Kosmatka

Indexer: Sharon Hilgenberg

QA Manuscript Reviewer: Serge Palladino

Art Director: Cheryl Pearl, GEX

Cover Designer: Lisa Kuhn, Curio Press, LLC

Cover Photo: Tom Kates Photography

Text Designer: Joel Sadagursky

Compositor: PreMediaGlobal

For product information and technology assistance, contact us at
Cengage Learning Customer & Sales Support, www.cengage.com/support

For permission to use material from this text or product,
submit all requests online at **cengage.com/permissions**
Further permissions questions can be emailed to
permissionrequest@cengage.com

Library of Congress Control Number: 2013941329

ISBN-13: 978-1-285-19799-9
ISBN-10: 1-285-19799-2

Cengage Learning
200 First Stamford Place, 4th Floor
Stamford, CT 06902
USA

Cengage Learning is a leading provider of customized learning solutions with
office locations around the globe, including Singapore, the United Kingdom,
Australia, Mexico, Brazil, and Japan. Locate your local office at:
international.cengage.com/region

Cengage Learning products are represented in Canada by Nelson Education, Ltd.

To learn more about Cengage Learning, visit **www.cengage.com**

Purchase any of our products at your local college bookstore or at our
preferred online store at **www.cengagebrain.com**

Printed in the United States of America
1 2 3 4 5 6 7 19 18 17 16 15 14 13

CONTENTS

PREFACE

The Shelly Cashman Series® offers the finest textbooks in computer education. This *Microsoft Visual Basic 2012* book utilizes an innovative step-by-step pedagogy, which integrates demonstrations of professional-quality programs with in-depth discussions of programming concepts and techniques and opportunities for hands-on practice and reinforcement. The popular Guided Program Development section supports students as they work independently to create useful, realistic, and appealing applications, building their confidence and skills while guiding them to select appropriate Visual Basic 2012 programming methods. Online Reinforcement boxes direct students to online videos that show how to perform a series of steps. Other marginal elements, such as In the Real World boxes, provide expert tips to add interest and depth to topics. A robust and varied collection of exercises, including a series of practical case-based programming projects, ensures students gain the knowledge and expertise they need to succeed when developing professional programs.

Visual Basic 2012 builds on the features of Visual Basic 2010, which emphasized coding once and deploying on multiple devices. Some of the major enhancements to Visual Basic 2012 include enhanced code editing, a robust collection of online samples, an improved interface that makes it easier to access frequently used files, and more efficient build management. Using Visual Basic 2012, you can design, create, and deploy Windows, Mobile, Web, Database, Office, and Windows Store applications. Visual Studio 2012 includes several productivity enhancements including debugging tools, more powerful searching tools, Windows Store sample applications, and more.

Objectives of this Textbook

Microsoft Visual Basic 2012 for Windows and Mobile Applications: Introductory is intended for a one-credit course that introduces students to the correct ways to design and write programs using Visual Basic 2012. The goal of this text is to provide an introductory-level course in computer programming for students with little or no previous programming experience. The objectives of this book are:

* To teach the fundamentals of the Microsoft Visual Basic 2012 programming language
* To understand and apply graphical user interface design principles
* To emphasize the development cycle when creating applications, which mirrors the same approach that professional developers use
* To illustrate well-written and readable programs using a disciplined coding style, including documentation and indentation standards
* To create Visual Basic applications that deploy on multiple platforms such as mobile computers, Web pages, and Windows Office environments
* To demonstrate how to implement logic involving sequence, selection, and repetition using Visual Basic 2012

- To write useful, well-designed programs for personal computers and mobile computers that solve practical business problems
- To encourage independent study and help those who are working on their own in a distance education environment

The Shelly Cashman Approach

Features of this *Microsoft Visual Basic 2012* book include:

- **Realistic, Up-to-Date Applications** Each programming chapter focuses on building a sample project, a complete, useful application that showcases Visual Basic 2012 features and the latest technology.
- **Guided Steps to Encourage Independence** After observing how a professional developer would build the chapter project and exploring related programming concepts and Visual Basic 2012 techniques, students create the sample application on their own in the Guided Program Development section. This step-by-step section provides enough guidance for students to work independently, with Hint Screens that verify students are performing the tasks correctly.
- **More Than Step-By-Step** Each chapter offers clear, thorough discussions of the programming concepts students need to understand to build the sample application. Important Visual Basic 2012 design and programming features are also highlighted, including time-saving techniques such as using IntelliSense, code snippets, and the Toolbox. As appropriate, students design and prepare for applications the way professional developers do — by creating or analyzing requirements documents, use case definitions, and event planning documents.
- **Online Reinforcement Boxes** The Online Reinforcement boxes send students to the Student Companion site at CengageBrain.com to watch videos illustrating each step in the chapter project. Students can refer to the Online Reinforcement boxes when they work through or review the chapter, watching videos as they prepare to create the chapter application on their own.
- **Heads Up Boxes** Heads Up boxes appear in the margin to give advice for following best programming practices and tips about alternative ways of completing the same task.
- **In the Real World Boxes** This marginal feature provides insight into how developers use Visual Basic tools or programming techniques to save time or enhance professional development projects.
- **Watch Out For Boxes** These boxes explain how to avoid common pitfalls when using a particular command, programming structure, or technique.
- **Consider This Boxes:** This element encourages critical thinking and independent problem solving by posing thought-provoking questions and providing answers related to programming and Visual Basic.

Organization of this Textbook

Microsoft Visual Basic 2012 for Windows and Mobile Applications: Introductory provides detailed instructions on how to use Visual Basic 2012 to build authentic, effective, and appealing applications for Microsoft Windows personal computers and mobile devices. The material is divided into six chapters and three appendices as follows:

Chapter 1 — Introduction to Visual Basic 2012 Programming Chapter 1 provides an overview of programming with Visual Basic 2012. The chapter defines a computer program, describes the role of a developer in creating computer programs, and discusses event-driven programs that have a graphical user interface (GUI). The chapter also explains the roles of input, processing, output, and data when running a program on a computer; examines the basic arithmetic and logical operations a program can perform; and explores the use of databases and computer programming languages in general. Finally, the chapter introduces Visual Studio 2012 and the .NET 4.5 Framework, including the .NET class libraries and related features, and surveys the types of Visual Basic 2012 applications.

Chapter 2 — Program and Graphical User Interface Design Chapter 2 introduces students to the major elements of the Visual Studio 2012 integrated development environment (IDE) while designing a graphical user interface mock-up. Topics include opening Visual Studio 2012, creating a Windows Forms Application project, adding objects to a Windows form, assigning properties to objects, aligning objects on the Windows form, and saving Visual Basic projects. The chapter also discusses how to apply GUI design principles and examines the first two phases of the program development life cycle (PDLC).

Chapter 3 — Program Design and Coding Chapter 3 provides students with the skills and knowledge necessary to complete phases 2, 3, and 4 of the PDLC by enhancing a GUI mock-up, designing program processing objects, and coding a program. Topics include using IntelliSense when writing code and enhancing a Visual Basic 2012 form by changing the BackColor property of an object and displaying images. This chapter also explains how to enter Visual Basic 2012 code, correct errors, and run a completed program. Finally, the chapter discusses the value of creating an event planning document.

Chapter 4 — Variables and Arithmetic Operations Chapter 4 introduces variables and arithmetic operations used in the coding of a Visual Basic application. The chapter provides in-depth coverage of declaring variables, gathering input for an application, differentiating data types, performing mathematical calculations, and understanding the proper scope of variables. The chapter also shows how to use various types of TextBox objects.

Chapter 5 — Decision Structures Chapter 5 explains how to create a Visual Basic 2012 Windows application that uses decision structures to take different actions depending on the user's input. Topics include using If...Then statements, If...Then... Else statements, nested If statements, logical operators, and Case statements. The chapter also explores how to use the GroupBox object, place RadioButton objects, display a message box, insert code snippets, and test input to ensure it is valid.

Chapter 6 — Loop Structures Chapter 6 presents another type of fundamental programming structure — the repetition structure, including Do While, Do Until, For...Next, For Each...Next, and While...End While loops. Topics include repeating a process using the For...Next and Do loops; priming a loop; creating a nested loop; selecting the best type of loop; avoiding infinite loops; validating data; and understanding compound operators, counters, and accumulators. The chapter also shows how to insert a MenuStrip object, use the InputBox function, display data using the ListBox object, debug programs using DataTips at breakpoints, and publish a finished application using ClickOnce technology.

Appendices This book concludes with three appendices. Appendix A explains the purpose of Unicode and provides a table listing Unicode characters and their equivalents. Appendix B examines the My namespace element of Visual Basic 2012 in detail. Appendix C lists the common data types used in Visual Basic 2012, including the recommended naming convention for the three-character prefix preceding variable names.

End-of-Chapter Activities

A notable strength of this *Microsoft Visual Basic 2012* book is the extensive student activities at the end of each chapter. Well-structured student activities can make the difference between students merely participating in a class and retaining the information they learn. These end-of-chapter activities include the following:

- **Learn Online** The Learn Online section directs students to Web-based exercises, which are fun, interactive activities that include chapter reinforcement (true/false, multiple choice, and short answer questions), practice tests, and a crossword puzzle challenge to augment concepts, key terms, techniques, and other material in the chapter.

- **Knowledge Check** The Knowledge Check section includes short exercises and review questions that reinforce concepts and provide opportunities to practice skills.

- **Debugging Exercises** In these exercises, students examine short code samples to identify errors and solve programming problems.

- **Program Analysis** The Program Analysis exercises let students apply their knowledge of Visual Basic 2012 and programming techniques. In some exercises, students write programming statements that meet a practical goal or solve a problem. In other exercises, students analyze code samples and identify the output.

- **Case Programming Assignments** Nine programming assignments for each chapter challenge students to create applications using the skills learned in the chapter. Each assignment presents a realistic business scenario and requires students to create programs of varying difficulty.

  - Easiest: The first three assignments provide most of the program design information, such as a requirements document and use case definition, for a business application. Students design an application, create an event planning document, and write the code for the application.

  - Intermediate: The next three assignments provide some of the program design information, such as a requirements document. Students create other design documents, such as a use case definition and event planning document, and then build the user interface and code the application.

  - Challenging: The final three assignments provide only a description of a business problem, and students create all the design documents, design the user interface, and code the application.

To the Instructor

Each chapter in this book focuses on a realistic, appealing Visual Basic 2012 application. A chapter begins with a completed application, which you can run to demonstrate how it works, the tasks it performs, and the problems it solves. The chapter introduction also identifies the application's users and their requirements, such as running the program on a mobile computer or validating input data.

The steps in the next section of a chapter show how to create the user interface for the application. You can perform these steps in class — each step clearly explains an action, describes the results, and includes a figure showing the results, with callouts directing your attention to key elements on the screen. Some marginal features, such as the Heads Up boxes, provide additional tips for completing the steps. The Online Reinforcement boxes direct students to videos that replay the steps, which is especially helpful for review and for distance learning students.

This section also explains the Visual Basic 2012 tools and properties needed to understand and create the user interface. For example, while placing a text box in an application, the chapter describes the purpose of a text box and why you should set its maximum and minimum size. You can discuss these ideas and strategies, and then continue your demonstration to show students how to apply them to the chapter application.

After completing the user interface, the chapter explores the programming concepts students should understand to create the application, such as proper syntax, variables, data types, conditional statements, and loops. This section uses the same types of steps, figures, and marginal features to demonstrate how to enter code to complete and test the application.

To prepare students for building the application on their own, the chapter next considers the program design and logic by examining planning documents:

- *Requirements document* — The requirements document identifies the purpose, procedures, and calculations of the program, and specifies details such as the application title, restrictions, and comments that help to explain the program.
- *Use case definition* — The use case definition describes what the user does and how the program responds to each action.
- *Event planning document* — The event planning document lists each object in the user interface that causes an event, the action the user takes to trigger the event, and the event processing that must occur.

You can discuss these documents in class and encourage students to review them as they create a program, reinforcing how professional developers create applications in the modern workplace.

In the innovative Guided Program Development section, students work on their own to create the chapter application. They complete the tasks within each numbered step, referring to Hint Screens when they need a reminder about how to perform a step or which method to use. Many tasks reference figures shown earlier in the chapter. Students can refer to these figures for further help — they show exactly how to use a particular technique for completing a task. Steps end with a results figure, which illustrates how the application should look if students performed the tasks correctly. To reinforce how students learned the chapter material, the Guided Program Development section also focuses first on designing the user interface and then on coding the application. A complete program listing appears at the end of this section, which students can use to check their work.

At the end of each chapter, you'll find plenty of activities that provide review, practice, and challenge for your students, including a summary table that lists skills and corresponding figures and videos, descriptions of online learning opportunities, and exercises ranging from short, focused review questions to assignments requiring complete programs and related planning documents. You can assign the Learn Online, Knowledge Check, Debugging Exercises, and Program Analysis activities as necessary to reinforce and assess learning. Depending on the expertise of your class, you can assign the Case Programming Assignments as independent projects, selecting one from each level of difficulty (easiest, intermediate, and challenging) or concentrating on the level that is most appropriate for your class.

INSTRUCTOR RESOURCES

The following resources are available through www.cengage.com to instructors who have adopted this book. Search for this title by ISBN, title, author, or keyword. From the Product Overview page, select the Instructor's Companion Site to access your complementary resources.

- **Instructor's Manual** The Instructor's Manual consists of Microsoft Word files, which include chapter objectives, lecture notes, teaching tips, classroom activities, lab activities, quick quizzes, figures and boxed elements summarized in the chapters, and a glossary page.

- **Syllabus** Sample syllabi, which can be customized easily to a course, cover policies, assignments, exams, and procedural information.

- **Figure Files** Illustrations for every figure in the textbook are available in electronic form. Figures are provided both with and without callouts.

- **PowerPoint Presentation** PowerPoint is a multimedia lecture presentation system that provides slides for each chapter. Presentations are based on chapter objectives. Use this presentation system to present well-organized lectures that are both interesting and knowledge based. PowerPoint Presentations provide consistent coverage at schools that use multiple lecturers.

- **Solutions to Exercises** Solutions are included for all end-of-chapter and chapter reinforcement exercises.

- **Test Bank & Test Engine** Test Banks include a wide range of questions for every chapter, featuring objective-based and critical-thinking question types, and include page number references and figure references, when appropriate. Also included is the test engine, ExamView, the ultimate tool for your objective-based testing needs.

- **Printed Test Bank** A printable Rich Text File (.rtf) version of the test bank is included.
- **Data Files for Students** Includes all the files that are required by students to complete the exercises.
- **Additional Activities for Students** These additional activities consist of Chapter Reinforcement Exercises, which are true/false, multiple-choice, and short answer questions that help students gain confidence in the material learned.

About Our Covers

The Shelly Cashman Series® is continually updating our approach and content to reflect the way today's students learn and experience new technology. This focus on student success is reflected on our covers, which feature real students from University of Rhode Island using the Shelly Cashman Series in their courses, and reflect the varied ages and backgrounds of the students learning with our books. When you use the Shelly Cashman Series®, you can be assured that you are learning computer skills using the most effective courseware available.

To the Student

Getting the Most Out of Your Book

Welcome to *Microsoft Visual Basic 2012 for Windows and Mobile Applications: Introductory*. To save yourself time and gain a better understanding of the elements in this text, spend a few minutes reviewing the descriptions and figures in this section.

Introduction and Initial Chapter Figures
Each chapter presents a programming project and shows the solution in the first figure of the chapter. The introduction and initial chapter figure let you see first-hand how your finished product will look and illustrate your programming goals.

Guided Program Development After reading through the chapter and observing how to create the chapter application, the Guided Program Development section takes you through building the chapter project step by step. As you perform each task, you can refer to Hint Screens that remind you how to complete a step or use a particular technique. If you need further help, some steps include references to figures shown earlier in the chapter — you can revisit these figures to review exactly how to perform a task. Each step ends with a results figure, so you can make sure your application is on the right track. A complete program listing also appears at the end of the Guided Program Development section, which you can use to check your work.

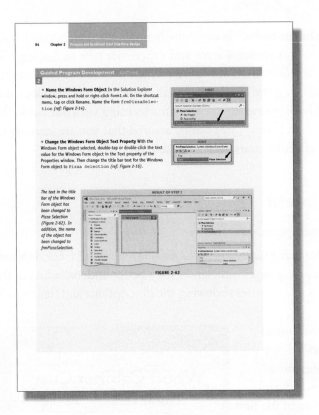

Visual Basic 2012 Online Reinforcement Videos The first of their kind, the Shelly Cashman Online Companion provides video reenactments of every new Visual Basic process that is introduced in each chapter. These animated tutorials provide a Web-based visual instruction on how to complete a Visual Basic task. You can watch these videos to learn how to perform the steps shown in the book or to review the steps and techniques.

To access the Online Reinforcement videos, you need only a computer with an Internet connection. Use your Web browser to visit cengagebrain.com, navigate to the resources for this title, tap or click the link to the appropriate chapter, and then tap or click the link to a video to play a video.

Marginal Boxes Marginal elements include Heads Up boxes, which offer tips and programming advice, In the Real World boxes, which indicate how professional developers use Visual Basic 2012 tools, and Watch Out For boxes, which identify common errors and explain how to avoid them.

Learn Online Reinforcing what you're learning is a snap with the Chapter Reinforcement exercises, Practice Tests, and other learning games on the Student Companion site. Visit cengagebrain.com to access these fun, interactive exercises.

Knowledge Check To verify you've learned the essential information in the chapter, you can work through the Knowledge Check exercises. Use these short exercises to test your knowledge of concepts and tools and to prepare for longer programming assignments.

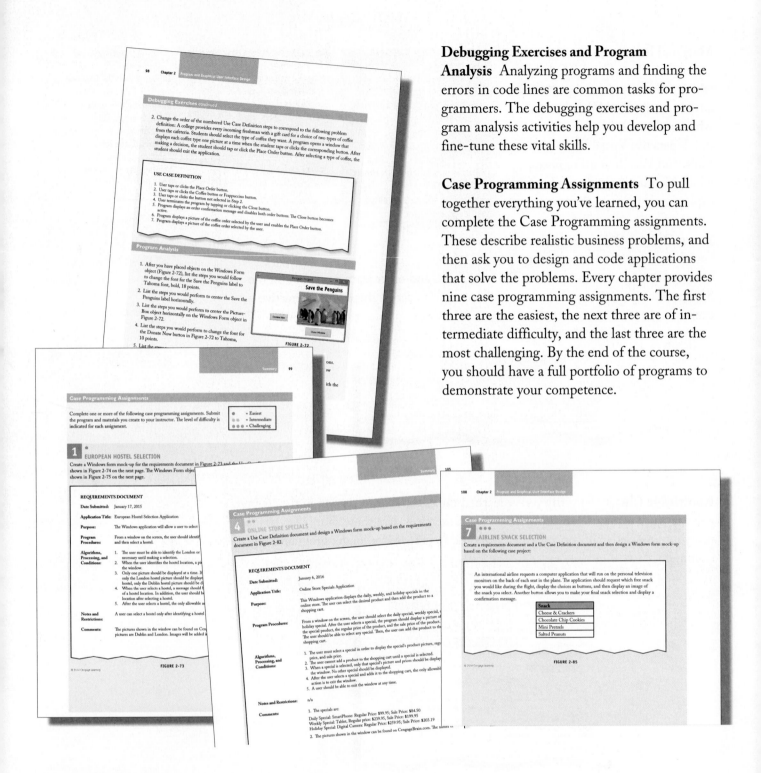

Debugging Exercises and Program Analysis Analyzing programs and finding the errors in code lines are common tasks for programmers. The debugging exercises and program analysis activities help you develop and fine-tune these vital skills.

Case Programming Assignments To pull together everything you've learned, you can complete the Case Programming assignments. These describe realistic business problems, and then ask you to design and code applications that solve the problems. Every chapter provides nine case programming assignments. The first three are the easiest, the next three are of intermediate difficulty, and the last three are the most challenging. By the end of the course, you should have a full portfolio of programs to demonstrate your competence.

Acknowledgements

To Tim, my husband, for sharing this wonderful world that is full of beauty, adventure, and frequent flyer miles. To Liam, my grandson, without whose loving attention this book would have been finished in half the time. To Gary Shelly, for teaching me to write with passion and clarity. To Lisa Ruffolo, my editor, for her analytical flair and creative panache. To Melinda White (Seminole State College) and John Hoye (Kellogg Community College), my reviewers, for their brilliant insight.

— Corinne Hoisington

CHAPTER 1

Introduction to Visual Basic 2012 Programming

OBJECTIVES

You will have mastered the material in this chapter when you can:

- Understand software and computer programs

- State the role of a developer in creating computer programs

- Specify the use of a graphical user interface and describe an event-driven program

- Specify the roles of input, processing, output, and data when running a program on a computer

- Describe the arithmetic operations a computer program can perform

- Explain the logical operations a computer program can perform

- Define and describe the use of a database

- Identify the use of a computer programming language in general, and Visual Basic 2012 in particular

- Explain the use of Visual Studio 2012 when developing Visual Basic 2012 programs

- Specify the programming languages available for use with Visual Studio 2012

- Explain .NET Framework 4.5

- Explain RAD

- Describe classes, objects, and the .NET Framework 4.5 class libraries

- Explain ADO.NET 4.5, ASP.NET 4.5, MSIL, and CLR

- Specify the types of Visual Basic 2012 applications

Introduction

A computer is an electronic device that completes tasks under the direction of a sequence of instructions to produce useful results for people. Computers include desktop models, laptops, tablets, and smartphones. The set of instructions that directs a computer to perform tasks is called **computer software**, or a **computer program**. A computer program on a mobile device or Windows 8 computer is also called an **app**.

When controlled by programs, computers and mobile devices can accomplish a wide variety of activities. For example, computers can interpret and display a page from the web, compute and write payroll checks for millions of employees, display video and play audio from the web, post to a social network on a smartphone, and be used to write a book (Figure 1-1).

FIGURE 1-1

© Palto / Photos.com; © Wesley Thornberry / Thinkstock; © Jimeone / Photos.com; Microsoft Corporation; © iStockphoto / Michael Phillips; © iStockphoto / TommL; © iStockphoto / Hocus Focus Studio

internal hard drive
(storage)

on-screen keyboard
(input device)

monitor
(output device)

system unit
(processing)

DVD
(storage)

keyboard
(input device)

mouse
(input device)

speakers
(output device)

RAM
(storage)

printer
(output device)

scanner
(input device)

digital camera
(input device)

FIGURE 1-2

© Carlos Andre Santos / Photos.com; © Chesky_W / Photos.com; © Vetkit / Photos.com; © Alex Max / Photos.com; © Hayri Kodal / Photos.com; © Tatiana Popova /Photos.com; © Murat Baysan / Photos.com; © iStockphoto / muratkoc; © iStockphoto / camilla wisbauer; Szemeno / Photos.com

Two vital components of a computer must interact with one another for any activity to be performed. These components are computer hardware and computer software. **Computer hardware** is the physical equipment associated with a computer. This includes the keyboard (traditional or on-screen), mouse, touch screen or monitor, central processing unit (CPU), smartphone, random access memory (RAM), hard disk, and other devices (Figure 1-2).

A computer program or app is a set of electronic instructions that directs the hardware to perform tasks such as displaying a character on the screen when a key is pressed on the keyboard, adding an employee's regular pay and overtime pay to calculate the employee's total pay, or displaying a picture from an attached digital camera on the monitor. Computer hardware cannot perform any activity unless an instruction directs that hardware to act. In most cases, the instruction is part of a computer program a developer has created to carry out the desired activity. A third component required is data. **Data** includes words, numbers, videos, graphics, and sound that programs manipulate, display, and otherwise process. The basic function

FIGURE 1-3

© Chesky_W / Photos.com; © iStockphoto / Paige Foster; © iStockphoto / camilla wisbauer; © Szemeno / Photos.com; © iStockphoto / muratkoc; © iStockphoto / Michael Phillips; © Tatiana Popova / Photos.com; © Alex Max / Photos.com; © Palto / Photos.com; Mr.Reborn55 / Shutterstock.com; © Anna Khomulo / Photos.com

of many programs is to accept some form of data (sometimes called **input data**), manipulate the data in some manner (sometimes called **processing**), and create some form of data that is usable by people or other computers (sometimes called **output data**, or **information**) (Figure 1-3). In short, many computer programs perform the following general steps: accept input data, process the data, and create output data. The data that acts as input to a program, the processing that occurs, and the output that is created vary with the requirements of the program.

In order for the computer to execute a program, both the program and the data must be placed in the computer's **random access memory (RAM)** (Figure 1-4). Once the program is stored in RAM, the computer's **central processing unit (CPU)** can access the program instructions and the data in RAM to perform activities as directed by the program.

One other activity that hardware and software typically carry out is saving both the data and other software. **Saving**, or **storing**, data refers to placing the data or software electronically on a storage medium such as a hard disk or Universal Serial Bus (USB) drive or saving to a cloud storage server. The software and data are stored so they can be accessed and retrieved at a later time. Stored local data is said to be **persistent** because it remains available even after the computer power is turned off.

```
Program:
If Hours > 40
        Regular Pay = 40 * Hourly Rate
        Overtime Pay = ((Hours Worked - 40) * 1.5) * Hourly Rate
        Total Pay = Regular Pay + Overtime Pay
```

```
Data:
Hours Worked: 43
Hourly Rate: 23.50
```

FIGURE 1-4

© Tatiana Popova / Photos.com; © 2014 Cengage Learning

Computer Programmers and Developers

A computer program is designed and developed by people known as **computer programmers**, or developers. **Developers** are people skilled in designing computer programs and creating them using programming languages. Some computer programs are small and relatively simple, but often a problem to be solved on a computer requires more than one program. Developers speak of developing an **application**, which can mean several computer programs working together to solve a problem.

When designing a program, developers analyze the problem and determine how to solve it. Once a computer program or an application is designed, the developer must create it so it can be executed on a computer. In most cases, the developer creates the program by writing code using a **programming language**, which is a set of words and symbols that can be interpreted by special computer software and eventually executed as instructions by a computer. In this book, you will learn the skills required both to design and create computer programs and apps using the Visual Basic 2012 programming language (Figure 1-5 on the next page).

Will I be able to find a job in computer programming?

According to the National Association of Colleges and Employers (NACE), the top employable degrees for 2013 include the following majors, which all require programming skills:

- Computer & Information Science — #2
- Management Information Systems — #6
- Computer Engineering — #8

(www.thebestschools.org/blog/2012/10/15/20-best-it-jobs-2013/)

CONSIDER THIS

```
 9 ⊟Public Class frmHotelRoomSelection
10
11 ⊟    Private Sub btnStandardRoom_Click(ByVal sender As System.Object, ByVal e As System.E
12            ' This code is executed when the user
13            ' clicks the Standard Room button. It
14            ' displays the Standard Room picture,
15            ' hides the Deluxe Room picture, and
16            ' enables the Select Room button.
17
18            picStandardRoom.Visible = True
19            picDeluxeRoom.Visible = False
20            btnSelectRoom.Enabled = True
21
22        End Sub
23
24 ⊟    Private Sub btnSelectRoom_Click(ByVal sender As System.Object, ByVal e As System.Eve
25            ' This code is executed when the user
26            ' clicks the Select Room button. It
27            ' disables the Standard Room button,
28            ' the Select Room button, and the
29            ' Deluxe Room button. It hides the
30            ' Instructios label, displays the
31            ' Confirmation Message label, and
32            ' enables the Exit Window button.
33
34            btnStandardRoom.Enabled = False
35            btnSelectRoom.Enabled = False
36            btnDeluxeRoom.Enabled = False
37            lblInstructions.Visible = False
38            lblConfirmationMessage.Visible = True
39            btnExitWindow.Enabled = True
40
41        End Sub
```

FIGURE 1-5

Event-Driven Computer Programs with a Graphical User Interface

Most Visual Basic 2012 programs are **event-driven programs** that communicate
with the user through a **graphical user interface (GUI)**. The GUI usually consists
of a window that contains a variety of objects and that can be displayed on various
devices such as a computer monitor or a smartphone screen. Users employ the GUI
objects to select options, enter data, and cause events to occur. An **event** is an action
the user initiates and causes the program to perform a type of processing in response.
For example, a user might enter data into the program, and then tap or click a
button. The button action triggers an event, resulting in the program performing the
appropriate processing in response.

To illustrate the process of entering data when using a graphical user interface
and then triggering an event, consider the window shown in Figure 1-6.

FIGURE 1-6

This window is part of a banking application. When it is displayed, the teller at the bank or a user on the web can enter an account number. Then the user can click the Display Account Balance button (that is, trigger an event) and the program displays the account balance. The following steps illustrate the dynamics of the interaction with the program:

STEP 1   The user enters the account number in the Account Number box.

The account number the user entered is displayed in the Account Number text box (Figure 1-7). The Account Balance label displays no information.

FIGURE 1-7

STEP 2   The user clicks the Display Account Balance button.

The account balance is displayed in the Account Balance label (Figure 1-8). Clicking the Display Account Balance button triggered the event that caused the program to determine and display the account balance based on data that the program accessed.

FIGURE 1-8

STEP 3   The user clicks the Reset Window button to clear the text box and the label and prepare the user interface for the next account number.

Clicking the Reset Window button triggers another event. The text box and the label are cleared and the insertion point is placed in the Account Number text box (Figure 1-9). The user now can enter a new account number to determine the account balance.

FIGURE 1-9

The events in the previous example consist of clicking the Display Account Balance button and clicking the Reset Window button. The program reacts to the events by performing specific actions (showing the account balance and resetting the text box and label). This is an example of an event-driven program. The Visual Basic developer designs the user interface and writes the program code that performs these event-triggered actions.

Basic Program Operations

All programs, regardless of their size and complexity, execute only a few fundamental operations: input, output, basic arithmetic operations, and logical operations. These operations can be combined in countless different ways to accomplish the tasks required of the program. The following pages describe these basic program operations.

Input Operation

As noted previously, a fundamental operation in most computer programs involves a user who enters data. For instance, in Figure 1-7 on the previous page, the user entered the account number. The steps that occurred when the user typed the account number are shown in Figure 1-10.

Step 1:
User types the account
number on the keyboard.

Step 2:
The data is stored in RAM.

73-0529

73-0529

Step 3:
Data is displayed on the
computer screen.

Account Balance	– ☐ ✕

Account Number   [73-0529]

Account Balance   _____

[Display Account Balance]

[Reset Window]

FIGURE 1-10

© Wesley Thornberry / Thinkstock; © Tatiana Popova / Photos.com; © 2014 Cengage Learning

In Figure 1-10, the banking computer program that processes the user's request is stored in RAM. The data entered by the user also is stored in RAM. Depending on the input device, entered data might also be displayed on the computer screen. The input device used to enter data depends on the application. In Figure 1-10, the user typed the account number on a keyboard. Other applications might allow data to be entered with a scanner, digital camera, video camera, mouse, or other device. In each instance, the data is stored in the computer's RAM. When the data is in RAM, instructions in the program can operate on the data.

Output Operation

The second basic program operation is creating output, or information. As you learned previously, a major goal of most computer programs is to create output data, or information, that is useful to people. In Figure 1-8 on page 7, the information requested of the program is the account balance. The process of creating output is shown in Figure 1-11 on the next page.

As always, the program must be stored in RAM to control the operations of the computer. In the example, the program sets the text of the Account Balance label equal to the account balance, and then displays it on the screen.

FIGURE 1-11

© Tatiana Popova / Photos.com; © 2014 Cengage Learning

As with input operations, a variety of devices can present output. In addition to computer monitors, common output devices include printers, gaming console screens, and smartphone screens (Figure 1-12).

Input and output operations are basic to all computers and most computer programs. The ability to enter data, process it in some manner, and create output in the form of useful information is what makes a computer valuable. Understanding input/output operations is essential because they provide the foundation for many of the programs you will write in this text.

Basic Arithmetic Operations

Once data is stored in main computer memory as a result of an input operation, the program can process it in some manner. In many programs, arithmetic operations (addition, subtraction, multiplication, and division) are performed on numeric data to produce useful output.

Prior to performing arithmetic operations, the numeric data used in calculations must be stored in RAM. Then, program instructions that also are stored in RAM can direct the computer to add, subtract, multiply, or divide the numbers. The answers from arithmetic operations can be used in additional calculations and processing, stored for future use, and used as output from the program.

The example in Figure 1-13 on page 12 illustrates the steps an application performs to calculate an average test score. The average score is calculated from the three test scores a user enters.

smartphones

printer

FIGURE 1-12

In the example in Figure 1-13 on the next page, the program adds the three test scores the user enters, and then divides the total by 3 to obtain the average score. As always, both the program and the data required to calculate the average test score must be stored in the computer's RAM. As you can see, when the user enters data in a text box, the data is stored in RAM and is available for arithmetic and other operations.

This example demonstrates the three fundamental operations of input (entering the three test scores), processing (calculating the average test score), and output (displaying the average test score). Although most applications are more complex than the one illustrated, the input, process, and output operations are used; arithmetic operations are commonly part of the processing step.

Logical Operations

The ability of a computer to perform logical operations separates it from other types of calculating devices. Computers, through the use of programs, can compare numbers, letters of the alphabet, and special characters. Based on the result of these comparisons, the program can perform one processing task if the tested condition

Program: (Test 1 Score + Test 2 Score + Test 3 Score) / 3 = Average Test Score

Data: (90 + 83 + 94) / 3 = 89

add these
values together

divide the sum
by 3 to determine
the average test
score

FIGURE 1-13

© Tatiana Popova / Photos.com; © 2014 Cengage Learning

is true and another processing task if the condition is not true. Using a program to compare data and perform alternative operations allows the computer to complete sophisticated tasks such as predicting weather, formatting and altering digital photographs, editing digital video, and running high-speed games.

A program can perform the following types of logical operations:

- Comparing to determine if two values are equal
- Comparing to determine if one value is greater than another value
- Comparing to determine if one value is less than another value

Based on the results of these comparisons, the program can direct the computer to take alternative actions.

Comparing — Equal Condition

A program can compare two values stored in RAM to determine whether they are equal. If the values are equal, one set of instructions will be executed; if they are not equal, another set of instructions will be executed.

Comparing to determine if two values are equal requires comparing one value to another. In an application for calculating student tuition, different rates might apply based on the student's residence. If the school is located in Texas and the student resides in Texas, the tuition per unit is one value; if the student does not reside in Texas, the tuition per unit is another value (Figure 1-14).

BEFORE:

State of Residence
is equal to TX

AFTER:

Tuition per
Unit for TX
resident

BEFORE:

State of
Residence is
equal to NY

AFTER:

Tuition per Unit
for non-TX
resident

FIGURE 1-14

When the Display Tuition button is clicked and the state is equal to TX, the program displays the in-state tuition per unit. If the state is not equal to TX, the program displays the out-of-state tuition per unit.

Comparing can be used to determine if a condition is selected. For example, in Figure 1-15 on the next page, the Campus Parking Fees window contains a Student Name text box that provides space for the student's name and On-Campus Housing and Off-Campus Housing option buttons, or radio buttons, that allow the user to select either on-campus housing or off-campus housing. When the user clicks the Calculate Parking Fees button, the program displays the appropriate parking fee.

In Example 1, the user name is Athir Gomez and the On-Campus Housing option button is selected. When the user clicks the Calculate Parking Fees button, the program performs a comparison and determines that the On-Campus Housing button is selected. Because it is selected, the result of the comparison is true and the program displays the parking fee for on-campus housing. In Example 2, the Off-Campus Housing button is selected, so the program displays the parking fee for off-campus housing.

EXAMPLE 1:

On-Campus
Housing selected

Parking fee for
On-Campus Housing

EXAMPLE 2:

Off-Campus
Housing selected

Parking fee for
Off-Campus Housing

FIGURE 1-15

Comparing — Less than Condition

A second type of comparison a computer program can perform is to determine if one value is less than another value. If it is, one set of instructions will be executed; if it is not, another set of instructions will be executed. For example, in the Student Dorm Assignment program in Figure 1-16, the user clicks the Submit Application button and the program makes a comparison to determine if the person registering for a dorm room is less than 18 years old. If so, the person is considered a minor and a parent's signature is required. If not, no signature is required. An instruction is performed in the program to place a check in the Parent Signature Required check box if the age is less than 18, and the instruction is not executed if the age is 18 or more.

BEFORE:

Student Age
is less than 18

AFTER:

parent
signature is
required
because
Student Age
is less than 18

FIGURE 1-16 *(continues)*

BEFORE:

AFTER:

Student Age is not less than 18

parent signature is not required because Student Age is greater than 18

FIGURE 1-16 *(continued)*

Comparing — Greater than Condition

The other condition a computer program can determine is whether one value is greater than another value. For example, in a payroll application, the hours worked by an employee can be compared to the value 40. If the hours worked are greater than 40, then overtime pay (1.5 times the hourly rate) is calculated for the hours over 40. If the employee worked 40 hours or less, no overtime pay is calculated. This comparing operation is shown in Figure 1-17.

In Figure 1-17a, the Hours Worked box contains 42, so the program calculates overtime pay for employee Lisa Hueve. In Figure 1-17b, Mia Ortega worked 30 hours, so no overtime pay is calculated. When the Hours Worked value is greater than 40, the program executes one set of instructions; if the Hours Worked value is not greater than 40, the program executes another set of instructions.

Hours Worked is greater than 40

Overtime Pay is calculated

FIGURE 1-17a

Hours Worked is not greater than 40

no Overtime Pay calculated

FIGURE 1-17b

Logical Operations Summary

While the logical operations shown in the previous examples might seem simple, the ability of a computer running under program control to perform millions of these comparisons in a single second provides the computer's processing power. For example, if you are participating in a road race computer game, the game program uses comparisons to determine where your car is located on the screen, which graphic road elements should be displayed on the screen, whether your car has collided with your competitor, and so on. All of the many decisions that are required to display your game on the screen and respond to your actions are based on comparisons to determine if one value is equal to, greater than, or less than another value. As you can imagine, millions of these decisions must be made every second for your high-speed game to provide an enjoyable experience.

Saving Software and Data

When you develop and write a program, the code you write and other features, such as the graphical user interface, must be saved on disk. Then, when you want the program to run, you can make the program load into RAM and execute. By saving the program on disk, you can execute the same program many times without rewriting it each time you want to run it.

The program you write, however, also can save data. This data, which can be generated from the processing in the program, can be saved on disk for future use. For example, in a banking application, a customer might open an account. The computer program that is used to open the account saves the customer's information, such as name, address, account number, and account balance, to a local file on the device or in the cloud on a remote server. Later, when the customer makes a deposit or withdrawal, the customer information will be retrieved and modified to reflect the deposit or withdrawal.

In most cases, data such as a customer's name and address is saved in a database. A **database** is a collection of data organized in a manner that allows access, retrieval, and use of that data. Once the data is saved in the database, any programs with permission can reference the data. You will learn more about databases and their use when programming using Visual Basic 2012 later in this textbook.

Visual Basic 2012 and Visual Studio 2012

To write a computer program, a developer uses a programming language. As you learned previously, a programming language is a set of written words, symbols, and codes, with a strict set of usage rules called the language **syntax**, that a developer uses to communicate instructions to a computer. An example of code statements in the Visual Basic 2012 programming language is shown in Figure 1-18.

Each program statement causes the computer to perform one or more operations. When written, these instructions must conform to the rules of the Visual Basic 2012 language. Coding a program is a precise skill. The developer must follow the syntax,

```
41        Do Until intNumberOfEntries > intMaxNumberOfEntries Or strVehicleSpeed = strCancelC
42
43            If IsNumeric(strVehicleSpeed) Then
44                decVehicleSpeed = Convert.ToDecimal(strVehicleSpeed)
45                If decVehicleSpeed > 0 Then
46                    lstRadarSpeed.Items.Add(decVehicleSpeed)
47                    decTotalOfAllSpeeds += decVehicleSpeed
48                    intNumberOfEntries += 1
49                    strInputMessage = strNormalMessage
50                Else
51                    strInputMessage = strNegativeError
52                End If
53            Else
54                strInputMessage = strNonNumericError
55            End If
56
57            If intNumberOfEntries <= intMaxNumberOfEntries Then
58                strVehicleSpeed = InputBox(strInputMessage & intNumberOfEntries, strInputHe
59            End If
60
61        Loop
62
63        ' Makes label visible
64        lblAverageSpeed.Visible = True
65
66        'Calculates and displays average speed
67        If intNumberOfEntries > 1 Then
68            decAverageSpeed = decTotalOfAllSpeeds / (intNumberOfEntries - 1)
69            lblAverageSpeed.Text = "Average speed at checkpoint is " & _
70                decAverageSpeed.ToString("F1") & " mph"
71        Else
72            lblAverageSpeed.Text = "No speed entered"
73        End If
```

FIGURE 1-18

or **programming rules**, of the programming language precisely. Even a single coding error can cause a program to execute improperly. Therefore, the developer must pay strict attention to coding an error-free program.

When writing Visual Basic 2012 programs, most developers use a tool called Visual Studio 2012. **Visual Studio 2012** is a software application that allows you to develop Visual Basic 2012 programs using code you write, code prewritten by others that can be incorporated into your program, and sophisticated tools that speed up the programming process significantly while building better executing and more reliable programs. In this book, you will use Visual Studio 2012 to write Visual Basic 2012 programs.

Visual Studio 2012 is a type of **integrated development environment (IDE)**, which provides services and tools that enable a developer to code, test, and implement a single program, or sometimes the series of programs that comprise an application. Visual Studio 2012, which was developed by Microsoft Corporation, works specifically with Visual Basic 2012 as well as other programming languages to develop program code.

Visual Basic, part of Visual Studio 2012, can be installed on a Windows 7 computer with Service Pack 1, a Windows 8 computer, Windows Server 2008, or Windows Server 2012. Visual Studio 2012 can be installed on a 32-bit or 64-bit computer. Students, educators, and academic institutions can access a free copy of Visual Studio 2012 at *www.dreamspark.com*. DreamSpark (Figure 1-19 on the next page) is a Microsoft program that supports technical education by providing access to Microsoft software for learning, teaching, and research purposes. This text uses the Microsoft Visual Studio 2012 Professional version to present the programming topics.

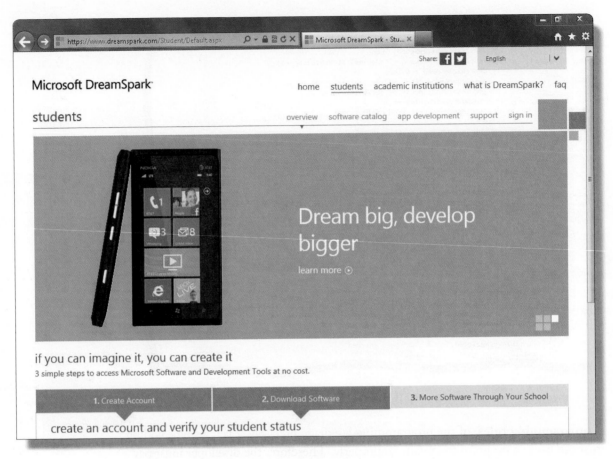

FIGURE 1-19

After you start the Visual Studio 2012 application, the Visual Studio 2012 window is displayed. In this window, you can develop and write your Visual Basic 2012 program, as shown in Figure 1-20.

The following elements help you use the Visual Studio 2012 window. In subsequent chapters, you will learn to use each of the elements found in this window.

Title bar: The title bar identifies the window and the application open in the window. In Figure 1-20, the open application is Payroll.

Menu bar: The menu bar displays the Visual Studio 2012 menu names. The menus contain lists of commands that allow you to create, edit, save, print, test, and run a Visual Basic program, and to perform other functions that are critical to developing Visual Basic programs.

Standard toolbar: The Standard toolbar contains buttons that execute frequently used commands such as Open Project, New Project, Save, Cut, Copy, Paste, and Undo.

Toolbox: The Toolbox contains **.NET components** that help you develop the graphical user interface for your program. For example, you can use the Toolbox to place buttons, picture boxes, labels, radio buttons, and other Windows GUI objects in the windows of your program.

title bar

menu bar

Standard
toolbar

Toolbox

Solution
Explorer

Properties
window

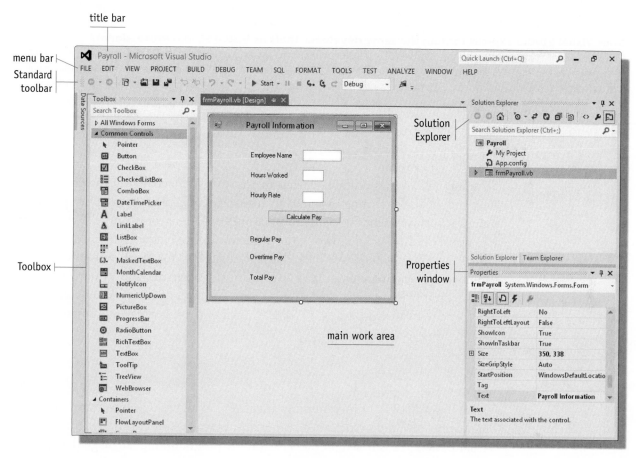

main work area

FIGURE 1-20

Main work area: The main work area contains the item you are currently developing. In Figure 1-20, this area contains the Payroll Information window of the Payroll program.

Solution Explorer: The Solution Explorer window displays the elements of the Visual Basic **solution**, which is the name for the Visual Basic program and other items generated by Visual Studio to help the program execute properly. You will learn about these items and how to use the Solution Explorer window throughout this book.

Properties window: An item that is a visible part of a graphical user interface, such as the Calculate Pay button in Figure 1-20, is called an **object** or **control**. Each object in a Visual Basic program has a set of characteristics called the **properties** of the object. These properties, such as the size of the button and the text displayed within the button, can be set in the Properties window within Visual Studio. You will learn about the properties of many objects throughout this book.

To code a Visual Basic program, the developer starts the Visual Studio program, identifies the kind of program to be developed, and then uses the tools and features of Visual Studio to create the program.

Does Visual Studio Express contain the same developer tools as Visual Studio Professional?
Microsoft Visual Studio Express is a free software IDE developed by Microsoft with multiple products that include lightweight versions of the Microsoft Visual Studio product line. The Visual Studio Express product line includes a subset of the full Visual Studio Professional product. Express 2012 products include Express for Web, Express for Windows 8, Express for Windows Desktop, Express for Windows Phone, and Team Foundation Server Express.

Programming Languages

Several thousand programming languages exist today. Each language has its own rules and syntax for writing instructions. Languages often are designed for specific purposes, such as scientific applications, business solutions, or webpage development.

Visual Studio can be used to write programs in five languages: Visual Basic, Visual C++ (pronounced Cee Plus Plus and called C++ for short), Visual C# (pronounced Cee Sharp and called C# for short), JavaScript, and Visual F# (pronounced F Sharp and called F# for short). You can develop a Windows Store app coded with Visual Basic, C++, or C#. Each of these languages is described in the following sections.

Visual Basic

Visual Basic 2012 is a programming language that allows developers to easily build complex Windows and Web programs, as well as other software tools. Visual Basic 2012 is based on the Visual Basic programming language that Microsoft developed in the early 1990s. Visual Basic, in turn, was based on the BASIC (Beginner's All-purpose Symbolic Instruction Code) language, which was developed in the 1960s.

Visual Basic's popularity evolved from the wide range of productivity features that enabled developers to quickly generate high-quality software applications for Windows. Today, Visual Basic is one of the most widely used programming languages in the world because it is English-like and is considered one of the easier enterprise-level programming languages to learn. Visual Basic is the only language in Visual Studio that is not case sensitive, which makes it easy for entry-level program-mers. It is as powerful as the other programming languages in the Visual Studio suite, such as C++ or C#. An example of Visual Basic 2012 code is shown in Figure 1-18 on page 17.

In this book, you will learn to become a proficient Visual Basic developer.

C++

C++ is a derivative of the programming language C, which originally was developed at Bell Labs in the 1970s. It gives developers exacting control of their applications through optimized code and access to system-provided services. It contains powerful language constructs, though at the price of added complexity. C++ provides unrivaled performance and precision for applications that require a high degree of control.

Visual C#

Introduced in 2001 by Microsoft, Visual C# offers a synthesis of the elegance and syntax of C++ with many of the productivity benefits enjoyed in Visual Basic. Visual C# can be used to create both Windows and Web applications, as well as other types of software tools. Microsoft designed Visual C# to overcome some of the limitations of C++ while still providing the depth of control that C++ developers demand. Visual C# includes aspects of several other programming languages, such as C++, Java, and Delphi, with a strong emphasis on code simplification.

JavaScript

JavaScript (JS) is fully included in the Visual Studio 2012 version. JS is an open source client-side scripting language that enhances web browser user interfaces and dynamic websites. Visual Studio 2012 provides complete IntelliSense and debugging support for all JavaScript objects and methods.

Visual F#

A Microsoft .NET object-oriented language that debuted with Visual Studio 2010 is called F#. A multipurpose language similar to Visual Basic and C#, the F# language is known for its math-intensive focus, making it perfect for heavy-duty scientific programming applications. The language is relatively new and is just beginning to gain popularity in the business and science environments.

.NET Framework 4.5

In 2000, Microsoft announced a set of software technologies and products under the umbrella name of .NET. The .NET technologies and products were designed to work together to allow businesses to connect information, people, systems, and devices through software. Much of this connection occurs over the Internet.

The software environment in which programs and applications can be developed for .NET is called the **.NET Framework**, which provides tools and processes developers can use to produce and run programs. The .NET Framework is a development platform for building apps for Windows, Windows Phone, Windows Server, and Windows Azure (Microsoft's professional cloud computing platform). The most recent version is called **.NET Framework 4.5**. Visual Studio 2012 provides the development environment for the developer to have access to the .NET Framework 4.5 tools and processes.

Major features of .NET Framework 4.5 include the .NET class library, ADO.NET 4.5 (provides the ability to read and write data in databases), ASP. NET 4.5 (provides the ability to develop Web applications), Windows Presentation Foundation (WPF), Windows services, and the Common Language Runtime (allows programs to run on different computers under different operating systems). Each of these features is explained in the following sections.

.NET Class Library

As you have learned, most programs written using Visual Basic 2012 are event-driven programs in which a user performs an action, such as clicking a button, and the program executes the appropriate instructions. The instructions a program executes when a user clicks a button are normally written by the Visual Basic developer and are unique to the processing required by the program. For example, when a user clicks a button in one program, the overtime pay is calculated for an employee, whereas in another program parking fees are calculated. Each program responds to the events triggered by users with unique processing based on the requirements of the program.

In many programs, however, much of the programming code that must be developed is common for all the programs. For example, in all the programs you have seen in this chapter, a button was used to trigger an event in the program. The button appears in a window on a screen and senses when it has been clicked through the use of program instructions.

When certain code is common to multiple programs, the best approach is to write the code one time and then reuse it when appropriate. For example, when a button is required in the graphical user interface of a program, it is more efficient to use common programming code to insert the button than to require a developer to write all the code for a button each time one is required. When a common task must be performed or a new object such as a button is required, a developer can write the code one time and save it as a class. That class then can be referenced by all other programs when the task or object is required.

In short, the coding required for a button can be placed in a class. A **class** is a named group of program code. Once the class is coded, it can be stored in a **class library**, which makes the class available to all developers who need to use it. For example, when you as a developer need to place a button in the user interface, you can use the Button class stored in a class library to create the button without writing all the programming code associated with the button (Figure 1-21).

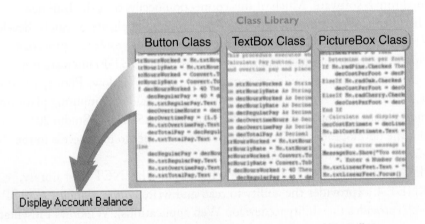

FIGURE 1-21

A button created from a class is called an **object**, or sometimes an **instance** of a class. In programming terminology, the process of creating a Button object from the Button class is called **instantiation**. In other words, a class acts as a general template, while an object is a specific item that is generated based on the class template. All buttons can be generated, or instantiated, from the Button class. The Display Account Balance button in Figure 1-21 is a specific Button object instantiated from the Button class.

To create a Button object from the Button class in Visual Studio 2012, you only need to drag the Button .NET component from the Toolbox to a Windows Form object, as you will learn in Chapter 2.

A button in a graphical user interface is only a single example of using classes and class libraries. The .NET Framework 4.5 class library contains thousands of classes and many class libraries for Visual Basic developers who use Visual Studio to create programs.

With so many classes available in .NET Framework 4.5, developers use a method of program development called rapid application development. **Rapid application development (RAD)** refers to the process of using prebuilt classes to make application development faster, easier, and more reliable. Throughout this book, you will gain a further understanding of classes and their use in modern computer programming, and will see how the classes in the .NET Framework 4.5 class libraries can be used for RAD.

ADO.NET 4.5

Often, programs you write must access data stored in a database. A set of prewritten classes called ADO.NET 4.5 (ADO stands for ActiveX Data Objects) provides the functionality for a program to perform the four primary tasks required when working with a database: getting the data, examining the data, editing the data, and updating the data.

Getting the data refers to retrieving it from the database and making it available to the program. Once the data is retrieved from the database, ADO.NET 4.5 provides the tools for the program to examine the data and determine how to use it. For example, a program might retrieve data from a database to create a printed report. The program can examine the data to determine its use for the report.

In other applications, the program might examine the data to determine if it is appropriate to display for a user. Thus, in a banking application such as in Figure 1-22 on the next page, the program might require the user to enter a special value, such as her mother's maiden name, to verify her identity before displaying the requested information. The program, using ADO.NET 4.5 classes, can compare the special value to the data retrieved from the database to determine if the user is permitted to access the data.

specify value to verify user

FIGURE 1-22

A third facility provided by ADO.NET 4.5 is the ability to edit the data, which means to make changes to it. For example, if you change your address or telephone number, those values should be changed in your account database information. ADO.NET 4.5 supports the ability to make those changes.

Finally, once changes have been made to data, ADO.NET 4.5 enables a program to update the database with the new information by writing the data into the database.

ADO.NET 4.5 is a powerful and necessary part of .NET Framework 4.5. The developer uses Visual Studio 2012 to access the ADO.NET 4.5 classes.

ASP.NET 4.5

The Internet and the web are integral technological resources. Modern websites provide services from selling products to sharing the latest medical research on any known disease. The development and maintenance of these websites is a constant requirement and consumes many developer hours.

Recognizing the importance of the web, Microsoft developed .NET Framework 4.5 to include a programming framework called ASP.NET 4.5. Developers can use this framework through Visual Studio 2012 to build powerful and sophisticated Web applications on a web server. Using ASP.NET 4.5 classes, Visual Basic 2012 programmers can create websites that perform any function available on the web today. In addition to traditional websites, you can automatically adapt Web applications to target mobile devices with enhanced ASP.NET support for mobile browsers.

ASP.NET 4.5 offers several advantages for developers. First, almost all the objects available in the .NET framework, such as buttons, text boxes, and picture boxes, are available in ASP.NET 4.5. Developers can use the same techniques to create a Web application that they use to create Windows applications, such as those shown in this chapter. In addition, deploying the Web application on a web server almost is automatic. Visual Studio 2012 incorporates a new Web designer interface into ASP.NET 4.5 that uses the design engine of a popular webpage designing program named Microsoft Expression Web. This design engine greatly improves moving between HTML5 (Hypertext Markup Language) source code, cascading style sheets (CSS3) that assist in layout, and Visual Basic code. The new ASP.NET 4.5 editor within Visual Studio provides tools to develop interactive HTML5 Web applications easily and efficiently with JavaScript and jQuery.

Important web requirements such as performance and security are enhanced and maximized through use of the tools offered with ASP.NET 4.5. In short, ASP.NET 4.5 offers a complete solution for developing modern Web applications for computers, tablets, and smartphones.

Microsoft Intermediate Language (MSIL) and Common Language Runtime (CLR)

After a developer writes a program in a programming language such as Visual Basic 2012 using Visual Studio 2012, the programming statements must be translated into a collection of instructions that eventually can be understood by the electronics of the computer. These electronic instructions then are executed by the computer to carry out the tasks of the program. This process of translation is called **program compilation**.

Program compilation for a Visual Basic 2012 program creates a set of electronic code expressed in an intermediate language called the **Microsoft Intermediate Language (MSIL)**. When the program is executed, a portion of .NET 4.5 called the **Common Language Runtime (CLR)** reads the MSIL and causes the instructions within the program to be executed (Figure 1-23 on the next page).

In Figure 1-23, the Visual Basic program written by a developer is compiled, which translates the human-readable statements in Visual Basic into MSIL, the set of electronic code that forms the input to CLR. Then, when the program is ready for execution, the CLR reads the MSIL in RAM in a form that allows the computer's CPU to execute the instructions in the program.

The use of MSIL and CLR offers multiple benefits that provide speed and flexibility for both the development and execution environments of a program. Utmost among these benefits is that a program written using Visual Studio 2012 and compiled into MSIL can be executed on any computer using any operating system, as long as .NET Framework 4.5 is available on the computer. For example, with no changes to a program you write, the program could be executed on a Dell computer running Windows 8 or an older operating system or on an IBM computer using the Linux operating system. This ability to execute programs on different computers running different operating systems is a primary benefit of using .NET Framework 4.5.

```
Public Class frmPayroll

    Private Sub frmPayroll_Load(ByVal sender As System.Object, ByVal e As System.EventArgs) Handles MyBase.Load
        ' The eventhandler is executed when the form is loaded.  It
        ' clears the Label objects for the hours worked and weekly pay.

        lblHoursWorked.Text = ""
        lblExtraMinutesWorked.Text = ""
        lblRegularPay.Text = ""
        txthoursWorked.Focus()
    End Sub

    Private Sub btnWeeklyPay_Click(ByVal sender As System.Object, ByVal e As System.EventArgs) Handles btnWeeklyPay.Click
        ' This event handler is executed when the user clicks the Weekly
        ' Pay button.  It calculates and displays the hours worked, minutes
        ' worked, and weekly pay.

        Dim strHoursWorked As String
        Dim strHourlyPay As String
        Dim decHourlyPay As Decimal
        Dim intHoursWorked As Integer
        Dim decRegularPay As Decimal
        Dim decOverTimeHours As Decimal
        Dim decOvertimePay As Decimal

        ' Convert the user input from string to a numeric value
        strHourlyPay = txtHourlyPayRate.Text
        decHourlyPay = Convert.ToDecimal(strHourlyPay)
        strHoursWorked = txtHoursWorked.Text
        intHoursWorked = Convert.ToInt32(strHoursWorked)
        If intHoursWorked > 40 Then
            decRegularPay = decHourlyPay * 40
            lblRegularPay.Text = decRegularPay.ToString("C")
            decOvertimePay = 1.5D * decOverTimeHours + decHourlyPay
        Else
            decRegularPay = decHourlyPay * decHourlyPay

        End If
```

Compiler

MSIL Stored on
Disk Storage

CLR

Payroll Information

Employee Name   Robert Terrell

Hours Worked   42

Hourly Rate   18.00

Calculate Pay

Regular Pay $720.00

Overtime Pay $54.00

Total Pay $774.00

FIGURE 1-23

Types of Visual Basic 2012 Applications

When you begin creating a new Visual Basic 2012 program in Visual Studio 2012, you must choose the type of application you will be developing. Based on your choice, Visual Studio 2012 provides the classes, tools, and features required for that type of application.

Five major types of applications are Windows applications, Windows Store apps, website applications, Office applications, and database applications. A **Windows application** means the program will run on a computer or other device that supports the Windows GUI. You can run Windows applications on a variety of computers.

You can create **Windows Store apps** that are designed to run on Windows 8 computers and mobile devices such as smartphones and tablets. Windows Store apps have a new look and feel, run on a variety of devices, and can be sold in the Windows Store. Unlike traditional desktop apps, a Windows Store app has a single, chromeless window that fills the entire screen by default. (Chrome consists of the borders, controls, and other features of a window that frame the content.) To develop a Windows Store app, you must have Visual Studio 2012 installed on a Windows 8 computer. You cannot develop Windows Store apps on Windows 7 or Windows Server products. You must obtain a free developer license to develop and test Windows Store apps before the Windows Store can certify them. The free developer license is provided on a per-machine basis and for a fixed amount of time.

You create a **Web application** using ASP.NET 4.5. The application runs on a web server. It produces HTML5 code that is downloaded to the client computer, where the browser interprets the HTML and displays the contents of a webpage. In a Web application created with ASP.NET 4.5, the developer can include items such as security and forms processing to provide all the services required of a modern website on a computer or mobile device.

An **Office application** includes writing Visual Basic 2012 code to automate and manipulate documents created using Microsoft Office 2010 and Office 2013.

A **database application** is written using ADO.NET 4.5 to reference, access, display, and update data stored in a database. The Visual Basic 2012 developer writes the code to process the data.

Other types of applications Visual Basic 2012 developers can create include console applications, classes for class libraries, certain controls to use in Windows applications, Web services, and device-specific applications.

Summary

In this chapter, you have learned the fundamentals of computer programming and have been introduced to the Visual Studio 2012 and Visual Basic 2012 program development environments. In subsequent chapters, you will learn to use Visual Studio 2012 and Visual Basic 2012 to create Windows applications, Windows Store apps, database applications, and Web applications.

Knowledge Check

1. Explain the differences between computer hardware and computer software.

2. The basic functions of many programs are: a. _____; b. _____;
   c. _____.

3. Match the following terms and their definitions:

   a. Developer

   b. Persistent data

   c. Programming language

   d. Graphical user interface

   e. Database

   f. Class library

   g. Rapid application development (RAD)

   1. A collection of classes that are available for use in programs

   2. Someone skilled in designing computer programs and implementing them in programming languages

   3. A window with a variety of objects that can be displayed on a variety of devices

   4. Data that is stored on a storage medium

   5. The process of using prebuilt classes to make application development faster, easier, and more reliable

   6. A collection of data organized in a manner that allows access, retrieval, and use of that data

   7. A set of words and symbols that can be interpreted by special computer software and eventually can be executed as instructions by a computer

4. Explain what an event is in the context of event-driven programs. Give two examples.

5. Give examples of the differences between an input operation and an output operation.

6. What are the four primary arithmetic operations a computer program can perform? Give an example of each.

7. In the following examples, identify the condition a program would detect (the first exercise is solved for you):

   a. 4 is _____ 3   a. greater than

   b. 9 is _____ 9   b. _____

   c. 17 is _____ 17.8   c. _____

   d. 75 is _____ 85   d. _____

   e. "Microsoft" is _____ "Microsoft"   e. _____

8. Describe three different databases where you think information about yourself might be stored.

9. What is programming language syntax? Why is it important?

10. What is a Toolbox in Visual Studio 2012? Why is it valuable?

11. Name two properties that a Button object can possess.

12. What are the five programming languages you can use with Visual Studio 2012?

13. Where can you sell the Windows Store apps that you develop?

14. State three reasons that Visual Basic is one of the most widely used programming languages in the world.

15. What are four major features of .NET Framework 4.5?

16. Why is a class developed? How are classes organized and stored?

17. Differentiate between a class and an object. Give three examples each of classes and objects.

18. What is the primary use of ADO.NET 4.5?

19. What do you call the process of translating statements written by a developer? What is the result of this process?

20. What are five types of applications you can create in Visual Basic 2012?

CHAPTER 2

Program and Graphical User Interface Design

OBJECTIVES

You will have mastered the material in this chapter when you can:

- Open and close Visual Studio 2012

- Create a Visual Basic 2012 Windows Application project

- Name and set the title bar text in a Windows Form object; resize a Windows Form object

- Add a Label object to a Windows Form object; name the Label object; set the text in the Label object; change the

Font properties of the text in the Label object

- Add a PictureBox object to the Windows Form object; name the PictureBox object; resize the PictureBox object

- Add a Button object to the Windows Form object; name the Button object; set the text in the Button object; change the Button object's size

- Align objects on the Windows Form object

- Save and open Visual Basic projects

- Understand and implement design principles of the graphical user interface

- Understand and implement the first two phases of the program development life cycle

Introduction

Before a program can be coded using Visual Basic 2012, it must be designed. Designing a program can be compared to constructing a building. Before cement slabs are poured, steel beams are put in place and walls are built. Architects and engineers must design a building to ensure it will perform as required and be safe and reliable. The same holds true for a computer program. Once the program is designed, it can be implemented through the Visual Basic 2012 programming language to perform its intended functions.

To illustrate the process of creating a computer program in Visual Basic 2012 using **Visual Studio 2012** as the integrated development environment, you will design and implement the application shown in Figure 2-1 throughout this chapter and Chapter 3.

The application in Figure 2-1 could be part of a larger menu application used to select your pizza order. The program that creates the window in Figure 2-1 will run on a personal computer using the Windows operating system. The program will allow customers to select their favorite pizza type between the two options of Chicago deep-dish pizza and New York thin-crust pizza.

FIGURE 2-1a

FIGURE 2-1b

In Figure 2-1a, the program begins by displaying the Pizza Selection window on a PC monitor. The program provides instructions for the user to choose the pizza type by tapping or clicking the Deep Dish or Thin Crust button, and then to complete the selection by tapping or clicking the Select Pizza button. If the user taps or clicks the Deep Dish button, a picture of a deep-dish pizza is displayed (Figure 2-1b). If the user taps or clicks the Thin Crust button, a picture of a thin-crust pizza is displayed (Figure 2-1c). After choosing a pizza type, the user can tap or click the Select Pizza button and the program informs the user that pizza selection has been completed (Figure 2-1d). To close the window and exit the program, the user can tap or click the Exit Window button after making a pizza selection.

By the end of Chapter 3, you will have completed the design and implementation of this program.

ONLINE REINFORCEMENT

To view a video of the process described in the preceding paragraphs, visit CengageBrain.com and navigate to the resources for this title. Tap or click the link for Chapter 2 and then navigate to Video 2-1. Turn on your speakers to listen to the audio walkthrough of the steps.

FIGURE 2-1c

FIGURE 2-1d

© Brand X Pictures / Getty Images

Use Visual Studio 2012

When designing an event-driven program that uses a graphical user interface (GUI), such as the program in this chapter, one of the first steps after defining the purpose for the program is to design the user interface itself. Recall that the user interface is the window that appears on the screen when the program is running. The user interface includes a variety of objects such as buttons that are displayed in the window. Before beginning to design the user interface, however, the developer should know how to use Visual Studio and Visual Basic **rapid application development** (**RAD**) tools in the design process. For example, you use the Visual Studio tools to place a button on the window. Before starting the design of the program shown in Figure 2-1, you should know how to accomplish the Visual Studio tasks described on the following pages. In this text, you can complete steps by tapping if you are using a touch screen or by clicking if you are using a mouse.

Open Visual Studio 2012

To design a user interface using Visual Studio, the developer opens Visual Studio 2012 and then uses the tools the program provides. To open Visual Studio 2012, you can complete the following steps:

STEP 1   In Windows 8, open the Search charm and type Visual Studio 2012. In Windows 7, tap or click the Start button on the Windows taskbar, point to All Programs on the Start menu, and then tap or click Microsoft Visual Studio 2012 on the All Programs submenu.

The program name, Microsoft Visual Studio 2012, is displayed on the left side of the Windows 8 Apps screen (Figure 2-2).

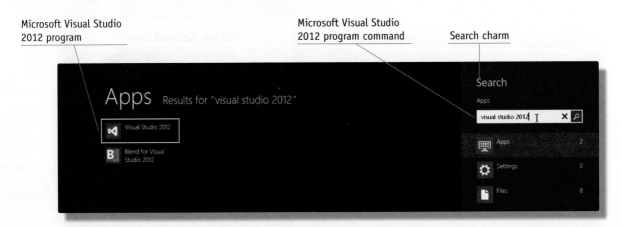

FIGURE 2-2

STEP 2   Tap or click Visual Studio 2012.

A Visual Studio splash screen appears briefly, and then Microsoft Visual Studio 2012 opens (Figure 2-3). The title of the window is Microsoft Visual Studio. The menu bar and the Standard toolbar are displayed at the top of the window. The Start Page contains information about Visual Basic. To close the Start Page, tap or click the Close button on the Start Page title bar. You will learn the other elements of this window as you progress through this book.

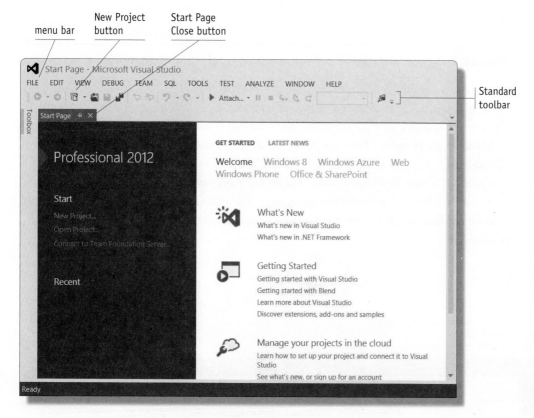

FIGURE 2-3

Create a New Visual Basic 2012 Windows Application Project

A **project** is equivalent to a single program created using Visual Studio. A **Windows Application project** is a program that includes a user interface whose windows are created using the Windows operating system. When the program is executed, the user interacts with the program by using its windows and components (the user interface).

To create a new project using Visual Studio, you must specify the programming language you want to use and the type of program or application you will create. To create a new Visual Basic Windows Application project, you can take the following steps:

STEP 1   Tap or click the New Project button on the Standard toolbar.

Visual Studio opens the New Project window (Figure 2-4). The New Project window on your computer might be displayed differently, depending on selections made when Visual Studio was installed on your computer. For example, if you are using Windows 7, you will not see the Windows Store templates listed because you need Windows 8 to develop a Windows Store app. The left pane contains the programming languages and other types of templates available in Visual Studio. The middle pane contains the types of applications you can create within each programming language. The right pane displays a description of the selected application. At this point, you want to create a Windows Forms Application using Visual Basic.

FIGURE 2-4

STEP 2 If necessary, tap or click Windows in the left pane so it is selected.

Windows is highlighted in the left pane and the types of Windows projects you can create using Visual Basic are listed in the middle pane (Figure 2–5).

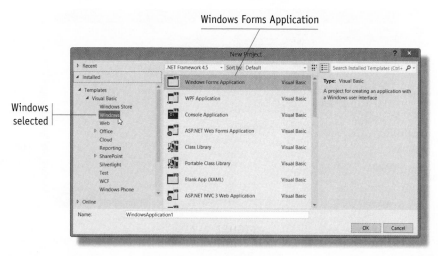

FIGURE 2-5

STEP 3 If necessary, tap or click Windows Forms Application in the middle pane.

Windows Forms Application is selected in the middle pane (Figure 2–6). By making this selection, you have specified you want to create a program that will run under the Windows operating system using the Windows graphical user interface.

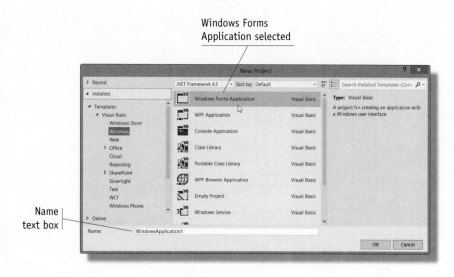

FIGURE 2-6

STEP 4 Type the project name. For this example, you could type Pizza Selection as the name.

The project name appears in the Name text box (Figure 2-7).

FIGURE 2-7

STEP 5 Tap or click the OK button in the New Project window.

Visual Studio creates a new project (Figure 2-8). The project name is displayed in the title bar of the window.

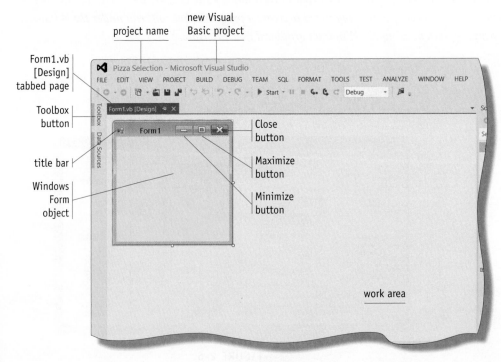

FIGURE 2-8

The Visual Studio window contains several important features you should know. First, in the portion of the window known as the **work area**, a tabbed page named Form1.vb [Design] contains a Windows Form object called Form1. A **Windows Form object** is the window you will use to build the program and then display it on your screen when you execute the program. The Windows Form object is the fundamental object in the graphical user interface you will create using Visual Studio tools. Notice in Figure 2-8 that the Windows Form object contains a blue title bar, a window title (Form1), a Minimize button, a Maximize button, and a Close button.

A second important element is displayed on the left side of the window. Depending on the settings in Visual Studio, the left portion of the window will appear as shown in Figure 2-8 or Figure 2-9. In Figure 2-8, the left margin contains the Toolbox button. The Toolbox button also appears on the Standard toolbar.

Display the Toolbox

You can use the **Toolbox button** to display the Toolbox. The **Toolbox** is the primary tool you use to place objects such as buttons on the Windows Form object. Items in the Toolbox are grouped into sections called **tabs**. To display the Toolbox, you can take the following steps:

STEP 1   If the window does not already display the Toolbox, tap or click the Toolbox button in the left margin of the window. If necessary, tap or click Common Controls to display the Common Controls tab.

When you point to the Toolbox button, the Toolbox is displayed on the window (Figure 2-9). Notice that the Toolbox hides the Form1 Windows Form object.

FIGURE 2-9

WATCH OUT FOR

In Figure 2-9, the Common Controls category of tools is open and all its tools are visible. If the Common Category tab is not expanded, a right triangle appears to the left of the Common Controls tab. To open the tab, tap or click the right triangle.

ONLINE REINFORCEMENT

To view a video of the process in the previous steps, visit CengageBrain.com and navigate to the resources for this title. Tap or click the link for Chapter 2 and then navigate to Video 2-4.

Among other things, the Toolbox contains many graphical elements called **controls** that you can place on the Windows Form object as graphical user interface objects. For example, the Toolbox contains buttons that can be placed on the Windows Form object. You will learn how to perform this activity in the next section of this chapter.

Permanently Display the Toolbox

When you tap or click outside the Toolbox, it no longer is displayed. When you are designing the graphical user interface, normally it helps to display the Toolbox at all times. To always display the Toolbox, you can complete the following step:

STEP 1 If necessary, tap or click the Toolbox button in the left margin of the window to display the Toolbox. Then, tap or click the **Auto Hide button** (Pushpin icon) on the Toolbox title bar.

When you tap or click the Auto Hide button, the Pushpin icon on the button changes from being horizontal, which indicates Auto Hide, to vertical, which indicates the Toolbox has been "pinned" to the window and will remain there (Figure 2-10). Form1 is moved to the right so you can see both the Toolbox and all of Form1.

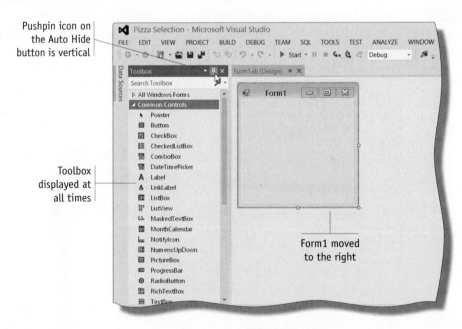

Pushpin icon on
the Auto Hide
button is vertical

Toolbox
displayed at
all times

Form1 moved
to the right

FIGURE 2-10

When the Pushpin icon is vertical, the Toolbox is said to be in Dockable mode, which means it can be dragged around and placed anywhere within the Visual Studio window. In most applications, it should remain on the left side of the window, as shown in Figure 2-10. Later, you can change the Toolbox back to Auto Hide mode by tapping or clicking the Auto Hide button again.

View Object Properties

Every object you create in the user interface, including the Windows Form object, has properties. **Properties** can describe a multitude of characteristics about the object, including its color, size, name, and position on the screen. You will learn about the properties of all the objects you create using the Toolbox.

To view the properties for an object in Visual Studio, you use the Properties window. By default, the Properties window is displayed in the lower-right section of the Visual Studio window (Figure 2-11).

FIGURE 2-11

HEADS UP

If the Solution Explorer window is not displayed on your screen, you can display the window by taking the following steps:
1) Tap or click VIEW on the menu bar;
2) Tap or click Solution Explorer on the VIEW menu. The Solution Explorer window will be displayed in the location shown in Figure 2-11.

In the **Properties window** shown in Figure 2-11, the property names in the left list appear in Alphabetical view. Many developers find the Alphabetical view the easiest to use when searching for properties. Some developers, however, prefer the Categorized view, in which properties are organized according to type. You can change the order of the properties to Categorized if you tap or click the Categorized button on the Properties window toolbar (see Figure 2-11). In this book, the properties are shown in Alphabetical view, which you select by tapping or clicking the Alphabetical button on the Properties window toolbar.

HEADS UP

If you want to reset your Visual Basic window to its original installed layout, you can take the following steps:
1) Tap or click WINDOW on the menu bar;
2) Tap or click Reset Window Layout on the WINDOW menu.

Name the Windows Form Object

Visual Studio assigns a default name to every object in a Visual Basic graphical user interface. For example, the first Windows Form object in a project is named Form1. In virtually every instance, a developer should assign a meaningful name to an object so the program can reference it if required. The name of an object should reflect the object's use. For example, a good name for the Pizza Selection window might be frmPizzaSelection. Notice in the name that each word is capitalized and the remaining letters are lowercase. You should always follow this naming method when naming objects.

No spaces or other special characters are allowed in the object name. Also, by convention, each object name should begin with a prefix that identifies the type of object. For Windows Form objects, the prefix is frm. Therefore, the complete name for the Windows Form object would be frmPizzaSelection. The form name should be changed from Form1 to a more descriptive name in the Solution Explorer.

To give the name frmPizzaSelection to the form in Figure 2-11 on the previous page, you can complete the following steps:

STEP 1   Tap or click anywhere in the Windows Form object to select it.

When you tap or click within any object, including a Windows Form object, it is selected (Figure 2-12). Sizing handles and a heavier border surround the selected object. In addition, the Properties window displays the properties of the selected object.

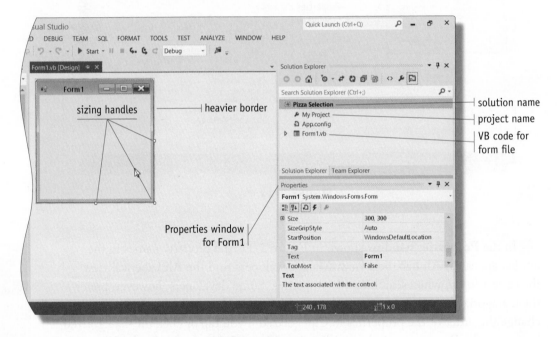

FIGURE 2-12

STEP 2   In the Solution Explorer window, press and hold or right-click the Form1. vb filename. On the shortcut menu, point to Rename.

The shortcut menu for the Form1.vb file appears in the Solution Explorer. Rename is highlighted (Figure 2-13).

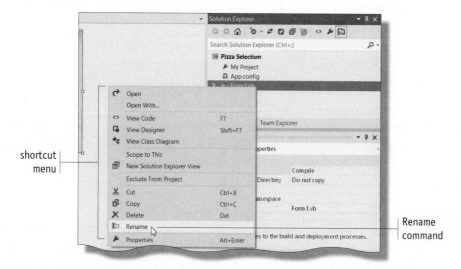

FIGURE 2-13

STEP 3 Tap or click Rename. Type `frmPizzaSelection.vb` and press the ENTER key.

The Form1.vb form file is given the new name frmPizzaSelection.vb in the Solution Explorer window (Figure 2-14).

FIGURE 2-14

ONLINE REINFORCEMENT

To view a video of the process in the previous steps, visit CengageBrain.com and navigate to the resources for this title. Tap or click the link for Chapter 2 and then navigate to Video 2-6.

Why should you name the Form object?

Later in this text, you add multiple Form objects. It can become confusing if you do not have unique identifying names for each of the Form objects within the project.

Set the Title Bar Text in a Windows Form Object

After you name the Windows Form object, often the next step in graphical user interface design is to change the title bar text to reflect the function of the program. In this example, the name used is Pizza Selection. The **Text property** in the Properties window for the Windows Form object contains the value displayed in the title bar of the window. You can set the Text property using the following steps:

STEP 1 With the Windows Form object selected, scroll in the Properties window as necessary until you find the Text property. (Remember that the properties are in alphabetical order.) Then, double-tap or double-click the Text property in the right column.

The text, Form1, is selected in the Properties window (Figure 2-15). Form1 is the default text value for the first Windows Form object created in a project. Whenever a property is selected, you can change the property.

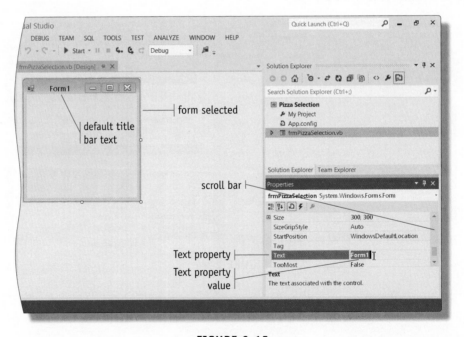

FIGURE 2-15

STEP 2   Type `Pizza Selection` and then press the ENTER key.

The value, Pizza Selection, is displayed for the Text property in the Properties window and is partially displayed in the title bar of the Windows Form object (Figure 2-16). You can enter any value you like for the Text property of the Windows Form object.

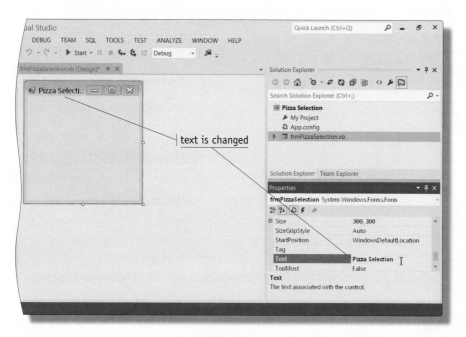

text is changed

FIGURE 2-16

You can change many of the properties for any object in the graphical user interface using the techniques just illustrated.

Resize a Form

To resize a Windows Form object, you can change the **Size property** in the Properties window to the exact number of horizontal and vertical pixels you desire. You can change the Size property in the Properties window, or you can drag the vertical border to change the width of the window and the horizontal border to change the height. Another way to change the size is to drag a corner sizing handle, which allows you to change the width and height at the same time.

The following steps illustrate how to change the Size property of the Windows Form object shown in Figure 2-17:

STEP 1 With the Windows Form object selected, double-click the Size property in the right column.

The Size property is selected in the Properties window (Figure 2-17).

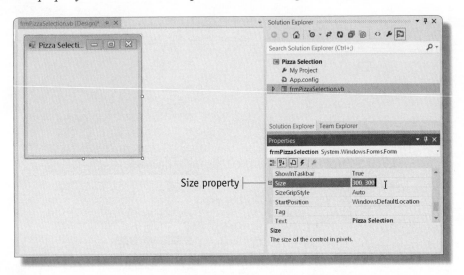

FIGURE 2-17

STEP 2 Type 430, 395 and then press the ENTER key.

The Windows Form object has been resized (Figure 2-18). The exact size of the Windows Form object is shown on the status bar as (number of horizontal pixels, number of vertical pixels). In Figure 2-18, the size of the Windows Form object is 430 pixels horizontally by 395 pixels vertically.

FIGURE 2-18

ONLINE REINFORCEMENT

To view a video of the process in the previous steps, visit CengageBrain.com and navigate to the resources for this title. Tap or click the link for Chapter 2 and then navigate to Video 2-8.

Add a Label Object

After sizing the Windows Form object, you can use the Toolbox to add other GUI objects as required. For example, a graphical user interface often displays a message or labels an item in the window. To accomplish this, you can use the **Label .NET component** in the Toolbox to place a **Label object** on the Windows Form object. To add a Label object to a Windows Form object, you can complete the following steps.

STEP 1 Drag the Label .NET component from the Common Controls tab in the Toolbox over the Windows Form object to the approximate location where you want to place the Label object.

The pointer changes to a crosshair and small rectangle when you place it over the Windows Form object (Figure 2-19). The Label object will be placed on the form at the location of the small rectangle in the pointer.

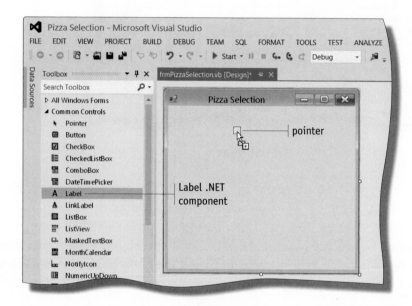

FIGURE 2-19

IN THE REAL WORLD

In addition to dragging a .NET component from the Toolbox to the Windows Form object, you can place an object on the Windows Form object by double-tapping or double-clicking the .NET component in the Toolbox. You can move and resize the object after placing it on the Windows Form object. You also can tap or click the .NET component in the Toolbox and then tap or click the Windows Form object at the desired location for the object. The object will be placed where you tapped or clicked. Developers use the technique they find most convenient.

ONLINE REINFORCEMENT

To view a video of the process in the previous steps, visit CengageBrain.com and navigate to the resources for this title. Tap or click the link for Chapter 2 and then navigate to Video 2-9.

STEP 2   When the Label object is in the correct location, release the left mouse button.

The Label object is placed on the Windows Form object at the location you selected (Figure 2-20). The label is selected, as identified by the dotted border surrounding it. The default text within the label is Label1. In virtually all cases, you must change the label text to reflect the needs of the interface.

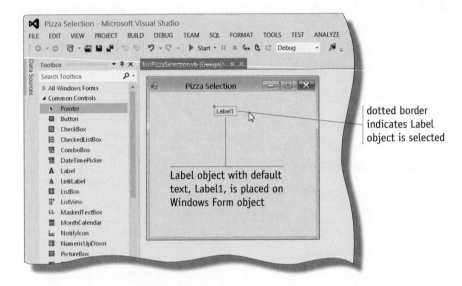

FIGURE 2-20

Name the Label Object

As with most objects you place on the Windows Form object, the first step after creating the object should be to name it. To give the Label object the name Heading with the Label prefix lbl, complete the following steps:

STEP 1   With the Label object selected, scroll in the Properties window until you find the (Name) property. Then, double-click the (Name) property in the right column.

The default name, Label1, is selected (Figure 2-21). When a property is selected, you can change the property.

FIGURE 2-21

STEP 2 Type the new name as `lblHeading` and then press the ENTER key.

The name you entered is displayed in the Name property in the Properties window (Figure 2-22). You now can reference the Label object by its name in other parts of the program.

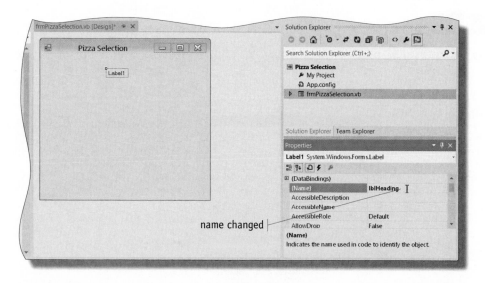

FIGURE 2-22

WATCH OUT FOR

If you make an error while typing a property, such as the name, you can press the backspace key to erase your mistake and then type the correct data. You also can double-tap or double-click the property you want to change and start over.

ONLINE REINFORCEMENT

To view a video of the process in the previous steps, visit CengageBrain.com and navigate to the resources for this title. Tap or click the link for Chapter 2 and then navigate to Video 2-10.

Change the Text in a Label Object

The default text in a Label object, Label1, normally is not the text you want to display in the label. Therefore, you should change the Text property for the Label object to the value you want. To change the text on the label in Figure 2-21 to Pizza Selection, you can complete the following steps:

STEP 1   With the Label object selected, scroll in the Properties window until you find the Text property. Then, double-tap or double-click the Text value in the right column.

The text value is selected in the right column of the Text property. The same text is displayed on the label (Figure 2-23). When the Text value is selected, you can change it.

Text property —

Text value selected

FIGURE 2-23

STEP 2   Type Pizza Selection for the Text property.

The text you typed, Pizza Selection, is displayed in the Text property for the Label object (Figure 2-24).

text entered into Text property

FIGURE 2-24

STEP 3   To enter the Text property, press the ENTER key.

The text you entered, Pizza Selection, is displayed in the Text property and in the label itself (Figure 2-25). By default, the text is 8 points in size. The Label object automatically expanded horizontally to accommodate the text you typed. By default, Label objects change to be the right size for the text in the Text property.

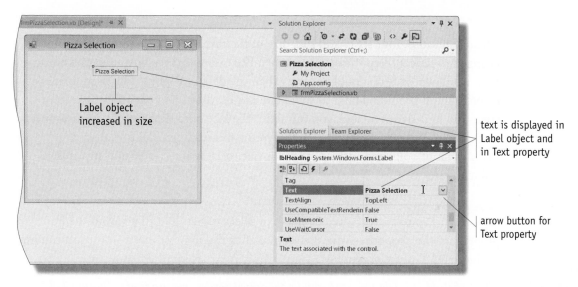

FIGURE 2-25

The text in a Label object can span multiple lines. To enter multiple lines for a Label object, you can complete the following steps:

STEP 1 With the Label object selected, tap or click the Text property name in the left column of the Properties window. Then, tap or click the arrow button in the right column of the Text property.

A box opens in which you can enter multiple lines (Figure 2-26). As you type, you can move the insertion point to the next line by pressing the ENTER key. To accept the text for the label, press CTRL + ENTER. (In other words, hold down the CTRL key, press the ENTER key, and then release both keys.)

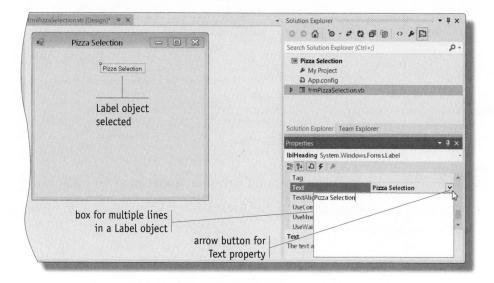

FIGURE 2-26

Change the Label Font, Font Style, and Font Size

The default font, font style, and font size of the text in a Label object often must be changed to reflect the purpose of the label. For example, in a label used as a heading for a window, the text should be larger than the default 8-point font used for Label objects, and it should be bold to stand out as a heading. To change the font, font style, and font size of a label, you can select the label and then use the **Font property** to make the change. To change the text in the lblHeading label to Tahoma font, make the font bold, and increase the font size to 16 points, you can complete the following steps:

STEP 1   Tap or click the Label object to select it. Scroll until you find the Font property in the Properties window. Tap or click the Font property in the left column of the Label Properties window.

The Label object is selected, as shown by the dotted border surrounding it (Figure 2-27). When you tap or click the Font property in the Properties window, a button with an ellipsis (three dots) is displayed in the right column. In the Properties window, an ellipsis button indicates that multiple choices for the property will be made available when you tap or click the button.

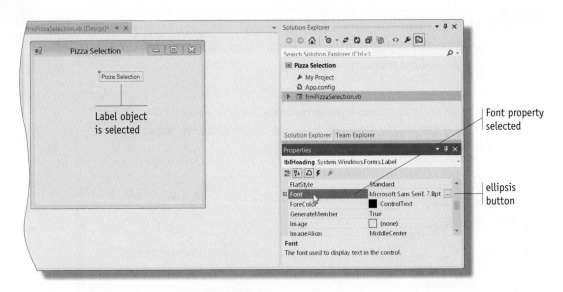

FIGURE 2-27

STEP 2   Tap or click the ellipsis button for the Font property.

The Font dialog box is displayed (Figure 2-28). Using the Font dialog box, you can change the font, font style, and size of the text in the Label object.

FIGURE 2-28

STEP 3   In the Font dialog box, scroll in the Font list until you find Tahoma and then tap or click it. Tap or click Bold in the Font style list. Tap or click 16 in the Size list.

The selections are highlighted in the Font dialog box (Figure 2-29).

FIGURE 2-29

STEP 4 Tap or click the OK button.

The font, font style, and font size in the Label object are changed as specified in the Font dialog box (Figure 2-30). The Label object automatically expands to accommodate the changed font. The changes also are made for the Font property in the Properties window.

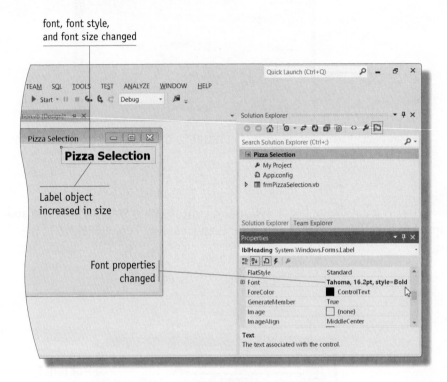

FIGURE 2-30

Center a Label Object in the Windows Form Object

When you place an object on the Windows Form object, your object may not be located in precisely the correct position. So, you must align the object in the window. A single label often is centered horizontally in the window; that is, the distance from the left frame of the window to the beginning of the text should be the same as the distance from the end of the text to the right frame of the window. To horizontally center the label that contains the heading, you can complete the following steps:

STEP 1 With the Label object selected, tap or click FORMAT on the menu bar and then point to Center in Form on the FORMAT menu.

The FORMAT menu is displayed and the pointer is located on the Center in Form command (Figure 2-31). The Center in Form submenu also is displayed. The two choices on the Center in Form submenu are Horizontally and Vertically. Horizontally means the label will be centered between the left and right edges of the window. Vertically means the label will be centered between the top edge and the bottom edge of the window.

FORMAT on menu bar

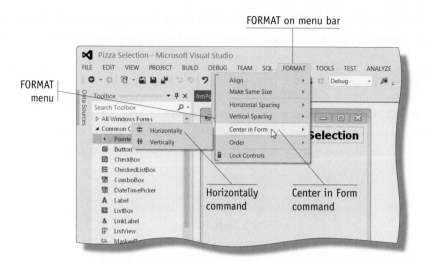

FORMAT menu

Horizontally command

Center in Form command

FIGURE 2-31

STEP 2 Tap or click Horizontally on the Center in Form submenu.

The label is centered horizontally in the window (Figure 2-32).

Label object is centered horizontally

FIGURE 2-32

Aligning objects is an important aspect of user interface design because it makes objects and the interface easy to use. Centering within the Windows Form object is the first of several alignments you will make in this chapter.

Delete GUI Objects

In some instances, you might add an object to the Windows Form object and later discover you do not need the object in the user interface. When this occurs, you should delete the object from the Windows Form object. Visual Studio provides two primary ways to delete an object from the Windows Form object: the keyboard and a shortcut menu. To delete an object using the keyboard, perform the following steps:

STEP 1 Select the object to delete by tapping or clicking it.

When you tap or click an object, such as the label in Figure 2-33, the object is selected. When a label is selected, it is surrounded by a dotted border. As you saw with the Windows Form object (Figure 2-12), other objects are surrounded by a heavier border and sizing handles.

FIGURE 2-33

STEP 2 Press the DELETE key.

When you press the DELETE key, Visual Studio removes the object from the screen (Figure 2-34).

FIGURE 2-34

ONLINE REINFORCEMENT

To view a video of the process in the previous steps, visit CengageBrain.com and navigate to the resources for this title. Tap or click the link for Chapter 2 and then navigate to Video 2-15.

A second way to delete an object is to use a shortcut menu. To do so, press or right-click the object to be deleted and then select Delete on the shortcut menu.

Use the Undo Button on the Standard Toolbar

As you work in Visual Studio to create a graphical user interface, you might delete an object or perform another activity that you realize was an error. You can undo an action you just performed by tapping or clicking the Undo button on the Standard toolbar. To undo the action of deleting the heading label, you can perform the following step:

STEP 1 Tap or click the Undo button on the Standard toolbar.

When you tap or click the Undo button, the last action performed in Visual Studio is "undone." In Figure 2-35, the action that deleted the label (Figure 2-34) is undone and the Label object now appears on the Windows Form object again.

FIGURE 2-35

You can use the Undo button to undo more than just the last action performed. If you tap or click the Undo button arrow (Figure 2-35), many of the previous activities are shown in a list. You can undo any displayed activity by tapping or clicking it in the list.

When you use the Undo button, you might undo something you do not want to undo. You can tap or click the Redo button on the Standard toolbar to redo an action.

Learning to use the Undo and Redo buttons on the Standard toolbar means you can add or delete items in the graphical user interface with the assurance that any error you make can be corrected immediately.

Add a PictureBox Object

When you want to display a picture in a window, such as the pizza pictures shown in Figure 2-1b and Figure 2-1c on pages 32 and 33, you must place a PictureBox object on the Windows Form object. Then, you place the picture in the PictureBox object.

In this section, you will learn to add a PictureBox object to the Windows Form object. In Chapter 3, you will learn how to place a picture in the PictureBox object.

A **PictureBox** is an object much like a label. To add a PictureBox object to the window, you can use the Toolbox, as shown in the following steps:

STEP 1   With the Toolbox visible, drag the PictureBox .NET component on the Toolbox over the Windows Form object to the approximate location where you want the PictureBox object to be displayed.

The pointer changes when you place it over the Windows Form object (Figure 2-36). The upper-left corner of the PictureBox object will be placed on the form at the location of the small square in the pointer.

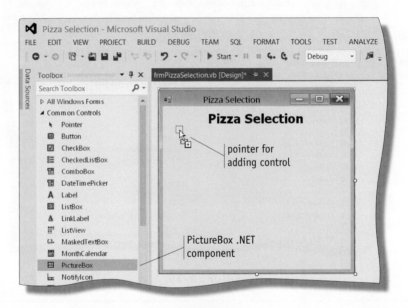

FIGURE 2-36

STEP 2   When the pointer is in the correct location, release the left mouse button.

A PictureBox object is placed on the Windows Form object in the default size (Figure 2-37). The PictureBox object is selected, as indicated by the sizing handles and the heavier border. Notice that when the pointer is inside the PictureBox object, it changes to a crosshair with four arrowheads. This indicates you can drag the PictureBox object anywhere on the Windows Form object.

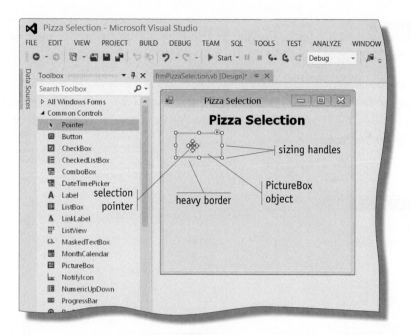

FIGURE 2-37

ONLINE REINFORCEMENT

To view a video of the process in the previous steps, visit CengageBrain.com and navigate to the resources for this title. Tap or click the link for Chapter 2 and then navigate to Video 2-17.

As you can see, placing a PictureBox object on the Windows Form object is similar to placing a Label object on the Windows Form object. You can use the same technique for most objects within the Toolbox.

Name a PictureBox Object

When you add an object to the Windows Form object, your next action should be to name the object. The technique for naming a PictureBox object is identical to that for a Label object, except that the prefix for a PictureBox object is pic. For example, to give the name picDeepDish to the PictureBox object just added to the form, you can complete the following steps:

1. Select the PictureBox object.
2. Locate the (Name) property in the Properties window for the PictureBox object.
3. Double-tap or double-click the value in the right column for the (Name) property, type picDeepDish as the name, and then press the ENTER key.

Resize a PictureBox Object

When you place a PictureBox object on the Windows Form object, it often is not the size required for the application. You can resize a PictureBox object using the same technique you used to resize the Windows Form object. The step on the next page will resize the PictureBox object:

STEP 1 Double-tap or double-click to the right of the Size property of the PictureBox object, type 185,150, and then press the ENTER key.

When you change the Size property, the width and height of the PictureBox object are changed. In Figure 2-38, the width and height of the PictureBox object are increased. The actual size of the PictureBox object in pixels (185 horizontal pixels, 150 vertical pixels) is shown on the status bar.

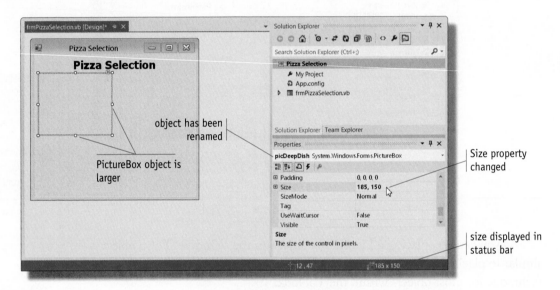

FIGURE 2-38

Add a Second PictureBox Object

You can add a second PictureBox object to the Windows Form object by performing the same technique you used previously, as in the following step:

STEP 1   Drag the PictureBox .NET component in the Toolbox to any location in the Windows Form object, and then release the left mouse button.

The PictureBox object is placed on the Windows Form object (Figure 2-39). Notice that the PictureBox objects in Figure 2-39 are different sizes. If you see a blue line as you drag the PictureBox object onto the Windows Form object, ignore it. You will learn about these lines later in this chapter.

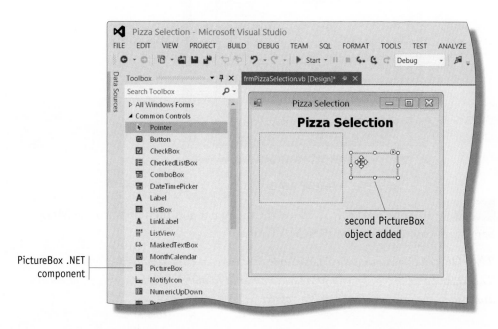

FIGURE 2-39

ONLINE REINFORCEMENT

To view a video of the process in the previous step, visit CengageBrain.com and navigate to the resources for this title. Tap or click the link for Chapter 2 and then navigate to Video 2-19.

As with all objects you add to the Windows Form object, you should name the PictureBox object immediately after adding it. A good name for the second PictureBox object is picThinCrust.

Make Objects the Same Size

Often you will want picture boxes and other GUI elements in your user interface to be the same size. You can use the FORMAT menu to make GUI objects the same size, as shown in the steps on the next page:

STEP 1 Select the object whose size you want to duplicate (in this example, the left PictureBox object in the window), and then hold down the CTRL key and tap or click the object you want to resize (the right PictureBox object in the window).

The left and right PictureBox objects are selected (Figure 2–40). The left PictureBox object is surrounded by white sizing handles and the right PictureBox object is surrounded by black sizing handles, which indicates the left PictureBox object is the "controlling" object when sizing or alignment commands are executed. The first object selected always is the controlling object.

FIGURE 2-40

STEP 2 Tap or click FORMAT on the menu bar and then point to the Make Same Size command on the FORMAT menu.

The FORMAT menu and the Make Same Size submenu are displayed (Figure 2–41). The Make Same Size submenu provides commands to make the width, height, or both dimensions the same as the controlling object.

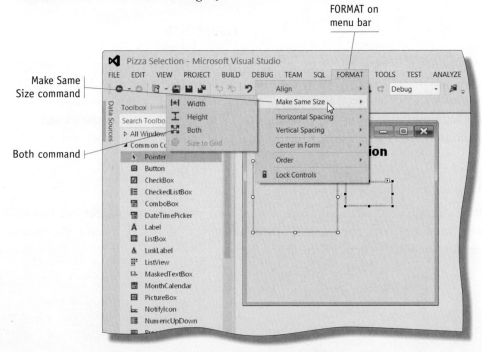

FIGURE 2-41

STEP 3   Tap or click Both on the Make Same Size submenu.

Visual Studio changes the size of the right PictureBox object to match the size of the left PictureBox object (Figure 2-42). Both the width and the height of the right PictureBox object are changed.

PictureBox objects
are the same size

FIGURE 2-42

Align the PictureBox Objects

Notice in Figure 2-42 that the left PictureBox object is higher in the form than the right PictureBox object. When designing a graphical user interface, you should consider aligning the elements to create a clean, uncluttered look for the user. **Alignment** means one element in the GUI is lined up horizontally (left and right) or vertically (up and down) with another element in the window. For example, in Figure 2-42 the GUI would look better if the PictureBox objects were aligned horizontally so their tops and bottoms were even across the window.

When you want to align objects that are already on the Windows Form object, select the objects to align and then specify the alignment you want. As you saw when changing the object size, the first object selected is the controlling object; when aligning, this means the other selected objects will be aligned with the first object selected. To horizontally align the two PictureBox objects in Figure 2-42, you can perform the steps on the next page:

STEP 1 With the left and right PictureBox objects selected, as shown in Figure 2-42 on the previous page, tap or click FORMAT on the menu bar and then point to Align on the FORMAT menu.

The FORMAT menu and the Align submenu are displayed (Figure 2-43). The left PictureBox object is the "controlling" object, as indicated by the white sizing handles, so the right PictureBox object will be aligned horizontally with the left PictureBox object.

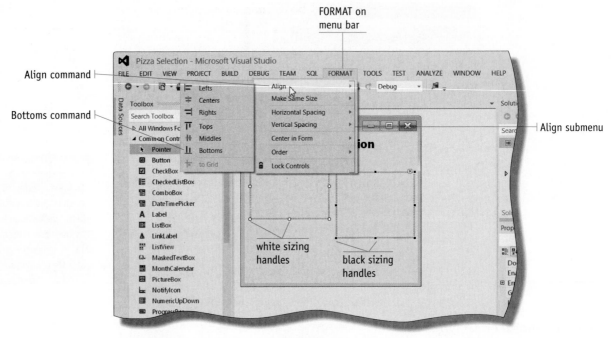

FIGURE 2-43

STEP 2 Tap or click Bottoms on the Align submenu.

The bottom of the right PictureBox object is aligned horizontally with the bottom of the left PictureBox object (Figure 2-44). Because the PictureBox objects are the same size, the tops also are aligned.

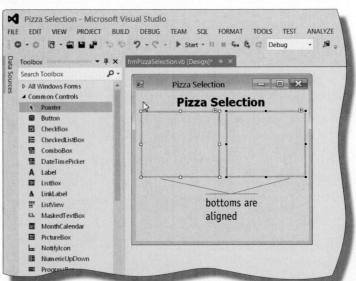

FIGURE 2-44

Notice on the Align submenu in Figure 2-43 that Visual Studio offers seven choices for alignment. When you are aligning objects horizontally, you should choose from the Tops, Middles, and Bottoms group. When you are aligning objects vertically, you should choose from the Lefts, Centers, and Rights group. You will learn how to align to a grid later in this book.

Center Multiple Objects Horizontally in the Window

From Figure 2-44, you can see that the PictureBox objects are not centered horizontally in the Windows Form object. As you learned, you can center one or more objects horizontally within the Windows Form object by using a command from the FORMAT menu. To center the two PictureBox objects as a unit, you can complete the following steps:

STEP 1   With both PictureBox objects selected, tap or click FORMAT on the menu bar and then point to the Center in Form command.

The FORMAT menu is displayed (Figure 2–45). The Center in Form submenu also is displayed.

FIGURE 2-45

STEP 2   Tap or click Horizontally on the Center in Form submenu.

The two PictureBox objects are centered horizontally as a unit in the Windows Form object (Figure 2-46). The left border of the left PictureBox object is the same distance from the window frame as the right border of the right PictureBox object.

FIGURE 2-46

Adding an object, naming it, sizing it, and aligning it are basic to graphical user interface design.

Add a Button Object

A **Button object** is a commonly used object in a graphical user interface. For example, you probably are familiar with the OK button used in many applications. Generally, when the program is executing, buttons are used to cause an event to occur. To place a Button object on the Windows Form object, you use the Toolbox. To create a Button object, you can complete the following steps:

STEP 1 With the Toolbox displayed in the Visual Studio window, drag the Button control in the Toolbox over the Windows Form object to the position where you want to place the button below the first PictureBox object.

When you drag the button over the Windows Form object, the pointer changes (Figure 2-47). The upper-left corner of the Button object will be placed at the lower-left corner of the rectangle.

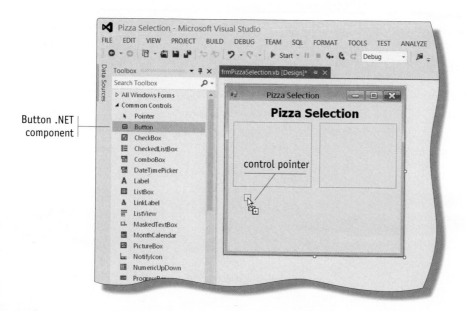

Button .NET component

control pointer

FIGURE 2-47

STEP 2 When the pointer is positioned properly, release the left mouse button.

A standard-sized Button object is added to the Windows Form object (Figure 2-48). The text on the button is the default, Button1. The button is selected, as indicated by the heavier border and sizing handles.

default text

Button object is selected

Button object added

FIGURE 2-48

ONLINE REINFORCEMENT

To view a video of the process in the previous steps, visit CengageBrain.com and navigate to the resources for this title. Tap or click the link for Chapter 2 and then navigate to Video 2-23.

Name and Set Text for a Button Object

As with other objects you add to the Windows Form object, the first step after adding the Button object is to name it. A Button object name should contain the prefix btn. For example, the name for the button you just added could be btnDeepDish.

In most cases, you also will change the text that appears on the Button object. To change the text on the btnDeepDish button, you can do the following:

STEP 1 With the Button object selected, scroll in the Properties window until you find the Text property. Double-click the Text value in the right column, type Deep Dish, and then press the ENTER key.

The text for the Deep Dish button is changed on the button and in the Properties window (Figure 2-49). The button is not large enough to contain the words Deep Dish, so only Deep is displayed. In the next set of steps, you will learn how to increase the size of the Button object.

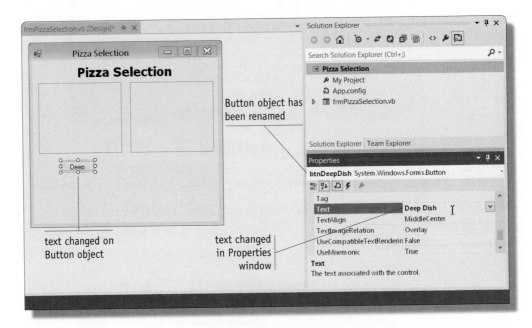

FIGURE 2-49

Change a Button Object's Size

Sometimes, a button may not be big enough to display the button text (see Figure 2-49). To change a Button object's size to accommodate the text, you can perform the following steps:

STEP 1 Place the pointer over the right edge of the Button object until the pointer changes to a double-headed arrow.

The pointer changes to a double-headed arrow, which indicates you can drag the border of the button to increase or decrease its size (Figure 2-50).

FIGURE 2-50

STEP 2 Drag the pointer to the right until the Button object is just big enough to display the text Deep Dish, and then release the left mouse button.

As you drag the pointer to the right, the button becomes bigger (Figure 2-51). When the button is big enough to display the text, it is the right size.

FIGURE 2-51

ONLINE REINFORCEMENT

To view a video of the process in the previous steps, visit CengageBrain.com and navigate to the resources for this title. Tap or click the link for Chapter 2 and then navigate to Video 2-25.

To move a Button object, first place the pointer on the button; when the pointer changes to a crosshair with four arrowheads, drag the button to any location on the Windows Form object. You can move other objects on the Windows Form object using the same technique.

Add and Align a Second Button

Often, a window requires more than one button. When a second button is added to the window, a normal requirement is to align the buttons. As with PictureBox objects, you can align Button objects horizontally or vertically.

With the PictureBox objects, you saw that you can align objects after placing them on the Windows Form object. You also can align objects when you place them on the Windows Form object. To add a second button to the Windows Form object in Figure 2-51 on the previous page and align it horizontally at the same time, you can complete the following steps:

STEP 1   Drag the Button .NET component from the Toolbox to the right of the Deep Dish button on the Windows Form object. Align the top of the rectangle in the pointer to the top of the Deep Dish button until a red line appears under the text of the buttons.

*The red line, called a **snap line**, indicates the text on the Deep Dish button is aligned with the text on the Button object being added to the Windows Form object (Figure 2-52). You can drag the Button object left or right to obtain the desired spacing between the buttons. If the red line disappears while you are dragging, move the pointer up or down until the red line reappears, signaling the objects are aligned horizontally.*

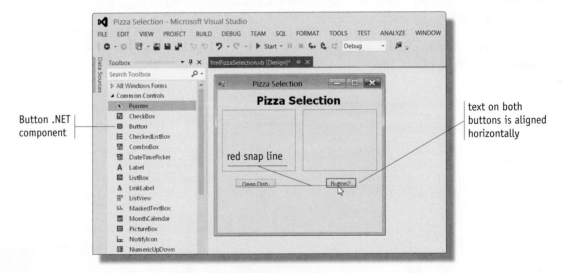

FIGURE 2-52

STEP 2 When the buttons are aligned and spaced as you like, release the left mouse button.

The Button2 object is aligned horizontally with the Deep Dish button (Figure 2-53). The text of each button is on the same line.

FIGURE 2-53

ONLINE REINFORCEMENT

To view a video of the process in the previous steps, visit CengageBrain.com and navigate to the resources for this title. Tap or click the link for Chapter 2 and then navigate to Video 2-26.

After adding the second Button object, you should name it, change the text as needed, and size the Button object if necessary. Assume you have named the second Button object btnThinCrust, changed the button text to Thin Crust, and made the two buttons the same size. Recall that you can make the Thin Crust button the same size as the Deep Dish button by completing the following steps:

Step 1: Tap or click the Deep Dish button and then, while holding down the CTRL key, tap or click the Thin Crust button.

Step 2: Tap or click FORMAT on the menu bar, point to Make Same Size on the FORMAT menu, and then tap or click Both on the Make Same Size submenu.

Step 3: To deselect the Button objects, tap or click anywhere on the Windows Form object except on another object.

Align Objects Vertically

The buttons in Figure 2-53 on the previous page are aligned horizontally, but they also can be aligned vertically. To illustrate this point and to use snap lines to align objects that are already on the Windows Form object, assume that the Deep Dish and Thin Crust buttons should be aligned vertically on the left side of the Windows Form object, with the Deep Dish button above the Thin Crust button. To align the Button objects vertically, you can complete the following steps:

STEP 1   If necessary, tap or click anywhere in the Windows Form object to deselect any other objects. Then, slowly drag the Thin Crust button below the Deep Dish button until vertical blue snap lines are displayed.

*As you drag, **blue snap lines** indicate when the sides of the objects are aligned vertically. In Figure 2-54, the buttons are the same size, so when the left side of the Deep Dish button is aligned with the left side of the Thin Crust button, the right sides are aligned as well. As a result, two blue vertical lines are displayed. If you drag the button a little more to the left or right, the buttons will not be aligned and the blue lines will disappear.*

FIGURE 2-54

STEP 2   When the blue lines appear, indicating the buttons are aligned vertically, drag the Thin Crust button up or down to create the proper spacing between the buttons, and then release the left mouse button.

The proper vertical distance between the buttons is a judgment call based on the needs of the application, the size of the Windows Form object, and the number of other elements in the window (Figure 2-55). As with many aspects of GUI design, the eye of the developer is critical when placing objects in the window.

FIGURE 2-55

ONLINE REINFORCEMENT

To view a video of the process in the previous steps, visit CengageBrain.com and navigate to the resources for this title. Tap or click the link for Chapter 2 and then navigate to Video 2-27.

In the previous examples, you have seen the use of blue snap lines. As you drag objects, you also might see red snap lines flash on the screen. A red snap line indicates text is aligned within an object. For example, if you drag a button that contains text and the text aligns horizontally with the text in another button, a red snap line will be displayed. The use of red and blue snap lines allows you to align objects on the Windows Form object by dragging instead of selecting the objects and using the FORMAT menu.

Visual Studio offers a variety of tools to create and align elements in the graphical user interface, and to make the user interface as effective and useful as possible.

Save a Visual Basic Project

As you are working on a Visual Basic project, you must save your work on a regular basis. Some developers save every 10 to 15 minutes, while others might wait for a natural break to save their work. Regardless, it is important to develop the habit of regularly saving your work.

To save the work you have completed, you can tap or click the Save All button on the Standard toolbar. The first time you save a project, the Save Project dialog box is displayed (Figure 2-56).

location for
saving project

FIGURE 2-56

Select the location where you want to store your program. You might use a USB drive, the hard drive on your computer, or a network drive. If you have questions about where to store your program, check with your instructor or network administrator.

After you save the program the first time, tap or click the Save All button on the Standard toolbar to save your program in the same location with the same name.

Close Visual Studio 2012

To close Visual Studio, you can tap or click the Close button to the right of the title bar in the Visual Studio window. If you try to close Visual Studio but you have never saved your program, Visual Studio will display the Close Project dialog box (Figure 2-57).

FIGURE 2-57

You can choose to save your program or discard it. If you tap or click the Save button, the Save Project dialog box will be displayed (Figure 2-56) and you can save the program. If you tap or click the Discard button, your program will be discarded and not saved.

If you try to close Visual Studio but you have done more work since last saving your project, Visual Studio will ask if you want to save your recent work. In most cases, you should choose Yes.

Open a Visual Basic Project

After you save a project and close Visual Studio, you often will want to open the project and work on it again. To open a saved project, you can use one of several methods:

Method 1: Double-tap or double-click the solution file in the folder where it is stored. This method will open the solution and allow you to continue your work.

Method 2: With Visual Studio open, tap or click the Open File button on the Standard toolbar, locate the solution file, and open it in the same manner you use for most Windows programs.

Method 3: With Visual Studio open, tap or click FILE on the menu bar and then point to Recent Projects and Solutions on the FILE menu. A list of recent projects is displayed. Tap or click the name of the project you want to open. This method might not work well if you are not using your own computer because other projects might be listed.

After using one of these methods, you can continue working on your project.

Program Development Life Cycle

Now that you have learned the necessary skills to design a user interface in Visual Studio and Visual Basic, you are ready to learn about the program development life cycle. The **program development life cycle** is a set of phases and steps that developers follow to design, create, and maintain a computer program. The phases of the program development life cycle are:

1. **Gather and Analyze the Program Requirements** — The developer must obtain information that identifies the program requirements and then document these requirements.
2. **Design the User Interface** — After the developer understands the program requirements, the next step is to design the user interface. The user interface provides the framework for the processing that will occur within the program.
3. **Design the Program Processing Objects** — A computer program consists of one or more processing objects that perform the tasks required by the program. The developer must determine what processing objects are required and then determine the requirements of each object.
4. **Code the Program** — After a processing object has been designed, the object must be implemented in program code. **Program code** is the set of instructions, written using a programming language such as Visual Basic 2012, that a computer executes.
5. **Test the Program** — As the program is being coded, and after the coding is completed, the developer should test the program code to ensure it is executing properly. The testing process is ongoing and includes a variety of stages.

6. **Document the Program/System** — As a program is being designed and coded, and after the process is completed, the developer should document the program. **Documenting a program** means using a prescribed method to write down the instructions for using the program, the way the program performs its tasks, and other items that users, developers, and management might require.

7. **Maintain the Program/System** — After a program is put into use, it probably will have to be modified in the future. For example, if a third type of pizza is added to the pizza selection program, it must be changed to reflect the new pizza type. The process of changing and updating programs is called **program and system maintenance**.

The program development life cycle rarely is accomplished in a linear fashion, with one phase completed before the next phase starts. Rather, programs are developed iteratively, which means phases and steps within phases might have to be repeated several times before the program is completed. For example, the requirements for a program might change after the developer has begun coding the program. If so, the developer must return to Phase 1 and gather and document the new requirements. Then, changes might be needed to the user interface or other parts of the program to accommodate the updated requirements. This process of moving back and forth within the program development cycle is normal when developing a computer program.

The next sections in this chapter explain Phase 1 and Phase 2 of the program development life cycle in more detail. The remaining phases are explained in Chapter 3.

Phase 1: Gather and Analyze the Program Requirements

An old programming adage states, "If you don't understand the problem to be solved, you will never develop a solution." While this seems self-evident, too often a program does not perform as desired because the designer did not understand the problem to be solved. Before beginning the user interface design, it is mandatory that the developer understand the problem.

In many programming projects, the developer is responsible for gathering program requirements by interviewing users, reviewing current procedures, and completing other fact-gathering tasks. The emphasis in this book is on learning to program using the Visual Basic 2012 language, so the process of gathering program requirements is beyond the scope of the book. You will be given the program requirements for each program in this book.

When the requirements have been determined, they must be documented so the developers can proceed to design and implement the program. The exact form of the requirements documentation can vary significantly. The format and amount of documentation might be dictated by the application itself or by the documentation standards of the organization for which the program is being developed. For Windows applications in this book, two types of requirements documentation will be provided for you. The first is the requirements document.

A **requirements document** identifies the purpose of the program being developed, the application title, the procedures to be followed when using the program, any equations and calculations required by the program, any conditions within the program that must be tested, notes and restrictions that the program must follow, and any other comments that would be helpful to understanding the problem.

Recall that the program being developed in this chapter and Chapter 3 is the Pizza Selection program (see Figure 2-1 on pages 32 and 33). The requirements document for the Pizza Selection program is shown in Figure 2-58.

REQUIREMENTS DOCUMENT

Date Submitted:	January 23, 2015
Application Title:	Pizza Selection Application
Purpose:	This Windows application will allow a user to select a type of pizza.
Program Procedures:	From a window on the screen, the user should view two different pizza types and then make a pizza selection.

Algorithms, Processing, and Conditions:

1. The user must be able to view choices for a deep-dish and thin-crust pizza until the user selects a pizza type.
2. When the user chooses a pizza type, a picture of the selected type should appear in the window.
3. Only one picture should be displayed at a time, so if a user chooses deep-dish pizza, only its picture should be displayed. If a user then chooses thin-crust pizza, its picture should be displayed instead of deep-dish pizza.
4. When the user makes a pizza selection, a confirming message should be displayed. In addition, the user should be prevented from identifying a pizza type after making the pizza selection.
5. After the user makes a pizza selection, the only allowable action is to exit the window.

Notes and Restrictions:	The user should only be able to make a pizza selection after choosing a pizza type.
Comments:	The pictures shown in the window should be selected from pictures available on the web.

FIGURE 2-58

The requirements document contains all the information a developer needs to design the program. In an event-driven program such as the Pizza Selection program, however, one additional document often is needed to clarify for the developer what should occur in the program. This document is the Use Case Definition.

A **use case** is a sequence of actions a user will perform when using the program. The **Use Case Definition** specifies each of these sequences by describing what the user will do and how the program will respond. The Use Case Definition for the Pizza Selection program is shown in Figure 2-59.

USE CASE DEFINITION

1. User clicks Deep Dish or Thin Crust button.
2. Program displays a picture of the pizza chosen by the user and enables the pizza selection button.
3. User clicks pizza type buttons to view the types of pizza as desired. Program displays the picture of the chosen pizza type.
4. User clicks the Select Pizza button.
5. Program displays a pizza selection confirmation message, and disables both pizza type buttons and the Select Pizza button. The Exit Window button becomes active.
6. User terminates the program by clicking the Exit Window button.

FIGURE 2-59

© 2014 Cengage Learning

As you can see, the Use Case Definition specifies the actions that the user performs and the actions the program must take in response.

The Use Case Definition is an important part of the requirements documentation for two reasons: 1) It defines for the developer exactly what will occur as the user operates the program; 2) It allows users to review the requirements documentation and ensure that the specifications are correct before the developer begins designing the program.

When gathering and documenting the program requirements, it is critical that users be involved. After all, the program is being developed for their use. When the users concur that the requirements documentation is correct, the developer can move forward into the design phases of the program with confidence that it will fulfill users' needs.

For the programs you will design in this book, the program requirements, including the requirements document and the Use Case Definition, will be provided to you. However, be aware that in many cases in industry, an experienced developer must gather the requirements as well as implement them in a program.

Phase 2: Design the User Interface

Virtually all programs developed for a graphical user interface are driven by the user's actions within the interface. These actions dictate the processing that the program should execute. Therefore, by designing the user interface, the developer will obtain a foundation for designing the rest of the program. By designing the user interface early in the design process, the developer also can interact with users and ensure that the interface will fulfill their requirements.

Expert program developers recognize the importance of the graphical user interface. These developers spend 25 to 40 percent of program design on the user interface, which sometimes is called the **presentation layer** of the program because it is so critical to the program's success. Mobile devices use small screens, so an easy-to-follow user interface assists in clear navigation that relies on fingers instead of keyboard input.

In the past, developers would draw the user interface on paper and present the drawings to users for their approval. When using Visual Studio 2012, however, the developer should use the program's rapid application development tools to create the user interface. The interface is created with no functionality; that is, none of the buttons or other GUI elements will cause processing to occur. Often, these interface designs are called **mock-ups** because they are provided only for approval of the design. When the users or others approve the interface design, the developer can design the program elements required to implement the functions of the program.

An additional benefit of using Visual Studio to design the user interface is that you can use the completed design in the actual program; you do not have to re-create the design using other software.

My boss at my programming job asked me to design a prototype for the layout of the user interface. What is a prototype?

A prototype is a model of a software product or information system built for customer approval. It is similar to a mock-up of a user interface.

CONSIDER THIS

Principles of User Interface Design

Because the presentation layer of the program is so important, a number of principles and guidelines have been developed over the years for user interface design. While the intent of this book is not to create experts in user interface design, you should understand some of the principles so you can develop programs that are useful and usable. The following are some **design principles** you should incorporate into your user interface designs:

1. The most important principle to remember is that the user's ability to operate the program effectively depends on the design of the interface. If the GUI is easy to use and follow, the user will have a productive and enjoyable experience. On the other hand, if the user struggles to figure out how to enter data or which button to tap or click, the user interface design is defeating the purpose of the program.
2. If the user interface is not easy to use, the user will not be satisfied with the application regardless of how well it works.
3. The user interface includes the windows, graphics, and text shown on the screen, as well as the methods that interact with your program and cause operations to occur. Four primary means of interacting with a user interface are the keyboard, a pointing device such as a mouse, a touch interface, and voice input. The correct use of these tools significantly increases the probability of success for a traditional or touch-based user interface.
4. Using the interface should feel natural and normal. The developer must be aware of who the user is and how the user is accustomed to working. For example, the interface for a banking program in which a teller enters account information will be different from that of a graphic arts program that allows manipulation of graphics and photographs. Each must reflect the needs of the user.

5. Visual Studio contains a wide variety of objects, many of which can be used for similar purposes in the GUI. A good user interface provides the most appropriate object for each requirement. You will learn about all these objects and their correct use throughout this text.

6. Once an object is used for a particular purpose in the user interface, such as a button that causes a particular action, the object should be used for the same purpose throughout the program interface.

7. Objects must be arranged in the sequence in which they are used so the user can move from item to item on the screen in a logical, straightforward manner. Following this principle helps create an interface that is clean and easy to use. Again, the developer must understand the needs of the user. When this principle is not followed, a confusing interface can result.

8. The interface should be kept as simple as possible while containing all required functionality. Generally, the simpler the interface is, the more effective it will be. Consider using colors that are "easy on the eyes" to prevent eye fatigue.

9. When implemented, the user interface should be intuitive, which means the user should be able to use it with little or no instruction. In fact, the user should feel that no other interface could have been designed because the one they are using is the most "natural."

By following these principles, you will create user interfaces that assist the user. The success of your program can depend on the user interface you design.

Sample Program

As you learned earlier, the Pizza Selection program is the sample program for this chapter and Chapter 3 (see Figure 2-1 on pages 32 and 33). The requirements document for this program is shown in Figure 2-58 on page 77, and the Use Case Definition is shown in Figure 2-59 on page 78. With these documents in hand, the first phase of the program development cycle is complete.

Sample Program — Phase 2: User Interface Design

When beginning the design of the user interface, the primary sources of reference are the requirements document and the Use Case Definition for the program. Using these documents, the developer must analyze the program requirements and determine which elements are required in the user interface.

On a line-for-line basis, the analysis of the requirements document in Figure 2-58 on page 77 could proceed as follows:

1. The application will be presented in a window on the screen, so a Windows Forms Application using a Windows Form object is the appropriate means for creating the program.

2. The user will choose either a deep-dish or thin-crust pizza and then make a pizza selection. When the pizza is chosen, a picture of the pizza should be displayed. To choose each pizza, the program uses a Button object, a common tool that is familiar to users. When a user taps or clicks a button, the user has made a choice and the program responds appropriately. In this application, a good design decision is to use buttons so the user can decide between pizza types and then make a pizza selection. When the user taps or clicks the Deep Dish button, a picture of deep-dish pizza will be displayed. When the user taps or clicks the Thin Crust button, a picture of thin-crust pizza will be displayed. The user then taps or clicks the Select Pizza button to make the selection.

3. Two pictures must be displayed in the user interface — a deep-dish picture and a thin-crust picture. Although it is possible to display two different pictures in a single PictureBox object depending on the user's choice, you can develop a simpler and more easily understood user interface if a PictureBox object and a button work together. In other words, when the user taps or clicks the Deep Dish button, the deep-dish picture is displayed in the Deep Dish PictureBox object; when the user taps or clicks the Thin Crust button, the thin-crust picture is displayed in the Thin Crust PictureBox object. In this way, the user can associate a button with a picture box location and the user interface is intuitive and easy to use.

4. When the user makes a pizza selection by tapping or clicking the Select Pizza button, a message must be displayed to confirm the pizza selection. Therefore, a Label object must be included for the confirmation message.

5. After the user makes a pizza selection, the only action available to the user is to exit the window, so an Exit Window button is required.

6. In addition to the requirements in the program requirements document, standard procedure usually dictates that a heading should appear in the program window. Also, it is common practice to include simple instructions in the window so the user is not confused while using the interface. The heading and instructions can be included as Label objects.

7. As a result of this analysis, the user interface should include the following items: a Windows Form object that will contain all the other objects; two PictureBox objects to contain pictures of deep-dish and thin-crust pizzas; four Button objects (Deep Dish button, Thin Crust button, Select Pizza button, and Exit Window button); and three Label objects (Heading, Instructions, and Pizza Selection Confirmation).

After determining the elements required for the user interface, the developer can use Visual Studio 2012 to create a mock-up of the user interface. The exact placement of objects in the window is a creative process, and is guided by the principles of user interface design you have learned. Usually, no "right answer" exists because each developer will see a slightly different solution, but you must adhere to the principles of good user interface design. Figure 2-60 shows the mock-up created for the Pizza Selection program.

FIGURE 2-60

Guided Program Development

This section on guided program development takes you step by step through the process of creating the sample program in this chapter. To create the mock-up shown in Figure 2-60, complete the steps on the following pages.

Guided Program Development

1

● **Open Visual Studio 2012**
Open Visual Studio using the
Search charm (Windows 8) or
the Start button on the Windows
taskbar and the All Programs
submenu (Windows 7) *(ref: Figure
2-2)*. If necessary, maximize the
Visual Studio window. If necessary, close the Start page.

HINT

● **Create a New Visual Basic Windows Forms
Application** Create a new Visual Basic Windows
Forms Application project by tapping or clicking the
New Project button, selecting Windows in the left
pane, selecting Windows Forms Application in the
middle pane, naming the project `Pizza Selec-
tion`, and then tapping or clicking the OK button
in the New Project window *(ref: Figure 2-4)*.

HINT

● **Keep the Toolbox Visible** If necessary, tap or
click the Auto Hide button to keep the Toolbox
visible *(ref: Figure 2-10)*.

HINT

*The Visual Studio
application opens
and a new project
is displayed in the
window (Figure
2-61). The Toolbox
remains visible
regardless of the
location of the
pointer.*

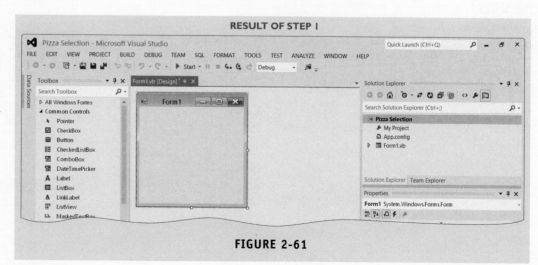

RESULT OF STEP I

FIGURE 2-61

(continues)

Guided Program Development   *continued*

2

● **Name the Windows Form Object** In the Solution Explorer window, press and hold or right-click Form1.vb. On the shortcut menu, tap or click Rename. Name the form `frmPizzaSelec-tion` *(ref: Figure 2-14).*

HINT

● **Change the Windows Form Object Text Property** With the Windows Form object selected, double-tap or double-click the text value for the Windows Form object in the Text property of the Properties window. Then change the title bar text for the Windows Form object to `Pizza Selection` *(ref: Figure 2-16).*

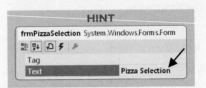

HINT

The text in the title bar of the Windows Form object has been changed to Pizza Selection (Figure 2-62). In addition, the name of the object has been changed to frmPizzaSelection.

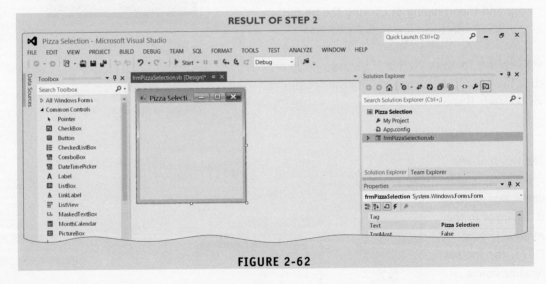

RESULT OF STEP 2

FIGURE 2-62

3

• **Resize the Windows Form Object** Resize the Windows Form object to the approximate size shown in Figure 2-60 (430 × 395) by changing the Size property in the Properties window to 430,395 *(ref: Figure 2-18)*.

4

• **Add a Label Object** Add a Label object by dragging the Label .NET component from the Toolbox to the Windows Form object. Place the label near the center and top of the Windows Form object *(ref: Figure 2-19)*.

• **Name the Label Object** Change the name of the Label object to lblHeading by using the (Name) property in the Properties window for the Label object *(ref: Figure 2-21)*.

• **Change the Label Object Text Property** Double-tap or double-click the text value for the Label object in the Text property of the Properties window, and then change the Text property of the lblHeading Label object to Pizza Selection *(ref: Figure 2-23)*.

• **Open the Font Dialog Box** Tap or click the Font property for the Label object in the Properties window, and then tap or click the ellipsis button (...) for the Font property *(ref: Figure 2-27)*.

• **Change the Font for the Label Object** In the Font list of the Font dialog box, change the font in the lblHeading Label object to Tahoma *(ref: Figure 2-29)*.

• **Change the Font Style for the Label Object** Using the Font style list in the Font dialog box, change the font style in the lblHeading Label object to Bold *(ref: Figure 2-29)*.

• **Change the Size for the Label Object** Using the Size list in the Font dialog box, change the font size in the lblHeading Label object to 16 points *(ref: Figure 2-29)*.

(continues)

Guided Program Development   *continued*

● **Center the Heading Horizontally** If necessary, select
the lblHeading Label object. Then, using the Center in Form
command on the FORMAT menu, tap or click the Horizontally command on the Center in Form submenu to center the
lblHeading Label object horizontally on the Windows Form
object *(ref: Figure 2-31)*.

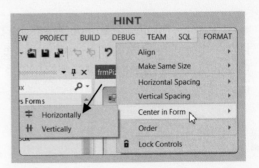

*The lbl Heading Label object text has been changed and the label object is centered horizontally on the Windows
Form object (Figure 2-63). The vertical placement of the label (that is, the distance from the top of the window
frame) depends on the eye of the developer, the size of the Windows Form object, and the other objects in
the graphical user interface. Although your label might be a little higher or lower, your window should closely
resemble the one in Figure 2-63.*

RESULT OF STEPS 3 AND 4

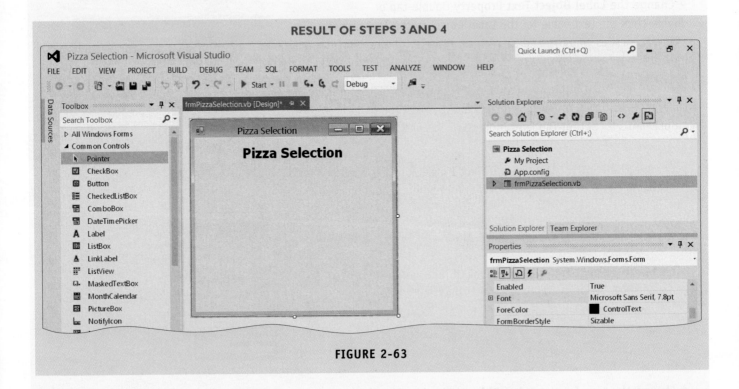

FIGURE 2-63

- **Add a PictureBox Object** Add a PictureBox object to the Windows Form object by dragging a PictureBox .NET component from the Toolbox to the Windows Form object. Place the Picture-Box object below and to the left of the heading label, as shown in Figure 2-64 *(ref: Figure 2-36)*.

- **Name the PictureBox Object** Using the (Name) property in the PictureBox Properties window, name the PictureBox object `picDeepDish`.

- **Resize the PictureBox Object** Resize the PictureBox object by changing its Size property to `139, 122` *(ref: Figure 2-38)*.

A properly sized PictureBox object is displayed in the Windows Form object (Figure 2-64). This PictureBox object will display a picture of a deep-dish pizza when the program is completed in Chapter 3.

RESULT OF STEP 5

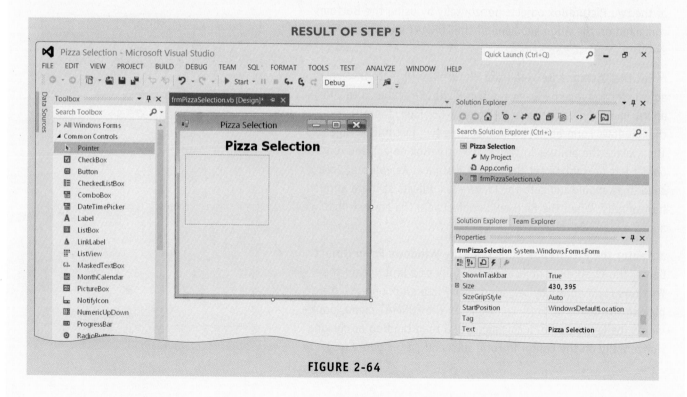

FIGURE 2-64

(continues)

6

• **Add a PictureBox Object** Add a second PictureBox object to the Windows Form object by dragging a PictureBox .NET component from the Toolbox to the Windows Form object. Place it to the right of the first PictureBox object in the Windows Form object *(ref: Figure 2-39)*.

• **Name the PictureBox Object** Using the (Name) property in the PictureBox Properties window, name the PictureBox object `picThinCrust`.

• **Size the PictureBox Object** Make the second PictureBox object on the Windows Form object the same size as the first by using the Both command on the Make Same Size submenu of the FORMAT menu *(ref: Figure 2-41)*.

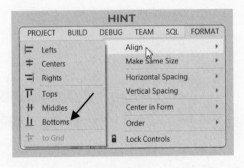

• **Align the PictureBox Objects Horizontally** Align the bottoms of the two PictureBox objects horizontally by using the Bottoms command on the Align submenu of the FORMAT menu *(ref: Figure 2-43)*.

• **Set the Distance Between the PictureBox Objects** If necessary, adjust the distance between the two PictureBox objects to the approximate distance shown in Figure 2-65. First, tap or click the Windows Form object to deselect the two PictureBox objects. Then, place the pointer in the right PictureBox object and drag the object left or right to set the correct distance. As you drag, red snap lines should indicate the PictureBox objects still are aligned horizontally. When the PictureBox objects are the correct distance apart, release the object.

• **Center the PictureBox Objects in the Windows Form Object** Center the PictureBox objects horizontally as a unit within the Windows Form object by selecting both PictureBox objects, displaying the Center in Form command on the FORMAT menu, pointing to the Center in Form command, and then tapping or clicking Horizontally on the Center in Form submenu *(ref: Figure 2-45)*.

The PictureBox objects are sized and located properly within the Windows Form object (Figure 2-65).

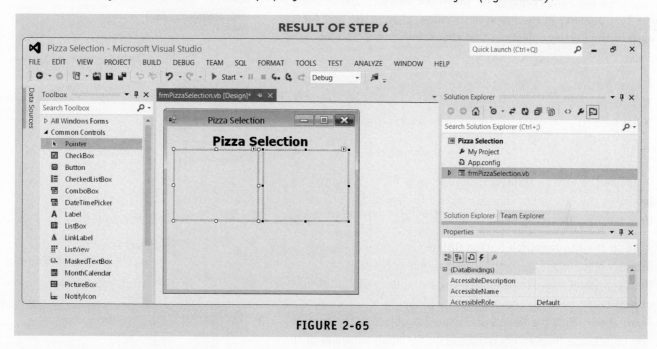

FIGURE 2-65

7

● **Add Three Button Objects to the Windows Form Object** Add three Button objects by dragging them onto the Windows Form object. Align them horizontally below the PictureBox objects at about the same locations shown in Figure 2-60 on page 82. Use blue snap lines to align horizontally the buttons on the Windows Form object as you drag them onto the form *(ref: Figure 2-47, Figure 2-52)*.

● **Name the Three Button Objects** Using the (Name) property in the Properties window, name the left Button object `btnDeep-Dish`, the center Button object `btnSelectPizza`, and the right Button object `btnThinCrust`.

(continues)

● **Change the Text Property for the Three Button Objects** Using the Text property in the Properties window, change the text for each of the Button objects to that shown in Figure 2-66 *(ref: Figure 2-49)*.

● **Change the Button Object Size** Change the size of the Select Pizza button to accommodate the Select Pizza text *(ref: Figure 2-50)*.

● **Resize the Button Objects** Using the same technique you used for sizing the PictureBox objects, make all three Button objects the same size as the Select Pizza Button object.

● **Align the btnDeepDish Button Object** Center the Deep Dish Button object under the Deep Dish PictureBox object. First, select the Deep Dish PictureBox and then select the Deep Dish Button object, either by using the CTRL key or by tapping or clicking *(ref: Figure 2-40)*. With the Deep Dish PictureBox object as the controlling object, use the Centers command on the Align submenu of the FORMAT menu to align the PictureBox object and the Deep Dish Button object *(ref: Figure 2-43)*.

● **Align the btnThinCrust Button Object** Using the same technique, center the Thin Crust Button object below the Thin Crust PictureBox object.

● **Center the btnSelectPizza Button Object** Center the Select Pizza Button object horizontally within the Windows Form object by selecting the Select Pizza Button object and then using the Horizontally command on the Center in Form submenu of the FORMAT menu *(ref: Figure 2-31)*.

The Button objects are sized and placed properly within the Windows Form object (Figure 2-66). All three buttons are the same size. The Deep Dish and Thin Crust buttons are centered under their respective PictureBox objects, and the Select Pizza button is centered in the Windows Form object.

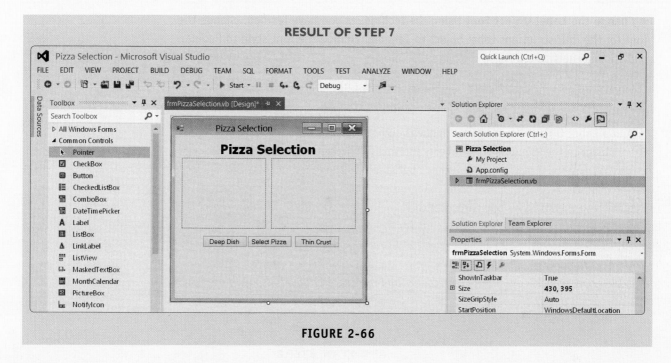

RESULT OF STEP 7

FIGURE 2-66

8

● **Add a Label Object** Add the instructions Label object to the Windows Form object by dragging a Label .NET object from the Toolbox to the Windows Form object. Place it below the Button objects at the approximate location shown in Figure 2-60 on page 82 *(ref: Figure 2-19)*.

● **Name a Label Object** Using the techniques you have learned, name the Label object `lblInstructions`.

HINT

(continues)

● **Change the Label Object Text Property** Using the techniques you have learned, change the text in the lblInstructions Label object to `Choose a pizza type and then click the Select Pizza button`.

● **Change the Label Object Font** Using the techniques you have learned, change the font for the lblInstructions Label object to Tahoma, change the font style to Regular, and change the size to 9 points.

● **Center the Label Object** Using the techniques you have learned, center the lblInstructions Label object horizontally within the Windows Form object.

● **Add a Label Object** Using the techniques you have learned, add the final message Label object to the Windows Form object. The text of the label should read `Enjoy your pizza selection`. Place the Label object in the location shown in Figure 2-67. Name it `lblConfirmation`. Change the font to Tahoma, the font style to Regular, and the size to 9 points. Center the Label object within the Windows Form object.

The two Label objects contain the correct text and are centered horizontally in the Windows Form object (Figure 2-67).

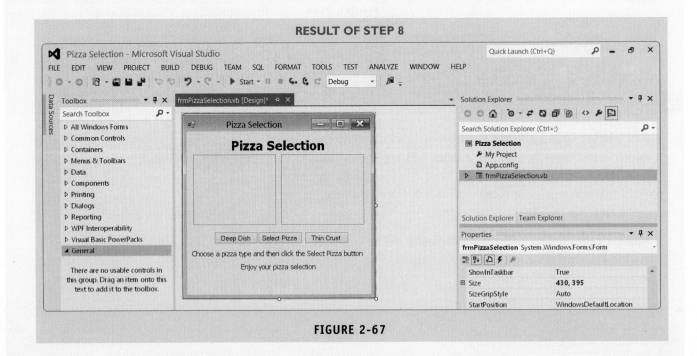

FIGURE 2-67

- **Add a Button Object** Add the Exit Window Button object by dragging a Button control onto the Windows Form object. Place it in the approximate location shown in Figure 2-68. Then, using the techniques you have learned, give the name `btnExit` to the Button object, change its text to `Exit Window`, make the Exit Window Button object the same size as the other Button objects in the window, and center the Exit Window Button object horizontally in the window.

The user interface mock-up is complete (Figure 2-68).

RESULT OF STEP 9

FIGURE 2-68

After completing the user interface mock-up, the designers will distribute the design to the users and others for approval. In many cases, the developers must implement changes the users request. Then they will resubmit the design for approval.

Summary

You have completed the steps to create the graphical user interface mock-up for the Pizza Selection program. As you can see, many of the required steps are somewhat repetitive; the same technique is used repeatedly to accomplish similar tasks. When you master these techniques and other principles of user interface design, you will be able to design user interfaces for a variety of different programs.

The items listed in the following table include all the new Visual Studio and Visual Basic skills you have learned in this chapter.

Visual Basic Skills		
Skill	**Figure Number**	**Video Number**
Run the completed program	Figure 2-1	Video 2-1
Open Visual Studio 2012	Figure 2-2	Video 2-2
Create a New Visual Basic 2012 Windows Application	Figure 2-4	Video 2-3
Display the Toolbox	Figure 2-9	Video 2-4
Permanently Display the Toolbox	Figure 2-10	Video 2-5
Name the Windows Form Object	Figure 2-12	Video 2-6
Set the Title Bar Text in a Windows Form Object	Figure 2-15	Video 2-7
Resize a Form	Figure 2-17	Video 2-8
Add a Label Object	Figure 2-19	Video 2-9
Name a Label Object	Figure 2-21	Video 2-10
Change the Text in a Label Object	Figure 2-23	Video 2-11
Enter Multiple Lines for a Label Object	Figure 2-26	Video 2-12
Change the Label Font, Font Style, and Font Size	Figure 2-27	Video 2-13
Center a Label Object in the Windows Form Object	Figure 2-31	Video 2-14
Delete GUI Objects	Figure 2-33	Video 2-15
Use the Undo Button on the Standard Toolbar	Figure 2-35	Video 2-16
Add a PictureBox Object	Figure 2-36	Video 2-17

Visual Basic Skills (continued)

Skill	Figure Number	Video Number
Resize a PictureBox Object	Figure 2-38	Video 2-18
Add a Second PictureBox Object	Figure 2-39	Video 2-19
Make Objects the Same Size	Figure 2-40	Video 2-20
Align PictureBox Objects	Figure 2-43	Video 2-21
Center Multiple Objects Horizontally	Figure 2-45	Video 2-22
Add a Button Object	Figure 2-47	Video 2-23
Name a Button Object	Figure 2-49	Video 2-24
Set Text for a Button Object	Figure 2-49	Video 2-24
Change the Button Object's Size	Figure 2-50	Video 2-25
Add a Button with Alignment (Use Snap Lines)	Figure 2-52	Video 2-26
Align Objects Vertically	Figure 2-54	Video 2-27
Save and Close a Visual Basic Project	Figure 2-56, 2-57	
Open a Visual Basic project	Page 75	

FIGURE 2-69

Learn Online

Reinforcement activities and resources are available at no additional cost on *www.cengagebrain.com*. Visit *www .cengage.com/ct/studentdownload* for detailed instructions about accessing the available resources at the Student Companion Site.

Knowledge Check

1–5. Label the following parts of the window:

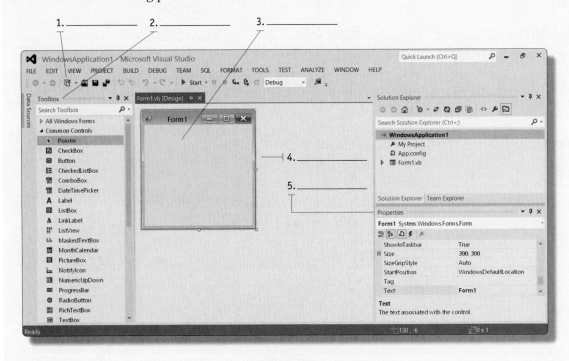

FIGURE 2-70

(continues)

Knowledge Check *continued*

6. What does RAD stand for?

7. What is the purpose of the Auto Hide button on the Toolbox title bar?

8. What is the difference between red and blue snap lines?

9. What is the prefix of the Form object?

10. A Button, a Label, and a PictureBox are all _____.

11. How do you select four Button objects on the Windows Form object at the same time for alignment purposes?

12. What is the purpose of a mock-up?

13. What are the first two phases of the program development life cycle?

14. Write the Label object name "Video" with the correct prefix.

15. Write the Button object name "Submit" with the correct prefix.

16. Write the PictureBox object name "Tablet" with the correct prefix.

17. Which property of the Label object do you use to change the name of the label from Label1?

18. Which button can you tap or click to sort the property names in the Properties window from A to Z?

19. How do you save the project you have created for the user interface mock-up?

20. Name the four objects you learned in Chapter 2 and briefly describe the purpose of each object.

Debugging Exercises

1. List the steps required to change the poorly aligned buttons on the left to the properly aligned buttons on the right.

BEFORE

FIGURE 2-71a

AFTER

FIGURE 2-71b

(continues)

2. Change the order of the numbered Use Case Definition steps to correspond to the following problem definition: A college provides every incoming freshman with a gift card for a choice of two types of coffee from the cafeteria. Students should select the type of coffee they want. A program opens a window that displays each coffee type one picture at a time when the student taps or clicks the corresponding button. After making a decision, the student should tap or click the Place Order button. After selecting a type of coffee, the student should exit the application.

USE CASE DEFINITION

1. User taps or clicks the Place Order button.
2. User taps or clicks the Coffee button or Frappuccino button.
3. User taps or clicks the button not selected in Step 2.
4. User terminates the program by tapping or clicking the Close button.
5. Program displays an order confirmation message and disables both order buttons. The Close button becomes active.
6. Program displays a picture of the coffee order selected by the user and enables the Place Order button.
7. Program displays a picture of the coffee order selected by the user.

Program Analysis

1. After you have placed objects on the Windows Form object (Figure 2-72), list the steps you would follow to change the font for the Save the Penguins label to Tahoma font, bold, 18 points.

2. List the steps you would perform to center the Save the Penguins label horizontally.

3. List the steps you would perform to center the Picture-Box object horizontally on the Windows Form object in Figure 2-72.

4. List the steps you would perform to change the font for the Donate Now button in Figure 2-72 to Tahoma, 10 points.

FIGURE 2-72

5. List the steps you would perform to align the two Button objects horizontally by the tops of the buttons.

6. List the steps you would perform to make the Donate Now button the same size as the Close Window button.

7. In the real world, why is it important to have a user interface mock-up approved before proceeding with the rest of the project?

Complete one or more of the following case programming assignments. Submit the program and materials you create to your instructor. The level of difficulty is indicated for each assignment.

●	= Easiest
● ●	= Intermediate
● ● ●	= Challenging

1
●
EUROPEAN HOSTEL SELECTION

Create a Windows form mock-up for the requirements document in Figure 2-73 and the Use Case Definition shown in Figure 2-74 on the next page. The Windows Form object and the other objects in the user interface are shown in Figure 2-75 on the next page.

REQUIREMENTS DOCUMENT

Date Submitted: January 17, 2015

Application Title: European Hostel Selection Application

Purpose: The Windows application will allow a user to select a location in London or Dublin.

Program Procedures: From a window on the screen, the user should identify a hostel location (London or Dublin) and then select a hostel.

Algorithms, Processing, and Conditions:
1. The user must be able to identify the London or Dublin hostel as many times as necessary until making a selection.
2. When the user identifies the hostel location, a picture of that hostel should appear in the window.
3. Only one picture should be displayed at a time. If a user identifies the London hostel, only the London hostel picture should be displayed; if a user identifies the Dublin hostel, only the Dublin hostel picture should be displayed.
4. When the user selects a hostel, a message should be displayed to confirm the selection of a hostel location. In addition, the user should be prevented from identifying another location after selecting a hostel.
5. After the user selects a hostel, the only allowable action is to exit the window.

Notes and Restrictions: A user can select a hostel only after identifying a hostel location.

Comments: The pictures shown in the window can be found on CengageBrain.com. The names of the pictures are Dublin and London. Images will be added in Chapter 3.

FIGURE 2-73

(continues)

Case Programming Assignments

European Hostel Selection (continued)

USE CASE DEFINITION

1. User taps or clicks London Hostel button or Dublin Hostel button.
2. Program displays a picture of the hostel identified by the user and enables the location selection button.
3. User taps or clicks hostel buttons to view hostel locations as desired. Program displays the picture of the identified hostel.
4. User taps or clicks the Select Location button.
5. Program displays a hostel selection confirmation message and disables both hostel buttons and the Select Location button. The Exit Window button becomes active.
6. User terminates the program by tapping or clicking the Exit Window button.

FIGURE 2-74

FIGURE 2-75

2 • STUDENT PICNIC

Create a Windows form mock-up for the requirements document shown in Figure 2-76 and the Use Case Definition shown in Figure 2-77 on the next page. The Windows Form object and the other objects in the user interface are shown in Figure 2-78 on the next page.

REQUIREMENTS DOCUMENT

Date Submitted:	January 14, 2015
Application Title:	Student Picnic Application
Purpose:	This Windows application displays a welcome screen for the Annual Spring Fling Picnic. The user can choose an option to view the date and location.
Program Procedures:	From a window on the screen, the user makes a request to see the picnic's date and location.
Algorithms, Processing, and Conditions:	1. The user first views a Student Picnic window that displays the picnic name (Annual Spring Fling Picnic), a picnic picture, and a phrase that states all students are welcome.
	2. When the user chooses to view the picnic date and location, the following information is displayed: April 17, 2015 Located in the Quad in front of the Barnard Building
	3. After the user views the picnic information, the only allowable action is to exit the window.
Notes and Restrictions:	n/a
Comments:	The picture shown in the window can be found on CengageBrain.com. The name of the picture is Picnic. Images will be added in Chapter 3.

FIGURE 2-76

© 2014 Cengage Learning

(continues)

Student Picnic (continued)

USE CASE DEFINITION

1. The window opens, displaying the name of the picnic, a picnic picture, and a message stating all students are welcome. All buttons are enabled.
2. User taps or clicks the View Picnic Information button.
3. Program displays the picnic time and location between the buttons. The View Picnic Information button is disabled.
4. User taps or clicks the Exit Window button to terminate the application.

FIGURE 2-77

© 2014 Cengage Learning

FIGURE 2-78

© 2014 Cengage Learning

3
VISUAL BASIC 2012 TERMS

Create a Windows form mock-up for the requirements document shown in Figure 2-79 and the Use Case Definition shown in Figure 2-80 on the next page. The Windows Form object and the other objects in the user interface are shown in Figure 2-81 on the next page.

REQUIREMENTS DOCUMENT

Date Submitted:	August 16, 2015
Application Title:	Visual Basic 2012 Terms Application
Purpose:	This Windows application displays the definitions of common Visual Basic terms. When the user chooses to view a definition, the term's definition is displayed.
Program Procedures:	From a window on the screen, the user makes a request to see one of three VB definitions.
Algorithms, Processing, and Conditions:	1. The user first views a screen that displays three VB terms.
	2. A logo is displayed at the top of the window throughout the running of the application.
	3. The user can select any of the three terms displayed on the buttons to view the definition.
	4. When the user taps or clicks a term button to display the definition, any previous definitions will disappear.
	5. An exit button is available at all times, allowing the user to end the application.
Notes and Restrictions:	Only one definition should be displayed at a time, so if a user selects a second term, only the second definition should be displayed.
Comments:	n/a

FIGURE 2-79

(continues)

Visual Basic 2012 Terms (continued)

USE CASE DEFINITION

1. The window opens and displays a logo (Professional 2012), a title (Visual Basic 2012 Terms), three buttons labeled with VB terms, and an Exit Window button. All buttons are enabled.
2. User taps or clicks each of the term buttons to review the definitions.
3. Program displays the definitions to the right of the buttons.
4. Only one definition is displayed at a time.
5. User taps or clicks the Exit Window button to terminate the application.

FIGURE 2-80

FIGURE 2-81

4 ●●

ONLINE STORE SPECIALS

Create a Use Case Definition document and design a Windows form mock-up based on the requirements document in Figure 2-82.

REQUIREMENTS DOCUMENT

Date Submitted:	January 6, 2016
Application Title:	Online Store Specials Application
Purpose:	This Windows application displays the daily, weekly, and holiday specials in the online store. The user can select the desired product and then add the product to a shopping cart.
Program Procedures:	From a window on the screen, the user should select the daily special, weekly special, or holiday special. After the user selects a special, the program should display a picture of the special product, the regular price of the product, and the sale price of the product. The user should be able to select any special. Then, the user can add the product to the shopping cart.
Algorithms, Processing, and Conditions:	1. The user must select a special in order to display the special's product picture, regular price, and sale price. 2. The user cannot add a product to the shopping cart until a special is selected. 3. When a special is selected, only that special's picture and prices should be displayed in the window. No other special should be displayed. 4. After the user selects a special and adds it to the shopping cart, the only allowable user action is to exit the window. 5. A user should be able to exit the window at any time.
Notes and Restrictions:	n/a
Comments:	1. The specials are:

Daily Special: SmartPhone: Regular Price: $99.95; Sale Price: $84.50
Weekly Special: Tablet, Regular Price: $239.95, Sale Price: $199.95
Holiday Special: Digital Camera: Regular Price: $259.95; Sale Price: $203.19

2. The pictures shown in the window can be found on CengageBrain.com. The names of the pictures are SmartPhone, Tablet, and DigitalCamera.

FIGURE 2-82

5 •• GUITAR STORE

Create a Use Case Definition document and design a Windows form mock-up based on the requirements document in Figure 2-83.

REQUIREMENTS DOCUMENT

Date Submitted:	March 21, 2015
Application Title:	Guitar Store Application
Purpose:	A local guitar store has three guitars on special this week. A customer can choose one of three guitar types. The program must display each of the guitars upon request. The customer can then select a guitar for purchase.
Program Procedures:	From a window on the screen, the user selects one of three guitars. A picture of the selected guitar is displayed in the window. The user then can choose a guitar for purchase.
Algorithms, Processing, and Conditions:	1. The user selects a guitar. Then, a picture of the guitar is displayed in the window.
	2. The user can select any of the three guitars. Only the picture of the selected guitar should be displayed.
	3. The user can select guitars as many times as necessary and display the pictures of the guitars.
	4. The user finds a guitar, chooses it for purchase, and taps or clicks the Purchase button.
	5. After the user chooses a guitar, a message stating "Enjoy your guitar!" should be displayed.
	6. After the user chooses a guitar, the only allowable action is to exit the window.
Notes and Restrictions:	The user should not be able to choose a guitar until viewing at least one guitar image.
Comments:	1. The available guitars are classical acoustic, steel-string acoustic, and electric.
	2. The pictures shown in the window can be found on CengageBrain.com. The names of the pictures are Classical, Electric, and Steel.

FIGURE 2-83

Case Programming Assignments

6 ●●
SONG VOTING

Create a Use Case Definition document and design a Windows form mock-up based on the requirements document in Figure 2-84.

REQUIREMENTS DOCUMENT

Date Submitted: February 22, 2015

Application Title: Song Voting Application

Purpose: In your mall, a music store named Millennium Music wants an application that shows the #1 song in each of three music genres and allows users to vote for their overall favorite. The user should be able to select one of three music genres and then vote for one.

Program Procedures: From a window on the screen, the user selects one of three music genres. The name of the #1 song in the selected genre is displayed with a picture of the performing artist or band. Then, the user can vote for that song or genre as his or her overall favorite.

Algorithms, Processing, and Conditions:
1. The user selects a music genre. The title of the #1 song in that genre and a picture of the artist or band are displayed in the window.
2. The user can select any of the three music genres. Only the name of the song and the picture for the selected genre should be displayed.
3. The user can select music genres as many times as necessary to see the #1 song for each genre and the associated artist or band.
4. After selecting a genre, the user should be able to vote for that genre and song as the favorite. The user can vote only after selecting a genre.
5. After the user votes, a message confirming the vote should be displayed.

Notes and Restrictions: The user should only be able to vote after selecting a musical genre.

Comments:
1. You (the developer) should select the three music genres and the #1 song for each of the genres.
2. The pictures of the artist or band will depend on your selection of music genres and the #1 song in those genres. You should download pictures of artists or bands from the web. You can search anywhere on the web for the pictures. You will find that *www.google.com/images* is a good source.

FIGURE 2-84

7 ●●●
AIRLINE SNACK SELECTION

Create a requirements document and a Use Case Definition document and then design a Windows form mock-up based on the following case project:

An international airline requests a computer application that will run on the personal television monitors on the back of each seat in the plane. The application should request which free snack you would like during the flight, display the choices as buttons, and then display an image of the snack you select. Another button allows you to make your final snack selection and display a confirmation message.

Snack
Cheese & Crackers
Chocolate Chip Cookies
Mini Pretzels
Salted Peanuts

FIGURE 2-85

8 ● ● ●
TRAVEL SPECIALS

Create a requirements document and a Use Case Definition document and then design a Windows form mock-up based on the following case project:

Your local travel agent requests a computer application that advertises the travel specials of the week from your city. This week's flight specials are:

Destination	Price
New York City	$399 round trip
Las Vegas	$419 round trip
Miami	$520 round trip
St. Thomas	$619 round trip
Hawaii	$828 round trip

Write an application that allows the user to select any of the five vacation destinations. When the user selects a vacation destination, the corresponding flight price and a picture of the destination should be displayed. Clear each prior price and picture when the user selects a different vacation destination. In addition to a picture of the destination, include a web page address that features the selected location. After selecting a destination, the user should be able to book the flight and then exit the window.

FIGURE 2-86

Case Programming Assignments

9 •••
LACROSSE TICKETS

Create a requirements document and a Use Case Definition document and then design a Windows form mock-up based on the following case project:

Your favorite university lacrosse team has asked you to develop a Windows application that allows the user to see the four types of game tickets offered, one at a time. Then, the user should be able to reserve a single game ticket for the selected seat type. The four types of stadium seating and their base prices are as follows:

Name of Ticket	Minimum Price
Upper Endline Seating	$15.00
Lower Endline Seating	$25.00
Sideline Seating	$30.00
Club Seats	$50.00

For each type of seating, your program should display the base price and a picture depicting an example of the seating type. Clear each price and picture when the user selects a different seating type. After selecting a ticket, the user should be able to purchase the ticket and then exit the window.

FIGURE 2-87

CHAPTER 3

Program Design and Coding

OBJECTIVES

You will have mastered the material in this chapter when you can:

- Change the color properties of an object

- Add images to a PictureBox object

- Locate and save an image from the World Wide Web

- Import an image into the Program Resources folder

- Size an image

- Set the Visible property in the Properties window

- Set the Enabled property in the Properties window

- Run a Visual Basic 2012 program

- Enter Visual Basic 2012 code

- Understand Visual Basic 2012 code statement formats

- Use IntelliSense to enter Visual Basic 2012 code statements

- Use code to set the Visible property of an object

- Use code to set the Enabled property of an object

- Enter comments in Visual Basic 2012 code

- Correct errors in Visual Basic 2012 code

- Write code to use the Close() procedure

- Print code

- Prepare an event planning document

Introduction

In Chapter 2 you completed the design of the graphical user interface (GUI) mock-up. While users and others can approve the mock-up as being functional, the developer normally must make a variety of changes to the GUI to prepare it for the actual production version of the program. Among these changes are:

- Adding color to the interface to make it more visually appealing
- Acquiring and including images that are required for the program
- Setting interface object properties in accordance with the needs of the program

Once these tasks have been completed, Phase 2 of the program development life cycle (PDLC) is complete.

The next two phases of the PDLC are:

- Phase 3: Design the program processing objects
- Phase 4: Code the program

This chapter will provide the skills and knowledge necessary to complete Phase 2 of the PDLC and then complete Phases 3 and 4.

Sample Program

You will recall that the sample program for Chapter 2 and this chapter is the Pizza Selection program. Windows for the program are shown in Figure 3-1.

FIGURE 3-1a

FIGURE 3-1b
© Brand X Pictures/Getty Images

picture of thin-crust pizza is displayed

Select Pizza button is enabled

Thin Crust button is clicked

Exit Window button is dimmed

FIGURE 3-1c
© Brand X Pictures/Getty Images

Select Pizza button is clicked

instructions are not displayed

confirmation message indicates pizza has been selected

Exit Window button is enabled

In the opening window (Figure 3-1a), no images appear in the PictureBox objects, and the Select Pizza button and Exit Window button are dimmed, which means they are disabled (visible, but not available for selection) when the program begins. In Figure 3-1b, the user tapped or clicked the Thin Crust button, so the picture is displayed. In addition, the Select Pizza button is enabled. The Exit Window button still is dimmed. In Figure 3-1c, the user has selected a type of pizza, so the pizza selection confirmation message is displayed. The Deep Dish, Select Pizza, and Thin Crust buttons are dimmed and the Exit Window button is enabled. When the program runs, each of these changes occurs through the use of code you enter into the program, as you will discover later in this chapter.

Fine-Tune the User Interface

You learned about some properties of Visual Basic objects in Chapter 2, including the Name property and the Text property. As you probably noted while viewing the Properties window in Chapter 2, more properties are available for each of the objects in a graphical user interface. In many cases, you set these properties to fine-tune the user interface and make it more usable. In the sample program, the BackColor and ForeColor properties make the user interface more attractive and effective.

BackColor and ForeColor Properties

The **BackColor** of an object is the color displayed in its background. For example, in Figure 3-1 on the previous page the BackColor of the Windows Form object is white instead of the default gray color, and the BackColor of the Button objects is a wheat shade. You can select the BackColor of an object by using the **BackColor property** in the Properties window. The **ForeColor** of an object is the color displayed in the text of the object. The heading Label object that displays the Pizza Selection text uses a text color called Firebrick. To change the BackColor of a Windows Form object from its default color of Control (gray) to White, you can complete the following steps:

STEP 1   Tap or click the Windows Form object to select it. (Do not tap or click any of the objects on the Windows Form object.)

The Windows Form object is selected, as indicated by the thick border and the sizing handles (Figure 3-2).

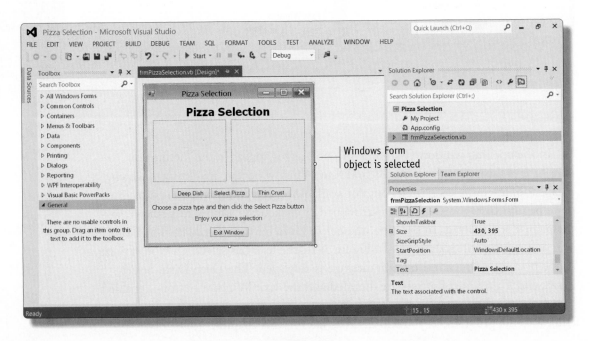

FIGURE 3-2

STEP 2   If necessary, scroll in the Properties window until the BackColor property is displayed, and then tap or click the right column of the BackColor property.

The BackColor property is selected, and the BackColor arrow is displayed (Figure 3-3).

BackColor property
is selected

FIGURE 3-3

STEP 3   Tap or click the BackColor arrow. Then, tap or click the Web tab to display the Web tabbed page.

The color window opens within the Properties window (Figure 3-4). The Web tabbed page contains more than 100 named colors you can display as the BackColor for the selected object, which in this case is the Windows Form object.

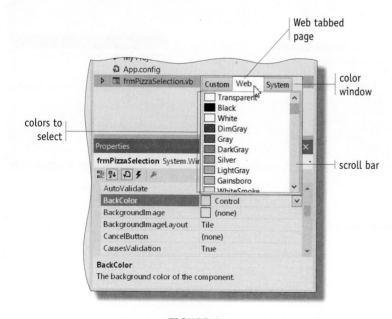

Web tabbed
page

color
window

colors to
select

scroll bar

FIGURE 3-4

IN THE REAL WORLD

Visual Studio 2012 offers three palettes for BackColors and ForeColors: the Custom palette, the Web palette, and the System palette. In the Custom palette, 48 colors are available for selection; in addition, 16 white color chips are available. You can select your own color by pressing and holding or right-clicking a chip and then identifying the color you want from the Define Color window. Be aware that some colors you select from the Define Color window might not be displayed properly on all computers. When the Web palette is open, you can choose from 141 colors that are guaranteed to be displayed properly on every computer. The System palette contains fewer colors; it lists only those that correspond to colors selected in other areas of the computer system.

STEP 4 If necessary, scroll until the color White is displayed in the list of colors.

The name and a sample of the White color are displayed (Figure 3-5).

FIGURE 3-5

STEP 5 Tap or click White on the color list.

The background color in the Windows Form object is changed to White (Figure 3-6).

FIGURE 3-6

You can use the same technique to change the BackColor or ForeColor on any object that contains the BackColor or ForeColor properties, including Button and Label objects.

Add Images to a PictureBox Object

PictureBox objects are used to display a graphic image. The sample program can display a picture of a deep-dish pizza and a thin-crust pizza. You must specify the image that will be displayed in a particular PictureBox object. Before specifying the image, however, you must locate the image and then place it in the Resources folder that is linked to the application. The general steps for displaying an image in a PictureBox object are:

1. Locate the image to be displayed in the PictureBox object. You might locate this image on the Web, in which case you must store the image in a folder on your computer, or the image might already be stored on your computer or a local network.
2. Import the image into the **Resources folder**. This step makes the image available for display within the PictureBox object. Multiple images can be placed in the Resources folder.
3. Specify the image to be displayed within the PictureBox object.

Each of these steps will be explained on the following pages.

Locate and Save an Image from the World Wide Web

Images are available from a multitude of sources, from your own digital camera to millions of publicly available images on the Web. If you work for a company, it might have photos and graphic images that can be used in company applications.

In this book, you can use the Student Companion Site to retrieve an image. For example, to retrieve the DeepDish image from this site, you could complete the following steps:

STEP 1   Open your Web browser. (This example uses Internet Explorer; steps for other browsers might vary slightly.) Enter www.cengagebrain.com in the Address box, and then press the ENTER key. Enter 9781285197975 (the book's ISBN) in the Search text box, and then click the Search button. Select the Free Materials tab, and then click the Access Now button to display your student resources.

> **HEADS UP**
>
> While many websites offer images you can select, three sites are particularly useful: *bing.com/images, www.google.com/images*, and *www.webshots.com*. When you visit sites, not all images are available for free download. In some cases, the images are copyrighted and you must acquire rights to use them. In addition, some sites require a fee before the image can be used. Therefore, you should download only images for which you have paid, acquired the rights to use, or that are free of copyright restrictions and available to everyone.

The browser window opens and the Student Companion Site for this book is displayed (Figure 3-7).

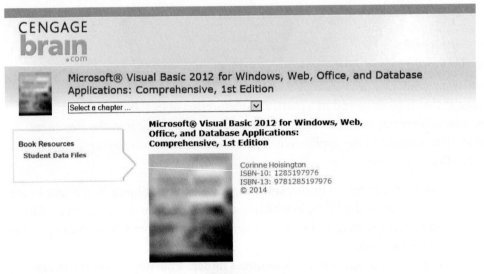

FIGURE 3-7

© 2014 Cengage Learning

STEP 2   In the left pane, click Student Data Files, and then click the Download Now link for Chapters 1-6.

The Information bar is displayed at the bottom of the browser window (Figure 3-8).

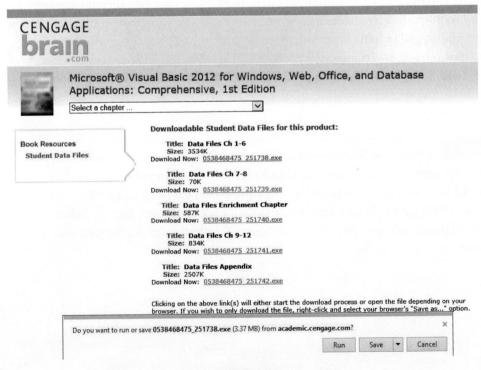

FIGURE 3-8

© 2014 Cengage Learning

STEP 3 Click Save as, and then navigate to the location on your computer where you store downloaded files.

In the Save As dialog box (Figure 3-9), you must identify the drive and folder in which you want to store the image files. The location depends on your computer and drives. In all sample programs in this book, images are stored on a USB drive that is designated as drive E.

Save As
dialog box

FIGURE 3-9

STEP 4 Click the Save button to save the zipped file. Navigate to the location of the downloaded file, and then double-click the file. Click the Browse button, navigate to the folder where you want to store files for this book, and then click the OK button. Click the Extract all button on the Extract tab to extract the files to the selected folder. Click the Extract button. Open the extracted folder for Chapter 3 to display its contents.

The image files for Chapter 3 are displayed in a folder window (Figure 3-10). Remember where you save the images because later you must locate and import them into the Resources folder for use in the program. Image file names should not contain spaces.

drive E: is
selected

FIGURE 3-10

ONLINE REINFORCEMENT

To view a video of the process in the preceding steps, visit CengageBrain.com and navigate to the resources for this title. Tap or click the link for Chapter 3 and then navigate to Video 3-3.

Import the Image into the Program Resources Folder

After you have saved an image on a storage device that is available to your computer, you should import the image into the program's Resources folder so the image is available for use. To import the DeepDish image into the Resources folder, you can complete the following steps:

STEP 1   If necessary, open Visual Studio 2012 and the Pizza Selection Visual Basic program. Select the picDeepDish PictureBox object by tapping or clicking it. Scroll in the PictureBox Properties window until the Image property is visible. Tap or click the Image property name in the left list of the Properties window.

*With the PictureBox object selected, the Properties window displays all the properties of the object (Figure 3-11). The **Image property** specifies the image that should be displayed in the selected PictureBox object. The Image property is selected in the Properties window. The Image property's ellipsis button is displayed in the right column of the Image property.*

picDeepDish PictureBox object is selected

Image property

ellipsis button for Image property

FIGURE 3-11

STEP 2   Tap or click the ellipsis button in the right column of the Image property.

*The **Select Resource dialog box** opens (Figure 3-12) and displays the resources that have been imported for the program. In Figure 3-12, no resources have been imported.*

FIGURE 3-12

STEP 3   Tap or click the Import button in the Select Resource dialog box. Use the features of the Open dialog box to locate the file you want to import into the program. In this case, you want to import the DeepDish.jpg file stored on drive E, which is a USB drive.

The Open dialog box opens when you tap or click the Import button (Figure 3-13). The DeepDish.jpg file is stored on drive E.

FIGURE 3-13

STEP 4 Select DeepDish.jpg. Tap or click the Open button in the Open dialog box.

The Select Resource dialog box is displayed again, but now the DeepDish image is identified in the Project resource file list (Figure 3-14). The image appears in the preview window. This means the image is now part of the resources for the program. You no longer need to locate the image on the USB drive to include the image in a PictureBox object.

Select Resource
dialog box

DeepDish image
is selected

DeepDish image in
preview window

© Brand X Pictures/Getty Images

FIGURE 3-14

STEP 5 With the DeepDish file name selected in the Project resource file list, tap or click the OK button in the Select Resource dialog box.

The DeepDish image is displayed in the picDeepDish PictureBox object (Figure 3-15). In addition, the Resources folder is added to the Solution Explorer window, indicating the Resources folder now is part of the program.

Resources
folder

DeepDish image
in picDeepDish
PictureBox object

© Brand X Pictures/Getty Images

FIGURE 3-15

Size an Image

In most cases, when you import an image into a program, the image will not fit in the PictureBox object perfectly because the two items have different sizes or dimensions. The developer must adjust the size of the image to fit in the PictureBox object or adjust the size of the PictureBox object to accommodate the image.

By comparing the images in Figures 3-14 and 3-15, you can see that the image is larger than the PictureBox object. Because the PictureBox object must remain its current size, the image must be adjusted using the **SizeMode property**. To adjust an image's size to fit in a PictureBox object, you can complete the following steps:

STEP 1 Select the PictureBox object that contains the DeepDish image, and then scroll in the picDeepDish Properties window until you see the SizeMode property. Tap or click the SizeMode property name in the left column, and then tap or click the SizeMode arrow in the right column of the SizeMode property.

The SizeMode property list is displayed (Figure 3-16). The list contains five choices you can use to change either the size of the image or the size of the PictureBox object. Normal is selected because it is the default value.

© Brand X Pictures/Getty Images

FIGURE 3-16

In the example, StretchImage is selected from the SizeMode list in the Properties window for PictureBox objects (see Figure 3-16). The other choices and their actions are:

- **Normal** — No changes are made to the image size or the size of the PictureBox object. Visual Studio places the image in the PictureBox object and aligns the upper-left corner of the image with the upper-left corner of the PictureBox object.

- **AutoSize** — Visual Studio increases or decreases the size of the PictureBox object to accommodate the size of the image. The entire image is visible and fits precisely in the PictureBox object.

- **CenterImage** — No changes are made to the image size or the size of the PictureBox object. Visual Studio places the image in the PictureBox object and aligns the center of the image with the center of the PictureBox object.

- **Zoom** — The image size is either reduced or enlarged to fit in the PictureBox object. The fit can be left and right or up and down, depending on the dimensions of the image and the PictureBox object. If the image and PictureBox object are not exactly proportional to one another, the image will not fill out the entire PictureBox object.

STEP 2   Tap or click StretchImage in the SizeMode list.

*The SizeMode list is closed and the image is resized to fit within the picDeepDish PictureBox object (Figure 3-17). When you use the **StretchImage option**, some image distortion might occur to make it fit within the PictureBox object. Therefore, you should select an image that has the same approximate dimensions (or at least the same aspect ratio) as the selected PictureBox object.*

image is resized

StretchImage is selected

© Brand X Pictures/Getty Images

FIGURE 3-17

Set the Visible Property

As you have learned, when the Pizza Selection program begins, neither of the two pizza types is pictured in the window. When the user taps or clicks the Deep Dish button, the program displays the appropriate picture in the Deep Dish PictureBox object. When the user taps or clicks the Thin Crust button, the program displays the appropriate picture in the other PictureBox object.

The **Visible property** controls whether an object is displayed on the Windows Form object. By default, the Visible property is set to True so that any object you place on the Windows Form object is displayed when the program runs. If you do not want an object to be displayed, you must set the Visible property to False. To set the Visible property to False for the picDeepDish PictureBox object, you can complete the following steps:

STEP 1 If necessary, select the picDeepDish PictureBox object. Scroll in the Properties window until the Visible property is displayed. Tap or click the Visible property name in the left column, and then tap or click the Visible arrow in the right column of the Visible property.

When you tap or click the Visible arrow, the list displays the words True and False (Figure 3–18). To make the object visible when the program starts, select True. If you do not want the object to be visible when the program starts, select False.

© Brand X Pictures/Getty Images

FIGURE 3-18

STEP 2 Tap or click False on the Visible property list.

The Visible property is set to False (Figure 3–19). When the program begins, the DeepDish picture will not be displayed on the Windows Form object. Note that the image and object are displayed on the frmPizzaSelection.vb [Design] tabbed page regardless of the Visible property setting.

© Brand X Pictures/Getty Images

FIGURE 3-19

Once you have set an object's Visible property to False, the only way to display the object on the Windows Form object while the program is running is to set the Visible property to True. You can do this by writing code, as you will see later in this chapter.

Set the Enabled Property

In an event-driven program, objects such as Button objects can be used to make events occur. For example, when you tap or click the Deep Dish button, a picture of a deep-dish pizza is displayed in the PictureBox object. In addition, the Select Pizza Button object becomes **enabled**, which means it can be tapped or clicked to make an event occur. When the program begins, however, the Select Pizza button is **disabled**, which means nothing will happen when you tap or click the button. A disabled button is displayed as dimmed (see Figure 3-1a on page 112).

The **Enabled property** controls when a Button object is enabled. The property also controls when a Button object is not enabled, which means tapping or clicking the button causes no action. The default selection for the Enabled property is True, which means the associated Button object is enabled. To set the Enabled property to False for the Select Pizza button, you can complete the following steps:

STEP 1   Select the btnSelectPizza object. Scroll in the Properties window until the Enabled property is displayed. Tap or click the Enabled property name in the left column, and then tap or click the Enabled arrow in the right column of the Enabled property.

When you tap or click the Enabled arrow, the list contains the words True and False (Figure 3-20). To make the object enabled when the program starts, select True. If you do not want the object to be enabled when the program starts, select False.

FIGURE 3-20

© Brand X Pictures/Getty Images

STEP 2   Tap or click False on the Enabled property list.

The Enabled property is set to False (Figure 3-21). When the program begins, the btnSelectPizza Button object will not be enabled on the Windows Form object.

Enabled property is set to False

FIGURE 3-21

© Brand X Pictures/Getty Images

ONLINE REINFORCEMENT

To view a video of the process in the previous steps, visit CengageBrain.com and navigate to the resources for this title. Tap or click the link for Chapter 3 and then navigate to Video 3-7.

Once you have set the Enabled property to False, the only way to enable a Button object on the Windows Form object while the program is running is to set the Enabled property to True. You can do this by writing code, as you will see later in this chapter.

Run a Program

When you set some object properties, the effect of their changes might not be evident until you run the program. For example, you have set the Visible property to False for the picDeepDish PictureBox object, and you have set the Enabled property to False for the btnSelectPizza Button object. Neither change is evident, however, when you view the Pizza Selection Windows Form object on the frmPizzaSelection.vb [Design] tabbed page in Visual Studio. These settings are applied only when you actually run the program.

To ensure the settings are correct for the user interface, you must run the program. **Running the program** means it is compiled, or translated, from the instructions you have written or generated in Visual Basic into a form of instructions that the computer can execute. These instructions are saved and then executed as a program.

To run the program you have created, you can tap or click the Start Debugging button on the Standard toolbar, as shown in the steps on the next page:

STEP 1   Point to the Start Debugging button on the Standard toolbar.

The pointer appears over the Start Debugging button (Figure 3-22).

FIGURE 3-22

© Brand X Pictures/Getty Images

STEP 2   Tap or click the Start Debugging button on the Standard toolbar.

The program is compiled and saved, and then it runs on the computer. When the program runs, the Pizza Selection window is displayed on the screen (Figure 3-23). Notice that the DeepDish image is not displayed in the window because the Visible property was set to False for the picDeepDish PictureBox object (see Figure 3-19 on page 125). Notice also that the Select Pizza button is dimmed, which indicates its Enabled property is set to False.

FIGURE 3-23

Once you start running the program, it continues to run until you close it. To close a program, tap or click the Close button on the right side of the window title bar (see Figure 3-23).

After you set all the properties for the objects in the user interface, the design of the user interface is complete. You now are ready to move to the next phase of the program development life cycle — designing the program processing objects.

Visual Basic Program Coding

Before beginning to design the program processing objects, the developer must understand certain program coding principles and techniques. **Program code** is the set of instructions written by the developer that direct the program to carry out its required processing. The following sections explain the Visual Basic 2012 code required for the Pizza Selection program.

Enter Visual Basic Code for Event Handling

As you have learned, most processing in an event-driven program occurs when the user triggers an event. For example, when a user taps or clicks a button on the graphical user interface, the activity can trigger an event and the program performs the required processing. The developer writes program code to carry out the processing. This code is placed in a section of the program called an **event handler** — it "handles" the event that the user action triggers by executing code that performs the required processing.

To write the code for an event handler, the developer first must identify the GUI object that will be used to trigger the event. For example, when the Deep Dish button is tapped or clicked in the sample program, the DeepDish picture should appear in the picDeepDish PictureBox object. To write the code that will display the DeepDish picture, the developer must inform Visual Studio that the Deep Dish button is the object for which the code is being written, and that an event handler must be created for the tap or click event. You can create the event handler using the steps on the next page:

STEP 1   If necessary, open Visual Studio 2012 and the Pizza Selection program and make the frmPizzaSelection.vb [Design] tabbed window visible. Point to the Deep Dish Button object in the Windows Form object.

The pointer appears over the Deep Dish Button object (Figure 3-24). The four-headed arrow pointer indicates you can drag the Button object to another location in the window.

pointer is on
Deep Dish
Button object

FIGURE 3-24

STEP 2   Double-click the Deep Dish Button object.

The code window is displayed on the frmPizzaSelection.vb* tabbed page (Figure 3-25). The code in the window is generated by Visual Studio. This code identifies an event handler, which is the code that executes when an event is triggered. When the Deep Dish button is tapped or clicked, the program will execute the code in this event handler. The list box in the upper-left corner of the tabbed page identifies the object for which the event handler will execute — in this case, the btnDeepDish object. The list box in the upper-right corner of the tabbed page identifies the event that must occur to execute the code in the event handler. The event identified in Figure 3-25 is "Click." When the user taps or clicks the Deep Dish button, the program executes the code between the Private Sub statement and the End Sub statement. In Figure 3-25, no code has been entered other than the event handler identification code generated by Visual Studio. The insertion point is located where the developer should begin entering the code that executes when the user taps or clicks the btnDeepDish Button object.

Toolbox
Close button

frmPizzaSelection.vb*
tabbed page

object for which event
handler will execute

event handler
identification code
generated by
Visual Studio

insertion point

event that must occur for
this code to be executed

FIGURE 3-25

Visual Basic 2012 Coding Statements

A Visual Basic 2012 coding statement contains instructions that the computer
eventually executes. Visual Basic has a set of rules, or **syntax,** that specifies how each
statement must be written.

When the user taps or clicks the Deep Dish button while the Pizza Selection
program is running, the DeepDish image should be displayed in the picDeepDish
PictureBox object. Figure 3-26 shows a Visual Basic coding statement that sets the
Visible property to True for the picDeepDish PictureBox object so the image is
displayed in the picture box after the statement executes.

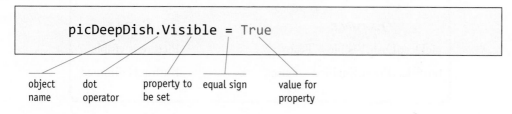

```
picDeepDish.Visible = True
```

object   dot   property to   equal sign   value for
name   operator   be set   property

FIGURE 3-26

The first part of the statement, picDeepDish, identifies the object that contains the property to set. The name of the object is followed by the dot operator (period) with no intervening spaces. The dot operator separates the name of the object from the next entry in the statement and is required.

Following the dot operator is the name of the property to set. In Figure 3-26 on the previous page, the name of the property is Visible. You will recall that the Visible property determines whether an image is displayed in the PictureBox object when the program is running. In Figure 3-19 on page 125, the Visible property was set to False for the picDeepDish PictureBox object so the image would not be displayed when the program started. This statement sets the Visible property to True so the image will be displayed.

The property name is followed by a space and then an equal sign. The space is not required, but good coding practice dictates that elements within a statement should be separated by a space so the statement is easier to read. One or more spaces can be used, but most developers use only one space. The equal sign is required because it indicates that the value to be used for setting the property follows. A space follows the equal sign for readability.

The word True follows the space. The value True in the Visible property indicates that the image should be displayed in the PictureBox object. When the program is running and the Visible property is set to True, the image appears in the picture box.

Each entry within the program statement must be correct or the program will not compile. This means the object name must be spelled properly, the dot operator must be placed in the correct location, the name of the property must be spelled properly, the equal sign must be present, and a valid entry for the property must follow the equal sign. For the Visible property, the only valid entries are True and False.

General Format of a Visual Basic Statement

The general format of the Visual Basic statement shown in Figure 3-26 appears in Figure 3-27.

General Format: Property Value Assignment Statement
`objectname.property = propertyvalue`

EXAMPLE	RESULT
picDeepDish.Visible = True	Picture is visible
btnSelectPizza.Enabled = False	Button is dimmed

FIGURE 3-27

In the general format, the object name always is the first item in the Visual Basic statement. The object name is the name you specified in the (Name) property of the Properties window. In Figure 3-26 on page 131, the object name is picDeepDish because that name was given to the Deep Dish PictureBox object.

The dot operator (period) is required. It follows the object name with no space between them. Immediately following the dot operator is the name of the property that will be set by the statement. The property name must be spelled correctly and must be a valid property for the object named in the statement. Valid properties that can be specified in the statement are identified in the Properties window associated with the object.

The equal sign must follow the property name in the statement. Visual Basic statements do not require spaces, nor is there a limit to how many spaces you can place between elements in the statement. The equal sign identifies the statement as an **assignment statement**, which means the value on the right side of the equal sign is assigned to the element on the left side of the equal sign. When setting properties, the element on the left side of the equal sign is the property.

The property value specified in the assignment statement must be a valid value for the property identified on the left side of the equal sign. You can see the valid values for a given property by looking in the Properties window for the object whose property you are setting.

After you have entered the property value, the Visual Basic statement is complete. Because correct programming protocol dictates that only one statement should appear on a line, the next step is to press the ENTER key to move the insertion point to the next line in the code window.

The general statement format shown in Figure 3-27 is used for all statements in which the code sets the value of an object property.

IntelliSense

In Figure 3-25 on page 131, the insertion point is located in the code window. To enter the statement in Figure 3-26 into the program using the code window, you can type the entire statement. Visual Studio, however, provides help so that you will be less prone to make a typing error when entering the statement. This help feature is called IntelliSense.

IntelliSense displays all allowable entries you can make in a Visual Basic statement each time a dot (period), equal sign, or other special character is required for the statement. When you type the prefix pic as shown in Figure 3-28, an IntelliSense window opens with all the objects that begin with the prefix. Instead of possibly misspelling the object name, you can select it from the IntelliSense list. The complete Visual Basic statement is shown in Figure 3-28.

```
picDeepDish.Visible = True
```

FIGURE 3-28

When you type the first few letters of the object name, IntelliSense displays a list of all the objects and other entries that can be specified in the statement.

Enter a Visual Basic Statement

To enter the Visual Basic statement in Figure 3-28 on the previous page using IntelliSense, you can complete the following steps:

> **STEP 1** Tap or click the Close button to close the Toolbox. With the code window open and the insertion point positioned as shown in Figure 3-25 on page 131, type pic.

The characters "pic" are displayed in the code window (Figure 3-29). IntelliSense displays a list of all the entries that can follow the prefix in the statement. Sometimes the selected entry is correct for the statement you are entering, but often it is not. Therefore, you must identify the correct statement in the list before entering it.

FIGURE 3-29

> **STEP 2** To identify the correct entry, type its next letter until the entry is selected. In this case, type d.

As you type, IntelliSense highlights an entry in the list that begins with the letters you enter (Figure 3-30). When you enter picd, IntelliSense highlights the only term in the list that begins with picd, which is picDeepDish. This is the object name you want to enter into the Visual Basic statement.

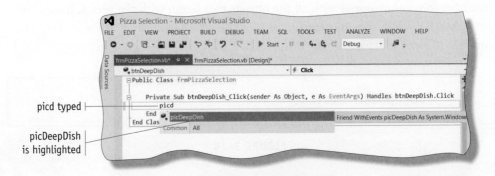

FIGURE 3-30

STEP 3   When IntelliSense highlights the correct object name, press the key corresponding to the entry that follows the object name. In this case, press the PERIOD key.

IntelliSense automatically enters the entire object name into the Visual Basic statement and the period you typed following the object name (Figure 3-31). In addition, IntelliSense realizes that the dot you entered means more information is required in the statement, so it displays a list of the allowable entries following the dot.

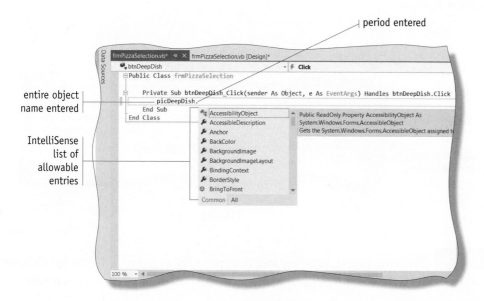

FIGURE 3-31

STEP 4   As with the object name in Step 2, the next step is to enter one or more characters until IntelliSense highlights the desired property in the list. Type the letter v for the Visible property.

IntelliSense highlights the properties in the list that begin with the letter v (Visible) or that contain the letter v, such as ProductVersion (Figure 3-32). Because the Visible property is highlighted, no further action is required to select it.

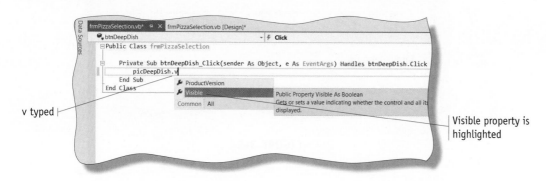

FIGURE 3-32

STEP 5 Press the key for the character that follows the property name. In this case, press the SPACEBAR.

IntelliSense enters the highlighted property name (Visible) followed by the space you typed (Figure 3-33). The space indicates to Visual Basic that the object name and property name entry is complete. Notice also that the IntelliSense tip specifies what the statement will do. In Figure 3-33, the statement gets or sets a value indicating whether the control is displayed. This means the Visible property indicates whether the picDeepDish PictureBox object is displayed.

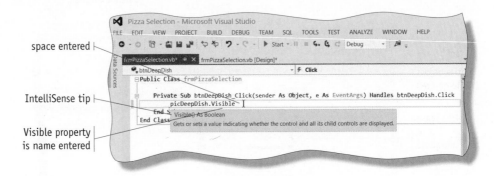

FIGURE 3-33

STEP 6 Press the EQUAL SIGN key and then press the SPACEBAR. In the IntelliSense list, tap or click the Common tab if necessary to display the most common results.

The equal sign and a space are displayed and then IntelliSense displays a list of the entries you can make (Figure 3-34). For the Visible property, the only possible entries following the equal sign are False and True. An entry of False indicates the PictureBox object should not be visible; True indicates the opposite.

FIGURE 3-34

STEP 7 Type t for True.

IntelliSense highlights the True entry (Figure 3-35).

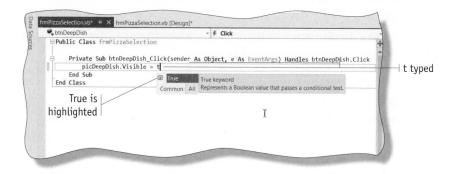

|→ t typed

True is
highlighted

FIGURE 3-35

STEP 8 Press the key for the character that follows the True entry. In this case, press the ENTER key.

Because you pressed the ENTER key, IntelliSense enters True into the statement and then Visual Studio moves the indented insertion point to the next line (Figure 3-36). The Visual Basic statement now is entered completely.

| True is entered
| in statement

FIGURE 3-36

Can I turn on line numbers to receive assistance while creating my program?
Line numbers help identify each line of code in the code window. They do not appear by default, however, so you must instruct Visual Studio to display the line numbers. If line numbers do not appear in the code window on your computer, you can display them by completing the following steps:
1. Tap or click TOOLS on the menu bar.
2. Tap or click Options on the TOOLS menu.
3. If necessary, tap or click the triangle next to Text Editor in the Options dialog box.
4. If necessary, tap or click the triangle next to Basic in the list below Text Editor.
5. Tap or click General in the list below Basic.
6. Place a check mark in the Line numbers check box.
7. Tap or click the OK button in the Options dialog box.

CONSIDER THIS

Visual Studio and IntelliSense automatically create the indentations in the program statements in Figure 3-36 on the previous page because indentations make the statements easier to read and understand. As programs become more complex, proper indentation of program statements can be an important factor in developing error-free programs.

The following general steps summarize the procedure for using IntelliSense to enter a Visual Basic statement that sets a property:

1. In the IntelliSense list, type the first letter(s) of the name of the object whose property will be set.
2. When the object name is selected in the list, press the PERIOD key.
3. Type the first letter(s) of the name of the property to be set until the name is highlighted in the IntelliSense list.
4. Press the SPACEBAR to complete the first portion of the statement.
5. Press the EQUAL SIGN key.
6. Press the SPACEBAR.
7. Press the first letter(s) of the entry you want to select in the list until the entry is highlighted. If IntelliSense does not display a list, type the value for the property.
8. Press the ENTER key.

Using IntelliSense to enter a Visual Basic statement provides two significant advantages. First, it is faster to enter a statement using IntelliSense than it is to type the statement. Second, using IntelliSense drastically reduces the number of errors when entering statements. By using only the entries in the IntelliSense lists, the developer seldom will make an invalid entry. In addition, because the entry is chosen from a list, it cannot possibly be misspelled or mistyped.

Entering a programming statement is a fundamental skill for a Visual Basic programmer. You should thoroughly understand how to enter a programming statement using IntelliSense.

Set the Visible Property to False

In Figure 3-36 on the previous page, the programming statement set the Visible property to True for the picDeepDish PictureBox object, which will display the image in the picture box when the statement is executed. The statement will execute when the user taps or clicks the Deep Dish button because the statement is part of the btnDeepDish_Click event handler.

When the user taps or clicks the Deep Dish button, the Visible property also must be set to False for the picThinCrust PictureBox so the ThinCrust picture is not displayed alongside the DeepDish picture. To set the Visible property to False for the picThinCrust PictureBox object, you could complete the following steps:

STEP 1   With the insertion point on the next line of the code window for the Deep Dish button click event, type pic.

The letters you typed are displayed in the code window and the IntelliSense list shows the valid entries you can choose (Figure 3-37). The entry picDeepDish is highlighted because it is the last entry that was selected from this list.

pic typed

IntelliSense list

picDeepDish is highlighted

FIGURE 3-37

STEP 2   Type t to highlight the picThinCrust entry in the IntelliSense list.

IntelliSense highlights picThinCrust in the list because it is the only entry that starts with the characters "pict" (Figure 3-38).

pict typed

picThinCrust is highlighted

FIGURE 3-38

STEP 3   Press the key for the character that follows the object name. In this case, press the PERIOD key.

The picThinCrust entry is placed in the statement followed by the dot operator (period) you typed (Figure 3-39 on the next page). In addition, IntelliSense displays the list of allowable entries.

The Visible entry is highlighted in the list because it was selected the last time the list was used. If Visible was not highlighted, you could type the letter v to highlight Visible in the list.

picThinCrust entered
in statement

period entered

Visible is
highlighted

FIGURE 3-39

STEP 4   Press the SPACEBAR, press the EQUAL SIGN key, and then press the SPACEBAR.

IntelliSense places the Visible entry in the statement (Figure 3-40). Next, the space you typed appears, followed by the equal sign and the second space you typed. When you typed the equal sign, IntelliSense displayed the list of allowable entries following the equal sign.

Visible
entered

space, equal
sign, and
space entered

IntelliSense
list

FIGURE 3-40

STEP 5   Type f and then press the ENTER key.

When you type the letter f, IntelliSense highlights False in the list. When you press the ENTER key, IntelliSense inserts False (Figure 3-41).

indented
insertion point

False inserted

ONLINE REINFORCEMENT

To view a video of the process in the previous steps, visit CengageBrain.com and navigate to the resources for this title. Tap or click the link for Chapter 3 and then navigate to Video 3-11.

FIGURE 3-41

Again, using IntelliSense to enter a Visual Basic programming statement results in a correct statement entered in minimal time with a reduced chance of errors.

Set the Enabled Property

You learned earlier that if the Enabled property is True for a Button object, the tap or click event code will be executed for the button when the user taps or clicks it. If the Enabled property is False for a Button object, the event code for the button will not be executed. In Figure 3-21 on page 127, the Enabled property was set to False for the Select Pizza button so that the button is not active when the program begins. When the user taps or clicks a picture button such as the Deep Dish button, however, the Enabled property must be set to True so the Select Pizza button is active. To set the Enabled property to True, the developer must enter a coding statement for the btnSelectPizza Button object. To enter the coding statement into the btnDeepDish_Click event handler, you can complete the following steps:

STEP 1 Type btn to display the IntelliSense list (Figure 3-42).

FIGURE 3-42

STEP 2 Type s (or more characters if necessary) until IntelliSense highlights the btnSelectPizza entry in the list.

IntelliSense highlights btnSelectPizza, the only entry that starts with the characters "btns" (Figure 3-43). Sometimes, the correct entry will be highlighted before you type all the distinguishing characters. If so, you need not type more characters.

FIGURE 3-43

STEP 3   Type a period, type e, press the SPACEBAR, press the EQUAL SIGN key, press the SPACEBAR again, and then type t to select True in the IntelliSense list.

IntelliSense places the highlighted entry (btnSelectPizza) in the statement and displays a list of the next allowable entries. When you typed e, Enabled was selected in the list. Pressing the SPACEBAR caused IntelliSense to place Enabled and then the space in the statement. When you typed the equal sign and second space, IntelliSense inserted both and displayed the list of entries that can follow the equal sign (Figure 3–44). When you typed the letter t, IntelliSense highlighted True in the list.

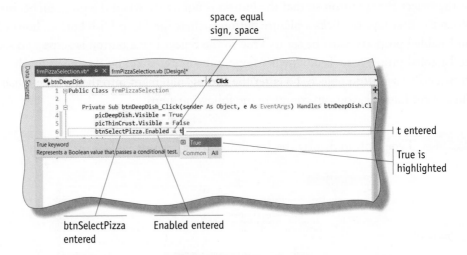

FIGURE 3-44

STEP 4   Press the ENTER key to enter the completed statement and place the insertion point on the next line.

IntelliSense enters True in the statement (Figure 3–45). Pressing the ENTER key completes the statement and moves the indented insertion point to the next line.

ONLINE REINFORCEMENT

To view a video of the process in the previous steps, visit CengageBrain.com and navigate to the resources for this title. Tap or click the link for Chapter 3 and then navigate to Video 3-12.

FIGURE 3-45

Learning how to enter program statements using IntelliSense is fundamental to writing programs using the Visual Basic 2012 language.

Comments in Program Statements

A well-written Visual Basic 2012 program normally contains **comment statements** within the code itself to document what the code is doing. The general purpose of comments is to help code readers understand the code and how it accomplishes its tasks. An example of comment statements used in code is shown in Figure 3-46.

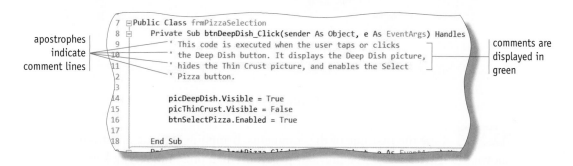

apostrophes indicate comment lines

comments are displayed in green

```
 7  Public Class frmPizzaSelection
 8      Private Sub btnDeepDish_Click(sender As Object, e As EventArgs) Handles
 9          ' This code is executed when the user taps or clicks
10          ' the Deep Dish button. It displays the Deep Dish picture,
11          ' hides the Thin Crust picture, and enables the Select
12          ' Pizza button.
13
14          picDeepDish.Visible = True
15          picThinCrust.Visible = False
16          btnSelectPizza.Enabled = True
17
18      End Sub
```

FIGURE 3-46

A comment is preceded by an apostrophe. Whenever the Visual Basic compiler encounters an apostrophe in the code, it ignores the remaining characters on the line. To the compiler, it's as if the comments do not exist.

The comments in the code are displayed in green text and describe the processing that will occur in the code that follows. Because comments are ignored by the Visual Basic compiler, developers must not include programming language syntax in the comments. Any letters or characters are allowed within comments.

To enter comments, first type an apostrophe in the code. All characters following the apostrophe on a line of code are considered a comment. To enter the comment code shown in Figure 3-46, you could complete the following steps:

STEP 1 To insert a blank line following the event code generated by Visual Studio that begins with the word Private, tap or click anywhere in that line and then press the END key.

Visual Studio positions the insertion point at the end of the line that you tapped or clicked (Figure 3-47).

code generated by Visual Studio

insertion point at end of line

FIGURE 3-47

STEP 2 Press the ENTER key.

Visual Studio inserts a blank line in the code and then moves the insertion point to the blank line (Figure 3-48). The comments can be inserted on the blank line.

insertion point
moved to next
line

Visual Studio
inserts blank
line

FIGURE 3-48

STEP 3 Type the first line of the comments, beginning with an apostrophe as shown in Figure 3-46 on the previous page, and then press the ENTER key.

The apostrophe identifies the rest of the line as a comment (Figure 3-49). The comment line is displayed in green text. When you press the ENTER key, Visual Studio creates a new blank line and places the indented insertion point on that line.

apostrophe
indicates
comment line

comment line
is displayed in
green

indented
insertion point

blank line

FIGURE 3-49

You can continue to enter lines of comments by typing an apostrophe and the comment and then pressing the ENTER key until all comments are completed.

Same-line Comments

Because the Visual Basic compiler treats all characters following an apostrophe as comments, it is possible to place a comment on the same line as executable code. In Figure 3-50, a comment is shown on the same line as the statement that sets the btnSelectPizza Enabled property to True.

```
 3  ⊟ Private Sub btnDeepDish_Click(sender As Object, e As EventArgs) Handles btnDeepDish.Cl
 4        ' This code is executed when the user taps or clicks
 5        ' the Deep Dish button. It displays the Deep Dish picture,
 6        ' hides the Thin Crust picture, and enables the Select
 7        ' Pizza button.
 8
 9        picDeepDish.Visible = True
10        picThinCrust.Visible = False
11        btnSelectPizza.Enabled = True ' Enable button
12
13     End Sub
14  End Class
15
```
apostrophe identifies comment

FIGURE 3-50

In Figure 3-50, the apostrophe specifies that subsequent characters on the line are to be treated as comments. Therefore, the Enable button text is displayed in green and is treated as a comment. To enter a comment on any line, enter an apostrophe and then type the comment. Remember that all characters after an apostrophe are treated as comments on a line of code.

Introductory Comments

Every program should begin with comments that state the name of the program, the developer's name, the date, and the purpose of the program. These introductory comments should precede all code in the program — even the code generated by Visual Studio (Figure 3-51).

introductory comments

```
  frmPizzaSelection.vb*  ↔ ✕  frmPizzaSelection.vb [Design]*
  (General)                              ▼  (Declarations)
 1 ⊟ ' Program Name:  Pizza Selection
 2     ' Developer:     Corinne Hoisington
 3     ' Date:          January 28, 2015
 4     ' Purpose:       This application displays two pizza types
 5     '                (deep dish and thin crust). The user can select a pizza type.
 6
 7 ⊟ Public Class frmPizzaSelection
```

FIGURE 3-51

To enter introductory comments, you can complete the steps on the next page:

STEP 1 Tap or click to the left of the word Public on line 1 of the program to place the insertion point on that line.

The insertion point is positioned at the beginning of line 1 in the code (Figure 3-52).

insertion point
positioned on line 1

FIGURE 3-52

STEP 2 Press the ENTER key and then press the UP ARROW key.

When you press the ENTER key, Visual Studio inserts a blank line on line 1 of the code and moves the line that begins with the words Public Class down to line 2 (Figure 3-53). Visual Studio also moves the insertion point to line 2 when you press the ENTER key. When you press the UP ARROW key, the insertion point moves to the first line, which is blank.

insertion point

blank line

Public Class line
now on line 2

FIGURE 3-53

STEP 3 Type an apostrophe, a space, the text `Program Name:`, and then press the TAB key.

The apostrophe identifies all characters and words that follow as comments, so those characters are displayed in green (Figure 3-54). The first line of introductory comments normally specifies the name of the program. Pressing the TAB key moves the insertion point to the right.

FIGURE 3-54

STEP 4 Type Pizza Selection as the name of the program, and then press the ENTER key.

The program name appears in the first line of comments and the insertion point is moved to line 2 (Figure 3-55).

FIGURE 3-55

You can enter the remaining comments using the same techniques. Press the TAB key one or more times to vertically align the paragraphs on the right so they appear as shown in Figure 3-51 on page 145.

What do the yellow and green lines represent to the left of the code?
The yellow lines indicate lines that have not been saved. The green lines indicate the changes in code that have been saved. The yellow and green lines are a method of tracking your most recent changes in code.

CONSIDER THIS

Correct Errors in Code

Using IntelliSense to help you enter code reduces the likelihood of coding errors considerably. Nevertheless, because you could create errors when entering code, you should understand what to do when a coding error occurs.

One possible error would be to forget an apostrophe in a comment statement. In Figure 3-56, a comment was entered without a leading apostrophe.

FIGURE 3-56

In Figure 3-56, the comment words are displayed in black and blue text, which indicates an error because comment characters normally are displayed in green text. Visual Studio gives no other indication that an error has occurred.

From this point where the error occurred, the developer might take any course of action. For example, she might immediately run the program. Or, she might tap or click anywhere in the window to move the insertion point, or press the ENTER key to insert a blank line. If the program in Figure 3-56 is executed immediately by tapping or clicking the Start Debugging button on the Standard toolbar, the window shown in Figure 3-57 will be displayed.

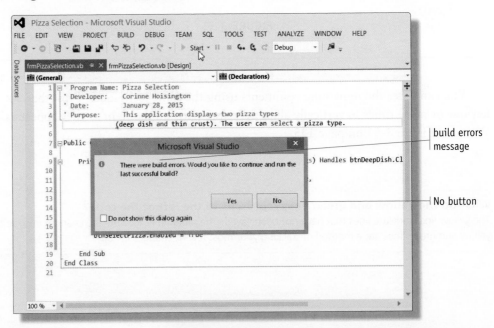

FIGURE 3-57

The **build errors message** means the Visual Basic compiler detected a coding error in the program. An absolute requirement when creating Visual Basic programs is that when you see the build errors message, you *always tap or click the No button.* Under no circumstances should you tap or click the Yes button in the dialog box. When you tap or click the No button, you can perform the following steps to make corrections in your program:

STEP 1   Tap or click the No button in the Microsoft Visual Studio dialog box that informs you of a build error (see Figure 3-57).

*When you tap or click the No button, Visual Studio displays the program code and the Error List window (Figure 3-58). The **Error List window** identifies the number of errors that occurred and displays descriptions of the errors. For example, the Syntax error in Figure 3-58 means Visual Studio expected to find a different type of statement. The window also contains the file name in which the error occurred (frmPizzaSelection.vb), the line number of the statement in error (5), and the vertical column within the statement where the error was detected (15). In the code window, the location of the error is noted by a blue squiggly line.*

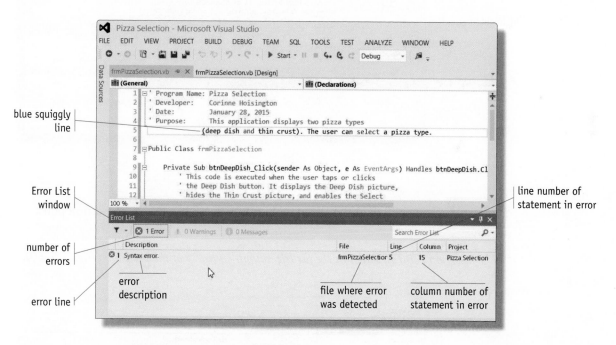

FIGURE 3-58

STEP 2 Double-click anywhere on the error line.

Visual Studio highlights the error with a blue squiggly line. The developer can type and replace the highlighted text with the correct code (Figure 3-59). With the error highlighted, the developer must examine the statement to determine the error. By looking at line 5, column 15, where the left parenthesis is highlighted, it is clear that the developer created a line that was intended to be a comment. Further examination reveals the required apostrophe is missing.

FIGURE 3-59

STEP 3 Tap or click in the far left column on line 5 to place the insertion point there.

The insertion point is placed in the far left column on line 5 of the program (Figure 3-60).

FIGURE 3-60

STEP 4 Type an apostrophe.

The apostrophe is placed in the first column on line 5 of the program (Figure 3-61).

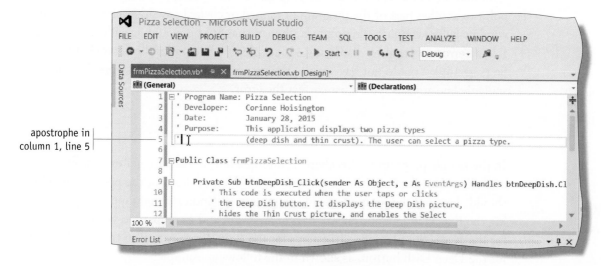

apostrophe in
column 1, line 5

FIGURE 3-61

STEP 5 Tap or click anywhere in the code window.

When you tap or click anywhere in the window, the insertion point moves to that location (Figure 3-62). If the statement has been corrected, the error line is removed from the Error List window, and the number of errors is reduced by one. In Figure 3-62, the number of errors now is zero because the one error found in the program has been corrected. Multiple errors can be detected when the program is compiled.

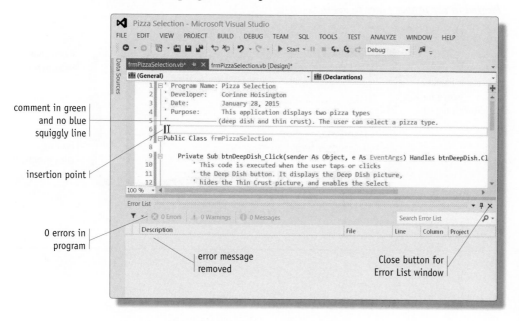

comment in green
and no blue
squiggly line

insertion point

0 errors in
program

error message
removed

Close button for
Error List window

FIGURE 3-62

ONLINE REINFORCEMENT

To view a video of the process in the previous steps, visit CengageBrain.com and navigate to the resources for this title. Tap or click the link for Chapter 3 and then navigate to Video 3-15.

You can close the Error List window by tapping or clicking its Close button (see Figure 3-62 on the previous page).

In Figure 3-57 on page 148, the example assumed that the developer made an error and then immediately ran the program. If the developer moved the insertion point to another part of the program or tapped or clicked any other element in the window before running the program, then Visual Studio would provide a visual cue that an error occurred by displaying a blue squiggly line under the error (Figure 3-58 on page 149). You do not have to run the program to find coding errors. If a blue squiggly line appears, you must correct the error.

Additional Tap or Click Events

In the sample program in this chapter, multiple buttons can trigger events. For example, when the user taps or clicks the Exit Window button, the program window should close and the program should terminate. To indicate that tapping or clicking the Exit Window button will trigger an event, and to prepare to write the code for the event, complete the same steps for the Exit Window button that you learned for the Deep Dish button, as shown in the following example:

STEP 1 On the frmPizzaSelection.vb [Design] tabbed page, double-click the Exit Window Button object.

Visual Studio opens the code window and displays the frmPizzaSelection.vb tabbed page (Figure 3-63). Visual Studio also inserts the event handler code for the tap or click event on the btnExit object. Two horizontal lines separate the event handler code for the btnExit object from code for other event handlers that might be in the program. The developer must write the code that will be executed when the tap or click event occurs. The insertion point is located in the proper place to begin writing code.

FIGURE 3-63

Enter Comments

As you have learned, you can enter code in the code window using the IntelliSense tools. The first code written for an event, however, should be comment code that identifies the event and the processing that will occur. The comment code for the Exit Window event handler is shown in Figure 3-64.

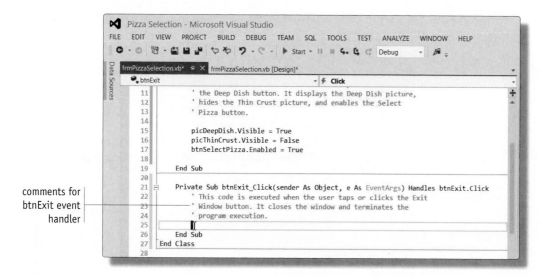

comments for btnExit event handler

FIGURE 3-64

Close Procedure

The Visual Basic statement to close the window and terminate the program calls a procedure that performs the actual processing. A **procedure** is a set of prewritten code that can be called by a statement in the Visual Basic program. When the procedure is called, the program processes the code. The procedure used to close a window and terminate a program is the Close procedure.

You can use the statement in Figure 3-65 to call the Close procedure.

procedure name

FIGURE 3-65

The word Close specifies the name of the procedure to be called. The left and right parentheses immediately following the procedure name identify the Visual Basic statement as a **procedure call statement**.

When the statement in Figure 3-65 is executed, the Close procedure will be called and control will be given to the prewritten programming statements in the Close procedure. These statements will close the window and terminate the application.

To enter the Close statement into the program, you can type "clo" and then select Close in the IntelliSense list, as shown in the following steps.

STEP 1   With the insertion point positioned as shown in Figure 3-64 on the previous page, type `clo` to highlight Close in the IntelliSense list.

When you type the letters "clo," IntelliSense highlights the word Close in the IntelliSense list (Figure 3-66).

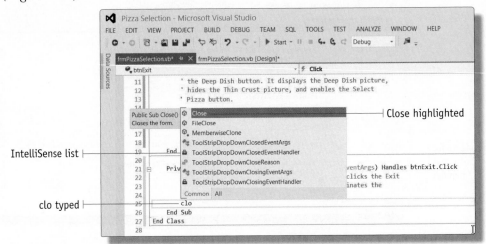

FIGURE 3-66

STEP 2   Press the ENTER key.

IntelliSense enters Close in the statement and, because it knows Close is a procedure call, automatically appends the open and closed parentheses to the statement (Figure 3-67). Then, Visual Studio returns the insertion point to the next line.

FIGURE 3-67

Prewritten procedures are an important element when using rapid application development in Visual Basic and Visual Studio because the developer is not required to write the procedure code. The developer merely writes a single statement to call the procedure. You will use many procedures in this book for a variety of reasons.

Print Code

In some instances, you will need to print the code in the program. While reviewing code, you might find it easier to read and understand the code on a printed page rather than on your computer screen. In other cases, you might want to share the code with another developer; the printed page often is a better tool for sharing than a monitor screen. To print the code in a program, you can complete the following steps:

1. Tap or click FILE on the menu bar to display the File menu.
2. Tap or click Print on the FILE menu to display the Print dialog box.
3. Ensure that a check mark appears in the Include line numbers check box if you want to include line numbers on your printout. Most developers prefer line numbers on printouts.
4. Make any other needed selections in the Print dialog box.
5. Tap or click the OK button in the Print dialog box to print the code.

If you have a color printer, the code will be printed with correct color. Otherwise, shades of gray will represent the colors shown in the code window. If a line of code extends beyond one printed line, an arrow will appear at the end of the first line to indicate it continues to the next printed line.

Coding Summary

Writing code is the essence of programming in Visual Basic 2012. Much of the emphasis in this book will be on writing the code required to implement applications of all kinds.

Once you understand coding and the statements shown in this chapter, you are ready to continue the process of designing and implementing the Pizza Selection program.

Phase 3 — Design the Program Processing Objects

The next phase in the program development life cycle requires determining the processing objects for the program and creating the event planning document. In the Pizza Selection program and programs of similar complexity, the designer need not be concerned about determining the processing objects. The only processing object required for the program is the Windows Form object. In more complex programs, determining processing objects will become important.

For the Pizza Selection program, the next task is to design the event planning document.

Event Planning Document

As you have learned, programs written using a graphical user interface normally are event-driven programs. An **event** means the user has initiated an action that causes the program to perform the appropriate type of processing in response. Once the mock-up has been created for the user interface, the developer must document the events that can occur based on the user interface.

The **event planning document** is a table that specifies objects in the user interface that will cause events, the actions taken by the user to trigger the events, and the event processing that must occur. The event planning document for the Pizza Selection program is shown in Figure 3-68.

EVENT PLANNING DOCUMENT

Program Name:	Developer:	Object:	Date:
Pizza Selection	Corinne Hoisington	frmPizzaSelection	January 28, 2015

Object	Event Trigger	Event Processing	
btnDeepDish	Tap or click	Display the DeepDish picture Hide the ThinCrust picture Enable the Select Pizza button	
btnSelectPizza	Tap or click	Disable the Deep Dish button Disable the Select Pizza button Disable the Thin Crust button Hide the Instructions label Display the Confirmation Message label Enable the Exit Window button	
btnThinCrust	Tap or click	Display the ThinCrust picture Hide the DeepDish picture Enable the Select Pizza button	
btnExitWindow	Tap or click	Close the window and terminate the program	

FIGURE 3-68

The left column in the event planning document identifies the object in the graphical user interface that can trigger an event. In the Pizza Selection program, each of the four Button objects can be used to trigger an event, so each must be included in the event planning document. Notice each Button object is identified by its name. Using this technique ensures that the documentation is precise, and provides little room for error when the developer creates the code to implement these events.

The middle column identifies the event trigger, which is the action a user takes to cause the event. In all four event cases in Figure 3-68, tapping or clicking a button triggers the event. As you will learn in this book, users can perform a variety of acts to trigger an event. For example, a user might point to an object, press or right-click the object, or double-tap or double-click the object. Each event trigger could trigger a different event.

The right column in the event planning document specifies the event processing that the program must perform when the event occurs. This list of tasks for each event is a critical element in the program design. It must be precise and accurate. No processing step that must occur should be left out of the event processing column. The tasks should be listed in the same sequence as they will be performed in the program.

For example, the first task for the btnDeepDish_Click event is to display the DeepDish picture. This is the primary task for the Deep Dish button. However, several other tasks must be completed. When the program begins, the ThinCrust picture is not visible, but if the user taps or clicks the Thin Crust button, then the picture will be visible. When the user taps or clicks the Deep Dish button, however, the ThinCrust picture should not be visible. Therefore, each time the user taps or clicks the Deep Dish button, the processing must hide the ThinCrust picture.

You also will recall that when the program begins, the Select Pizza button is dimmed (disabled). After the user taps or clicks a pizza type button, the Select Pizza button must be enabled. For example, each time the user taps or clicks the Deep Dish button, the Select Pizza button must be enabled.

As you review the event planning document in Figure 3-68, be sure you understand the processing that must occur for each event.

You should note that the event processing tasks in the right column identify *what* processing must be done when the event occurs. *How* these tasks will be accomplished is not identified specifically, although the information in the event planning document must be precise enough that the developer can easily write the code to implement the specified tasks.

Phase 4 — Code the Program

After the events and tasks within the events have been identified, the developer is ready to code the program. As you have learned in this chapter, coding the program means entering Visual Basic statements to accomplish the tasks specified in the event planning document. As the developer enters the code, she also will implement the logic to carry out the required processing.

Guided Program Development

To fine-tune the user interface in the Pizza Selection program and enter the code required to process each event in the program, complete the following steps to create the program shown in Figure 3-1 on pages 112 and 113.

NOTE TO THE LEARNER

In the following activity, you should complete the tasks within the specified steps. Each of the tasks is accompanied by a Hint Screen. The purpose of the Hint Screen is to indicate where you should perform the activity in the Visual Studio window and to remind you which method to use. If you need further help completing a step, refer to the figure identified by *ref:*.

Guided Program Development

1

● **Open the Mock-Up File** Open Visual Studio and then open
the mock-up file for the user interface you created in Chapter 2.
(If you did not create a mock-up file in Chapter 2, consult
with your instructor to obtain the file.)

● **Show the Windows Form Object's BackColor Property**
To finish the user interface, you must specify the BackColor
of the Windows Form object. Select the frmPizzaSelection
Windows Form object. In the Properties window, scroll until
the BackColor property is visible, tap or click the BackColor
property name in the left column, and then tap or click the
BackColor arrow in the right column. If necessary, tap or click
the Web tab (ref: Figure 3-3).

● **Choose the Windows Form Object's BackColor** Scroll the
Web tabbed page until White is visible, and then tap or click
White in the list (ref: Figure 3-5).

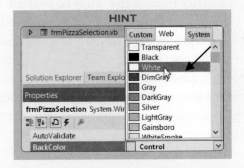

● **Select the BackColor for Buttons** Next, you must specify
the BackColor for the Button objects. Select the four buttons
in the window using techniques you have learned and change
the color to Wheat.

● **Change the ForeColor of a Label Object** Select lblHeading
and tap or click the ForeColor property name in the left
column, and then tap or click the ForeColor arrow in the right
column. If necessary, tap or click the Web tab and select
Firebrick in the list.

1

The BackColor for the Windows Form object is changed to White, the ForeColor of the heading is changed to Firebrick, and the BackColor for the buttons in the window is changed to Wheat (Figure 3-69).

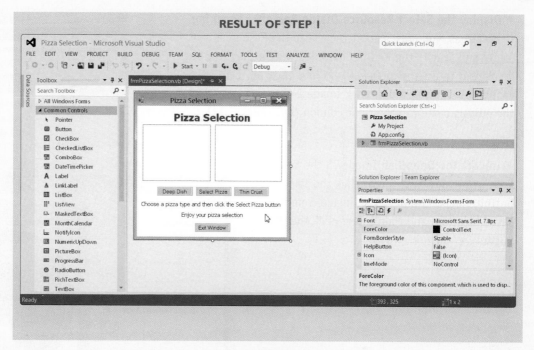

FIGURE 3-69

2

- **Download the DeepDish Image** To display the pictures in the PictureBox object, you might need to use your Web browser to download the pictures from the book's Web page at *CengageBrain.com* and store them on your computer. After downloading the files for Chapter 3, save the DeepDish image on a USB drive or other available storage media on your computer (*ref: Figure 3-7*).

- **Download the ThinCrust Image** Save the ThinCrust image on a USB drive or other storage media on your computer (*ref: Figure 3-7*).

(continues)

Guided Program Development   *continued*

3

● **Display the Select Resource Dialog Box** After acquiring
the pictures, you must import them into the Resources
folder and specify the PictureBox object where they will be
displayed. Select the picDeepDish PictureBox object. In the
Properties window, tap or click Image and then tap or click
the ellipsis button in the right column (*ref: Figure 3-11*).

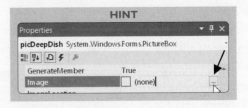

● **Import the DeepDish Image** In the Select
Resource dialog box, tap or click the Import
button, import the DeepDish image from its
saved location, and then tap or click the OK
button (*ref: Figure 3-14*).

© Brand X Pictures/Getty Images

● **Import the ThinCrust Image** Using the same
technique, specify the ThinCrust image as the
image for the picThinCrust PictureBox object.

© Brand X Pictures/Getty Images

● **Set the SizeMode Property to StretchImage for the DeepDish Image** When you import a picture, normally you must resize it or the PictureBox object so the picture is displayed properly. To resize the DeepDish image, select the picDeepDish PictureBox object. In the Properties window for the picDeepDish PictureBox object, tap or click the SizeMode property name, tap or click the SizeMode arrow, and then set the property to StretchImage (*ref: Figure 3-16*).

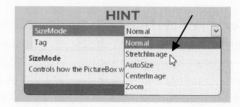

● **Set the SizeMode Property to StretchImage for the ThinCrust Image** Using the same technique, set the SizeMode property to StretchImage for the picThinCrust PictureBox object.

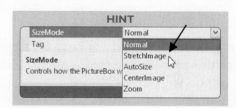

The images are displayed in the correct PictureBox objects (Figure 3-70).

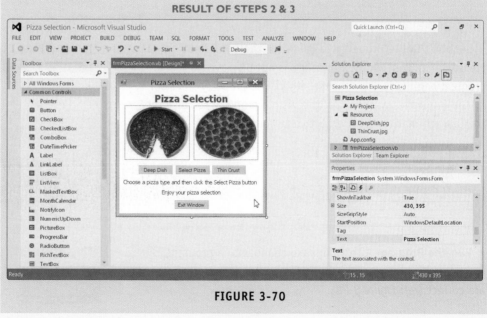

FIGURE 3-70

© Brand X Pictures/Getty Images

(continues)

● **Set the Visible Property to False for the DeepDish Image**
When the program begins, the pictures are not displayed in
the window, so you must set their Visible property to False.
In the Properties window for the picDeepDish PictureBox
object, tap or click the Visible property name in the left
column, tap or click the Visible arrow for the Visible property,
and then set the Visible property to False for the picDeepDish
PictureBox object (*ref: Figure 3-18*).

● **Set the Visible Property to False for the ThinCrust
Image** Using the same technique, set the Visible property to
False for the picThinCrust PictureBox object (*ref: Figure 3-18*).

● **Set the Visible Property to False for the Confirmation
Message** The confirmation message is not displayed when the
program begins, so you must set its Visible property to False.
In the Properties window, set the Visible property to False for
the lblConfirmation Label object (*ref: Figure 3-18*).

● **Run the Program** After you make changes to a program,
you should run it to ensure your changes work properly and
are correct (*ref: Figure 3-22*).

In Figure 3-71, the pizza type pictures are not displayed. In addition, the confirmation message is not displayed.

FIGURE 3-71

5

• **Set the Select Pizza Button's Enabled Property to False**
Initially, the Select Pizza button and the Exit Window button must be dimmed. In the Properties window for the btnSelect-Pizza object, tap or click the Enabled property name, tap or click the Enabled arrow, and then set the Enabled property to False for the btnSelectPizza Button object (*ref: Figure 3-20*).

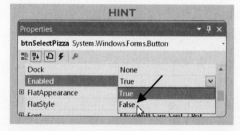

• **Set the Exit Window Button's Enabled Property to False**
Using the same technique, set the Enabled property to False for the btnExit Button object (*ref: Figure 3-20*).

• **Run the Program** Again, after you make changes, always ensure the changes are correct. Run the program.

Both the Select Pizza button and the Exit Window button are dimmed, indicating the Enabled property for both buttons is False (Figure 3-72).

FIGURE 3-72

(continues)

- **Open the Code Window for the btnDeepDish Event Handler** The user interface now is complete, so you should begin writing the code for the program. To write code, you must open the code window. Double-click the Deep Dish button to open the code window for the btnDeepDish_Click event (*ref: Figure 3-24*).

- **Position the Insertion Point** Close the Toolbox window. When you begin writing the code for a program, the first step is to write the introductory comments. Tap or click in the far left position of the first line of code (Public Class) (*ref: Figure 3-52*).

- **Create a Blank Line and Position the Insertion Point** Press the ENTER key and then press the UP ARROW key (*ref: Figure 3-53*).

- **Enter the First Line of the Introductory Comments** The introductory comments provide the code reader with important information about the program. The first line normally specifies the name of the program. Type an apostrophe, press the SPACEBAR, type Program Name:, press TAB, type Pizza Selection, and then press the ENTER key (*ref: Figure 3-55*).

- **Enter the Developer Identification Comment Line** Type an apostrophe, press the SPACEBAR, type Developer:, press TAB, type your name, and then press the ENTER key.

- **Enter the Date Comment Line** Type an apostrophe, press the SPACEBAR, type Date:, press TAB three times, enter the current date, and then press the ENTER key.

- **Enter the First Program Purpose Comment Line** Type an apostrophe, press the SPACEBAR, type Purpose:, press TAB two times, enter the first line of your own comments about the program, and then press the ENTER key.

- **Enter the Remaining Program Purpose Comment Lines**
Insert additional lines of comments about the purpose of the
program as you see fit.

*The comments appear at
the top of the program
code (Figure 3-73).*

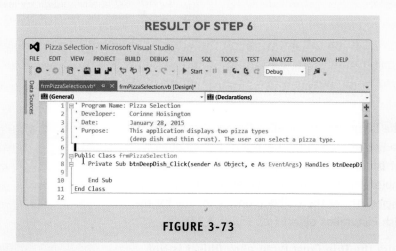

FIGURE 3-73

7

- **Position the Insertion Point Inside
the Click Event Handler** With the
insertion point located on the line
above the line of code that begins
with Public Class (see Figure 3-73),
press the DOWN ARROW key four times
and then press TAB two times to position
the insertion point (*ref: Figure 3-48*).

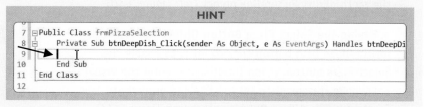

- **Enter the First Line of the Event
Handler Comments** Each event handler
should begin with comments describing
what the event handler accomplishes.
Type an apostrophe, press the SPACEBAR,
and then enter the first line of comments
for the btnDeepDish_Click event handler.
Press the ENTER key (*ref: Figure 3-49*).

(continues)

- **Enter the Remaining Event Handler Comments** Enter the remaining comments for the btnDeepDish_Click event handler.

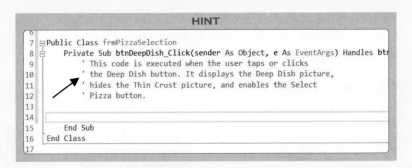

HINT

```
6
7  ☐Public Class frmPizzaSelection
8  ☐   Private Sub btnDeepDish_Click(sender As Object, e As EventArgs) Handles btn
9          ' This code is executed when the user taps or clicks
10         ' the Deep Dish button. It displays the Deep Dish picture,
11         ' hides the Thin Crust picture, and enables the Select
12         ' Pizza button.
13
14
15         End Sub
16 End Class
17
```

- **Make the Deep Dish PictureBox Object Visible** The first executable line of code in the Deep Dish Button object click event handler must make the Deep Dish PictureBox object visible. Using IntelliSense, enter the Visual Basic code statement to set the Visible property to True for the picDeepDish PictureBox object (*ref: Figure 3-32*).

HINT

```
14         picDeepDish.v
15    End Sub              ▸ ProductVersion
16 End Class               ▸ Visible
17                         Common | All
```

- **Make Sure the Thin Crust PictureBox Object is Not Visible** As documented in the event planning document, the next task is to make sure the ThinCrust picture is not visible in the window. Using IntelliSense, enter the Visual Basic code statement to set the Visible property to False for the picThinCrust PictureBox object (*ref: Figure 3-40*).

HINT

```
3  ☐   Private Sub btnDeepDish_Click(sender As
4          picDeepDish.Visible = True
5          picThinCrust.Visible =
False keyword                      ▣ False
```

- **Enable the Select Pizza Button Object** The last task for the Deep Dish button click event is to enable the Select Pizza button. Using IntelliSense, enter the Visual Basic code statement to set the Enabled property to True for the btnSelectPizza Button object (*ref: Figure 3-44*).

HINT

```
14         picDeepDish.Visible = True
15         picThinCrust.Visible = False
16         btnSelectPizza.Enabled = t
keyword                             ▣ True
```

The lines of code are entered in the Deep Dish Button object's click event handler (Figure 3-74). The code will set the Visible property to True for the picDeepDish PictureBox object, set the Visible property to False for the picThinCrust PictureBox object, and set the Enabled property to True for the btnSelectPizza Button object.

HEADS UP

As you enter executable code, you should refer to the event planning document to ensure the code implements the identified tasks. The event planning document is the guide to the code you write in each event handler.

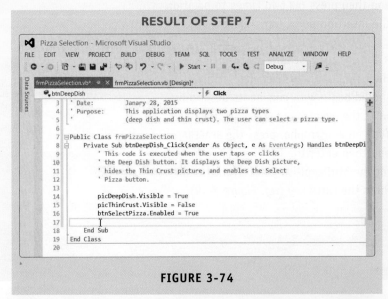

RESULT OF STEP 7

```
Pizza Selection - Microsoft Visual Studio
FILE  EDIT  VIEW  PROJECT  BUILD  DEBUG  TEAM  SQL  TOOLS  TEST  ANALYZE  WINDOW  HELP

frmPizzaSelection.vb* ╳  frmPizzaSelection.vb [Design]*
⬥ btnDeepDish                          ⚡ Click
3  ' Date:        Janary 28, 2015
4  ' Purpose:     This application displays two pizza types
5  '              (deep dish and thin crust). The user can select a pizza type.
6
7  ☐Public Class frmPizzaSelection
8  ☐   Private Sub btnDeepDish_Click(sender As Object, e As EventArgs) Handles btnDeepDi
9          ' This code is executed when the user taps or clicks
10         ' the Deep Dish button. It displays the Deep Dish picture,
11         ' hides the Thin Crust picture, and enables the Select
12         ' Pizza button.
13
14         picDeepDish.Visible = True
15         picThinCrust.Visible = False
16         btnSelectPizza.Enabled = True
17
18         End Sub
19 End Class
20
```

FIGURE 3-74

8

- **Run the Program** When the code for an event handler is complete, good practice dictates that you should run the program to ensure the event handler code works properly. Run the program. Tap or click the Deep Dish button.

When you tap or click the Deep Dish button, the DeepDish picture is displayed, the ThinCrust picture is not displayed, and the Select Pizza button is enabled (Figure 3-75). These are the correct results. Note that if you tap or click any of the other buttons in the window, nothing happens because you have not yet written the event handler code for these objects.

RESULT OF STEP 8

FIGURE 3-75

© Brand X Pictures/Getty Images

9

- **Display the Design Window** When the code for an event handler is completed, the next task is often to write the code for another event handler. To do so, you must go to the Design tabbed page and indicate the object for which the code will be written. Tap or click the frmPizzaSelection.vb [Design] tab to return to the Design tabbed page.

HINT

- **Open the Code Window for the btnSelectPizza Event Handler** You must open the code window for the btnSelectPizza Button object to enter code for the event handler. Double-tap or double-click the Select Pizza button to open the code window for the btnSelectPizza_Click event *(ref: Figure 3-24)*.

HINT

```
19
20    Private Sub btnSelectPizza_Click(sender As Object, e As EventArgs) Handles btnSel
21        |
22    End Sub
```

- **Enter Event Handler Comments** When beginning the code for an event handler, the first step is to enter the event handler comments. Enter the comments that describe the processing in the btnSelectPizza_Click event handler.

HINT

```
19    Private Sub btnSelectPizza_Click(sender As Object, e As EventArgs) Handles
20        ' This code is executed when the user taps or clicks the
21        ' Select Pizza button. It disables the Deep Dish button, the
22        ' Select Pizza button, and the Thin Crust button.
23        ' It hides the Instructions label, displays the
24        ' Confirmation label, and enables the Exit Window button.
25
26        |
27    End Sub
```

(continues)

• **Disable the btnDeepDish Button Object** According to the event planning document (Figure 3-68 on page 156), the next task is to disable the Deep Dish button. Using IntelliSense, enter the Visual Basic code statement to set the Enabled property to False for the btnDeepDish Button object (*ref: Figure 3-42*).

```
HINT
26        btnDeepDish.Enabled = False  ◄
27
28    End Sub
```

• **Disable the btnSelectPizza Button Object** The next task is to disable the Select Pizza button. Using IntelliSense, enter the Visual Basic code statement to set the Enabled property to False for the btnSelectPizza Button object (*ref: Figure 3-42*).

```
HINT
26        btnDeepDish.Enabled = False
27        btnSelectPizza.Enabled = False  ◄
28
29    End Sub
```

• **Disable the btnThinCrust Button Object** Using IntelliSense, enter the Visual Basic code statement to set the Enabled property to False for the btnThinCrust Button object (*ref: Figure 3-42*).

• **Hide the Instructions Label Object** When the Select Pizza button is tapped or clicked, the instructions should not be displayed. Using IntelliSense, enter the Visual Basic code statement to set the Visible property to False for the lblInstructions Label object (*ref: Figure 3-32*).

```
HINT
25
26        btnDeepDish.Enab    ⚲ ProductVersion
27        btnSelectPizza.E    ⚲ Visible  ◄
28        btnThinCrust.Ena   Common  All
29        lblInstructions.v
30
```

• **Display the Confirmation Message** The confirmation message must be displayed when the user taps or clicks the Select Pizza button. Using IntelliSense, enter the Visual Basic code statement to set the Visible property to True for the lblConfirmation Label object (*ref: Figure 3-32*).

```
HINT
26        btnDeepDish.Enabled = False
27        btnSelectPizza.Enabled = False
28        btnThinCrust.Enabled = False
29        lblInstructions.Visible = False
30        lblConfirmation.Visible = t

e keyword                              ▣ True
presents a Boolean value that passes a conditional test.  Common  All
```

• **Enable the Exit Window Button** After the user taps or clicks the Select Pizza button, the only allowable action is to tap or click the Exit Window button and close the application. Therefore, the Exit Window button must be enabled. Using IntelliSense, enter the Visual Basic code statement to set the Enabled property to True for the btnExit Button object (*ref: Figure 3-42*).

```
HINT
26        btnDeepDish.Enabled = False
27        btnSelectPizza.Enabled = False
28        btnThinCrust.Enabled = False
29        lblInstructions.Visible = False
30        lblConfirmation.Visible = True
31        btnExit.Enabled = True  ◄
```

• **Run the Program** Save and then run the program to ensure that it works correctly. Tap or click the Deep Dish button and then tap or click the Select Pizza button.

After tapping or clicking the two buttons, the DeepDish picture is displayed; the Deep Dish, Select Pizza, and Thin Crust buttons are disabled; the Instructions label is not displayed; the Confirmation Message label is displayed; and the Exit Window button is enabled (Figure 3-76).

RESULT OF STEP 9

FIGURE 3-76

© Brand X Pictures/Getty Images

10

• **Display the Design Window** The next task is to write the code for the btnThinCrust event handler. To return to the Design tabbed page so you can select the Thin Crust button, tap or click the frmPizzaSelection.vb [Design] tab.

HINT

• **Open the Code Window for the btnThinCrust Event Handler** Double-tap or double-click the Thin Crust button to open the code window for the btnThinCrust_Click event (*ref: Figure 3-24*).

HINT

```
35  |    Private Sub btnThinCrust_Click(sender As Object, e As EventArgs) Handles btnThinCrust.C
36  |
37  |    End Sub
38  |  End Class
```

• **Enter the Event Handler Comments** Using the techniques you have learned, enter the comments that describe the processing in the btnThinCrust_Click event handler.

• **Make the ThinCrust PictureBox Object Visible** According to the event planning document, the next task is to make the ThinCrust picture visible. Using IntelliSense, enter the Visual Basic code statement to set the Visible property to True for the picThinCrust PictureBox object (*ref: Figure 3-32*).

• **Make Sure the DeepDish Picture is Not Visible** Using IntelliSense, enter the Visual Basic code statement to set the Visible property to False for the picDeepDish PictureBox object (*ref: Figure 3-32*).

(continues)

● **Enable the Select Pizza Button** Using IntelliSense, enter the
Visual Basic code statement to set the Enabled property to True for
the btnSelectPizza Button object (*ref: Figure 3-42*).

● **Run the Program** Run the program and then tap or click the Thin
Crust button to ensure your code works correctly.

*The completed code for
the Select Pizza button
event handler and the Thin
Crust button event handler
is shown in Figure 3-77.*

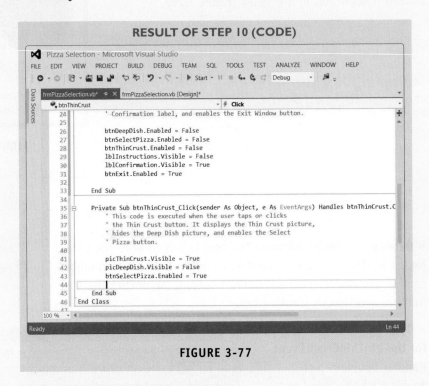

RESULT OF STEP 10 (CODE)

```
24        ' Confirmation label, and enables the Exit Window button.
25
26        btnDeepDish.Enabled = False
27        btnSelectPizza.Enabled = False
28        btnThinCrust.Enabled = False
29        lblInstructions.Visible = False
30        lblConfirmation.Visible = True
31        btnExit.Enabled = True
32
33     End Sub
34
35     Private Sub btnThinCrust_Click(sender As Object, e As EventArgs) Handles btnThinCrust.C
36        ' This code is executed when the user taps or clicks
37        ' the Thin Crust button. It displays the Thin Crust picture,
38        ' hides the Deep Dish picture, and enables the Select
39        ' Pizza button.
40
41        picThinCrust.Visible = True
42        picDeepDish.Visible = False
43        btnSelectPizza.Enabled = True
44
45     End Sub
46  End Class
```

FIGURE 3-77

*When you tap or click the
Thin Crust button, the
ThinCrust picture is displayed,
the DeepDish picture is not
displayed, and the Select Pizza
button is enabled (Figure 3-78).
The program is working properly.*

**RESULT OF STEP 10
(PROGRAM EXECUTION)**

FIGURE 3-78

11

- **Display the Design Window** Tap or click the frmPizzaSelection. vb [Design] tab to return to the Design tabbed page.

HINT

frmPizzaSelection.vb*   ⇥ ✕ frmPizzaSelection.vb [Design]*

- **Open the Code Window for the btnExit Event Handler** Double-tap or double-click the Exit Window button to open the code window for the btnExit_Click event (*ref: Figure 3-24*).

- **Enter the Event Handler Comments** Using the techniques you have learned, enter the comments that describe the processing in the btnExit_Click event handler.

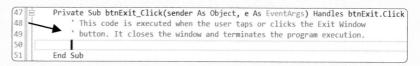

```
47    Private Sub btnExit_Click(sender As Object, e As EventArgs) Handles btnExit.Click
48        ' This code is executed when the user taps or clicks the Exit Window
49        ' button. It closes the window and terminates the program execution.
50
51    End Sub
```

- **Enter the Close() Procedure Call** Using IntelliSense, enter the Visual Basic code statement to close the window and terminate the program (*ref: Figure 3-66*).

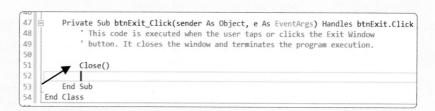

```
47    Private Sub btnExit_Click(sender As Object, e As EventArgs) Handles btnExit.Click
48        ' This code is executed when the user taps or clicks the Exit Window
49        ' button. It closes the window and terminates the program execution.
50
51        Close()
52
53    End Sub
54 End Class
```

The Close() procedure call statement is entered (Figure 3-79). When the procedure call is executed, the application will be closed.

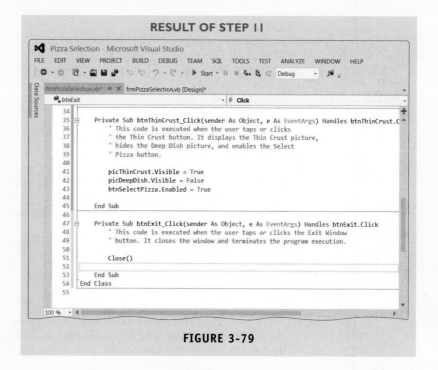

RESULT OF STEP 11

Pizza Selection - Microsoft Visual Studio

FILE   EDIT   VIEW   PROJECT   BUILD   DEBUG   TEAM   SQL   TOOLS   TEST   ANALYZE   WINDOW   HELP

▶ Start ▾   Debug

frmPizzaSelection.vb*   ⇥ ✕ frmPizzaSelection.vb [Design]*

btnExit   ↓ ⨍ Click

```
34
35    Private Sub btnThinCrust_Click(sender As Object, e As EventArgs) Handles btnThinCrust.C
36        ' This code is executed when the user taps or clicks
37        ' the Thin Crust button. It displays the Thin Crust picture,
38        ' hides the Deep Dish picture, and enables the Select
39        ' Pizza button.
40
41        picThinCrust.Visible = True
42        picDeepDish.Visible = False
43        btnSelectPizza.Enabled = True
44
45    End Sub
46
47    Private Sub btnExit_Click(sender As Object, e As EventArgs) Handles btnExit.Click
48        ' This code is executed when the user taps or clicks the Exit Window
49        ' button. It closes the window and terminates the program execution.
50
51        Close()
52
53    End Sub
54 End Class
55
```

100 %

FIGURE 3-79

12

- **Run the Program** Run the program to ensure that it works correctly. Tap or click the Deep Dish button, the Thin Crust button, the Select Pizza button, and the Exit Window button.

Code Listing

The complete code for the sample program is shown in Figure 3-80.

```vb
 1  ' Program Name: Pizza Selection
 2  ' Developer:      Corinne Hoisington
 3  ' Date:           January 28, 2015
 4  ' Purpose:        This application displays two pizza types
 5  '                 (deep dish and thin crust). The user can select a pizza type.
 6
 7  Public Class frmPizzaSelection
 8      Private Sub btnDeepDish_Click(sender As Object, e As EventArgs) Handles btnDeepDish.Click
 9          ' This code is executed when the user taps or clicks
10          ' the Deep Dish button. It displays the Deep Dish picture,
11          ' hides the Thin Crust picture, and enables the Select
12          ' Pizza button.
13
14          picDeepDish.Visible = True
15          picThinCrust.Visible = False
16          btnSelectPizza.Enabled = True
17
18      End Sub
19      Private Sub btnSelectPizza_Click(sender As Object, e As EventArgs) Handles btnSelectPizza.Click
20          ' This code is executed when the user taps or clicks the
21          ' Select Pizza button. It disables the Deep Dish button,
22          ' the Select Pizza button, and the Thin Crust button.
23          ' It hides the Instructions label, displays the Confirmation
24          ' label, and enables the Exit Window button.
25
26          btnDeepDish.Enabled = False
27          btnSelectPizza.Enabled = False
28          btnThinCrust.Enabled = False
29          lblInstructions.Visible = False
30          lblConfirmation.Visible = True
31          btnExit.Enabled = True
32
33      End Sub
34
35      Private Sub btnThinCrust_Click(sender As Object, e As EventArgs) Handles btnThinCrust.Click
36          ' This code is executed when the user taps or clicks
37          ' the Thin Crust button. It displays the Thin Crust picture,
38          ' hides the Deep Dish picture, and enables the Select
39          ' Pizza button.
40
41          picThinCrust.Visible = True
42          picDeepDish.Visible = False
43          btnSelectPizza.Enabled = True
44
45      End Sub
46
47      Private Sub btnExit_Click(sender As Object, e As EventArgs) Handles btnExit.Click
48          ' This code is executed when the user taps or clicks the Exit Window
49          ' button. It closes the window and terminates the program execution.
50
51          Close()
52
53      End Sub
54  End Class
```

FIGURE 3-80

Summary

In this chapter you have learned to fine-tune a graphical user interface to maximize its usefulness and to enter code for object event handlers.

The items listed in the table in Figure 3-81 include all the new Visual Studio and Visual Basic skills you have learned in this chapter. Video 3-1 demonstrates the complete program execution.

Visual Basic Skills		
Skill	**Figure Number**	**Video Number**
Run the completed program	Figure 3-1	Video 3-1
Set the BackColor Property	Figure 3-2	Video 3-2
Locate and Save an Image from the World Wide Web	Figure 3-7	Video 3-3
Import an Image into the Program Resources Folder	Figure 3-11	Video 3-4
Size an Image	Figure 3-16	Video 3-5
Set the Visible Property in the Properties Window	Figure 3-18	Video 3-6
Set the Enabled Property in the Properties Window	Figure 3-20	Video 3-7
Run a Visual Basic 2012 Program	Figure 3-22	Video 3-8
Enter Visual Basic 2012 Code for Event Handling	Figure 3-24	Video 3-9
Enter a Visual Basic 2012 Statement Using IntelliSense	Figure 3-29	Video 3-10
Enter a Visual Basic 2012 Statement to Set the Visible Property to True	Figure 3-29	Video 3-10
Enter a Visual Basic 2012 Statement to Set the Visible Property to False	Figure 3-37	Video 3-11
Enter a Visual Basic 2012 Statement to Set the Enabled Property to True	Figure 3-42	Video 3-12
Enter Comments in Visual Basic 2012 Code	Figure 3-47	Video 3-13
Enter Introductory Comments in Visual Basic Code	Figure 3-52	Video 3-14
Correct Errors in a Visual Basic 2012 Program	Figure 3-58	Video 3-15
Enter Additional Tap or Click Events	Figure 3-63	Video 3-16
Enter a Close() Statement into Visual Basic 2012 Code	Figure 3-66	Video 3-17
Print Code	Pages 155	

FIGURE 3-81

Learn Online

Reinforcement activities and resources are available at no additional cost on *www.CengageBrain.com*. Visit *www .cengage.com/ct/studentdownload* for detailed instructions about accessing the available resources at the Student Companion Site.

Knowledge Check

1. Which property controls the background color of the Form object?

2. Which property controls the text color of a Label object?

3. Which color palette is guaranteed to be displayed properly on every computer?

4. When a PictureBox object is placed on the form, what is the default SizeMode property setting?

5. When you place a PictureBox object on a Windows form, in which project folder is the image stored in the Solution Explorer?

6. When you tap or click the ellipsis button for the Image property of a PictureBox object (Figure 3-82), what action does Visual Studio 2012 take?

FIGURE 3-82

7. In which property of the PictureBox object do you tap or click the ellipsis button to select the correct picture?

8. Which option should be selected in the SizeMode property to make the image fit within the PictureBox object?

9. Which property has been set to False if a Button object is dimmed in a window when the program begins?

10. Which property has been set to False if a PictureBox object is not displayed when you run the application?

11. What two options can you select for the Visible property in the Properties window?

12. Write a line of code that would set the Visible property to False for a PictureBox object named picHomeTown.

13. Write a line of code that would set the Enabled property to True for a Button object named btnDiet.

14. Write a line of code that would set the Visible property to True for a PictureBox object named picHeadphones.

15. Write a comment line of code that states, "This code displays the headphone image."

16. What color is used to display comments in the code window of Visual Basic 2012?

17. Write a line of code that will close an application window and terminate the application.

18. What does a blue squiggly line mean in the code window?

19. Which symbol is associated with the assignment statement?

20. Why is it best to use IntelliSense when you enter code in the code window? List two reasons.

Debugging Exercises

1. Fix the following line of code to set the Enabled property to False for the btnDisplayCartoon Button object.

   ```
   btnCartoon.Enable.False
   ```

2. Fix the following line of code to change the visibility of the btnExitProgram Button object so that you can view it when the program runs.

   ```
   btnExitProgram.Visibilty = Yes
   ```

3. Fix the following line of code to set the Visible property to False for the lblDirections Label object.

   ```
   lblDirections.Visible = ' False
   ```

4. Fix the following comment line of code.

   ```
   The ' following line of code makes the college logo visible
   ```

5. Fix the following line of code.

   ```
   Close
   ```

6. Examine the code window and the Error List window in Figure 3-83. Then, write a line of code to replace the erroneous line.

FIGURE 3-83

Program Analysis

1. For the hiking application shown in Figure 3-84, write the Visual Basic 2012 coding statement to view the picture when the user taps or clicks the btnView button, assuming the Visible property had been set to False for the picHike PictureBox object in the Properties window.

FIGURE 3-84

Photo courtesy of Corinne Hoisington

2. Which property in the Properties window controls whether the picHike image is displayed when the program begins? Which option for the property would you select to make the button dimmed when the program begins?

3. When you import the picture into the Resources folder and select the image to use in the picHike PictureBox object, which SizeMode property option would you select to view the complete picture?

4. Write the Visual Basic 2012 coding statement for the btnView click event that would cause the image to be displayed.

5. To change the window background color to Bisque as shown in Figure 3-84, what property should you modify?

6. What property is used to display the text "Enjoy your Italian Hike" in the window title bar?

Case Programming Assignments

Complete one or more of the following case programming assignments. Submit the program and materials you create to your instructor. The level of difficulty is indicated for each assignment.

● = Easiest
●● = Intermediate
●●● = Challenging

1 ●

EUROPEAN HOSTEL SELECTION

Based on the Windows form mock-up you created in Chapter 2, complete the European Hostel Selection program by changing the window background color, downloading and adding the images, and writing the code that will execute according to the program requirements shown in Figure 3-85 and the Use Case Definition shown in Figure 3-86 on the next page. Before writing the code, create an event planning document for each event in the program. The completed Windows Form object and the other objects in the user interface are shown in Figure 3-87a, Figure 3-87b, and Figure 3-87c on the next page.

REQUIREMENTS DOCUMENT

Date Submitted:	January 17, 2015
Application Title:	European Hostel Selection Application
Purpose:	The Windows application will allow a user to select a location in London or Dublin.
Program Procedures:	From a window on the screen, the user should identify a hostel location (London or Dublin) and then select a hostel.
Algorithms, Processing, and Conditions:	1. The user must be able to identify the London or Dublin hostel as many times as necessary until making a selection.
	2. When the user identifies the hostel location, a picture of that hostel should appear in the window.
	3. Only one picture should be displayed at a time. If a user identifies the London hostel, only the London hostel picture should be displayed; if a user identifies the Dublin hostel, only the Dublin hostel picture should be displayed.
	4. When the user selects a hostel, a message should be displayed to confirm the selection of a hostel location. In addition, the user should be prevented from identifying another location after selecting a hostel.
	5. After the user selects a hostel, the only allowable action is to exit the window.
Notes and Restrictions:	A user can select a hostel only after identifying a hostel location.
Comments:	The pictures shown in the window can be found on CengageBrain.com. The names of the pictures are Dublin and London.

FIGURE 3-85

(continues)

Case Programming Assignments

European Hostel Selection (continued)

USE CASE DEFINITION

1. User taps or clicks London Hostel button or Dublin Hostel button.
2. Program displays a picture of the hostel identified by the user and enables the location selection button.
3. User taps or clicks hostel buttons to view hostel locations as desired. Program displays the picture of the identified hostel.
4. User taps or clicks the Select Location button.
5. Program displays a hostel selection confirmation message and disables both hostel buttons and the Select Location button. The Exit Window button becomes active.
6. User terminates the program by tapping or clicking the Exit Window button.

FIGURE 3-86

© 2014 Cengage Learning

In Figure 3-87a, no button has been tapped or clicked. In Figure 3-87b, the user has tapped or clicked the Dublin Hostel button. In Figure 3-87c, the user has tapped or clicked the Select Location button.

FIGURE 3-87a

FIGURE 3-87b
© DreamPictures/Photodisc/Getty Images

FIGURE 3-87c
© DreamPictures/Photodisc/Getty Images

Case Programming Assignments

2 STUDENT PICNIC

Based on the Windows form mock-up you created in Chapter 2, complete the Student Picnic program by changing the window background color, downloading and adding the image, and writing the code that will execute according to the program requirements shown in Figure 3-88. The Use Case Definition is shown in Figure 3-89 on the next page. Before writing the code, create an event planning document for each event in the program. The completed Windows Form object and the other objects in the user interface are shown in Figure 3-90a and Figure 3-90b on the next page.

REQUIREMENTS DOCUMENT

Date Submitted:	January 14, 2015
Application Title:	Student Picnic Application
Purpose:	This Windows application displays a welcome screen for the Annual Spring Fling Picnic. The user can choose an option to view the date and location.
Program Procedures:	From a window on the screen, the user makes a request to see the picnic's date and location.
Algorithms, Processing, and Conditions:	1. The user first views a Student Picnic window that displays the picnic name (Annual Spring Fling Picnic), a picnic picture, and a phrase that states all students are welcome.
	2. When the user chooses to view the picnic date and location, the following information is displayed:
	April 17, 2015 Located in the Quad in front of the Barnard Building
	3. After the user views the picnic information, the only allowable action is to exit the window.
Notes and Restrictions:	n/a
Comments:	The picture shown in the window can be found on CengageBrain.com. The name of the picture is Picnic.

FIGURE 3-88

(continues)

Case Programming Assignments

Student Picnic (continued)

USE CASE DEFINITION

1. The window opens, displaying the name of the picnic, a picnic picture, and a message stating all students are welcome. All buttons are enabled.
2. User taps or clicks the View Picnic Information button.
3. Program displays the picnic time and location between the buttons. The View Picnic Information button is disabled.
4. User taps or clicks the Exit Window button to terminate the application.

FIGURE 3-89

© 2014 Cengage Learning

In Figure 3-90a, no button has been tapped or clicked. In Figure 3-90b, the user has tapped or clicked the View Picnic Information button.

background color is Azure

button background color is YellowGreen

FIGURE 3-90a

© Angela Sorrentino/E+/Getty Images

FIGURE 3-90b

© Angela Sorrentino/E+/Getty Images

3

VISUAL BASIC 2012 TERMS

Based on the Windows form mock-up you created in Chapter 2, complete the Visual Basic 2012 Terms program by changing the window background color and writing the code that will execute according to the program requirements shown in Figure 3-91. The Use Case Definition is shown in Figure 3-92 on the next page. Before writing the code, create an event planning document for each event in the program. The completed Windows Form object and the other objects in the user interface are shown in Figure 3-93a and Figure 3-93b on the next page.

REQUIREMENTS DOCUMENT

Date Submitted:	August 16, 2015
Application Title:	Visual Basic 2012 Terms Application
Purpose:	This Windows application displays the definitions of common Visual Basic terms. When the user chooses to view a definition, the term's definition is displayed.
Program Procedures:	From a window on the screen, the user makes a request to see one of three VB definitions.
Algorithms, Processing, and Conditions:	1. The user first views a screen that displays three VB terms. 2. A logo is displayed at the top of the window throughout the running of the application. 3. The user can select any of the three terms displayed on the buttons to view the definition. 4. When the user taps or clicks a term button to display the definition, any previous definitions will disappear. 5. An exit button is available at all times, allowing the user to end the application.
Notes and Restrictions:	Only one definition should be displayed at a time, so if a user selects a second term, only the second definition should be displayed.
Comments:	n/a

FIGURE 3-91

(continues)

Visual Basic 2012 Terms (continued)

USE CASE DEFINITION

1. The window opens and displays a logo (Professional 2012), a title (Visual Basic 2012 Terms), three buttons labeled with VB terms, and an Exit Window button. All buttons are enabled.
2. User taps or clicks each of the term buttons to review the definitions.
3. Program displays the definitions to the right of the buttons.
4. Only one definition is displayed at a time.
5. User taps or clicks the Exit Window button to terminate the application.

FIGURE 3-92

In Figure 3-93a, no button has been tapped or clicked. In Figure 3-93b, the user has tapped or clicked the Developer button.

background color is White

button background color is Gray

FIGURE 3-93a

Developer button clicked

definition of developer

FIGURE 3-93b

4 •• ONLINE STORE SPECIALS

Based on the Windows form mock-up you created in Chapter 2, complete the Online Store Specials program by finishing the user interface, downloading and adding the images, and writing the code that will execute according to the program requirements shown in Figure 3-94. Before writing the code, create an event planning document for each event in the program.

REQUIREMENTS DOCUMENT

Date Submitted: January 6, 2016

Application Title: Online Store Specials Application

Purpose: This Windows application displays the daily, weekly, and holiday specials in the online store. The user can select the desired product and then add the product to a shopping cart.

Program Procedures: From a window on the screen, the user should select the daily special, weekly special, or holiday special. After the user selects a special, the program should display a picture of the special product, the regular price of the product, and the sale price of the product. The user should be able to select any special. Then, the user can add the product to the shopping cart.

Algorithms, Processing, and Conditions:
1. The user must select a special in order to display the special's product picture, regular price, and sale price.
2. The user cannot add a product to the shopping cart until a special is selected.
3. When a special is selected, only that special's picture and prices should be displayed in the window. No other special should be displayed.
4. After the user selects a special and adds it to the shopping cart, the only allowable user action is to exit the window.
5. A user should be able to exit the window at any time.

Notes and Restrictions: n/a

Comments:
1. The specials are:
    Daily Special: SmartPhone: Regular Price: $99.95; Sale Price: $84.50
    Weekly Special: Tablet: Regular Price: $239.95; Sale Price: $199.95
    Holiday Special: Digital Camera: Regular Price: $259.95; Sale Price: $203.19
2. The pictures shown in the window can be found on CengageBrain.com. The names of the pictures are SmartPhone, Tablet, and DigitalCamera.

FIGURE 3-94

5
GUITAR STORE

Based on the Windows form mock-up you created in Chapter 2, complete the Guitar Store program by finishing the user interface, downloading and adding the images, and writing the code that will execute according to the program requirements shown in Figure 3-95. Before writing the code, create an event planning document for each event in the program.

REQUIREMENTS DOCUMENT

Date Submitted:	March 21, 2015
Application Title:	Guitar Store Application
Purpose:	A local guitar store has three guitars on special this week. A customer can choose one of three guitar types. The program must display each of the guitars upon request. The customer can then select a guitar for purchase.
Program Procedures:	From a window on the screen, the user selects one of three guitars. A picture of the selected guitar is displayed in the window. The user then can choose a guitar for purchase.
Algorithms, Processing, and Conditions:	1. The user selects a guitar. Then, a picture of the guitar is displayed in the window.
	2. The user can select any of the three guitars. Only the picture of the selected guitar should be displayed.
	3. The user can select guitars as many times as necessary and display the pictures of the guitars.
	4. The user finds a guitar, chooses it for purchase, and taps or clicks the Purchase button.
	5. After the user chooses a guitar, a message stating "Enjoy your guitar!" should be displayed.
	6. After the user chooses a guitar, the only allowable action is to exit the window.
Notes and Restrictions:	The user should not be able to choose a guitar until viewing at least one guitar image.
Comments:	1. The available guitars are classical acoustic, steel-string acoustic, and electric.
	2. The pictures shown in the window can be found on CengageBrain.com. The names of the pictures are Classical, Electric, and Steel.

FIGURE 3-95

6 SONG VOTING

Based on the Windows form mock-up you created in Chapter 2, complete the Song Voting program by finishing the user interface, downloading and adding the images, and writing the code that will execute according to the program requirements shown in Figure 3-96. Before writing the code, create an event planning document for each event in the program.

REQUIREMENTS DOCUMENT

Date Submitted:	February 22, 2015
Application Title:	Song Voting Application
Purpose:	In your mall, a music store named Millennium Music wants an application that shows the #1 song in each of three music genres and allows users to vote for their overall favorite. The user should be able to select one of three music genres and then vote for one.
Program Procedures:	From a window on the screen, the user selects one of three music genres. The name of the #1 song in the selected genre is displayed with a picture of the performing artist or band. Then, the user can vote for that song or genre as his or her overall favorite.
Algorithms, Processing, and Conditions:	1. The user selects a music genre. The title of the #1 song in that genre and a picture of the artist or band are displayed in the window.
	2. The user can select any of the three music genres. Only the name of the song and the picture for the selected genre should be displayed.
	3. The user can select music genres as many times as necessary to see the #1 song for each genre and the associated artist or band.
	4. After selecting a genre, the user should be able to vote for that genre and song as the favorite. The user can vote only after selecting a genre.
	5. After the user votes, a message confirming the vote should be displayed.
Notes and Restrictions:	The user should only be able to vote after selecting a musical genre.
Comments:	1. You (the developer) should select the three music genres and the #1 song for each of the genres.
	2. The pictures of the artist or band will depend on your selection of music genres and the #1 song in those genres. You should download pictures of artists or bands from the web. You can search anywhere on the web for the pictures. You will find that *www.google.com/images* is a good source.

FIGURE 3-96

7 ●●●
AIRLINE SNACK SELECTION

Based on the problem definition (Figure 3-97) and the Windows form mock-up you created in Chapter 2, complete the airline snack selection program by finishing the user interface, downloading and adding any required images, and writing the code that will execute according to the program requirements. Before writing the code, create an event planning document for each event in the program.

An international airline requests a computer application that will run on the personal television monitors on the back of each seat in the plane. The application should request which free snack you would like during the flight, display the choices as buttons, and then display an image of the snack you select. Another button allows you to make your final snack selection and display a confirmation message.

Snack
Cheese & Crackers
Chocolate Chip Cookies
Mini Pretzels
Salted Peanuts

FIGURE 3-97

8 ●●●
TRAVEL SPECIALS

Based on the problem definition (Figure 3-98) and the Windows form mock-up you created in Chapter 2, complete the Travel Specials program by finishing the user interface, downloading and adding any required images, and writing the code that will execute according to the program requirements. Before writing the code, create an event planning document for each event in the program.

Your local travel agent requests a computer application that advertises the travel specials of the week from your city. This week's flight specials are:

Destination	Price
New York City	$399 round trip
Las Vegas	$419 round trip
Miami	$520 round trip
St. Thomas	$619 round trip
Hawaii	$828 round trip

Write an application that allows the user to select any of the five vacation destinations. When the user selects a vacation destination, the corresponding flight price and a picture of the destination should be displayed. Clear each prior price and picture when the user selects a different vacation destination. In addition to a picture of the destination, include a Web page address that features the selected location. After selecting a destination, the user should be able to book the flight and then exit the window.

FIGURE 3-98

9 ●●●
LACROSSE TICKETS

Based on the problem definition (Figure 3-99) and the Windows form mock-up you created in Chapter 2, complete the Lacrosse Tickets program by finishing the user interface, downloading and adding any required images, and writing the code that will execute according to the program requirements. Before writing the code, create an event planning document for each event in the program.

Your favorite university lacrosse team has asked you to develop a Windows application that allows the user to see the four types of game tickets offered, one at a time. Then, the user should be able to reserve a single game ticket for the selected seat type. The four types of stadium seating and their base prices are as follows:

Name of Ticket	Minimum Price
Upper Endline Seating	$15.00
Lower Endline Seating	$25.00
Sideline Seating	$30.00
Club Seats	$50.00

For each type of seating, your program should display the base price and a picture depicting an example of the seating type. Clear each price and picture when the user selects a different seating type. After selecting a ticket, the user should be able to purchase the ticket and then exit the window.

FIGURE 3-99

CHAPTER 4
Variables and Arithmetic Operations

OBJECTIVES

You will have mastered the material in this chapter when you can:

- Create, modify, and program a TextBox object

- Use code to place data in the Text property of a Label object

- Use the AcceptButton and CancelButton properties

- Understand and declare String and Numeric variables

- Use assignment statements to place data in variables

- Use literals and constants in coding statements

- Understand scope rules for variables

- Convert string and numeric data

- Understand and use arithmetic operators and arithmetic operations

- Format and display numeric data as a string

- Create a form load event

- Create a concatenated string

- Debug a program

Introduction

In the Pizza Selection program you developed in Chapter 2 and Chapter 3, you tapped or clicked buttons in the user interface to trigger events, but you did not enter data. In many applications, users must enter data that the program then uses in its processing.

When processing data entered by a user, a common requirement is to perform arithmetic operations on the data to generate useful output. Arithmetic operations include adding, subtracting, multiplying, and dividing numeric data.

To illustrate user data input and arithmetic operations, the application in this chapter allows the user to specify a number of songs to download from the World Wide Web. The application then calculates the total cost of downloading the files. The user interface for the program is shown in Figure 4-1.

FIGURE 4-1
© Luca Pierro PHOTOGRAPHY/Flickr/Getty Images

ONLINE REINFORCEMENT

To view a video of program execution, visit CengageBrain.com and navigate to the resources for this title. Tap or click the link for Chapter 4 and then navigate to Video 4-1. Turn on your speakers to listen to the audio walkthrough of the steps.

In Figure 4-1, the user entered 5 as the number of songs to download. When the user tapped or clicked the Calculate Cost button, the program multiplied 5 by the cost per song (99 cents) and then displayed the result as the total cost of downloads. When the user taps or clicks the Clear button, the values for the number of song downloads and the total cost of downloads are cleared so the next user can enter a value. Tapping or clicking the Exit button closes the window and terminates the program.

To create this application, the developer must understand how to perform the following processes, among others:

1. Define a text box for data entry.
2. Define a label to hold the results of arithmetic operations.
3. Convert data in a text box to data that can be used for arithmetic operations.
4. Perform arithmetic operations on data entered by a user.

The following pages describe the tools and techniques required to create the program shown in Figure 4-1.

Design the User Interface

As you have learned in Chapter 2 and Chapter 3, the next step after completing the program requirements document for an application is to define the graphical user interface. In this chapter, three new elements are introduced:

- TextBox objects
- Labels intended for variable text property values
- Accept buttons

Each of these elements is described in the following sections.

TextBox Objects

A **TextBox object** allows users to enter data into a program. In Figure 4-2, the user can enter a value into the text box.

FIGURE 4-2
© Luca Pierro PHOTOGRAPHY/Flickr/Getty Images

In Figure 4-2 on the previous page, the TextBox object is placed on the Windows Form object. A TextBox object automatically allows the user to enter data in the text box. To place a TextBox object on the Windows Form object, you can complete the following steps. (Note that the examples in this chapter illustrate new objects in the user interface. Portions of the user interface have already been completed for you. You should not expect to "tap or click along" with these examples unless you create all the elements or follow the steps using an unformatted user interface.)

STEP 1   With Visual Studio open, the Digital Downloads Windows application created, and the frmDownloads.vb [Design] tabbed page visible, point to the TextBox .NET component in the Toolbox.

The TextBox .NET component is highlighted in the Toolbox (Figure 4-3).

TextBox .NET component

FIGURE 4-3
© Luca Pierro PHOTOGRAPHY/Flickr/Getty Images

STEP 2   Drag the TextBox .NET component onto the Windows Form object at the desired location.

While you drag, the mouse pointer changes to indicate a TextBox object will be placed on the Windows Form object (Figure 4-4). Snap lines indicate where the TextBox object aligns with other objects on the Windows Form object. In Figure 4-4, the bottom of the TextBox object aligns with the bottom of the Label object. When adding a TextBox object to the Windows Form object, bottom alignment often provides a good beginning position.

upper-left corner
of pointer

snap line

pointer

FIGURE 4-4
© Luca Pierro PHOTOGRAPHY/Flickr/Getty Images

STEP 3 When the upper-left corner of the pointer is located where you want to
place the TextBox object's upper-left corner, release the left mouse button.

*Visual Studio places the TextBox object at the location identified by the mouse pointer
(Figure 4-5). The default size of the TextBox object is 100 pixels wide by 22 pixels high.
Notice that by default the TextBox object contains no text. You can change that by entering
text in the Text property of the TextBox object.*

TextBox object placed on
Windows Form object

TextBox object
contains no text

FIGURE 4-5
© Luca Pierro PHOTOGRAPHY/Flickr/Getty Images

ONLINE REINFORCEMENT

To view a video of the process
in the preceding steps, visit
CengageBrain.com and navigate
to the resources for this title.
Tap or click the link for Chapter 4
and then navigate to Video 4-2.

As you have learned, whenever you place an object on the Windows Form object, you must name the object. When naming a TextBox object, the prefix should be txt. Therefore, the name of the TextBox object in Figure 4-5 on the previous page could be txtNumberOfDownloads.

Size and Position a TextBox Object

To properly place a TextBox object on the Windows Form object, you need to know the minimum and maximum size of the text box. The minimum size normally is determined by the maximum number of characters the user will enter into the text box. For example, if the user can enter 999 in the sample program as the maximum number of downloads, the minimum size of the text box must be large enough to display three numbers. Although it can be larger, it should not be smaller.

The maximum size of the text box often is determined by the design of the user interface; that is, the size should "look and feel good" in the user interface. To determine the minimum size of the text box, you can use the technique in the following steps:

STEP 1   Select the TextBox object. Select the (Name) property and name the TextBox object `txtNumberOfDownloads`. Scroll in the Properties window until the Text property is visible and then tap or click the right column for the Text property.

The TextBox object is selected, as shown by the thick border and sizing handles (Figure 4-6). The TextBox object is named txtNumberOfDownloads. The Text property for the TextBox object is highlighted and the insertion point indicates you can enter text for the Text property.

FIGURE 4-6

© Luca Pierro PHOTOGRAPHY/Flickr/Getty Images

STEP 2 Type the maximum number of characters the user normally will enter
into the text box and then press the ENTER key. Programmers often use the digit 8 in
this situation because it is wider than other digits. This example uses the value 888
because three digits is the maximum number the user normally will enter.

*When the value is entered in the Text property of the TextBox object, the value is displayed
in the TextBox object (Figure 4-7).*

FIGURE 4-7
© Luca Pierro PHOTOGRAPHY/Flickr/Getty Images

STEP 3 Using the Properties window, change the Font property to the correct font
and font size. For this application, change the font to Century Gothic and change the
font size to 11. Then, drag the right edge of the TextBox object and resize it to be
slightly wider than the 888 entry.

*As you drag, the size of the TextBox object changes (Figure 4-8). When you release the left
mouse button, the text box will be resized. When the font size is changed, the horizontal
alignment of the text will change.*

FIGURE 4-8
© Luca Pierro PHOTOGRAPHY/Flickr/Getty Images

STEP 4 To horizontally align the text in the label and the text in the text box, drag the text box up until a red snap line indicates the bottoms of the text are aligned (Figure 4-9). Then, release the left mouse button.

As you drag the TextBox object, the red snap line indicates when the bottoms of the text are aligned (Figure 4-9). When you release the left mouse button, the TextBox object will be placed so the bottoms of the text are aligned.

FIGURE 4-9
© Luca Pierro PHOTOGRAPHY/Flickr/Getty Images

CONSIDER THIS

Are smaller details like alignment important in design and programming?
The user interface is more important than ever with Windows application and mobile design. Many colleges teach entire courses on interface design. Remember, your users need consistency in your design layout. Language is another interface element that needs consistency. A consistent interface enables your users to have a better understanding of how things will work and increases their efficiency.

Align Text in a TextBox Object

In Figure 4-9, the numbers are left-aligned in the text box. Often, the user interface will be more useful if the value the user enters is centered in the text box. To align the text in a TextBox object, you can use the following method:

Select the TextBox object. In the Properties window, scroll until the TextAlign property is visible, tap or click the TextAlign property in the left column, and then tap or click the list arrow in the right column of the TextAlign property.

The TextAlign property list contains the values Left, Right, and Center (Figure 4-10).

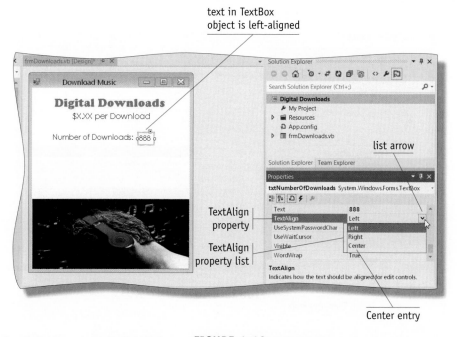

FIGURE 4-10

Tap or click Center in the TextAlign property list.

The text in the TextBox object is centered (Figure 4-11). When a user enters data in the text box, the data also will be centered.

FIGURE 4-11

STEP 3 Because the TextBox object is sized properly, remove the digits in the TextBox object. Select the characters 888 in the Text property, press the DELETE key on your keyboard, and then press the ENTER key.

The TextBox object contains no text and is ready for use in the user interface (Figure 4-12).

© Luca Pierro PHOTOGRAPHY/Flickr/Getty Images

FIGURE 4-12

Enter Data in a TextBox Object

When the program is executed, the user can enter data in the text box. Users can enter letters, numbers, and other characters. If the user enters more characters than the text box can display, the characters that have already been entered scroll to the left and no longer are visible. A text box does not contain a scroll bar, so if a user enters more characters than the text box can display, the user must move the insertion point left or right with the arrow keys on the keyboard to view the data in the text box. In most situations, a user should not enter more characters than are expected, and the text box should be designed to display all expected characters.

In a default text box, only a single line of text can be entered regardless of the number of characters in the line. However, programmers can select a special option for a text box to allow the user to enter multiple lines of text. Additionally, the MaskedTextBox object can be used to control the format of data that a user enters. These types of text boxes are explained in the following sections.

Create a MultiLine Text Box

A MultiLine text box allows the user to enter multiple lines in the text box. The TextBox object must be resized vertically to display the multiple lines. To create a TextBox object that can accept multiple lines, you can complete the following steps:

STEP 1   Select the TextBox object, tap or click the Action tag, and then point to the MultiLine check box.

The TextBox Tasks list is displayed with the MultiLine check box (Figure 4-13). When you tap or click the MultiLine check box, the TextBox object will be able to accept multiple lines.

FIGURE 4-13

STEP 2   Tap or click the MultiLine check box.

The text box is enabled to accept multiple lines.

In addition to enabling multiple lines, you should increase the vertical size of the TextBox object so the multiple lines will be visible when the user enters them.

Create a MaskedTextBox Object

The MaskedTextBox object allows you to specify the data format of the value typed into the text box. Using the MaskedTextBox object removes confusion about which format should be used for data the user enters. The term *mask* refers to a predefined layout for the data. Figure 4-14 shows three examples of the MaskedTextBox used for the Short date input mask, the Phone number input mask, and the Social Security number input mask.

FIGURE 4-14

In Figure 4-14, before the user enters data, the mask demonstrates the format of the data to be entered. To enter data, the user selects the text box and then types data into it. The user need not enter punctuation or spacing. To enter the date in the Order Date text box, the user typed 09302014 with no spaces, punctuation, or other keystrokes. Similarly, for the phone number, the user typed 9455553281, again with no spaces or other keystrokes. For the Social Security number, the user typed 999999999.

To place a MaskedTextBox object on the Windows Form object, you can complete the following steps:

STEP 1   Drag a MaskedTextBox .NET component from the Toolbox to the Windows Form object. Then, tap or click the Action tag on the TextBox object and point to the Set Mask command.

The MaskedTextBox object is placed on the Windows Form object (Figure 4-15). When the Action tag is tapped or clicked, the MaskedTextBox Tasks list is displayed. The Set Mask command is the only command in the list.

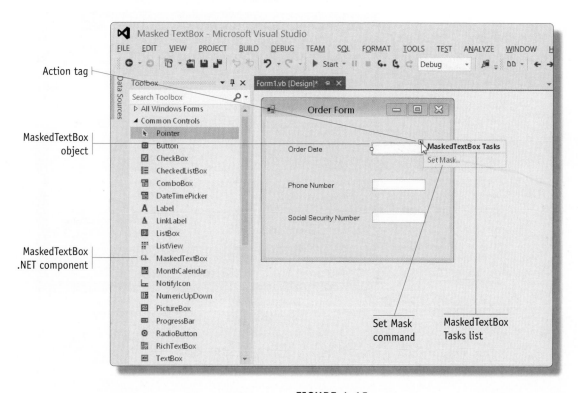

FIGURE 4-15

STEP 2 Tap or click Set Mask on the MaskedTextBox Tasks list and then tap or click the Short date mask description in the Input Mask dialog box.

Visual Studio displays the Input Mask dialog box (Figure 4-16). The Mask Description column contains all the masks that can be used for the MaskedTextBox object. The Short date mask description is highlighted. In the Preview box, you can type data to see how the mask will perform when it is used in the MaskedTextBox object. The Use Validating Type check box is selected to verify that the user entered valid numeric data.

FIGURE 4-16

STEP 3 Tap or click the OK button in the Input Mask dialog box and then tap or click anywhere in the Windows Form object.

The mask is placed in the MaskedTextBox object (Figure 4-17).

Short date mask in MaskedTextBox object

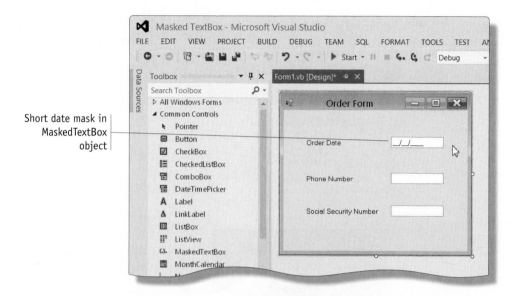

FIGURE 4-17

ONLINE REINFORCEMENT

To view a video of the process in the preceding steps, visit CengageBrain.com and navigate to the resources for this title. Tap or click the link for Chapter 4 and then navigate to Video 4-7.

You can use the same technique to place the phone number and Social Security number in the MaskedTextBox.

Label Objects

In the sample program, a Label object is used to display the total cost of downloads (see Figure 4-1 on page 190). The developer must accomplish two tasks to prepare the label for this purpose: Place the label on the Windows Form object in the correct location, and then ensure that when the Label object contains its maximum value, its location will work within the user interface design.

To accomplish these two tasks, you can complete the steps on the next page:

STEP 1 Drag a Label object onto the Windows Form object to the correct location. Name the label `lblTotalCost`. Change the label to the appropriate font and size (Century Gothic, 11 points). In the Text property for the Label object, enter the maximum number of characters ($888.88) that will appear in the label during execution of the program.

The properly sized characters appear in the label (Figure 4-18). The label is aligned vertically, but should be moved up to align horizontally with the Total Cost of Downloads label.

FIGURE 4-18
© Luca Pierro PHOTOGRAPHY/Flickr/Getty Images

STEP 2 Drag the Label object up until the red snap line appears (Figure 4-19). Then release the left mouse button.

The label is aligned (Figure 4-19).

FIGURE 4-19
© Luca Pierro PHOTOGRAPHY/Flickr/Getty Images

When program execution begins, the label that will contain the total cost of downloads should be blank. In Figure 4-19, however, it contains the value in the Text property of the Label object ($888.88). If the Text property in a Label object is set to hold no content, it will not be displayed in the Windows Form object during the design phase, which makes the Label object difficult to work with in Design mode. Therefore, most designers place a value in the Text property of the Label object and leave it there during user interface design. Then, when the program begins, the label Text property will be set to blank. You will learn to perform this task later in the chapter.

Accept Button in Form Properties

Computer users often press the ENTER key to enter data in a text box and cause processing to occur. For instance, in the sample program for this chapter, users might prefer to type the number of downloads and press the ENTER key instead of typing the number and tapping or clicking the Calculate Cost button.

You can assign a button to be an Accept button in the user interface, which means the program will carry out the event handler processing associated with the button if the user taps or clicks it or presses the ENTER key. To assign the Calculate Cost button as the Accept button, you can complete the following steps:

> **STEP 1**   After the Button objects are added, tap or click a blank area in the Windows Form object to select it. Scroll in the Properties window until the Accept-Button property is visible. Tap or click the AcceptButton property name in the left column and then tap or click the AcceptButton property list arrow in the right column.

The AcceptButton property list displays the names of the Button objects on the selected Windows Form object (Figure 4-20). Any of these buttons can be specified as the Accept button.

FIGURE 4-20

STEP 2   Tap or click btnCalculate in the AcceptButton property list.

The btnCalculate Button object is designated as the Accept button. When the program is running, the user can press the ENTER key after entering data to execute the event handler processing for the Calculate Cost button.

Cancel Button in Form Properties

In the same manner as the Accept button, you can designate a Cancel button for the Windows Form object. When the user presses the esc key, the event handler processing will be executed for the button identified as the Cancel button. In the sample program, the Cancel button will be used to clear the text box and the total cost of downloads and place the insertion point in the text box. Thus, it performs the same activity that occurs when the user taps or clicks the Clear button. To specify the Cancel button for the sample program, you complete the following steps:

Step 1:   Tap or click a blank area in the Windows Form object to select it.
Step 2:   Tap or click the CancelButton property name in the left column of the Properties window for the Windows Form object, and then tap or click the CancelButton list arrow.
Step 3:   Tap or click the button name (btnClear) in the CancelButton property list.

When the program is executed, the user can press the esc key to perform the same processing as when the Clear button is tapped or clicked.

Visual Studio Preparation for Code Entry

When you are designing and creating the user interface, the Toolbox in Visual Studio 2012 provides the objects that you can place in the interface. When you write the code in the code window, however, the Toolbox is of little use. Therefore, many developers close the Toolbox when writing code to increase the space used for coding. To close the Toolbox, you can complete the following step:

STEP 1 With the Toolbox visible (Figure 4-21), tap or click the Toolbox Close button. The Toolbox closes and the work area expands in size. To display the Toolbox after it has been closed, tap or click the VIEW menu and then tap or click Toolbox.

Figure 4-21 illustrates the screen before the Toolbox is closed. The Toolbox Close button is visible.

FIGURE 4-21

© Luca Pierro PHOTOGRAPHY/Flickr/Getty Images

In the following sections, the Toolbox has been closed in the windows that show code.

Introduction to Data Entry and Data Types

As you have seen, the user can enter data into the program by using the TextBox object. When the user enters data, it becomes the value stored in the Text property of the object. For example, if the user enters 15 as the number of downloads, the Text property for the txtNumberOfDownloads TextBox object will contain the value 15.

String Data Type

When data is stored in RAM, it is stored as a particular data type. Each data type allows data to be used in a specific manner. For example, to add two values together, the values must be stored in one of the numeric data types. The **String** data type is used for values that the user enters in a TextBox object and that are stored in the Text property of the TextBox object. A String data type can store any character available on the computer.

When the user enters data into a TextBox object, it is good programming style to copy the entered value from the Text property of the TextBox object to a String variable. A **variable** is a named location in RAM where data is stored. A **String variable** is a named location in RAM that can store a string value. Thus, a person's name, a dollar amount, a telephone number, or the number of song downloads can be stored in a String variable.

The programmer defines a variable during the coding of the program. The statement in Figure 4-22 defines a string.

FIGURE 4-22

VARIABLE NAME RULES

Variable names in Visual Basic must follow a few simple rules. The name must begin with a letter or an underline symbol (_). The name can contain letters, numbers, and the underline symbol. It cannot contain spaces or other special characters. Reserved words in Visual Basic cannot be used for variable names; reserved words appear in blue in the code window.

To begin the statement, the keyword Dim is required. This keyword stands for *variable dimension*. It indicates to the Visual Basic compiler that the entries after Dim are defining a variable.

The next entry is the variable name. Every variable must have a name so it can be referenced in other statements within the program. By convention, every String variable name begins with the letters str followed by a descriptive name. The name in Figure 4-22 (strNumberOfSongs) indicates a String variable that will contain the number of songs entered by the user.

The keyword As must follow the name of the variable, as shown in Figure 4-22. If it is not included, a compilation error will occur. Following the word As is the declaration for the variable's data type. In Figure 4-22, the data type is specified as String.

As a result of the statement in Figure 4-22, when the program is compiled, the Visual Basic compiler will allocate an area in RAM that is reserved to contain the value in the string.

The general format to define a variable is shown in Figure 4-23.

General Format: Define a Variable

```
Dim VariableName As DataType
```

EXAMPLE	*RESULT*
Dim strNumberOfSongs As String	String variable
Dim intNumberOfSongs As Integer	Integer variable
Dim decFinalCosts As Decimal	Decimal variable

FIGURE 4-23

© 2014 Cengage Learning

The Integer and Decimal variables defined as examples in Figure 4-23 are numeric variables. You will learn about numeric variables shortly.

Assignment Statements

When a variable is defined as shown in Figure 4-22, the variable does not contain any data. One method used to place data in the variable is an **assignment statement**. The assignment statement shown in Figure 4-24 will copy the data from the Text property of the txtNumberOfDownloads TextBox object into the strNumberOfSongs String variable.

FIGURE 4-24

© 2014 Cengage Learning

The variable name to the left of the assignment statement (strNumberOfSongs) identifies the variable to which a value will be copied. The equal sign indicates to the Visual Basic compiler that the statement is an assignment statement. The equal sign is required.

The value to the right of the equal sign will be copied to the variable to the left of the equal sign. In Figure 4-24, the value in the Text property of the txtNumberOfDownloads TextBox object will be copied to the strNumberOfSongs variable.

To enter the definition of the strNumberOfSongs variable and then enter the assignment statement in Figure 4-24 on the previous page using IntelliSense, you can complete the following steps:

STEP 1 With Visual Studio open to the code window and the insertion point located in the desired column, type Dim followed by a space. Then, type the name of the String variable you want to define, strNumberOfSongs.

The Dim keyword and the string name you typed are displayed in the code window (Figure 4-25). Notice that Dim is blue to indicate it is a keyword.

name of
Dim keyword   String variable

FIGURE 4-25

STEP 2 Press the SPACEBAR, type the word As, and then press the SPACEBAR again.

The letters you typed are entered. When you typed the space following the word As, IntelliSense displayed a list (Figure 4-26). The list contains all the allowable entries that can follow the As keyword. To define a String variable, the correct entry is String.

As keyword

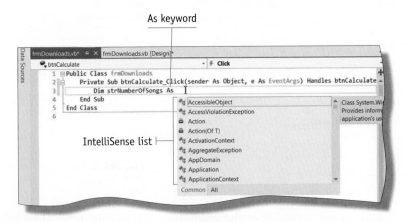

IntelliSense list

FIGURE 4-26

STEP 3   Because the correct entry is String, type `str`.

IntelliSense highlights String in the list (Figure 4-27).

str typed

FIGURE 4-27

STEP 4   Press the ENTER key.

The Dim statement is entered (Figure 4-28). The green squiggly underline indicates the variable is not referenced within the program. Visual Studio will remove the underline when the variable is used in an assignment statement or other statement.

variable not referenced   Dim statement is complete

FIGURE 4-28

STEP 5   To begin the assignment statement, type `strn`. IntelliSense displays the only variable name that starts with the letters strn, which is the String variable strNumberOfSongs.

IntelliSense displays a list of allowable entries for the statement (Figure 4-29). Whenever you want to reference a variable name in a statement, you can type the first few letters of the name to have IntelliSense display a list of allowable entries. The variable name strNumberOfSongs is highlighted because you typed strn.

FIGURE 4-29

STEP 6   Press the SPACEBAR, press the EQUAL SIGN key, and then press the SPACEBAR.

IntelliSense enters the highlighted variable name, the spaces, and the equal sign you typed (Figure 4-30). The spaces are not required in Visual Basic but should be included in the statement for ease of reading. An IntelliSense list automatically appears and displays the possible valid entries.

FIGURE 4-30

STEP 7   Type `txt` to display the IntelliSense list of Form objects, and then type `n` to identify the txtNumberOfDownloads TextBox object in the IntelliSense list.

The IntelliSense list contains the valid entries for the statement; in this case, only one object has the prefix of txt. The TextBox object txtNumberOfDownloads is highlighted in the list (Figure 4-31).

FIGURE 4-31

STEP 8   Press the PERIOD key. If necessary, next type `te` to highlight the Text entry in the IntelliSense list.

After the dot operator (period) and the txtNumberOfDownloads object name are entered, Visual Studio displays the IntelliSense list (Figure 4-32). When you typed te, the Text entry was highlighted in the IntelliSense list.

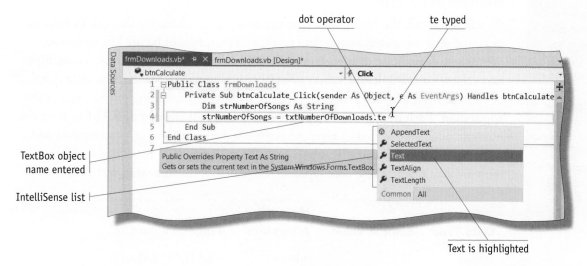

FIGURE 4-32

STEP 9 Press the ENTER key.

The assignment statement is entered (Figure 4-33). When the statement is executed, the value in the Text property of the txtNumberOfDownloads TextBox object will be copied to the location in memory identified by the strNumberOfSongs variable name. Notice also that the green squiggly lines in the Dim statement are removed because the variable now is referenced in a statement.

For any variable you define within a program, you can use the method shown in the previous steps to declare a variable name and include it in assignment statements. IntelliSense works the same with each variable name, regardless of the variable type.

completed assignment statement   no green squiggly line   IntelliSense entered Text

```
frmDownloads.vb*    frmDownloads.vb [Design]*
btnCalculate                                          Click
1  □Public Class frmDownloads
2   □    Private Sub btnCalculate_Click(sender As Object, e As EventArgs) Handles btnCalculate
3             Dim strNumberOfSongs As String
4             strNumberOfSongs = txtNumberOfDownloads.Text
5
6         End Sub
7  End Class
8
```

FIGURE 4-33

Numeric Data Types

As you will recall, the String data type can contain any character that can be entered or stored on a computer. String data types, however, cannot be used in arithmetic operations. A **numeric data type** must be used in arithmetic operations. To multiply two values, for example, the values must be stored in one of the numeric data types.

Visual Basic allows a variety of numeric data types depending on the need of the application. Each numeric data type requires a different amount of RAM to store the numeric value, and each data type can contain a different form of numeric data and a different maximum range of values. The table in Figure 4-34 lists three widely used numeric data types. These data types are explained in the following sections.

Data Type	Sample Value	Memory Allocation	Range of Values
Integer	48	4 bytes	−2,147,483,648 to +2,147,483,647
Decimal	3.14519	16 bytes	Decimal values that may have up to 28 significant digits
Double	5.3452307 or 673.6529	8 bytes	−1.79769313486232e308 to +1.79769313486232e308

FIGURE 4-34

Integer Data Type

An **Integer data type** holds a nondecimal whole number in Visual Basic. As you can see from Figure 4-34, an Integer data type can store a value that is greater or less than 2 billion. Examples of integers include the number of songs to download, the number of credit hours you are taking in a semester, and the number of points your favorite football team scored. Notice that each of these examples is a whole number.

Normally, an Integer data type is stored in an Integer variable. An **Integer variable** identifies a location in RAM where an integer value is stored. To define an Integer variable and place a value in the variable, you can use the Dim statement and the assignment statement, as shown in Figure 4-35.

```
6        Dim intNumberOfSongs As Integer
7        intNumberOfSongs = 34
```

FIGURE 4-35

The Dim statement in Figure 4-35 is similar to the Dim statement used to define the String variable (Figure 4-28 on page 211), except that the variable name begins with the prefix int and the word Integer follows the word As. Four bytes of RAM will be reserved for any value that is stored in the intNumberOfSongs Integer variable as a result of the Dim statement in Figure 4-35.

The definition in Figure 4-35 will not place a value in the intNumberOfSongs variable. To place a value in the variable, you can use an assignment statement. Enter the intNumberOfSongs variable that will hold the value on the left side of the equal sign, and enter the value to be placed in the variable (34) on the right side of the equal sign. When the statement is executed, the value 34 will be copied to the RAM location identified by the variable name intNumberOfSongs.

You also can place an initial value in the variable. For example, to define an Integer variable to hold the number of credit hours you are taking and to place the value 12 in that variable, you could write the Dim statement in Figure 4-36.

> **HEADS UP**
>
> Visual Basic 2012 now allows you to omit the data type without causing an error. For example, entering Dim intValue = 1 does not produce an error because the compiler infers that the value of intValue is an Integer data type. This feature is called type inference. While you are learning how to write programs, it is best to use the data types so you can understand the changes as you convert one data type to another.

value placed in
intCreditHours
Integer variable

```
9        Dim intCreditHours As Integer = 12
```

FIGURE 4-36

The statement in Figure 4-36 defines the Integer variable named intCreditHours. The equal sign after the word Integer indicates to the Visual Basic compiler that the value to the right of the equal sign should be placed in the variable. The value 12 will be placed in the intCreditHours Integer variable when the program is compiled.

Decimal Data Type

A **Decimal data type** accurately represents large or very precise decimal numbers. It is ideal for use in the accounting and scientific fields to ensure that numbers keep their precision and are not subject to rounding errors. The Decimal data type can be accurate to 28 significant digits. (Significant digits are those that contribute to the precision of a number.) Often, Decimal data types are used to store dollar amounts. For example, to define the Decimal variable for the total cost of downloads in the sample program, you can use the statement in Figure 4-37.

```
22          Dim decTotalCostOfDownloads As Decimal
```

FIGURE 4-37

The Dim statement is used to define the Decimal variable. The dec prefix is used for all Decimal variable names. When the compiler processes the statement in Figure 4-37, 16 bytes of RAM will be reserved for a value to be placed in the dec TotalCostOfDownloads variable. Initially, no value will be present in the variable unless you specify a value, as shown in Figure 4-36 on the previous page. You can use an assignment statement to place data into the decTotalCostOfDownloads variable.

Double Data Type

A **Double data type** can represent huge positive numbers and very small negative numbers that can include values to the right of the decimal point. Sometimes, a Double data type is said to represent floating-point numbers, which means the decimal point can be anywhere within the number. The Dim statement in Figure 4-38 declares a Double variable that could be used in a tax application.

```
13          Dim dblTaxRate As Double
14          dblTaxRate = 0.07875
```

FIGURE 4-38

In Figure 4-38, the dblTaxRate Double variable is declared and then the assignment statement places the value 0.07875 in the memory location identified by the variable name. Note that a Double variable begins with the dbl prefix.

Other Data Types

Visual Basic supports other data types that are used for more specialized situations. Two widely used data types are Char and Boolean (Figure 4-39).

Data Type	Sample Value	Memory Allocation	Range of Values
Char	A single character such as ? or M	2 bytes	Any single character
Boolean	True or False	2 bytes	True or False

FIGURE 4-39

Char Data Type

The **Char data type** represents a single keystroke such as a letter of the alphabet, a punctuation mark, or a symbol. The prefix for a Char variable name is chr. When you assign a value to a Char variable, you must place quotation marks around the value. For example, in Figure 4-40, the value A is assigned to the chrTopGrade Char variable.

```
16        Dim chrTopGrade As Char
17        chrTopGrade = "A"
```

FIGURE 4-40

The value A in the assignment statement has quotation marks around it. In addition, Visual Studio displays the letter and the quotation marks in red text, indicating they are not Visual Basic keywords, variable names, or object names. In fact, the value is called a literal. You will learn more about literals shortly.

Visual Studio allows 65,534 different characters in a program. These characters consist of numbers, letters, and punctuation symbols. In addition, a wide variety of technical characters, mathematical symbols, and worldwide textual characters are available, which allows developers to work in almost every known language, including Korean (Figure 4-41). These characters are represented by a coding system called Unicode. To learn more about Unicode, visit *www.unicode.org*.

유니코드에 대해 ?

어떤 플랫폼,
어떤 프로그램,
어떤 언어에도 상관없이
유니코드는 모든 문자에 대해 고유 번호를 제공합니다.

FIGURE 4-41

Even though you can assign a number to a Char variable, it cannot be used in arithmetic operations. A number to be used in an arithmetic operation must be assigned a numeric variable.

Boolean Data Type

A Boolean data variable can contain a value that Visual Basic interprets as either true or false. A Boolean variable name begins with the bln prefix. If a variable in your program should represent whether a condition is true or not true, then the variable should be Boolean. In Figure 4-42, a Boolean variable called blnFullTimeStudent is declared and then the assignment statement sets the Boolean variable to True.

```
19        Dim blnFullTimeStudent As Boolean
20        blnFullTimeStudent = True
```

FIGURE 4-42

In Figure 4-42, the Dim statement is used to declare the blnFullTimeStudent Boolean variable. The assignment statement sets the Boolean variable to True. This variable can be checked in the program to determine whether it is true or false, and appropriate processing can occur as a result.

Miscellaneous Data Types

Visual Basic has several other data types that are used less often than the ones you have seen so far. These data types are summarized in the table in Figure 4-43.

Data Type	Sample Value	Memory Allocation	Range of Values
Byte	A whole number such as 7	1 bytes	0 to 255
Date	April 22, 2014	8 bytes	Dates and times
Long	A whole number such as 342,534,538	8 bytes	$-9,223,372,036,854,775,808$ through $+9,223,372,036,854,775,807$
Object	Holds a reference	4 bytes	A memory address
Short	A whole number such as 16,546	2 bytes	$-32,786$ through 32,767
Single	A number such as 312,672.3274	4 bytes	$-3.4028235E+38$ through $1.401298E-45$ for negative values; and from $1.401298E-45$ through $3.4028235E+38$ for positive values

FIGURE 4-43

As a review, the prefixes for each of the data type variable names are shown in Figure 4-44.

Data Type	Prefix
String	str
Integer	int
Decimal	dec
Double	dbl
Char	chr
Boolean	bln
Byte	byt
Date	dtm
Long	lng
Short	shr
Single	sng

FIGURE 4-44

© 2014 Cengage Learning

Literals

When an assignment statement includes a value like the one in Figure 4-38 on page 216 or Figure 4-40 on page 217, the value is called a **literal** because it literally is the value required by the assignment statement. It is not a variable. The Visual Basic compiler determines the data type of the value you use for a literal based on the value itself. For example, if you type "Chicago," the compiler treats the literal as a String data type, and if you type 49.327, the compiler treats the literal as a Double data type. The table in Figure 4-45 displays the default literal types as determined by the Visual Basic compiler.

Standard Literal Form	Default Data Type	Example
Numeric, no fractional part	Integer	104
Numeric, no fractional part, too large for Integer data type	Long	3987925494
Numeric, fractional part	Double	0.99 8.625
Enclosed within double quotes	String	"Brittany"
Enclosed within number signs	Date	#3/17/1990 3:30 PM#

FIGURE 4-45

Forced Literal Types

Sometimes you might want a literal to be a different data type than the Visual Basic default type. For example, you may want to assign the number 0.99 to a Decimal data variable to take advantage of the precision of the Decimal data type. As you can see in Figure 4-45 on the previous page, Visual Basic will consider the value 0.99 a Double data type by default. To define the literal as a Decimal literal, you must use a special character to force Visual Basic to use a data type other than the default. Specifically, you place the literal-type character at the end of the literal value. The table in Figure 4-46 shows the available literal-type characters and examples of their use.

Literal-Type Character	Data Type	Example
S	Short	Dim shoAge As Short shoAge = 40S
I	Integer	Dim intHeight as Integer intHeight = 76I
D	Decimal	Dim decPricePerSong As Decimal decPricePerSong = 0.99D
R	Double	Dim dblWeight As Double dblWeight = 8491R
C	Char	Dim chrNumberOfDays As Char chrNumberOfDays = "7"C

FIGURE 4-46

In the first example, the value 40 will be processed by Visual Basic as a Short data type literal, even though the value would be considered an Integer value by default. In the second example, the literal-type character confirms that the value should be treated as an Integer data type. In the third example, the value 0.99 will be processed as a Decimal data type, even though it would be considered a Double data type by default. In the next example, the value 8491 would be considered an Integer data value by default, but because the R literal-type character is used, Visual Basic will treat it as a Double data type. In the final example, the value 7 will be treated as a Char data type.

Constants

Recall that a variable identifies a location in memory where a value can be stored. By its nature, the value in a variable can be changed by statements within the program. For instance, in the sample program in this chapter, one user might request 5 downloads and another user might request 12 downloads; the value in the strNumberOfSongs variable can change based on the user's needs. In some instances, however, you might not want the value to be changed. For example, the price per download in the sample program is $0.99 per song. This value will not change, regardless of how many songs the user wants to download.

When a value will remain the same throughout the execution of the program, you should assign a meaningful name to a value. A **constant** contains one permanent value throughout the execution of the program. It cannot be changed by any statement within the program. To define a constant value, you can use the code in Figure 4-47.

```
12      Const cdecPricePerDownload As Decimal = 0.99D
```

FIGURE 4-47

The following rules apply to a constant:

1. The declaration of a constant begins with the letters Const, not the letters Dim.
2. You must assign the value to be contained in the constant on the same line as its definition. In Figure 4-47, the value 0.99D is assigned to the constant on the same line as the Const definition.
3. You cannot attempt to change the value of the constant anywhere in the program. If you do, you will produce a compiler error.
4. The letter c often is placed before the constant name to identify it throughout the program as a variable that cannot be changed.
5. Other than the letter c, constant names are formed using the same rules and techniques as other variable names.

Using a named constant instead of a literal provides significant advantages:

1. The program becomes easier to read because the value is identified by the name. For example, instead of using the value 0.99D in a literal, you can use it in a constant called cdecPricePerDownload. This variable name describes the use of the value 0.99D and makes the program easier to read.
2. If you discover that a value must be changed in the code, it is much easier and more reliable to change the value one time in the constant as opposed to changing every occurrence of the value in a literal.

Reference a Variable

You learned earlier that when a variable is declared, it is underlined with a green squiggly line until it is referenced in a statement. This feature of Visual Basic is intended to ensure that you do not declare a variable and then forget to use it. It also helps ensure that you do not waste memory by declaring an unnecessary variable.

When using a variable in a program, it is mandatory that you define the variable before using the variable name in a statement. For example, the statements in Figure 4-48 *will cause an error* because the variable is used in an assignment statement before it is declared.

```
25          strNumberOfSongs = txtNumberOfDownloads.Text
26          Dim strNumberOfSongs As String
```

FIGURE 4-48

In the code in Figure 4-48, the variable strNumberOfSongs is referenced in an assignment statement (line 25) before it is defined (line 26). This creates a compile error, as indicated by the blue squiggly line beneath the variable name strNumberOfSongs on line 25. If you attempt to compile the statements on lines 25 and 26, you will receive a build error. Always define a variable before it is used in a statement.

Scope of Variables

When you declare a variable in Visual Basic, you not only declare the data type of the variable, you also implicitly define its scope. The **scope of a variable** specifies where the variable can be referenced in a Visual Basic statement within the program. In larger programs with multiple classes and forms, scope becomes critical, but it is important that you understand the concept at this point.

You declare a variable in a region within a program. For instance, in the sample program in this chapter, you can declare a variable in the tap or click event handler for the Calculate Cost button. You could declare another variable in the tap or click event handler for the Clear button. Scope determines where each of these variables can be referenced and used in the Visual Basic program. *The rule is: A variable can be referenced only within the region of the program where it is defined.* A region in the programs you have seen thus far in the book is the code between the Sub statement and the End Sub statement in the event handlers. The code between the Sub statement and the End Sub statement is a **procedure**.

Therefore, if you declare a variable within the tap or click event handler for the Calculate Cost button, that variable cannot be referenced in the tap or click event handler for the Clear button, and vice versa. A variable that can only be referenced within the region of the program where it is defined is called a **local variable**. This variable is defined in one region of the program and cannot be changed by a statement in another region of the program.

In addition, when a variable is defined in a procedure and the procedure ends, the values of the local variables within the procedure are destroyed. Thus, local variables have a certain **lifetime** in the program. They are only "alive" from the time the procedure begins until it ends. If the procedure is executed again, the value the variable once contained no longer is present. One execution of the procedure is a variable's lifetime. Therefore, if a user taps or clicks the Calculate Cost button, the values in the variables are valid until the tap or click event is completed. When the user taps or clicks the Calculate Cost button again, all values from the first tap or click are gone.

You can also define variables that can be used in multiple regions of a Visual Basic program. These variables are called **global variables**. In most programs, local variables should be used because they cause fewer errors than global variables.

Understanding the scope of a variable is important when developing a program. You will learn more about the scope of variables later in this chapter and throughout this book.

Convert Variable Data

Variables used in arithmetic statements in a Visual Basic program must be numeric. String variables cannot be used in an arithmetic statement. If you attempt to use them, you will create a compilation error.

A user often enters data in a text box. Data in the Text property of a TextBox object is treated as String data. Because String data cannot be used in an arithmetic statement, the String data entered by a user must be converted to numeric data before it can be used in an arithmetic statement.

For instance, in the sample program in this chapter, the user enters the number of songs to download. Before this number can be used in an arithmetic statement to determine the total cost of the downloads, the value must be converted to an Integer data type.

Visual Basic includes several procedures that allow you to convert one data type to another data type. You will recall that a procedure is a prewritten set of code that can be called by a statement in the Visual Basic program. When the procedure is called, it performs a particular task. In this case, the task is to convert the String value the user entered into an Integer data type that can be used in an arithmetic operation. One procedure that converts a String data type to an Integer data type is named ToInt32. The number 32 in the procedure name identifies that the representation of the integer will require 32 bits or 4 bytes, which is the amount of memory required for the Integer data type. The procedure is in the Convert class, which is available in a Visual Studio 2012 class library.

Use a Procedure

When you need to use a procedure to accomplish a task in your program, you must understand what the procedure does and how to code the procedure call in a program statement. A procedure can operate in one of two ways: It can perform its task and return a value, or it can perform its task without returning a value. You will recall in the Chapter 3 sample program that the Close() procedure closed the window and terminated the program. The procedure performed its task but did not return a value. A procedure of this type is called a **Sub procedure**.

In the Digital Downloads program in this chapter, the requirement is to convert the String value for the number of songs the user enters into an Integer data type. Then it can be used in an arithmetic operation. Therefore, the procedure must return a value (the Integer value for the number of songs). A procedure that returns a value is called a **Function procedure**, or a **function**.

In addition, a procedure might require data to be passed to it when called in order to carry out its processing. In the sample program in this chapter, the Function procedure to convert a String variable to an Integer variable first must be able to access the String variable. Therefore, in the statement that calls the Function procedure, the variable name for the String variable to be converted must be passed to the procedure. A value is passed to a procedure through the use of an argument.

An **argument** identifies a value required by a procedure. To pass the argument to the procedure, include its name within parentheses following the name of the procedure in the calling statement. For example, to pass the value stored in the strNumberOf-Songs variable to the ToInt32 procedure, you could use the statement in Figure 4-49.

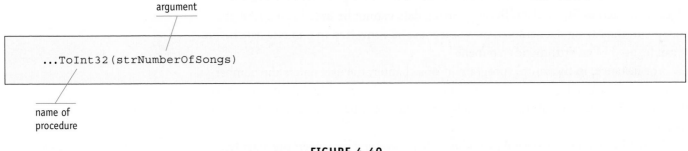

FIGURE 4-49

The name of the procedure is ToInt32. The argument is strNumberOfSongs, which is the String variable that contains the value to be converted to an Integer data type by the ToInt32 procedure. Notice that the argument is enclosed within parentheses.

Every procedure is part of a class in Visual Basic. You will recall from Chapter 1 that a **class** is a named grouping of program code. When the calling statement must call a procedure, it first must identify the class that contains the procedure. Thus, in Figure 4-49 the calling statement is incomplete because the class name is not included. The class that contains the ToInt32 procedure is the Convert class. To complete the procedure call statement, the class must be added, as shown in Figure 4-50.

FIGURE 4-50

In Figure 4-50, the class name Convert begins the procedure call. A dot operator separates the class name from the procedure name (ToInt32). The argument (strNumberOfSongs) within the parentheses completes the procedure call.

When a Function procedure returns a value, such as the ToInt32 procedure that returns an integer value, the returned value essentially replaces the Function procedure call in the assignment statement. So, in Figure 4-51, you can see that when the processing is completed within the Function procedure, the integer value is substituted for the procedure call in the assignment statement.

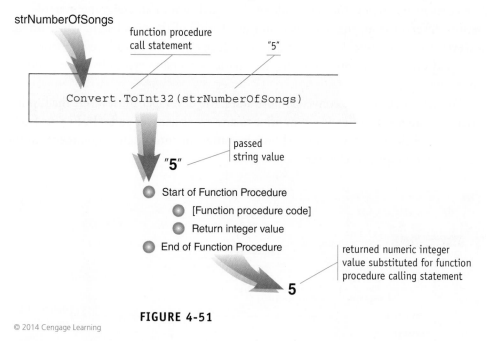

FIGURE 4-51

© 2014 Cengage Learning

Figure 4-52 shows the complete assignment statement to convert the String data type in the strNumberOfSongs variable to an Integer data type and place it in the intNumberOfSongs variable.

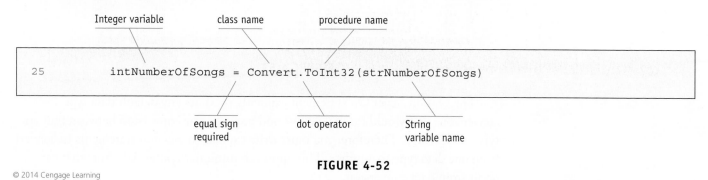

FIGURE 4-52

© 2014 Cengage Learning

The intNumberOfSongs variable name to the left of the equal sign identifies the Integer variable where the converted value will be copied. The equal sign in the assignment statement is required. As a result of the assignment statement in Figure 4-52, the ToInt32 Function procedure in the Convert class will convert the value in the strNumberOfSongs String variable to an integer value. The assignment statement will place that integer value in the intNumberOfSongs variable.

The use of Function procedures and arguments with procedure calls is common when programming in Visual Basic. You will encounter many examples of Function procedure calls throughout this book.

Option Strict On

In the previous section, you saw an example of how to explicitly change a value from one data type to another. By default, Visual Basic will automatically convert data types if the one on the right side of the equal sign in an assignment statement is different from the data type on the left side of the equal sign. Quite often, however, the automatic conversion can introduce errors and produce an incorrect converted value. Therefore, allowing automatic conversion typically is not good programming style.

To prevent automatic conversion of values, the developer must insert the Option Strict On statement in the program prior to any event handler code. In Figure 4-53, the Option Strict On statement is shown just after the introductory comments in the sample program for this chapter.

Option Strict On statement

FIGURE 4-53

The Option Strict On statement explicitly prevents any default data type conversions that would cause data loss and prevents any conversion between numeric types and strings. Therefore, you must write explicit conversion statements to convert from one data type to another. This approach minimizes potential errors that can occur from data conversion.

Arithmetic Operations

The ability to perform arithmetic operations on numeric data is fundamental to computer programs. Many programs require arithmetic operations to add, subtract, multiply, and divide numeric data. For example, in the Digital Downloads program in this chapter, the price per song downloaded must be multiplied by the number of songs downloaded to calculate the total cost. The formula is shown in Figure 4-54.

Total Cost of Downloads = Number of Song Downloads times Price per Download

FIGURE 4-54

An assignment statement is used in Visual Basic 2012 to perform the arithmetic operation shown in Figure 4-54. The statements used in the sample program and a depiction of the operation are shown in Figure 4-55.

```
20          Dim strNumberOfSongs As String
21          Dim intNumberOfSongs As Integer
22          Dim decTotalCostOfDownloads As Decimal
23          Const cdecPricePerDownload As Decimal = 0.99D
24
25          strNumberOfSongs = txtNumberOfDownloads.Text
26          intNumberOfSongs = Convert.ToInt32(strNumberOfSongs)
27          decTotalCostOfDownloads = intNumberOfSongs * cdecPricePerDownload
```

decTotalCostOfDownloads = intNumberOfSongs * cdecPricePerDownload

FIGURE 4-55

In the code in Figure 4-55, the variable strNumberOfSongs is assigned the user's entered value by the assignment statement on line 25. (See Figure 4-24 on page 209 for a detailed explanation of this statement.) The statement on line 26 converts the value in the strNumberOfSongs variable to an integer and copies it to the intNumberOfSongs variable. (See Figure 4-52 on page 225 for an explanation of this statement.)

The statement on line 27 multiplies the integer value in the intNumberOfSongs variable by the constant value in the cdecPricePerDownload variable, and then copies the result to the decTotalCostOfDownloads variable. For example, if the user enters 5 as the number of downloads, the value 5 is multiplied by 0.99 (the value in the cdecPricePerDownload variable), and the result (4.95) is copied to the decTotalCostOfDownloads variable.

Arithmetic Operators

The asterisk (*) is an important element on the right side of the equal sign in the assignment statement on line 27. This asterisk is the multiplication **arithmetic operator**. Whenever the compiler encounters this operator, the value to the left of the operator is multiplied by the value to the right of the operator, and these values then are replaced in the assignment statement by the product of the two numbers. Thus, in Figure 4-55 on the previous page the arithmetic expression intNumberOfSongs * cdecPricePerDownload is replaced by the value 4.95. Then, the assignment statement places the value 4.95 in the decTotalCostOfDownloads variable.

The multiplication arithmetic operator is only one of the arithmetic operators available in Visual Basic 2012. The table in Figure 4-56 lists the arithmetic operators in Visual Basic 2012, describes their use, and provides an example of their use.

Arithmetic Operator	Use	Assignment Statement Showing Use
+	Addition	decTotal = decPrice + decTax
−	Subtraction	decCost = decRegularPrice − decDiscount
*	Multiplication	decTax = decItemPrice * decTaxRate
/	Division	decClassAverage = decTotalScores / intNumberOfStudents
^	Exponentiation	intSquareArea = intSquareSide ^ 2
\	Integer Division	intResult = 13 \ 5
Mod	Modulus Arithmetic (remainder)	intRemainder = 13 Mod 5

FIGURE 4-56

The arithmetic operators shown in Figure 4-56 are explained in the following paragraphs:

Addition

The **addition arithmetic operator** (+) adds the numeric values immediately to the left and right of the operator and replaces the arithmetic expression in the assignment statement. For example, in Figure 4-57, the value in the decPrice variable is added to the value in the decTax variable.

decTotal   decPrice   decTax

FIGURE 4-57

In Figure 4-57, the arithmetic expression (decPrice + decTax) is evaluated, and then the assignment statement copies the sum to the decTotal variable in RAM.

An arithmetic expression that uses the addition operator can contain more than two numeric values to be added. For example, in Figure 4-58, three variables are used in the arithmetic expression.

```
47          decTotalPay = decRegularPay + decOvertimePay + decBonusPay
```

FIGURE 4-58

In Figure 4-58, the value in decRegularPay is added to the value in decOvertimePay. The result then is added to decBonusPay, and that sum is copied to the decTotalPay variable. Visual Basic imposes no limit on the number of variables in an arithmetic expression.

In addition to variables, arithmetic expressions can contain literals. The assignment statement in Figure 4-59 uses a literal.

```
53          decTicketCost = decInternetTicketCost + 10.25
```

FIGURE 4-59

In Figure 4-59 on the previous page, the value 10.25 is added to the value in the decInternetTicketCost variable, and that sum is placed in the decTicketCost variable. Generally, literals should not be used in arithmetic expressions unless you know that the value will not change. For example, if the extra cost for the ticket could change in the future, good program design would dictate that the value be placed in a variable (perhaps even a constant).

Subtraction

To subtract one value from another in an assignment statement, Visual Basic 2012 uses the **subtraction arithmetic operator** (–), as shown in Figure 4-60.

```
59          decNetProfit = decRevenue - decCosts
```

FIGURE 4-60

In Figure 4-60, the value in the decCosts variable is subtracted from the value in the decRevenue variable. The result then is copied into the decNetProfit variable. If the value in decCosts is greater than the value in decRevenue, the value placed in the decNetProfit variable will be negative.

Use Arithmetic Results

After an arithmetic operation has been performed using an assignment statement, the values used in the operation and the resulting answer can be used in subsequent arithmetic operations or for other purposes within the program. For example, the result of one operation can be used in a subsequent calculation (Figure 4-61).

```
67          decComputerCost = decMonitorCost + decSystemUnitCost
68          decNetComputerCost = decComputerCost - decSystemDiscount
```

FIGURE 4-61

In Figure 4-61, the statement on line 67 determines the computer cost by adding the costs of the monitor and the system unit. The statement on line 68 calculates the net computer cost by subtracting the system discount from the computer cost calculated on line 67. Whenever a value is stored in a variable, it can be used in other statements within the program.

Multiplication

Multiplication is accomplished through the use of an assignment statement and the multiplication operator (*), as shown in Figure 4-62.

```
74              intLandPlotArea = intLandPlotLength * intLandPlotWidth
```

FIGURE 4-62

© 2014 Cengage Learning

In Figure 4-62, the value in the intLandPlotLength variable is multiplied by the value in the intLandPlotWidth variable. The product of the multiplication is placed in the intLandPlotArea variable.

If two positive numbers are multiplied, the answer is positive. If two negative numbers are multiplied, the answer is positive. If one positive number and one negative number are multiplied, the answer is negative.

When two numbers are multiplied, you must be aware of the size of the result. The largest number of digits that can appear as a result of multiplication is the sum of the number of digits in the values being multiplied. If the product is greater than the value that can be stored in the variable to the left of the assignment statement, an overflow error can occur and the program will be terminated.

How should I test my program to make sure it works properly?
When you allow user input, be sure to test every possible entry by the user. If a decimal value is input instead of an expected integer value, your program may stop functioning. As you learn more about coding in the next chapters, error validation will become an important part of developing your program.

CONSIDER THIS

Division

Visual Basic 2012 provides three arithmetic operators for division and related calculations: the slash (/), the backslash (\), and the MOD operator.

You use the slash for normal division. For example, in Figure 4-63, the value in the decTestScores variable is divided by 3 to obtain the average test score.

```
79              decAverageTestScore = decTestScores / 3
```

FIGURE 4-63

© 2014 Cengage Learning

You use the backslash (\) for integer division. With integer division, the quotient returned from the division operation is an integer. If the division operation produces a quotient with a remainder, the remainder is dropped, or truncated. The examples in Figure 4-64 on the next page illustrate the use of the integer division arithmetic operator.

WATCH OUT FOR

The divisor is the number to the right of the division operator. Make sure the divisor is not zero. If you attempt to divide by zero, your program will be terminated with an error.

Division Operation	Result
12\5	2
25\4	6
30\7	4

FIGURE 4-64

© 2014 Cengage Learning

Notice in each example in Figure 4-64 that the result is a whole number with the remainder truncated.

The MOD operator divides the number to the left of the operator by the number to the right of the operator and returns an integer value that is the remainder of the division operation. Integer division and the MOD operator often are used together, as shown in Figure 4-65.

```
86          intHours = intTotalNumberOfMinutes \ 60
87          intMinutes = intTotalNumberOfMinutes Mod 60
```

FIGURE 4-65

© 2014 Cengage Learning

In Figure 4-65, the operation on line 86 will return only the integer value of the division. For example, if the intTotalNumberOfMinutes variable contains 150, a result of 2 (2 = 150\60) will be placed in the intHours variable. The operation on line 87 will place the remainder in the intMinutes variable. The remainder in the example is 30; 150 divided by 60 is 2, with a remainder of 30.

Exponentiation

Exponentiation means raising a number to a power. It is accomplished in Visual Basic 2012 using the exponentiation arithmetic operator (^), as shown in Figure 4-66.

```
                                        exponentiation
                                        arithmetic operator
                                               |
                                               /
92          intCubeArea = intLengthOfCubeSide ^ 3
```

FIGURE 4-66

© 2014 Cengage Learning

In Figure 4-66, the arithmetic expression is the same as intLengthOfCubeSide *intLengthOfCubeSide* intLengthOfCubeSide. Therefore, the value is cubed and copied to the intCubeArea variable.

The exponent used in the operation can be a fraction. If so, the root is taken (Figure 4-67).

```
94            intLengthOfCubeSide = intCubeArea ^ (1 / 3)
```

FIGURE 4-67

In Figure 4-67, the cube root of the value in the intCubeArea variable is calculated and the result is copied to the intLengthOfCubeSide variable. Thus, if the area of the cube is 64, the value calculated for the length of the cube side would be 4 (4 * 4 * 4 = 64). The fractional exponent can never be negative, and it must be placed within parentheses.

Multiple Operations

A single assignment statement can contain multiple arithmetic operations. In Figure 4-68, the addition and subtraction operators are used to calculate the new balance in a savings account by adding the deposits to the old balance and subtracting withdrawals.

```
101           decNewBalance = decOldBalance + decDeposits - decWithdrawals
```

FIGURE 4-68

When the assignment statement is executed in Figure 4-68, the value in the decOldBalance variable is added to the value in the decDeposits variable. Then, the value in the decWithdrawals variable is subtracted from that sum and the result is copied to the decNewBalance variable.

Notice in Figure 4-68 that the calculations proceed from left to right in the arithmetic expression.

Hierarchy of Operations

When multiple operations are included in a single assignment statement, the sequence for performing the calculations is determined by the following rules:

1. Exponentiation (^) is performed first.
2. Multiplication (*) and division (/) are performed next.
3. Integer division (\) is next.
4. MOD then occurs.
5. Addition (+) and subtraction (−) are performed last.
6. Within each of the preceding five steps, calculations are performed from left to right.

As a result of this predetermined sequence, an arithmetic expression such as decBonus + decHours * decHourlyRate would result in the product of decHours * decHourlyRate being added to decBonus.

An arithmetic expression such as decGrade1 + decGrade2 / 2 would cause the value in the decGrade2 variable to be divided by 2 and then the quotient to be added to the value in decGrade1 because division is performed before addition. However, this calculation probably was not intended. Instead, the intent probably was to add the values in decGrade1 and decGrade2 and then divide the sum by 2. To force certain operations to be performed before others, you can use parentheses. Any arithmetic expression within parentheses is evaluated before expressions outside the parentheses, as shown in Figure 4-69.

```
108            decAverageGrade = (decGrade1 + decGrade2) / 2
```

FIGURE 4-69

In Figure 4-69, the addition operation is inside the parentheses, so it will be completed before the division operation. Therefore, the result of the arithmetic expression is that the value in decGrade1 is added to the value in decGrade2. That sum then is divided by 2 and the quotient is copied to the decAverageGrade variable.

If you want to make the sequence of operations explicitly clear, you can use parentheses around multiple arithmetic operations in an arithmetic expression even if the predetermined sequence of operations will produce the correct answer.

IN THE REAL WORLD

You know that a procedure is a collection of code that a program can call to perform a particular function, such as converting data stored in a numeric data type to data stored as a String data type. In some programming languages, a procedure is called a method. Therefore, as you search the index or other areas in Visual Studio Help, you might find the word method *used*. Just remember that the terms *method* and *procedure* are virtually synonymous.

Display Numeric Output Data

As you have learned, the result of an arithmetic expression is a numeric value that typically is stored in a numeric variable. To display the numeric data as information in a graphical user interface, usually the data must be placed in the Text property of a Label object or a TextBox object. The Text property of these objects, however, requires that the data be a String data type. Therefore, to display a numeric value in a label or a text box, the numeric data must be converted to a String data type.

Each of the numeric data types provides a function called ToString that converts data from the numeric data type to the String data type. The general format of the function call for a Decimal numeric variable is shown in Figure 4-70.

General Format: ToString Function

```
decimalvariable.ToString()
```

FIGURE 4-70

The statement shown in Figure 4-70 consists of the name of the Decimal variable that contains data to be converted, the dot operator (.), and the name of the function (ToString). Notice that the function name is followed immediately by closed parentheses, which indicates to the Visual Basic compiler that ToString is a procedure name. When the function call is executed, the value returned by the ToString function replaces the call.

The function call normally is contained within an assignment statement to assign the returned string value to the Text property of a Label or TextBox object. The example in Figure 4-71 shows the assignment statement to convert the numeric value in the decTemperature variable to a String value that then is placed in the Text property of the lblTemperature Label object.

name of decimal variable

ToString
function call

```
118         lblTemperature.Text = decTemperature.ToString()
```

FIGURE 4-71

© 2014 Cengage Learning

In Figure 4-71, the name of the Decimal variable (decTemperature) is followed by the dot operator and then the name of the function (ToString) with the required parentheses. When the statement on line 118 is executed, the ToString function is called. It converts the numeric value in the decTemperature variable to a String data type and returns the String data. The assignment statement then copies the returned String data to the Text property of the Temperature Label object.

Format Specifications for the ToString Function

In the example in Figure 4-71, the conversion from numeric value to String value is a straight conversion, which means the value is returned but not formatted in any manner. For example, if the numeric value in the Decimal variable was 47.235, then the same value was returned as a String value.

The ToString function, however, can convert numeric data to String data using a specified format. For example, the value 2317.49 could be returned as $2,317.49. The returned value is in the form of dollars and cents, or currency. To identify the format for the numeric data to be returned by the ToString function, the **format specifier** must be included as an argument in the parentheses following the ToString function name. The table in Figure 4-72 on the next page identifies the commonly used format specifiers; in the examples, the value in the numeric field is 8976.43561.

HEADS UP

Rounding is an important consideration when determining the formatting of a number. When using the ToString function, all values are rounded based on the digit after the last digit to be displayed. For example, if the value 729.837 is being converted to a Currency string from a numeric format, the returned result will be rounded up ($729.84). If the value to be converted is 575.371, the returned result will be rounded down ($575.37). Rounding also is used with the precision specifier.

Format Specifier	Format	Description	Output from the Function
General(G)	ToString("G")	Displays the numbers as is	8976.43561
Currency(C)	ToString("C")	Displays the number with a dollar sign, a thousands separator (comma), 2 digits to the right of the decimal and negative numbers in parentheses	$8,976.44
Fixed(F)	ToString("F")	Displays the number with 2 digits to the right of the decimal and a minus sign for negative numbers	8976.44
Number(N)	ToString("N")	Displays a number with a thousands separator, 2 digits to the right of the decimal and a minus sign for negative numbers	8,976.44
Percent(P)	ToString("P")	Displays the number multiplied by 100 with a % sign, a thousands separator, 2 digits to the right of the decimal and a minus sign for negative numbers	897,643.56%
Scientific(E)	ToString("E")	Displays the number in E-notation and a minus sign for negative numbers	8.976436E+03

FIGURE 4-72

In Figure 4-72, each format specifier is used as an argument within parentheses. The argument must be included in the quotation marks on each side of the format specifier, as shown. The letter for the format specifier can be uppercase or lowercase.

Precision Specifier

Each format specifier has a default number of digits that will be returned to the right of the decimal point. You can use a precision specifier, however, to override this default number. The **precision specifier** is a number included within the quotation marks in the function call that identifies the number of positions that should be returned to the right of the decimal point. The examples in Figure 4-73 illustrate the use of the precision specifier; assume that the value in the decNumericValue variable is 8976.43561.

Statement	Copied to Text Property of lblOutput Label Object
lblOutput = decNumericValue.ToString("C2")	$8,976.44
lblOutput = decNumericValue.ToString("C3")	$8,976.436
lblOutput = decNumericValue.ToString("F1")	8976.4
lblOutput = decNumericValue.ToString("N4")	8,976.4356
lblOutput = decNumericValue.ToString("P0")	897,644%

FIGURE 4-73

As you can see, the precision specifier identifies the number of digits that should be displayed to the right of the decimal point in the string returned from the ToString function. Notice that if the precision specifier is 0, no digits are returned to the right of the decimal point.

As with all conversions, when the number of positions to the right of the decimal point in the returned string is less than the number of digits to the right of the decimal point in the numeric value being converted, the returned value is rounded to the specified number of decimal places.

Clear the Form — Clear Procedure and Focus Procedure

Earlier in this chapter, you learned that when the user taps or clicks the Clear button in the Digital Downloads program (see Figure 4-1 on page 190), the event handler for the Clear button must clear the results from the window and allow the user to enter the next number of downloads. To clear the results, the Clear button event handler must complete the following tasks:

1. Clear the Text property of the TextBox object.
2. Clear the Text property of the Label object that displays the total cost of the downloads.
3. Set the focus on the TextBox object, which means placing the insertion point in the text box.

You will learn to accomplish these tasks in the following sections.

Clear Procedure

The Clear procedure clears any data in the Text property of a TextBox object. The general format of the Clear procedure is shown in Figure 4-74.

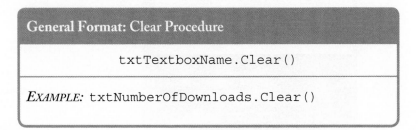

General Format: Clear Procedure

```
txtTextboxName.Clear()
```

EXAMPLE: `txtNumberOfDownloads.Clear()`

FIGURE 4-74

When the Clear procedure is executed, the Text property is cleared of data. As with every procedure call, the name of the procedure must be followed by parentheses.

Clear the Text Property of a Label

The Clear procedure cannot be used with a Label object. Instead, to clear the Text property of a Label object, you must write an assignment statement that assigns a null length string to the Text property. A null length string has no length, which means it is a string with no characters. A null length string is represented by two quotation marks with no character between them (""). To assign a null length string to the Text property, you can use the statement shown in Figure 4-75.

```
39              lblTotalCost.Text = ""
```

FIGURE 4-75

In Figure 4-75, the null length string represented by the two empty quotation marks is assigned to the Text property of the lblTotalCost Label object. As a result of the assignment statement, the Text property is cleared.

Set the Focus

When the focus is on a TextBox object, the insertion point is located in the text box (Figure 4-76).

insertion point
in text box

FIGURE 4-76

When the user taps or clicks a button or other item in the graphical user interface, the focus shifts to that item. Therefore, to place the focus on a text box, the user can tap or click it. However, the programmer can use the Focus procedure to place the focus on a text box automatically without requiring the user to tap or click it first, thus making it easier for the user to enter data in the text box (Figure 4-77).

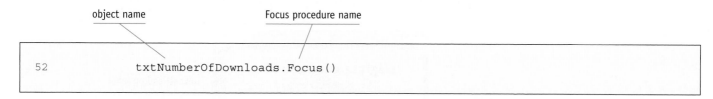

FIGURE 4-77

As with most procedure calls, the name of the object begins the statement, followed immediately by the dot operator (period). The name of the procedure (Focus) follows the dot operator. When the statement on line 52 is executed, the focus is placed on the txtNumberOfDownloads TextBox object, which means the insertion point is placed in the text box.

Form Load Event

In the sample programs in Chapter 3 and this chapter, you have seen that an event can occur when the user taps or clicks a button. The user's action triggers the code to execute in the event handler for the button tap or click. For example, in the Digital Downloads program in this chapter, the user taps or clicks the Calculate Cost button and the event handler code responds by multiplying the number of songs by the price per song and displaying the result (see Figure 4-1 on page 190).

Tapping or clicking a button is not the only action that can trigger an event. For example, a form load event occurs each time a program is started and the Windows Form object is loaded into computer memory. For the program in this chapter, a form load event occurs when the program starts and the Digital Downloads form is loaded. In some programs, an event handler is not written for this particular event and no processing occurs. In the Digital Downloads program, however, a form loading event handler is required. This event handler completes the following tasks:

1. Display the cost per download heading.
2. Clear the placeholder from the lblTotalCost Text property.
3. Set the focus on the txtNumberOfDownloads text box.

Concatenation

In the Digital Downloads program, the lblCostHeading Label object displays the cost per download (see Figure 4-1 on page 190). In the user interface design, the lblCostHeading Label contains placeholder information for the label, but does not contain the actual cost per download (Figure 4-78).

lblCostHeading label does not contain actual cost per download

FIGURE 4-78

© Luca Pierro PHOTOGRAPHY/Flickr/Getty Images

In Figure 4-78, the programmer had two reasons for not placing the actual download cost in the label during the design phase. First, in the original implementation of the program, the cost per download is 99 cents. In the future, however, the cost might change. Generally, data that might change should be placed in the Text property of a Label object during execution time, not at design time. Therefore, the cost per download should be placed in the label by the form load event handler when the form opens. Second, the cost per download is used in two places in the program — in the label and when the actual calculation is performed to determine the total cost (see Figure 4-55 on page 227). Instead of using the numeric value of 0.99 several times within the program, the value should be assigned to a variable. If the value must be changed in the future, only one change to the variable is necessary. For example, if the cost per download changes to 85 cents, the cost can be changed in the cost per download variable and then it will be correct for all uses of the variable. To illustrate, the variable for the cost per download is shown in Figure 4-79.

```
12      Const _cdecPricePerDownload As Decimal = 0.99D
```

FIGURE 4-79

As you can see, the price per download is declared as a constant that cannot be changed during program execution. If the price changes in the future, the developer can make one change to this declaration and all elements of the program that use the value will be correct.

To create the heading for the Digital Downloads program, the value in the variable declared in Figure 4-79 must be combined with the words Per Download and the result must be placed in the Text property of the lblCostHeading Label object. The process of joining two different values into a single string is called **concatenation**. When you use concatenation, the values being concatenated must be String data types. Note in Figure 4-79 that the _cdecPricePerDownload variable is a Decimal data type. Therefore, it must be changed to a String data type before being joined with the words in the heading.

The statement in Figure 4-80 converts the Decimal data type to a String data type, concatenates (or joins) the two strings together, and then places the result in the Text property of the lblCostHeading Label object.

In some instances, it is better to continue a line of code in the code window on a second line so that the entire line can be read without scrolling. To continue a line of code on a subsequent line, place a space in the statement and then place an underscore (_) character in the line of code. The underscore character indicates to the Visual Basic compiler that the line of code continues on the next line (see Figure 4-80).

HEADS UP

FIGURE 4-80

© 2014 Cengage Learning

In Figure 4-80, the string generated to the right of the equal sign will be placed in the Text property of the lblCostHeading Label object. The first entry to the right of the equal sign is the price variable name (see Figure 4-79). Following the dot operator is the ToString procedure name, followed by the currency argument within parentheses. Remember that the ToString procedure converts a numeric value to a String data type. When the currency argument ("C") is used, the String value returned is in a currency format. (See Figure 4-72 on page 236 for a detailed explanation.)

Following the conversion statement is the **concatenation operator (&)**. When the Visual Basic compiler encounters this operator, the string to the left of the operator is joined with the String data to the right of the operator to create a single concatenated string. The resulting string then is placed in the Text property of the lblCostHeading Label object.

The process that occurs to the right of the equal sign is illustrated in Figure 4-81.

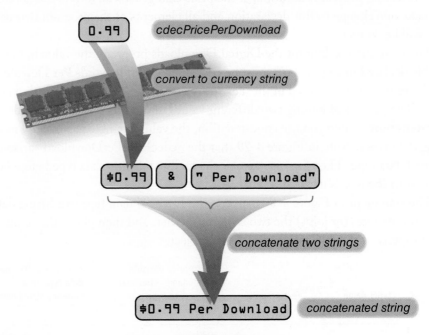

FIGURE 4-81

© 2014 Cengage Learning; © Tatiana Popova/Photos.com

In Figure 4-81 you can see that to obtain the concatenated string, the Decimal value in the cdecPricePerDownload Decimal variable is converted to a currency String data type. Then, that value is combined with the string literal to create the concatenated string. In the assignment statement in Figure 4-80 on the previous page, the concatenated string is assigned to the Text property of the lblCostHeading Label object.

Class Scope

Remember that when you declare a variable, you also define its scope. The scope of a variable identifies where within the program the variable can be referenced. For example, if a variable is declared within an event handler procedure, the variable can be referenced only within that procedure.

Sometimes, a variable must be referenced in multiple event handlers. In the Digital Downloads program, the value in the cdecPricePerDownload variable is referenced in the Calculate button event handler when the total cost is calculated (see Figure 4-55 on page 227). The value also is referenced in the form load event when the heading is displayed (see Figure 4-80 on the previous page). Because the variable is referenced in two different event handling procedures, it must be defined at the class level instead of the procedure (event handler) level. This means that the variable must be declared in the code before the first procedure in the program. As you can see in Figure 4-82, the declaration of the _cdecPricePerDownload variable follows the class definition statement but appears before the first event handler procedure.

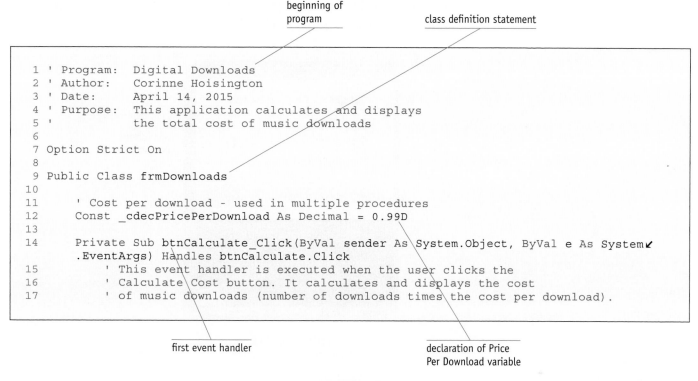

FIGURE 4-82

As a result of the code in Figure 4-82, the scope of the _cdecPricePerDownload variable will be all procedures within the class; that is, code in any event handler procedure within the class can reference the variable. Because the variable is declared as a constant, the value in the variable cannot be changed by code within the class; however, the value in the class can be referenced to calculate the total cost and to create the cost heading.

Debug Your Program

When your program processes numeric data entered by a user, you should be aware of several errors that can occur when the user enters data the program does not expect. The three errors that occur most often are Format Exceptions, Overflow Exceptions, and Divide By Zero Exceptions.

A **Format Exception** occurs when the user enters data that a statement within the program cannot process properly. In the Digital Downloads program, the user must enter a numeric value for the number of songs to download. When the user taps or clicks the Calculate Cost button, the program converts the entered value to

---

IN THE REAL WORLD

When a variable is declared for use throughout a class, the naming convention specifies that the name should begin with an underscore character (_). When you see a variable name that begins with the underscore character, you know the variable has class scope.

an integer and then uses the numeric value in the calculation (see Figure 4-52 on page 225). If the user enters a nonnumeric value, such as abc (Figure 4-83a), the conversion process cannot take place because the argument passed to the Convert class is not a numeric value. In this situation, a Format Exception error is recognized and the error box in Figure 4-83b is displayed.

FIGURE 4-83a

© Luca Pierro PHOTOGRAPHY/Flickr/Getty Images

FIGURE 4-83b

In Figure 4-83a, the user entered the value abc and then tapped or clicked the Calculate Cost button. When control was passed to the ToInt32 procedure to convert the String value in the text box to an Integer, the Format Exception was triggered because the value in the strNumberOfSongs variable was not numeric. When an exception occurs, the execution of the program is terminated. With Visual Studio running, tap or click the Stop Debugging button on the Standard toolbar.

An **Overflow Exception** occurs when the user enters a value greater than the maximum value the statement can process. For example, in the Digital Downloads program, if the user enters a value in the text box that is too large for the ToInt32 procedure to convert, an Overflow Exception occurs.

An Overflow Exception also can occur when a calculation creates a value larger than a procedure can process. For example, if two large but valid numbers are multiplied, the product of the multiplication might be too large to process.

The third type of common error is the **Divide By Zero Exception**. It is not possible to divide by zero, so if your program contains a division operation and the divisor is zero, the Divide By Zero Exception will occur.

Whenever an exception occurs, a window similar to that in Figure 4-83b will be displayed.

To avoid exceptions, which should always be your goal, you can use certain techniques for editing the data and ensuring that the user has entered valid data. In Chapter 5 and Chapter 6, you will learn how to write code that checks user input to ensure that exceptions do not occur.

Program Design

As you have learned, the requirements document identifies the purpose of the program being developed, the application title, the procedures to be followed when using the program, any required equations and calculations, any conditions within the program that must be tested, notes and restrictions that must be followed by the program, and any other comments that would be helpful to understanding the problem. The requirements document for the Digital Downloads application is shown in Figure 4-84 on the following page.

REQUIREMENTS DOCUMENT

Date Submitted:	April 14, 2015
Application Title:	Digital Downloads
Purpose:	The Digital Downloads program allows the user to enter the number of songs to be downloaded. The program calculates the total cost of the downloads based on a price of $0.99 per song.
Program Procedures:	In a Windows application, the user enters the number of songs she wants to download. The program calculates the total cost of downloads. The user can clear the values on the screen and enter a new value for the number of downloads.
Algorithms, Processing, and Conditions:	1. The user must be able to enter the number of songs to be downloaded. 2. The user can initiate the calculation and display the total cost of the downloads. 3. The application computes the total cost by multiplying the number of downloads by the cost per download ($0.99). 4. The total cost of downloads is displayed as a currency value. 5. The user should be able to clear the value entered for the number of downloads and the total cost of downloads. 6. The user should be provided with a button to exit the program.
Notes and Restrictions:	n/a
Comments:	A graphic should depict a musical image. A graphic named Music is available on CengageBrain.com.

FIGURE 4-84

The Use Case Definition for the Digital Downloads program is shown in Figure 4-85.

USE CASE DEFINITION

1. The Windows application opens with a text box in which the user can enter a number of song downloads. The user interface includes the text box, an area to display the total cost of downloads, a Calculate Cost button, a Clear button, and an Exit button.
2. The user enters the number of song downloads.
3. The user taps or clicks the Calculate Cost button.
4. The program displays the total cost of the song downloads.
5. The user taps or clicks the Clear button to clear the Number of Downloads text box and erase the Total Cost of Downloads amount.
6. The user can repeat steps 2 through 5.
7. The user taps or clicks the Exit button to terminate the application.

FIGURE 4-85

Event Planning Document

You will recall that the event planning document is a table that specifies which objects in the user interface will cause events, the action taken by the user to trigger each event, and the event processing that must occur. The event planning document for the Digital Downloads program is shown in Figure 4-86.

EVENT PLANNING DOCUMENT			
Program Name: Digital Downloads	**Developer:** Corinne Hoisington	**Object:** frmDownloads	**Date:** April 14, 2015
OBJECT	**EVENT TRIGGER**	**EVENT PROCESSING**	
btnCalculate	Tap or click	Assign data entered in text box to a String variable Convert entered data to numeric integer Calculate total cost of downloads (number of downloads * price per download) Display total cost of downloads	
btnClear	Tap or click	Clear Number of Downloads text box Clear Total Cost of Downloads label text Set focus on Number of Downloads text box	
btnExit	Tap or click	Close the window and terminate the program	
frmDownloads	Load	Display heading with price per download Clear the placement digits for Total Cost of Downloads Label object Set focus on Number of Downloads text box	

FIGURE 4-86

© 2014 Cengage Learning

Code the Program

You are now ready to code the program by entering Visual Basic statements to accomplish the tasks specified in the event planning document. You also will implement the logic to carry out the required processing.

Guided Program Development

To design the user interface for the Digital Downloads program and enter the code required to process each event in the program, complete the following steps:

NOTE TO THE LEARNER

In the following activity, you should complete the tasks within the specified steps. Each of the tasks is accompanied by a Hint Screen. The purpose of the Hint Screen is to indicate where you should perform the activity in the Visual Studio window and to remind you which method to use. If you need further help completing a step, refer to the figure identified by *ref:*.

Guided Program Development

Phase 1: Create the User Interface Mockup

1

- **Create a Windows Application** Open Visual Studio using the Search charm (Windows 8) or the Start button on the Windows taskbar and the All Programs submenu (Windows 7). Close the Start page by tapping or clicking the Close button. To create a Windows application, tap or click the New Project button on the Standard toolbar. If necessary, tap or click Windows in the Installed Templates pane, tap or

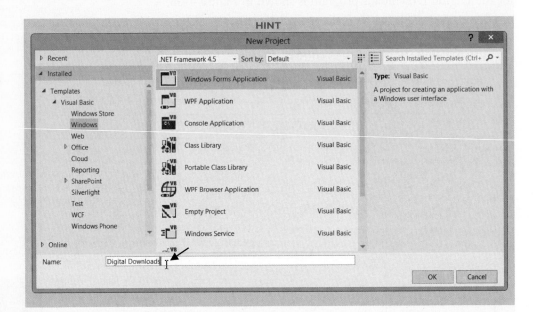

click Windows Forms Application in the center pane, and then type `Digital Downloads`. Tap or click the OK button in the New Project window.

- **Display the Toolbox** Ensure that the Toolbox is displayed in the Visual Studio window. If it is not, tap or click VIEW and then Toolbox. If necessary, tap or click the triangle next to the Common Controls category name in the Toolbox and tap or click the Auto Hide button to display the tools.

- **Name the Windows Form Object** In the Solution Explorer window, press and hold or right-click the Form1.vb form file name and select Rename. Type `frmDownloads.vb` and then press the ENTER key.

● **Change the Title on the Title Bar** To change the title on the Windows Form object, tap or click the form, scroll in the Properties window until the Text property is displayed, double-tap or double-click in the right column of the Text property, type Download Music, and then press the ENTER key.

● **Resize the Windows Form Object** Change the Size property of the form to 425,500.

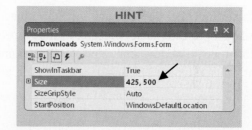

● **Add a PictureBox Object** Add a PictureBox object to the Windows Form object by dragging the PictureBox .NET component onto the Windows Form object. Place the object in the bottom of the Windows Form object.

● **Name the PictureBox Object** With the PictureBox object selected, scroll in the Properties window until the (Name) property is visible. Double-tap or double-click in the right column of the (Name) property, type picMusic, and then press the ENTER key.

● **Resize the PictureBox Object** To resize the picMusic PictureBox object, first select it if necessary. Tap or click to the right of the Size property and change it to 405, 175.

(continues)

● **Add a Heading Label** To insert the Digital Downloads heading label, drag the Label .NET component from the Toolbox to the Windows Form object. Position the Label object as shown in Figure 4-87.

● **Name the Label Object** Name the Label object lblHeading by scrolling to the (Name) property in the Properties window, double-tapping or double-clicking the (Name) property in the right column, typing lblHeading, and then pressing the ENTER key.

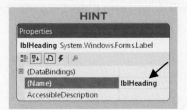

● **Change the Text of the Label Object** To change the text displayed in the Label object, scroll until the Text property is visible, double-tap or double-click in the right column of the Text property, type Digital Downloads, and then press the ENTER key.

● **Change the Heading Font, Font Style, and Size** To make the heading stand out on the Windows form, its font should be larger and more prominent. To change the font to Cooper, its style to Black, and its size to 18, select the Label object and then scroll in the Properties window until the Font property is visible. Tap or click the Font property in the right column, and then tap or click the ellipsis button. In the Font dialog box, scroll if necessary, tap or click Cooper (or a similar font) in the Font list, tap or click Black in the Font style list, and then tap or click 18 in the Size list. Tap or click the OK button in the Font dialog box.

● **Horizontally Center the Label Object** The Label object should be centered horizontally in the form. Tap or click FORMAT on the menu bar, point to Center in Form on the FORMAT menu, and then tap or click Horizontally on the Center in Form submenu.

The PictureBox object and the Label object are placed on the resized Windows Form object (Figure 4-87). The font and font size for the Label object are appropriate for a heading in the window.

RESULT OF STEP I

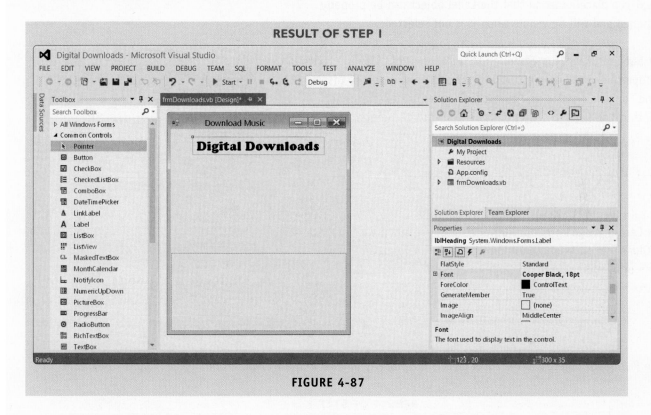

FIGURE 4-87

2

● **Add a Second Heading Label** To add the second heading label required for the window, drag a Label .NET component from the Toolbox to the Windows Form object. Place the second Label object below the lblHeading object.

● **Name the Label Object** Give the name `lblCostHeading` to the Label object you just placed on the Windows Form object.

(continues)

- **Change the Text in the Label Object** Change the text in the lblCostHeading object to `$X.XX per Download`. This text is a placeholder so that the Label object can be properly aligned and will be visible when it is not selected.

- **Set the Font, Font Style, and Size of the Font** Use the Font property and ellipsis button in the Properties window to display the Font dialog box, and then change the font to Century Gothic, the style to Regular, and the size to 12 points.

- **Center-Align the Label Object** Select the label, tap or click FORMAT on the menu bar, point to Center in Form, and then tap or click Horizontally.

The PictureBox object and the Label objects are properly aligned in the Windows Form object (Figure 4-88).

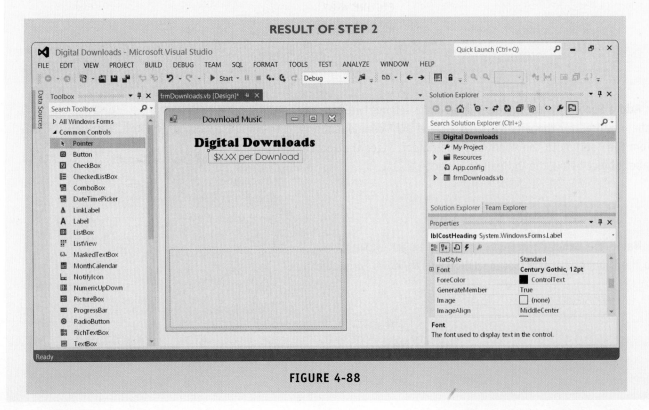

FIGURE 4-88

● **Add a Label for the Number of Song Downloads** Add the Label object for the number of song downloads by dragging it from the Toolbox. Place it below the two other Label objects, and then align the new Label object using the blue snap lines.

HEADS UP

As you work through the development of your program, remember to save the program frequently. To save the program, you can tap or click the Save All button on the Standard toolbar

● **Change the Name, Enter Text, and Change the Font for the Number of Song Downloads Label** Using techniques you have learned previously, change the name of the Label object to lblNumberOfDownloads. In the Text property, enter Number of Downloads:. Using the Font property in the Properties window, change the font to Century Gothic, Regular style, and 11-point size.

● **Add a TextBox Object for the Number of Song Downloads** Drag a TextBox object to the Windows Form object. Name the TextBox object txtNumberOfDownloads *(ref: Figure 4-3)*.

● **Enter Data into the Text Property** As you learned in this chapter, even though the TextBox object will not contain text when the program begins, it still is necessary to enter text in the Text property of the TextBox object to size it properly. To enter text into the TextBox, select the TextBox object. In the Properties window, change the Text property to 888 *(ref: Figure 4-6)*.

● **Change the Font and Size of the TextBox Object** Using the Properties window, change the font for the TextBox object to Century Gothic, Regular style, and 11-point size. Drag the right border of the TextBox object so the numbers fit properly in the text box *(ref: Figure 4-8)*.

(continues)

● **Align the Resized TextBox Object** To realign the resized TextBox object, drag it up until the red snap line indicates the text in the TextBox object is bottom-aligned with the label *(ref: Figure 4-9)*.

● **Center-Align Text in the TextBox Object** To center-align the text in the TextBox object, select the TextBox object, scroll in the Properties window until the TextAlign property is visible, tap or click the list arrow in the right column of the TextAlign property, and then tap or click Center in the TextAlign property list *(ref: Figure 4-10)*.

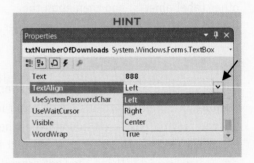

● **Remove Text from the TextBox Object** Because the TextBox object is sized properly, remove the digits from the TextBox object by selecting them in the Text property of the object and then pressing the DELETE key *(ref: Figure 4-12)*.

● **Add the Total Cost of Downloads Label Objects** A label that reports the total cost of the downloads must be displayed as the Text property of a Label object. A second label actually identifies the total cost. Drag two labels onto the Windows Form object and place them on the same horizontal line using the blue snap lines. Vertically align the left side of the left label with the label above it. Vertically align the left side of the right label with the text box above it. Name the Label object on the left lblTotalCostLabel. Name the label on the right lblTotalCost *(ref: Figure 4-18)*.

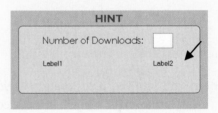

● **Enter Text for the Labels and Change the Font** Select the lblTotalCostLabel Label object and then double-tap or double-click the right column of the Text property for the label. Type the text Total Cost of Downloads: and then press the enter key. Select the lblTotalCost Label object and then double-tap or double-click the right column of the Text property for the label. Enter the value $888.88 to represent the widest expected value for the label. With the right label selected, hold down the ctrl key and then tap or click the left label. With both labels selected, change the font to Century Gothic, Regular style, 11-point size.

● **Add Buttons** Three buttons are required for the user interface: the Calculate Cost button, the Clear button, and the Exit button. Drag three buttons onto the Windows Form object below the labels. Use blue snap lines to horizontally align the tops of the buttons. Using the (Name) property for each button, name the first button btn-Calculate, the second button btnClear, and the third button btnExit.

● **Change the Button Text and the Font Style** Using the Text property for each button, change the text for the btnCalculate Button object to Calculate Cost and the text for the btnClear button to Clear. Change the text for the btnExit button to Exit. Select all three buttons by tapping or clicking the Calculate Cost button, holding down the CTRL key, and then tapping or clicking the other two buttons. Next, tap or click the Font property, tap or click the ellipsis button in the right column of the Font property, and then change the font style to Bold in the Font dialog box.

HINT

● **Change Button Size** The btnCalculate button does not display the entire Text property, so it must be enlarged. Drag the right border of the btnCalculate button until the entire Text property is visible.

● **Change the Size of the Other Buttons** Tap or click the btnCalculate button first, and then hold down the CTRL key and tap or click the other two buttons to select all three buttons. Make these buttons the same size by tapping or clicking FORMAT on the menu bar, pointing to Make Same Size on the FORMAT menu, and tapping or clicking Both on the Make Same Size submenu.

● **Space and Center the Buttons** With all three buttons selected, display the FORMAT menu, point to Horizontal Spacing on the FORMAT menu, and then tap or click Make Equal on the Horizontal Spacing submenu. Display the FORMAT menu, point to Center in Form on the FORMAT menu, and then tap or click Horizontally on the Center in Form submenu to center all three buttons horizontally in the Windows Form object.

(continues)

The mockup for the user interface is complete (Figure 4-89).

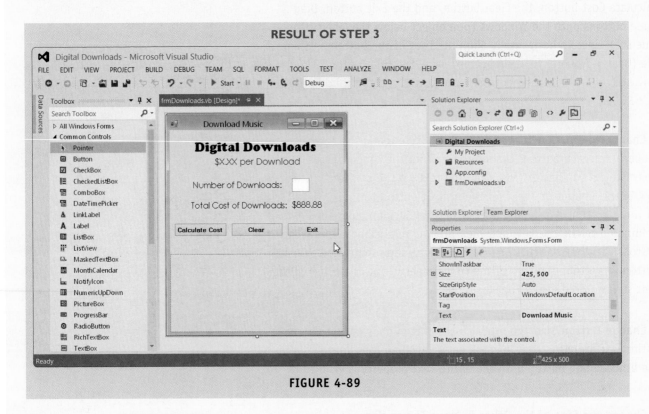

FIGURE 4-89

Phase 2: Fine-Tune the User Interface

4

• **Set the BackColor Property for the Windows Form Object** The user interface must be finished by setting the colors, adding images, and preparing for program execution. To set the BackColor property to White for the user interface, select the Windows Form object. In the Properties window, tap or click the BackColor property, and then tap or click the BackColor arrow in the right column of the BackColor property. If necessary, tap or click the Web tab. Scroll as required and then tap or click White in the BackColor list.

● **Set the ForeColor for the Button Objects and Label Object** To set the ForeColor to Red for the button objects and the first Label object, select all three buttons and the lblHeading object. Tap or click the ForeColor property in the Properties window, and then tap or click the ForeColor arrow in the right column of the ForeColor property. Tap or click the Web tab, if necessary. Scroll as required and then tap or click Red in the ForeColor list.

● **Set the Calculate Cost Button Object as the Accept Button** When the user enters the number of downloads, she should be able to calculate the total cost by tapping or clicking the Calculate Cost button or by pressing the ENTER key. To assign the Calculate Cost button as the Accept button, first select the Windows Form object by tapping or clicking anywhere in the window except on another object. Scroll in the Properties window until the AcceptButton property is visible, tap or click the AcceptButton property, tap or click the AcceptButton property arrow, and then tap or click btnCalculate *(ref: Figure 4-20)*.

● **Set the Clear Button Object as the Cancel Button** By pressing the ESC key, the user should cause the same action as tapping or clicking the Clear button. To set the Clear button as the Cancel button, tap or click the Windows Form object, tap or click the CancelButton property in the Properties window, tap or click the CancelButton arrow, and then tap or click btnClear *(ref: Page 206)*.

● **Insert the Music Image into the picMusic PictureBox Object** The last step to ready the user interface for execution is to insert the image into the PictureBox object. If necessary, download and save the Music image from the Student Companion Site. Then, with the picture box selected, tap or click the ellipsis button for the Image property in the Properties window, tap or click the Import button in the Select Resource dialog box, locate the Music image, and then import the image into the Resource folder. Tap or click the OK button in the Select Resource dialog box.

(continues)

Guided Program Development *continued*

● **Resize the Image** To resize the Music image, change the SizeMode property. With the picMusic PictureBox object selected, tap or click the SizeMode property in the Properties window, tap or click the SizeMode arrow in the right column, and then tap or click StretchImage.

The user interface is complete (Figure 4-90).

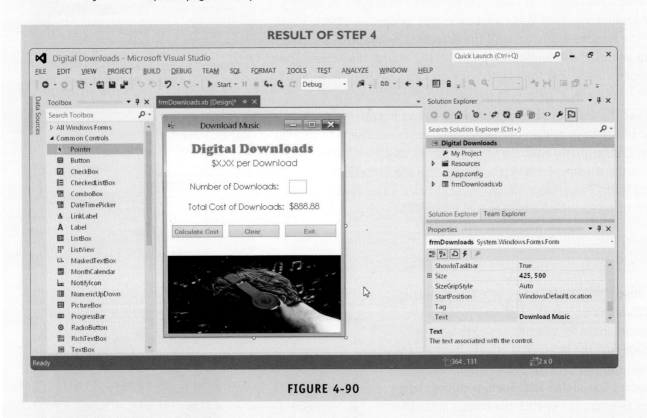

FIGURE 4-90

Phase 3: Code the Application

5

● **Code the Comments** Double-click the btnCalculate Button object on the frmDownloads Windows Form object to open the code window and create the btnCalculate_Click event handler. Tap or click the Close button on the Toolbox title bar to close the Toolbox. Tap or click in front of the first words, Public Class frmDownloads, and press the ENTER key to create a blank line. Press the UP ARROW key and then insert the first four standard comments. Insert the Option Strict On command at the beginning of the code to turn on strict type checking *(ref: Figure 4-53)*.

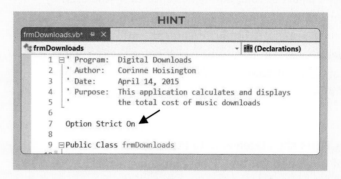

● **Enter the _cdecPricePer Download Class Variable** The next step is to enter the class variable that is referenced in more than one event handler in this program. This variable contains the price per download and is referenced in the heading and to calculate the total cost. To enter this variable, press the DOWN ARROW key until the insertion point is on the blank line following the Public Class command (line 10). Press the ENTER key to add a blank line, and then type the comment that identifies the variable. Press the ENTER key and then write the declaration for the _cdecPrice-PerDownload variable. The constant Decimal variable should contain the value 0.99. The underline character (_) in the name indicates a class variable that is referenced in multiple procedures within the class *(ref: Figure 4-47)*.

● **Comment the btnCalculate Tap or Click Event Handler** Following the Private statement for the btnCalculate_Click event handler, enter a comment to describe the purpose of the btnCalculate_Click event.

(continues)

Guided Program Development *continued*

- **Declare and Initialize the Variables** This event handler requires three variables: 1) strNumberOfSongs, which holds the number of song downloads entered by the user; 2) intNumberOfSongs, which holds the integer value for the number of song downloads entered by the user; and 3) decTotalCostOfDownloads, which holds the calculated total cost of downloads. Declare these three variables (ref: Figure 4-22, Figure 4-35, Figure 4-37).

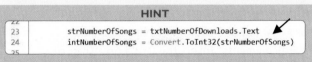

```
      HINT
19    Dim strNumberOfSongs As String
20    Dim intNumberOfSongs As Integer
21    Dim decTotalCostOfDownloads As Decimal
```

- **Write the Statements to Place the Number of Downloads in a Variable and Convert the Value to an Integer** The first steps in the event handler are to move the number of songs value from the Text property of the txtNumberOfDownloads TextBox object to a String variable and then convert that value to an Integer value. Using IntelliSense, write the code to complete these steps (ref: Figure 4-29, Figure 4-52).

```
                          HINT
22
23    strNumberOfSongs = txtNumberOfDownloads.Text
24    intNumberOfSongs = Convert.ToInt32(strNumberOfSongs)
25
```

- **Calculate the Total Cost of Downloads** To calculate the total cost of downloads and place the result in the decTotalCostOfDownloads variable, the number of songs is multiplied by the price per download. Using IntelliSense, write the statement to perform this calculation (ref: Figure 4-55).

```
                                HINT
25    decTotalCostOfDownloads = intNumberOfSongs * _cdecPricePerDownload
```

- **Convert the Decimal Total Cost of Downloads to a String Currency Value and Place It in the Text Property of the lblTotalCost Label Object** After

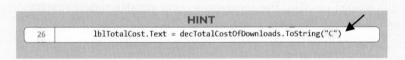

```
                          HINT
26    lblTotalCost.Text = decTotalCostOfDownloads.ToString("C")
```

calculating the total cost of downloads, the result must be converted from a Decimal value to a currency String value so it can be displayed as the value in the Text property of a Label object. Write the statement to perform this conversion and place the converted value in the Text property of the lblTotalCost Label object

The coding for the btnCalculate_Click event handler is complete (Figure 4-91).

```
RESULT OF STEP 5

14  ⊟    Private Sub btnCalculate_Click(ByVal sender As System.Object, ByVal e As System.Even
15           ' This event handler is executed when the user clicks the
16           ' Calculate button. It calculates and displays the cost
17           ' of music downloads (number of downloads times the cost per download).
18
19           Dim strNumberOfSongs As String
20           Dim intNumberOfSongs As Integer
21           Dim decTotalCostOfDownloads As Decimal
22
23           strNumberOfSongs = txtNumberOfDownloads.Text
24           intNumberOfSongs = Convert.ToInt32(strNumberOfSongs)
25           decTotalCostOfDownloads = intNumberOfSongs * _cdecPricePerDownload
26           lblTotalCost.Text = decTotalCostOfDownloads.ToString("C")
27
28       End Sub
```

FIGURE 4-91

6

• **Run the Application** After you have entered code, you should
run the application to ensure it is working properly. Run the Digital
Downloads application by tapping or clicking the Start Debugging
button on the Standard toolbar. Enter 10 for the number of song
downloads and then tap or click the Calculate Cost button. The Total
Cost of Downloads should be $9.90. Enter 15 for the number of song
downloads and then press the ENTER key.

When the number of downloads is 10 songs,
the total cost of the downloads is $9.90
(Figure 4-92).

RESULT OF STEP 6

FIGURE 4-92

(continues)

• Write the Code for the Clear Button Event Handler

Tap or click the frmDownloads.vb [Design] tab in the code window to return to the design window. Double-tap or double-click the Clear button to create the event handler for the Clear button. The Clear button event handler must accomplish the following tasks: Clear the txtNumberOfDownloads text box; clear the value in the Text property of the lblTotalCost Label object; and set the focus to the txtNumberOfDownloads text box. Write the comments for the event handler and then use IntelliSense to write the code for the event handler *(ref: Figure 4-74, Figure 4-75, Figure 4-77)*.

```
HINT
30   Private Sub btnClear_Click(ByVal sender As System.Object, ByVal e As System.EventArgs
31       ' This event handler is executed when the user clicks the
32       ' Clear button. It clears the number of songs text box
33       ' and the Text property of the Total Cost of Downloads label.
34       ' Then, it sets the focus on the txtNumberOfDownloads Textbox object.
35
36       txtNumberOfDownloads.Clear()
37       lblTotalCost.Text = ""
38       txtNumberOfDownloads.Focus()
39
40   End Sub
```

• Write the Code for the Form Load Event Handler

Tap or click the frmDownloads.vb [Design] tab in the code window to return to the design window. Double-tap or double-click the Windows Form object to create the event handler for the Form Load event. The Form Load event handler must accomplish the following tasks: Using concatenation, create and display the Price per Download heading in the Text property of the lblCostHeading Label object; clear the Text property of the lblTotalCost Label object; and set the focus to the txtNumberOfDownloads TextBox object. Write the comments for the event handler and then use IntelliSense to write the code for the event handler *(ref: Figure 4-75, Figure 4-77, Figure 4-80)*.

```
HINT
41
42   Private Sub frmDigitalDownloads_Load(ByVal sender As System.Object, ByVal e As System
43       ' This event handler is executed when the form is loaded.
44       ' It displays the cost heading, clears the Text property of the
45       ' Total Cost of Downloads label, and sets the focus on
46       ' the txtNumberOfSongs Textbox object.
47
48       lblCostHeading.Text = _cdecPricePerDownload.ToString("C") & " Per Download"
49       lblTotalCost.Text = ""
50       txtNumberOfDownloads.Focus()
51
52   End Sub
```

• Write the Code for the Exit Button Event Handler

Tap or click the frmDownloads.vb [Design] tab in the code window to return to the design window. Double-tap or double-click the Exit button to create its event handler. The Exit button event handler must close the window and terminate the application. Write the comments and code for this event handler.

```
HINT
54   Private Sub btnExit_Click(ByVal sender As System.Object, ByVal e As System.EventArgs)
55       ' Close the window and terminate the application
56
57       Close()
58
59   End Sub
60   End Class
```

The coding is complete for the Clear button event handler, the Form load event handler, and the Exit button event handler (Figure 4-93).

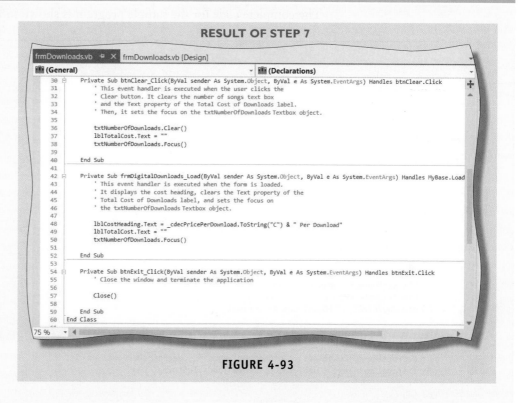

RESULT OF STEP 7

```
      frmDownloads.vb  ⊟ ✕  frmDownloads.vb [Design]
      ▦ (General)                                      ▼  ▦ (Declarations)                                      ▼
 30 ⊟       Private Sub btnClear_Click(ByVal sender As System.Object, ByVal e As System.EventArgs) Handles btnClear.Click
 31               ' This event handler is executed when the user clicks the
 32               ' Clear button. It clears the number of songs text box
 33               ' and the Text property of the Total Cost of Downloads label.
 34               ' Then, it sets the focus on the txtNumberOfDownloads Textbox object.
 35
 36               txtNumberOfDownloads.Clear()
 37               lblTotalCost.Text = ""
 38               txtNumberOfDownloads.Focus()
 39
 40           End Sub
 41
 42 ⊟       Private Sub frmDigitalDownloads_Load(ByVal sender As System.Object, ByVal e As System.EventArgs) Handles MyBase.Load
 43               ' This event handler is executed when the form is loaded.
 44               ' It displays the cost heading, clears the Text property of the
 45               ' Total Cost of Downloads label, and sets the focus on
 46               ' the txtNumberOfDownloads Textbox object.
 47
 48               lblCostHeading.Text = _cdecPricePerDownload.ToString("C") & " Per Download"
 49               lblTotalCost.Text = ""
 50               txtNumberOfDownloads.Focus()
 51
 52           End Sub
 53
 54 ⊟       Private Sub btnExit_Click(ByVal sender As System.Object, ByVal e As System.EventArgs) Handles btnExit.Click
 55               ' Close the window and terminate the application
 56
 57               Close()
 58
 59           End Sub
 60     End Class
      75 %  ▾  ◀
```

FIGURE 4-93

8

● **Test the Program** After finishing the coding, you should test the program to ensure it works properly. Run the Digital Downloads application by tapping or clicking the Start Debugging button on the Standard toolbar. Enter 20 for the number of song downloads and then tap or click the Calculate Cost button. The Total Cost of Downloads should be $19.80. Tap or click the Clear button to clear the text box and the label that contains the total cost of downloads. Enter 5 for the number of song downloads and then press the ENTER key on the keyboard. The Total Cost of Downloads should be $4.95. Press the ESC key to clear the text box and the label that contains the total cost of downloads. Enter other values to test the program completely.

The program runs properly (Figure 4-94).

RESULT OF STEP 8

FIGURE 4-94

(continues)

Code Listing

The complete code for the sample program is shown in Figure 4-95.

```vb
1  ' Program:  Digital Downloads
2  ' Author:   Corinne Hoisington
3  ' Date:     April 14, 2015
4  ' Purpose:  This application calculates and displays
5  '           the total cost of music downloads
6
7  Option Strict On
8
9  Public Class frmDownloads
10
11     ' Cost per download - used in multiple procedures
12     Const _cdecPricePerDownload As Decimal = 0.99D
13
14     Private Sub btnCalculate_Click(ByVal sender As System.Object, ByVal e As System.EventArgs) Handles btnCalculate.Click
15        ' This event handler is executed when the user clicks the
16        ' Calculate button. It calculates and displays the cost
17        ' of music downloads (number of downloads times the cost per download).
18
19        Dim strNumberOfSongs As String
20        Dim intNumberOfSongs As Integer
21        Dim decTotalCostOfDownloads As Decimal
22
23        strNumberOfSongs = txtNumberOfDownloads.Text
24        intNumberOfSongs = Convert.ToInt32(strNumberOfSongs)
25        decTotalCostOfDownloads = intNumberOfSongs * _cdecPricePerDownload
26        lblTotalCost.Text = decTotalCostOfDownloads.ToString("C")
27
28     End Sub
29
30     Private Sub btnClear_Click(ByVal sender As System.Object, ByVal e As System.EventArgs) Handles btnClear.Click
31        ' This event handler is executed when the user clicks the
32        ' Clear button. It clears the number of songs text box
33        ' and the Text property of the Total Cost of Downloads label.
34        ' Then, it sets the focus on the txtNumberOfDownloads Textbox object.
35
36        txtNumberOfDownloads.Clear()
37        lblTotalCost.Text = ""
38        txtNumberOfDownloads.Focus()
39
40     End Sub
41
42     Private Sub frmDigitalDownloads_Load(ByVal sender As System.Object, ByVal e As System.EventArgs) Handles MyBase.Load
43        ' This event handler is executed when the form is loaded.
44        ' It displays the cost heading, clears the Text property of the
45        ' Total Cost of Downloads label, and sets the focus on
46        ' the txtNumberOfDownloads Textbox object.
47
48        lblCostHeading.Text = _cdecPricePerDownload.ToString("C") & " Per Download"
49        lblTotalCost.Text = ""
50        txtNumberOfDownloads.Focus()
51
52     End Sub
53
54     Private Sub btnExit_Click(ByVal sender As System.Object, ByVal e As System.EventArgs) Handles btnExit.Click
55        ' Close the window and terminate the application
56
57        Close()
58
59     End Sub
60  End Class
61
```

FIGURE 4-95

Summary

In this chapter you have learned to declare variables and write arithmetic operations. The items listed in the table in Figure 4-96 include all the new Visual Studio and Visual Basic skills you have learned in this chapter.

Visual Basic Skills		
Skill	**Figure Number**	**Video Number**
Place a TextBox Object on the Windows Form Object	Figure 4-3	Video 4-2
Size and Position a TextBox Object	Figure 4-6	Video 4-3
Align Text in a TextBox Object	Figure 4-10	Video 4-4
Create a MultiLine TextBox Object	Figure 4-13	Video 4-5
Create a Masked TextBox Object	Figure 4-14	Video 4-6
Place a Masked TextBox Object on the Windows Form Object	Figure 4-15	Video 4-7
Place and Size a Label Object on the Windows Form Object	Figure 4-18	Video 4-8
Assign a Button Object as the Accept Button	Figure 4-20	Video 4-9
Assign a Button Object as the Cancel Button	Page 206	
Close the Toolbox	Figure 4-21	Video 4-10
Define a String Variable	Figure 4-22	
Write an Assignment Statement	Figure 4-24	
Use IntelliSense to Enter a Variable and an Assignment Statement	Figure 4-25	Video 4-11
Declare an Integer Data Type	Figure 4-35	
Declare a Decimal Data Type	Figure 4-37	
Declare a Char Data Type	Figure 4-40	
Declare a Boolean Data Type	Figure 4-42	
Declare a Constant	Figure 4-47	
Use an Argument in a Procedure Call Statement	Figure 4-49	
Write a Procedure Call Statement for the ToInt32 Procedure in the Convert Class	Figure 4-52	
Enter the Option Strict On Statement	Figure 4-53	
Perform Arithmetic Operations Using Arithmetic Operators	Figure 4-56	
Display Numeric Output Data	Figure 4-70	
Write a Procedure Call for the Clear Procedure	Figure 4-74	
Write a Procedure Call for the Focus Procedure	Figure 4-76	
Write a String Concatenation Statement	Figure 4-80	
Write a Variable with Class Scope	Figure 4-82	
Understand a Format Exception	Figure 4-83	

FIGURE 4-96

Learn Online

Reinforcement activities and resources are available at no additional cost on www.cengagebrain.com. Visit www.cengage.com/ct/studentdownload for detailed instructions about accessing the resources available at the Student Companion Site.

Knowledge Check

1. Name three numeric data types that can contain a decimal point.

2. Write a Dim statement for each of the following variables using the variable type and variable name that would be best for each value.

   a. The population of the state of Alaska

   b. Your weekly pay

   c. The smallest data type you can use for your age

   d. A constant for the first initial of your first name

   e. The minimum wage

   f. The name of the city where you live

   g. The answer to a true/false question

3. Determine whether each of the following variable names is valid or invalid. Explain the error in each invalid variable name.

   a. _intRadian

   b. PercentOfSales#

   c. first_Input_Value

   d. R743-L56

   e. 3CPO

   f. Close

   g. Name Of Client

4. List the steps that specify how you would perfectly align a group of TextBox objects along their left edges.

5. Which data type is best for currency amounts?

6. Explain the hierarchy in for the order of operations.

(continues)

7. What is the solution to each of the following arithmetic expressions?

   a. 3 + 4 * 2 + 6

   b. 16 / 2 * 4 − 3

   c. 40 − 6 ^ 2 / 3

   d. 68 Mod 9

   e. 9 \ 4 + 3

   f. 2 ^ 3 + (8 − 5)

   g. (15 Mod 2) − 1 + 4 * (16 \ 5)

8. What is the difference between a method and a procedure?

9. What is the difference between a variable and a literal?

10. Correct the following statements:

    a. `Dim itAge As Integr`

    b. `Dim dblDiscountRate As Dbl`

    c. `Constant cstrCollege As String = "CVCC"`

    d. `Dim strLastName As String`

    e. `strLastName = 'McNamara'`

    f. `1.5 * decHourlyPay = decOverTimePayRate`

11. Write a statement that sets the focus on the txtLastName TextBox object.

12. Write a statement that removes the contents of the txtAge TextBox object.

13. Write a statement that blanks the Text property of the lblEligibilityAge Label object.

14. Write a statement to convert the value in the String variable strWaistSize to an integer value and place the integer value in a variable named intWaistSize.

15. Write a statement to convert the value in the String variable strHourlyPay to a Decimal value and place the Decimal value in a variable named decWage.

16. Write a statement to close a form that currently is open.

17. Write a statement that declares a constant named decInsuranceDeductible as a Decimal data type and set its value to 379.25.

18. Which Windows Form property allows the user to press the enter key while the form is active and activate a button's event handler?

19. What is a local variable? How does its scope differ from that of a global variable?

20. When the following statements are executed, what would be displayed in the lblHourlyWage Label object?

```
decHourlyWage = 12.637
lblHourlyWage.Text = decHourlyWage.ToString("C")
```

Debugging Exercises

1. Fix the following code:

```
Option Strict On
Dim intDistance As Integer

intDistance = 17.5
```

2. Fix the following code:

```
Dim dblRegularPay As Double
Dim dblOvertimePay As Double

intRegularPay = 783.87
intOvertimePay = 105.92
lbl.TotalPay = (dblRegularPay + dblOvertimePay).ToString('C')
```

3. Analyze the code in Figure 4-97 and then correct it.

```
 1  Public Class Form1
 2
 3      Private Sub btnHeight_Click(sender As Object, e As EventArgs) Handles b
 4          Dim intFeet As Integer
 5          Dim strInches As String
 6          Dim intInches As Integer
 7
 8          intInches = Convert.ToInt32(strInches)
 9          intFeet = intInches / 12
10          lblFeet.Text = intFeet.ToString("P")
11
12      End Sub
13  End Class
14
```

FIGURE 4-97

Program Analysis

1. What will occur when the user taps or clicks the btnSlope Button in the following code?

```
Private Sub btnSlope_Click(ByVal sender As System.Object, ByVal e As System.
EventArgs) Handles btnSlope.Click
  Dim decRise As Decimal
  Dim decRun As Decimal
  Dim decSlope As Decimal
  decRise = 12.3D
  decRun = 2.1D
  decSlope = decRise / decRun
  lblSlope.Text = "The Line Slope is " & decSlope.ToString("F3")
End Sub
```

(continues)

Program Analysis *continued*

2. How would the number .0256 be displayed if the format specifier ("P") is used in a Convert.ToString statement?

3. How would the number 3746.35555 be displayed if the format specifier ("F3") is used in a Convert.ToString statement?

4. If you want the user to enter her telephone number with the area code, which .NET component would be best to use on the Windows Form object?

5. Using the format specifier with the ToString procedure, write the statement that would display:

   a. The value in the decDvdCost variable with a dollar sign and two places to the right of the decimal point in a label named lblDvd

   b. The value in the decWithholdingTaxRate variable with a percent sign and one place to the right of the decimal point in a label named lblWithholdingTaxRate

   c. The value in the decOilRevenue variable with commas as needed, two places to the right of the decimal point, and no dollar sign in a label called lblOilRevenue

6. Write a single line of code to declare a variable decWindSpeed as a Decimal data type and assign it the value 25.47. Use a forced literal to ensure that the compiler views this number as a Decimal data type.

7. What would the values of these variables be at the end of the code that follows?

   a. intParts

   b. intBoxes

   c. intLeftovers

```
Dim intParts As Integer
Dim intBoxes As Integer
Dim intLeftovers As Integer

intParts = 77
intPartsPerBox = 9

intBoxes = intParts \ intPartsPerBox
intLeftovers = intParts Mod intBoxes
```

8. Are the following statements written correctly? If not, how should they be written?

```
Dim dblPay as Double
lblPay.Text = dblPay.ToString("C2")
```

9. For a Button object named btnCalories, write the tap or click event handler to implement the following requirements and calculate the number of calories burned during a run:

   a. Declare variables named strMilesRan, decCaloriesConsumed, and decMilesRan.

   b. Declare a constant named cdecCaloriesBurnedPerHour and assign it the value 700. (Assume you burn 700 calories for every mile you run.)

   c. Allow the user to enter the number of miles she ran today.

   d. Convert the number of miles to a Decimal data type.

   e. Calculate the number of calories the user burned during her run.

   f. Display the result rounded to zero decimal places in a label named lblCaloriesBurned.

10. What would the output be when the user taps or clicks the btnDrivingAge Button?

```
Private Sub btnDrivingAge_Click(ByVal sender As System.Object, ByVal e As
System.EventArgs) Handles btnDrivingAge.Click
   Dim intPresentAge As Integer
   Const cintDrivingAge As Integer = 16
   Dim intYearsToDrive As Integer

   intPresentAge = 13
   intYearsToDrive = cintDrivingAge - intPresentAge
   lblYearsLeft.Text = intYearsToDrive.ToString() & " year(s) until you can
drive."
End Sub
```

Case Programming Assignments

Complete one or more of the following case programming assignments. Submit the program and materials you create to your instructor. The level of difficulty is indicated for each case programming assignment.

●	= Easiest
●●	= Intermediate
●●●	= Challenging

1 ●
STATE FAIR TICKETS

Design a Windows application and write the code that will execute according to the program requirements in Figure 4-98 and the Use Case Definition in Figure 4-99. Before writing the code, create an event planning document for each event in the program. The completed program is shown in Figure 4-100.

REQUIREMENTS DOCUMENT

Date Submitted: January 31, 2015

Application Title: State Fair Tickets Application

Purpose: This Windows application allows a user to purchase tickets for a full day at your state or regional fair.

Program Procedures: From a window on the screen, the user chooses the number of tickets needed for a group; the total cost of the tickets is displayed.

Algorithms, Processing, and Conditions:
1. The user must be able to enter the number of State Fair tickets.
2. A picture of women at the fair will be displayed throughout the entire process.
3. After entering the number of tickets needed, the user taps or clicks the Display Cost button.
4. Tickets cost $12.99 each; the total cost will be displayed in currency format.

Notes and Restrictions:
1. The user can use a Clear button to clear the number of tickets entered and the total cost and then enter another number of tickets.
2. An Exit button should close the application.
3. The cost per ticket can vary, so the program should allow a different price to be placed in any headings and be used in any calculations.

Comments: The picture is named Fair and is available on CengageBrain.com.

© 2014 Cengage Learning

FIGURE 4-98

(continues)

Case Programming Assignments

State fair tickets (continued)

USE CASE DEFINITION

1. The Windows application opens.
2. The user enters the number of State Fair tickets needed.
3. The user taps or clicks the Display Cost button.
4. The program displays the total cost of the State Fair tickets.
5. The user can tap or click the Clear button and repeat Steps 2 through 4.
6. The user terminates the program by tapping or clicking the Exit button.

FIGURE 4-99

FIGURE 4-100

Case Programming Assignments

2 TAXI FARE

Design a Windows application and write the code that will execute according to the program requirements in Figure 4-101 and the Use Case Definition in Figure 4-102. Before writing the code, create an event planning document for each event in the program. The completed program is shown in Figure 4-103.

REQUIREMENTS DOCUMENT

Date Submitted:	February 19, 2015
Application Title:	Taxi Fare Application
Purpose:	This Windows application computes the cost of a taxi fare.
Program Procedures:	From a window on the screen, the user enters the number of miles traveled in the taxi during one fare. The program calculates and displays the cost of the total fare.
Algorithms, Processing, and Conditions:	1. The user must be able to enter the number of miles traveled in a taxi cab for one fare.
	2. The title of the program and a taxi logo will be displayed throughout the entire process.
	3. After entering the number of miles traveled, the user taps or clicks the Display Fare button.
	4. The formula for calculating the fare is: Flat fee ($2.25) + (number of miles * $2.75 per mile).
	5. The program displays the fare in currency format.
Notes and Restrictions:	1. The user can clear the number of miles and make another entry.
	2. An Exit button should close the application.
Comments:	The taxi logo is named Taxi and is available on CengageBrain.com.

FIGURE 4-101

(continues)

Case Programming Assignments

Taxi Fare (continued)

USE CASE DEFINITION

1. The Windows application opens.
2. The user enters the number of miles traveled.
3. The user taps or clicks the Display Fare button.
4. The program displays the total fare.
5. The user can tap or click the Clear button and repeat Steps 2 through 4.
6. The user terminates the program by tapping or clicking the Exit button.

FIGURE 4-102

© 2014 Cengage Learning

FIGURE 4-103

© Rouzes/E+/Getty Images

Case Programming Assignments

3 DOG YEARS

Design a Windows application and write the code that will execute according to the program requirements in Figure 4-104 and the Use Case Definition in Figure 4-105. Before writing the code, create an event planning document for each event in the program. The completed program is shown in Figure 4-106.

REQUIREMENTS DOCUMENT

Date Submitted: October 20, 2015

Application Title: Dog Years Application

Purpose: This Windows application calculates the age of a dog in human years.

Program Procedures: From a window on the screen, a dog owner enters a dog's age. The program displays the age of the dog and the comparison in human years.

Algorithms, Processing, and Conditions:
1. The dog owner must be able to enter the dog's age.
2. A picture of a dog will be displayed throughout the entire process.
3. After entering the dog's age, the dog owner taps or clicks the Compute button.
4. The dog's age in human years is displayed with the dog's age.

Notes and Restrictions:
1. The user can clear the dog's age by tapping or clicking a Clear button. The dog owner then can enter another dog's age.
2. An Exit button should close the application.

Comments: The dog picture is named Dog and is available on CengageBrain.com.

FIGURE 4-104

© 2014 Cengage Learning

(continues)

Case Programming Assignments

Dog Years (continued)

USE CASE DEFINITION

1. The Windows application opens.
2. The dog owner enters the dog's age.
3. The dog owner taps or clicks the Compute button.
4. The program displays the dog's age and a computation of the age in human years.
5. The dog owner can tap or click the Clear button and then repeat Steps 2 through 4.
6. The user terminates the program by tapping or clicking the Exit button.

FIGURE 4-105

© 2014 Cengage Learning

FIGURE 4-106

Photo courtesy of Corinne Hoisington

Case Programming Assignments

4 ●● SALES TAX CALCULATOR

Design a Windows application and write the code that will execute according to the program requirements in Figure 4-107. Before designing the user interface, create a Use Case Definition. Before writing the code, create an event planning document for each event in the program.

REQUIREMENTS DOCUMENT

Date Submitted: June 6, 2014

Application Title: Sales Tax Calculator Application

Purpose: This Windows application will compute the tax and final cost of a purchased item.

Program Procedures: From a window on the screen, the user enters the item name and cost of the item purchased. The program calculates the tax for the item and the final total, and then displays these values.

Algorithms, Processing, and Conditions:
1. The user must be able to enter the name of the item purchased and the cost of the item before tax.
2. A store name and store picture will be displayed throughout the entire process.
3. After the user enters the item name and the cost of the item, the user taps or clicks the Display Cost button.
4. The program displays the item name with the cost, tax, and final total.
5. The cost, tax, and final total should appear in currency format.
6. The tax rate for all items is 8.75%.
7. The final total is calculated by adding the cost and the tax.

Notes and Restrictions:
1. The user can clear the item name, cost, tax, and final total with a Clear button.
2. The user can tap or click an Exit button to close the application.

Comments: The store picture shown in the window should be selected from pictures available on the Web.

FIGURE 4-107

5 ●● INCOME TAX CALCULATOR

Design a Windows application and write the code that will execute according to the program requirements in Figure 4-108. Before designing the user interface, create a Use Case Definition. Before writing the code, create an event planning document for each event in the program.

REQUIREMENTS DOCUMENT

Date Submitted:	January 4, 2015
Application Title:	Income Tax Calculator Application
Purpose:	This Windows application will compute and display the FICA tax, federal tax, and state tax for one year based on your income.
Program Procedures:	From a window on the screen, the user enters her yearly income. The program estimates the FICA tax, federal tax, and state tax for one year based on the user's income.
Algorithms, Processing, and Conditions:	1. Users must be able to enter their annual income. 2. The FICA tax (7.65%), federal tax (22%), and state income tax (3%) are computed. 3. The tax amounts should be displayed on separate lines and in currency format, two places past the decimal point. 4. The net pay should be displayed after the tax amounts have been deducted.
Notes and Restrictions:	1. The user can clear the income and taxes and then enter new data. 2. The user can use an Exit button to close the application.
Comments:	The designer should design the user interface, including all graphics and words displayed.

FIGURE 4-108

6 ●●
CONVERT CURRENCY

Design a Windows application and write the code that will execute according to the program requirements in Figure 4-109. Before designing the user interface, create a Use Case Definition. Before writing the code, create an event planning document for each event in the program.

REQUIREMENTS DOCUMENT

Date Submitted:	November 4, 2014
Application Title:	Convert Currency Application
Purpose:	This Windows application will display the value of U.S. dollars in euros, Canadian dollars, and Mexican pesos.
Program Procedures:	From a window on the screen, the user should enter the number of U.S. dollars to be converted. The program will display the equivalent value in euros, Canadian dollars, and Mexican pesos.
Algorithms, Processing, and Conditions:	1. The user must be able to enter the number of U.S. dollars to be converted. 2. After entering a number of U.S. dollars, the user taps or clicks the Convert Currency button. 3. The program converts the number of U.S. dollars entered into the equivalent number of euros, Canadian dollars, and Mexican pesos. The program displays all three currency amounts with the amount in U.S. dollars. 4. To find the conversion rates, the developer must consult appropriate Web sites. A possible site is *www.xe.com*. 5. Because currency rates change dynamically, the user should enter the date and time that the conversion rates were applied. The date and time should be displayed in U.S. format. 6. The user should be able to clear the date and time, the number of U.S. dollars entered, and the results of the calculations, and then enter new values.
Notes and Restrictions:	The user should be able to tap or click an Exit button to close the application.
Comments:	The designer must determine the design of the user interface and the words and graphics used in it.

FIGURE 4-109

7 ●●●
MULCH CALCULATOR

Create a requirements document and a Use Case Definition document and then design a Windows application based on the case project shown in Figure 4-110. Before writing the code, create an event planning document for each event in the program.

A local landscaping design business requests a Windows application that allows you to compute how much rubber mulch you need to fill a playground. The rubber mulch is designed for safety and costs $9.87 per cubic foot. In addition, the mulch supplier charges a one-time delivery fee of $25. The Windows application should request the playground's length, width, and average depth (for example, 0.25 of a foot equals a mulch depth of 3 inches). The program then determines the volume of the playground in cubic feet (volume = length * width * depth) and displays the final cost of landscaping the playground, including the delivery fee. Allow the user to enter values with decimal places. The user should be able to clear all entries and then reenter data. To close the program, the user should be able to tap or click a button.

FIGURE 4-110

8 ●●●
HOT TUB AREA AND CIRCUMFERENCE

Create a requirements document and a Use Case Definition document and then design a Windows application based on the case project shown in Figure 4-111. Before writing the code, create an event planning document for each event in the program.

You are interested in purchasing a hot tub. The listings on the Internet describe hot tubs that have a perfectly round shape. Each ad states the diameter of the hot tub. Create a Windows application that computes the area and circumference of a hot tub after the user enters the diameter in feet and inches (for example, 8 feet and 4 inches). The area and circumference results should display two decimal places. You should be able to clear the entry, enter a new diameter, and exit the form.

FIGURE 4-111

Case Programming Assignments

9 ●●● EXERCISE FOR A LIFETIME

Create a requirements document and a Use Case Definition document and then design a Windows application based on the case project shown in Figure 4-112. Before writing the code, create an event planning document for each event in the program.

The YMCA has asked you to write a Windows application that its members can use to determine the total number of hours they have exercised during their lifetimes, assuming they exercise an average of 3 hours per week. All users should enter their first name, their birth date, and the current date. For both dates, ask for the month, day, and year separately in numeric form. To calculate the number of hours exercised, assume 365 days per year and 30 days per month. The program must display the user's name and the number of hours the user has exercised in his or her lifetime. The user can tap or click a Clear button to clear all entries and results. An Exit button must be available to close the application.

FIGURE 4-112

CHAPTER 5
Decision Structures

OBJECTIVES

You will have mastered the material in this chapter when you can:

- Use the GroupBox object

- Place RadioButton objects in applications

- Display a message box

- Make decisions using If . . . Then statements

- Make decisions using If . . . Then . . . Else statements

- Make decisions using nested If statements

- Make decisions using logical operators

- Make decisions using Case statements

- Insert code snippets

- Test input to ensure a value is numeric

Introduction

Developers can code Visual Basic applications to make decisions based on the input of users or other conditions that occur. Decision making is one of the fundamental activities of a computer program. In this chapter, you will learn to write decision-making statements in Visual Basic 2012.

Visual Basic allows you to test conditions and perform different operations depending on the results. You can test whether a condition is true or false and change the flow of what happens in a program based on the user's input.

The sample program in this chapter is called the Wood Cabinet Estimate application. It is written for a carpenter or cabinetmaker who wants a program on the job site that can estimate the amount of wood needed for a job and the cost of building wood cabinets.

The application asks the user to enter the number of linear feet of cabinetry required and the desired wood type. The application then computes the cost of the cabinets based on a rate of $300.00 per linear foot for pine, $500.00 per linear foot for oak, and $650.00 per linear foot for cherry. Figure 5-1 shows the user interface for the application.

linear feet of cabinets

type of wood for cabinets

cost estimate to build cabinets

FIGURE 5-1

© Ivan Hunter/Digital Vision/Getty Images

In Figure 5-1, the Wood Cabinet Estimate Windows application displays the text "Wood Cabinet Estimate" in the title bar. The linear footage that the user enters in the TextBox object includes all cabinets for the job. The user chooses the wood type by selecting a RadioButton from the following list: Pine (the most common choice), Oak, or Cherry. After the user enters the number of linear feet of cabinetry and selects a type of wood, the user taps or clicks the Calculate button to obtain the cost estimate. The calculation is the linear feet multiplied by the cost of the selected wood. The cost estimate is displayed in currency format. In the example in Figure 5-1, the user entered 12 linear feet of cabinetry and selected cherry wood. After the user tapped or clicked the Calculate button, the application displayed a cost of \$7,800.00 (12 × \$650.00).

Tapping or clicking the Clear button clears the linear footage, resets the RadioButton selection to Pine, which is the most common wood type, and clears the calculation result.

Checking the validity of data the user entered is a requirement of the sample program in this chapter. In Chapter 4, you learned that if you enter nonnumeric data and attempt to use it in a calculation, the program will be terminated. To check for invalid data, the Wood Cabinet Estimate application ensures that the user enters a numeric value greater than zero in the Linear Feet TextBox object. A warning appears if the user leaves the TextBox blank or does not enter a valid number. Figure 5-2 displays the Input Error dialog box, called a Message Box, which directs the user to enter the linear feet for the cabinets.

FIGURE 5-2
© Ivan Hunter/Digital Vision/Getty Images

Checking input data for validity is an important task in Visual Basic programs. You will learn several data validation techniques in this chapter.

User Interface Design

The user interface for the Wood Cabinet Estimate application includes three new objects: a GroupBox, RadioButtons, and Message Boxes. The Message Boxes appear when the user enters a negative number or a nonnumeric value.

Use the GroupBox Object

The Wood Cabinet Estimate Form object requires a GroupBox object and RadioButton objects (Figure 5-3).

RadioButton objects

GroupBox object

FIGURE 5-3
© Ivan Hunter/Digital Vision/Getty Images

A **GroupBox** object associates items as a group, allowing the user to select one item from the group. It also includes caption text. RadioButton objects allow the user to make choices. In Figure 5-3, the GroupBox object groups the radio buttons for selecting the wood type. When RadioButton objects are contained in a group box, the user can select only one radio button. For example, in Figure 5-3 the Pine radio button is selected. If the user taps or clicks the Oak radio button, it will be selected and the Pine radio button automatically will be deselected.

The GroupBox object shown in Figure 5-3 is displayed with the Text property of Wood Type as the caption text. The prefix for the GroupBox object (Name) property is grp. To place a GroupBox object on the Form object, you can complete the following steps:

STEP 1   Drag the GroupBox object from the Containers category of the Toolbox to the approximate location where you want to place the GroupBox object on the Form object.

The pointer changes when you place it over the Form object (Figure 5-4). The GroupBox object will be placed on the form at the location of the outline in the pointer.

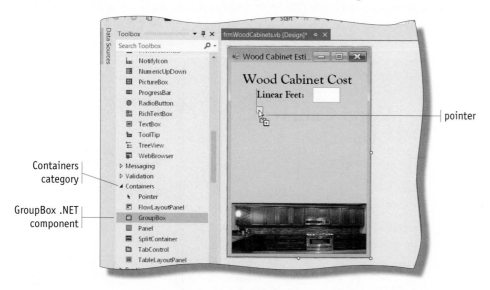

FIGURE 5-4

© Ivan Hunter/Digital Vision/Getty Images

STEP 2   When the pointer is in the correct location, release the object. With the GroupBox object selected, scroll in the Properties window to the (Name) property. Double-tap or double-click in the right column of the (Name) property, and then enter the name grpWoodType. Double-tap or double-click in the right column of the Text property to change the caption of the GroupBox object. Enter the text Wood Type. Click to the right of the Size property of the GroupBox object and enter 160, 100 as the size.

The name you entered is displayed in the (Name) property in the Properties window, the caption Wood Type is displayed, and the object is resized (Figure 5-5).

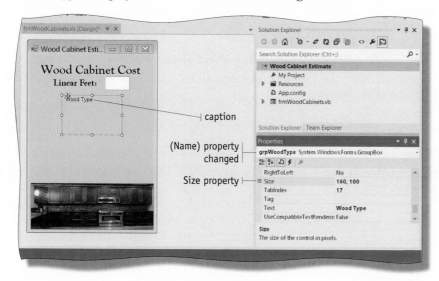

FIGURE 5-5

© Ivan Hunter/Digital Vision/Getty Images

STEP 3   Change the Font property to Goudy Old Style, Regular, 12 points. Change the BackColor property to White.

If you want to move the GroupBox to another location on the form, place the pointer over the drag box on the border of the GroupBox object and then drag it to the desired location. The Font property is set to Goudy Old Style, and the BackColor is white (Figure 5-6).

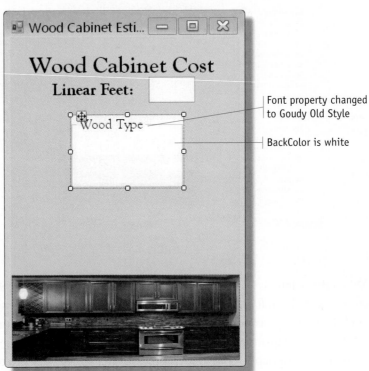

Font property changed to Goudy Old Style

BackColor is white

FIGURE 5-6
© Ivan Hunter/Digital Vision/Getty Images

Grouping all options in a GroupBox object gives the user a logical visual cue. Also, when you move the GroupBox object, all its contained objects move as well.

Add the RadioButton Objects

The GroupBox object in the Wood Cabinet Estimate application contains a set of RadioButton objects (see Figure 5-3 on page 286). The user may select only one type of wood: pine, oak, or cherry. To place RadioButton objects within the GroupBox object, you can complete the following steps:

STEP 1   Drag one RadioButton object from the Toolbox to the GroupBox object. Drag a second RadioButton object from the Toolbox into the GroupBox object, and use blue snap lines to align and separate the RadioButton objects vertically.

The second RadioButton object is aligned vertically with a blue snap line, which separates it vertically from the first RadioButton object (Figure 5-7).

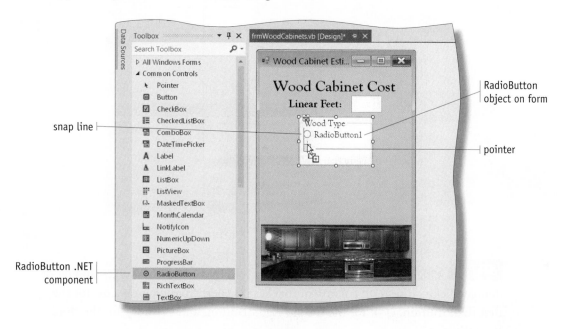

FIGURE 5-7

© Ivan Hunter/Digital Vision/Getty Images

STEP 2   Release the RadioButton object to place it within the GroupBox object. Using the same technique, add a third RadioButton object.

Three RadioButton objects are placed on the form and aligned within the GroupBox object (Figure 5-8).

FIGURE 5-8

STEP 3 Name the RadioButton objects by selecting them one at a time, double-tapping or double-clicking in the right column of the (Name) property in the Properties window, and entering the name. The names for the radio buttons, from top to bottom, should be radPine, radOak, and radCherry.

The (Name) property is selected. The names radPine, radOak, and radCherry are entered (Figure 5-9).

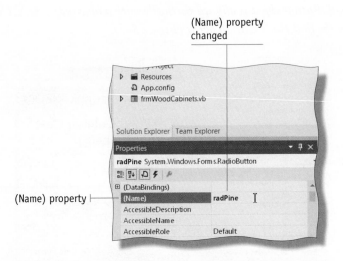

FIGURE 5-9

STEP 4 Change the Text property for each RadioButton by double-tapping or double-clicking the right column of the Text property and typing Pine for the first RadioButton, Oak for the second RadioButton, and Cherry for the third RadioButton.

The Text property is changed to the types of wood available: Pine, Oak, and Cherry (Figure 5-10).

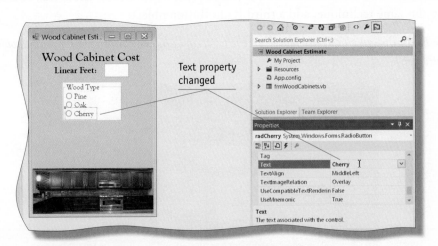

© Ivan Hunter/Digital Vision/Getty Images

FIGURE 5-10

ONLINE REINFORCEMENT

To view a video of the process in the previous steps, visit CengageBrain.com and navigate to the resources for this title. Tap or click the link for Chapter 5 and then navigate to Video 5-3.

A RadioButton object is best used when you have only one selection per group. What type of object would you use to select more than one option?
Checkbox objects are used with lists of options in which the user may select any number of choices. In other words, each Checkbox object is independent of all other check boxes in the list, so checking one box does not uncheck the others.

Use the Checked Property of RadioButton Objects

The RadioButton objects in the Wood Cabinet Estimate application allow the user to select one wood type. When the user selects Cherry, as shown in Figure 5-11, the RadioButton is selected, and the small circle in the radio button is shaded. When the Cherry RadioButton is selected, its Checked property changes from False (unselected) to True (selected).

FIGURE 5-11
© Ivan Hunter/Digital Vision/Getty Images

During design time, you usually set the Checked property to True for the most commonly selected RadioButton to save the user from having to select it. In the Wood Cabinet Estimate application, the cabinetmaker uses Pine most often. To cause the Pine RadioButton object named radPine to appear selected (shaded) when the program begins, you change the Checked property for the radPine RadioButton from False to True (Figure 5-12).

FIGURE 5-12

Windows Application Container Objects

The Panel object in a Windows application works like a GroupBox object. For Windows applications, Visual Basic provides four additional container objects: FlowLayoutPanel, SplitContainer, TabControl, and TableLayoutPanel. The GroupBox object is used most often; it provides several options that are not available with the Panel object. The table in Figure 5-13 shows the differences between the GroupBox and the Panel objects.

Option	GroupBox Object	Panel Object
Have a caption	Yes	No
Have scroll bars	Yes	No
Display a labeled border	Yes	No

FIGURE 5-13

Figure 5-14 shows the Windows application Toolbox and a GroupBox object and Panel object in a Windows Form. Notice in the Toolbox that the GroupBox and Panel objects are in a category called Containers.

FIGURE 5-14

GroupBox and Panel objects have the same purpose of grouping RadioButtons and other objects, but they differ in their appearance. The GroupBox object in Figure 5-14 displays a border around its edges, with a text area in the upper-left portion for a caption. The Panel object has a black dashed border that does not appear when the application is executed.

Related sets of RadioButtons should be placed in separate container objects so that the user can select one radio button from each group. Always place the container object on the form first, and then drag the RadioButton objects into the container object.

The Course Sign-Up example in Figure 5-15 displays a Windows application that allows the user to sign up for a technology course. Notice the two separate groups of RadioButton objects. In the Choose Course Level GroupBox object, the user should select a course level. In the Choose Semester GroupBox object, the user should identify the semester for the course. As you can see, the user selects one radio button from the left group and one radio button from the right group.

FIGURE 5-15

Display a Message Box

In the Wood Cabinet Estimate application, a message box, also called a dialog box, opens if the user does not enter the length of the cabinets correctly. The dialog box displays an error message if the user omits the length or enters nonnumeric data (Figure 5-16).

FIGURE 5-16
© Ivan Hunter/Digital Vision/Getty Images

If the user enters a negative number for the length of the cabinets, a message box appears and indicates that a positive number is necessary (Figure 5-17).

FIGURE 5-17
© Ivan Hunter/Digital Vision/Getty Images

This message box reminds the user to enter the linear feet of the cabinets as a positive number. A message box window must be closed before the application can continue. The user can continue the application by tapping or clicking the OK button in the message box.

In Visual Basic, the message in a message box window is displayed using a procedure named Show, which is found in the MessageBox class. The syntax for the statement that displays a message in a message box is shown in Figure 5-18.

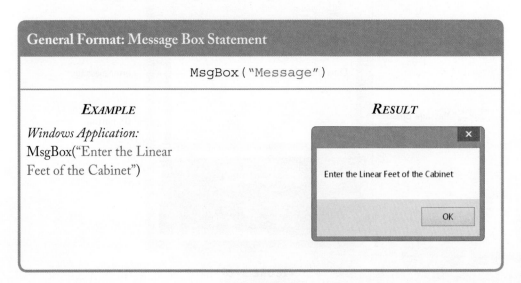

General Format: Message Box Statement
MsgBox ("Message")

EXAMPLE	RESULT
Windows Application: MsgBox("Enter the Linear Feet of the Cabinet")	Enter the Linear Feet of the Cabinet OK

FIGURE 5-18

The string message shown in the parentheses will appear in the message box when the code is executed. The string message is considered an argument of the procedure. You will recall that an argument is a value passed to a procedure. The first argument for the MsgBox command contains the message to be printed in the message box window during execution.

The example in Figure 5-19 illustrates the code that could be used in the Calculate button click event handler. This code could be executed if the user taps or clicks the Calculate button without entering a numeric value in the Linear Feet text box (Figure 5-16 on page 293).

Display Message Box Captions

A message box can be displayed during execution with a variety of arguments. For example, by using the syntax shown in Figure 5-19, a message box can display a message and a caption in the title bar (two arguments with two commas between the two arguments).

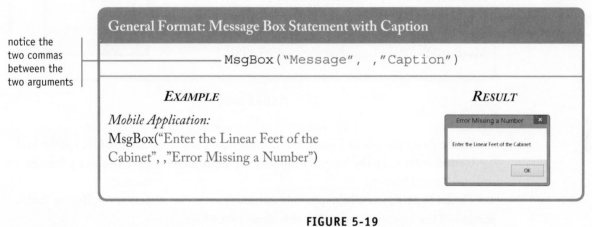

FIGURE 5-19

© 2014 Cengage Learning

The title bar in the example in Figure 5-19 displays a caption and the message box displays a message. In many applications, the caption is used to give further information to the user.

Message Box Buttons

The general format for changing the button command from OK to another button type is shown in Figure 5-20. The button entry can be a command or a value representing a command.

General Format: Message Box Statement with Caption and Button

```
MsgBox("Message", Button Entry, "Caption")
```

EXAMPLE	*RESULT*

Windows Application:
MsgBox("User name is missing", MsgBoxStyle.
OKCancel, "Entry Error")
or
MsgBox("User name is missing", 1, "Entry Error")

Windows Application:
MsgBox("You have been disconnected",
MsgBoxStyle.RetryCancel, "ISP")
or
MsgBox("You have been disconnected", 5, "ISP")

FIGURE 5-20

© 2014 Cengage Learning

In the first example in Figure 5-20, the buttons specified are the OK button and the Cancel button. In the second example, the buttons shown are the Retry button and the Cancel button.

Figure 5-21 shows all the possible entries that can be placed in the Button Entry portion of the argument passed to the Show procedure.

MsgBoxStyle Arguments	Value	Use
MsgBoxStyle.OKOnly	0	Displays an OK button — default setting
MsgBoxStyle.OKCancel	1	Displays an OK and Cancel button
MsgBoxStyle.AbortRetryIgnore	2	After a failing situation, the user can choose to Abort, Retry, or Ignore
MsgBoxStyle.YesNoCancel	3	Displays Yes, No, and Cancel buttons
MsgBoxStyle.YesNo	4	Displays Yes and No buttons
MsgBoxStyle.RetryCancel	5	After an error occurs, the user can choose to Retry or Cancel

FIGURE 5-21

© 2014 Cengage Learning

Message Box Icons

In the button entry portion of the argument (the second argument), you can add a message box icon (Figure 5-22). The word "or" connects the button entry to the icon entry.

General Format: Message Box Statement with Button and Icon

```
MsgBox("Message", Button Entry or Icon Picture, "Caption")
```

EXAMPLE

Windows Application:
MsgBox("User name is missing", MsgBoxStyle. OKCancel or MsgBoxStyle.Critical, "User Name Error")
or
MsgBox("User name is missing", 1 Or 16, "User Name Error")

Windows Application:
MsgBox("You have been disconnected", MsgBoxStyle.RetryCancel or MsgBoxStyle.Question, "ISP")
or
MsgBox("You have been disconnected", 5 Or 32, "ISP")

RESULT

FIGURE 5-22

The picture icon represents the MsgBoxStyle that can be displayed as a graphic icon in the message box. Both examples in Figure 5-22 show a graphic icon added to the message box.

The picture icon in the second argument can contain any of the entries shown in Figure 5-23.

MsgBoxStyle Icons	Value	Icon	Use
MsgBoxStyle.Critical	16		Alerts the user to an error
MsgBoxStyle.Question	32		Displays a question mark
MsgBoxStyle.Exclamation	48		Alerts the user to a possible problem
MsgBoxStyle.Information	64		Displays an information icon

FIGURE 5-23

In the general formats shown for a message box, you must follow the syntax of the statements exactly, which means the commas, quotation marks, and parentheses must be placed in the statement as shown.

You can also add values to display both the buttons and a picture icon. In Figure 5-24, the value of the message button type AbortRetryIgnore is 2 and the value of the critical icon is 16. If you add 16 plus 2, the result is 18.

General Format: MsgBox("Message", Button Entry Value + Icon Picture Value, "Caption")

EXAMPLE	RESULT
Windows Application: MsgBox("Enter a Number Only", 18, "Illegal Operation")	

FIGURE 5-24

Message Box IntelliSense

When you enter the code for a message box, IntelliSense can assist you. For example, the message box you create in the following steps contains a message, caption, and buttons. To use IntelliSense to enter the code, you can complete the following steps:

STEP 1   In the code window, inside the event handler you are coding, type msg to display MsgBox in the IntelliSense list.

IntelliSense displays a list of the allowable entries (Figure 5-25). When you type msg, MsgBox is selected in the IntelliSense list.

FIGURE 5-25

STEP 2   Press the tab key to select MsgBox in the IntelliSense list. Type the following
text: (`"You have been disconnected from the Internet"`, m)

*The first argument for the message box is entered (Figure 5-26). IntelliSense displays a list
of allowable entries for the second argument.*

first MsgBox argument entered

IntelliSense list

ScreenTip for selected command,
MsgBoxStyle.MsgBoxHelp

FIGURE 5-26

STEP 3   Select the MsgBoxStyle.AbortRetryIgnore argument by pressing the up
arrow until the correct argument is highlighted. Type a comma. Then type `"ISP"`
and a right parenthesis.

*The MsgBoxStyle.AbortRetryIgnore argument is selected. Next, the comma and the caption
"ISP" are entered with a right parenthesis (Figure 5-27).*

Start Debugging button

statement is entered   caption is entered

FIGURE 5-27

STEP 4   Tap or click the Start Debugging button on the Standard toolbar.

The application runs, displaying the message box that shows the message, buttons, and caption (Figure 5-28).

FIGURE 5-28

String Concatenation

Recall that when the Wood Cabinet Estimate application runs, the user enters the linear footage of the wood cabinets. If the user enters a number that is not greater than zero, such as –6, a message box displays "You entered –6. Enter a Positive Number", as shown in Figure 5-29.

FIGURE 5-29
© Ivan Hunter/Digital Vision/Getty Images

To create the message in the message box, you can use concatenation, which you learned about in Chapter 4. In Figure 5-29, the string message is constructed by joining a string ("You entered"), a variable named decFeet that contains the entered linear footage (which must be converted to a string), and a string for the final part of the message (". Enter a Positive Number"). The code in Figure 5-30 creates the message box.

```
46    MsgBox("You entered " & decFeet.ToString() & ". Enter a Positive Number", , "Input Error")
```

FIGURE 5-30

You will recall that the operator to concatenate strings is the ampersand (&). When the statement is executed, the three string elements are joined together (concatenated) to form the one string that is displayed in the message box.

Make Decisions with Conditional Statements

In the Wood Cabinet Estimate application, users can select one of three types of wood: pine, oak, or cherry. The price per linear foot is based on the user's choice of wood. To select the wood type, the user must tap or click one of three radio buttons titled Pine, Oak, and Cherry. Then, based on the choice, the application uses a different wood cost.

Visual Basic uses decision structures to deal with the different conditions that occur based on the values entered into an application. A **decision structure** is one of the three fundamental control structures used in computer programming. For example, if the user taps or clicks the Pine radio button, the wood cost is set to $300.00 per linear foot. The statement that tests the radio button is called a **conditional statement**. The condition to check is whether the Pine radio button is selected. If so, the wood cost is set to $300.00.

When a condition is tested in a Visual Basic program, the condition either is true or false. For example, when checking to determine if the Pine radio button is selected, the condition can either be true (the button is checked) or false (not checked). All conditional statements result in the tested condition either being true or false.

To implement a conditional statement and the statements that are executed when a condition is true or false, Visual Basic uses the If statement and its variety of formats. You will learn about the If statement in the following sections.

Use an If . . . Then Statement

In the sample program, an If . . . Then statement is used to determine the cost of the wood. The simplest form of the If . . . Then statement is shown in Figure 5-31.

```
5        If condition Then
6            Statement(s) executed when condition is true
7        End If
8
```

FIGURE 5-31

In Figure 5-31, when the condition tested in the If statement on line 5 is true, the statement(s) between the If and the End If keywords will be executed. If the condition is not true, no statements between the If and End If keywords will be executed, and program execution will continue with the statement(s) after the End If statement.

HEADS UP

In older versions of Visual Basic, the plus (+) sign was used to concatenate strings instead of the ampersand (&) symbol. The + sign still functions for concatenation, but it can be confusing because it looks like the plus sign used in addition. You should always use the ampersand.

Visual Basic automatically indents statements to be executed when a condition is true or not true to indicate which lines of code are within the conditional If . . . Then structure. This is why the statement on line 6 in Figure 5-31 on the previous page is indented. The End If keywords terminate the If . . . Then block of code. After executing the If . . . Then block, execution continues with any statements that follow the closing End If statement.

Relational Operators

In Figure 5-31, the condition portion of the If . . . Then statement means a condition is tested to determine if it is true or false. The conditions that can be tested are:

1. Is one value equal to another value?
2. Is one value not equal to another value?
3. Is one value greater than another value?
4. Is one value less than another value?
5. Is one value greater than or equal to another value?
6. Is one value less than or equal to another value?

To test these conditions, Visual Basic provides relational operators that are used within the conditional statement to express the relationship being tested. Figure 5-32 shows these relational operators.

	Relational Operator	Meaning	Example	Resulting Condition
1	=	Equal to	8 = 8	True
2	<>	Not equal to	6 <> 6	False
3	>	Greater than	7 > 9	False
4	<	Less than	4 < 6	True
5	>=	Greater than or equal to	3 >= 3	True
6	<=	Less than or equal to	7 <= 5	False

FIGURE 5-32

A condition tested using a relational operator is evaluated as true or false. Example 1 tests whether 8 is equal to 8. Because it is, the resulting condition is true. Example 2 tests whether 6 is not equal to 6. Because they are equal, the resulting condition is false. Similarly, Example 5 tests whether 3 is greater than or equal to 3. Because they are equal, the resulting condition is true.

As an example of using a conditional operator, consider the following problem, in which an If statement is used to determine if someone is old enough to vote. If the value in the intAge variable is greater than or equal to 18, then the person is old enough to vote. If not, the person is not old enough to vote. The If . . . Then statement to test this condition is shown in Figure 5-33.

```
8          If intAge >= 18 Then
9              lblVotingEligibility.Text = "You are old enough to vote"
10         End If
```

FIGURE 5-33

© 2014 Cengage Learning

In Figure 5-33, if the value in the intAge variable is greater than or equal to 18, the string value "You are old enough to vote" is assigned to the Text property of the lblVotingEligibility Label object. If not, then no processing occurs based on the conditional statement and any statement(s) following the End If keywords will be executed.

You can see in Figure 5-33 that several keywords are required in an If . . . Then statement. The word If must be the first item. Next, the condition(s) to be tested are stated, followed by the word Then. This keyword is required in an If statement.

The End If keywords follow the statements to be executed when the condition is true. This entry also is required. It signals to the Visual Basic compiler that the statements following it must be executed regardless of the result of the conditional statement; that is, the End If keywords are the last element within the If block and no subsequent statements depend on the If block for execution.

To enter the If . . . Then statement shown in Figure 5-33, you can complete the following steps:

STEP 1 With the insertion point in the correct location in the code, type if and then press the SPACEBAR.

The statement begins with the word if (Figure 5-34). The If command is displayed in blue because it is a Visual Basic keyword. You can type uppercase or lowercase letters.

FIGURE 5-34

STEP 2   Type `inta` to select the variable named intAge in the IntelliSense list. Type `>=18` as the condition to be tested. Press the ENTER key.

The If . . . Then statement is entered in the code window (Figure 5-35). When the ENTER key is pressed, Visual Basic adds the keyword Then to the end of the If statement line of code and inserts spaces between the elements of the statement for ease of reading. In addition, Visual Basic inserts the End If keywords following a blank line. Notice the keywords Then and End If are capitalized and displayed in blue.

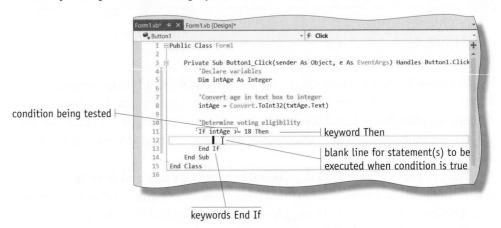

FIGURE 5-35

STEP 3   On the blank line (line 12 in Figure 5-35), enter the statement that should be executed when the condition is true. To place the message "You are old enough to vote" in the Text property of the lblVotingEligibility Label object, insert the code shown in Figure 5-33 on the previous page. Remember to use IntelliSense to reference the lblVotingEligibility Label object.

The resulting statement is entered between the If and End If keywords (Figure 5-36). Notice that Visual Basic automatically indents the line for ease of reading. The blank line allows you to enter more statements. If you have no further statements, you can press the DELETE key to delete the blank line in the If . . . Then statement.

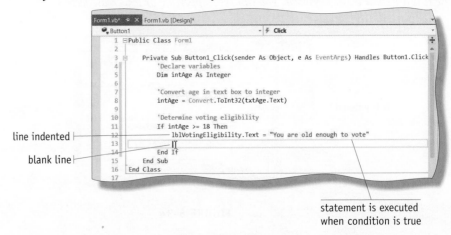

FIGURE 5-36

Compare Strings

You also can write an If . . . Then statement to compare string values using the
relational operators shown in Figure 5-32 on page 302. A string value comparison
compares each character in two strings, starting with the first character in each string.
For example, in the two strings in Figure 5-37, the comparison begins with the first
character (a) in each string. Because the characters are equal, the comparison continues with the second character in each string, which is b. Because these characters are
equal, the comparison continues with the third character in each string, c. Because all
three characters are equal, the strings are considered equal and the resulting condition
from the If statement is true.

```
13        Dim String1 As String = "abc"
14        Dim String2 As String = "abc"
15
16        If String1 = String2 Then
17              lblStringTest.Text = "Equal"
18        End If
```

FIGURE 5-37

All characters found in strings, including letters, numbers, and special characters,
are in a sequence based on how the characters are coded internally on the computer.
In Visual Studio 2012, characters are stored and sequenced in Unicode, which is a
coding methodology that can accommodate more than 60,000 characters. Appendix
A in this book shows the Unicode sequence for the standard keyboard characters.
You will find that numbers have lower Unicode values than uppercase letters, and
uppercase letters have lower values than lowercase letters.

Using the If . . . Then statement, the following comparisons produce the
following resulting conditions:

Example 1:
```
Dim String1 As String = "Powder"
Dim String2 As String = "Power"

If String1 < String2 Then
```

Resulting Condition: True because in the fourth character position, the letter d is
less than the letter e.

Example 2:
```
Dim String1 As String = "6"
Dim String2 As String = "T"

If String1 < String2 Then
```

Resulting Condition: True because in a string comparison, a number is less than
an uppercase letter.

Example 3:
```
Dim String1 As String = "12"
Dim String2 As String = "9"

If String1 < String2 Then
```

Resulting Condition: True because in a string comparison, the characters in the first position of the string are compared first. Because the value 1 in String1 is less than the value 9 in String2, the entire value in String1 is considered less than the value in String2.

Example 4:
```
Dim String1 As String = "anchor"
Dim String2 As String = "Anchorline"

If String1 > String2 Then
```

Resulting Condition: True because a lowercase letter (the a in the first position of String1) is considered greater than an uppercase letter (the A in the first position of String2).

Compare Different Data Types

Every type of data available in Visual Basic can be compared. Different numeric types can be compared to each other using an If statement. A single string character can be compared to a Char data type. The following examples illustrate some of the allowable comparisons.

Example 1: Decimal compared to Double

```
If decQuarterlySales > dblSalesQuota Then
```

If decQuarterlySales = 110,324.54 and dblSalesQuota = 112,435.54, the condition is false.

Example 2: Decimal compared to Integer

```
If decTirePressureReading > intTirePressureMaximum Then
```

If decTirePressureReading = 30.21 and intTirePressureMaximum = 30, the condition is true.

Example 3: Double compared to Integer

```
If dblCurrentTemperature >= intHeatDanger Then
```

If dblCurrentTemperature = 94.543 and intHeatDanger = 98, the condition is false.

Example 4: String compared to Char

```
If strChemistryGrade < chrPassingGrade Then
```

If strChemistryGrade = "B" and chrPassingGrade = "C", the condition is true.

Visual Basic allows comparisons between most data types. If you are unsure whether a comparison can be made, write an If statement to ensure the comparison is working properly.

Use the If . . . Then . . . Else Statement

An If . . . Then statement executes a set of instructions if a condition is true. If the condition is false, the instructions between the If statement and the End If statement are not executed and program execution continues with the statement(s) following the End If statement.

In many applications, the logic requires one set of instructions to be executed if a condition is true and another set of instructions to be executed if a condition is false. For example, a program requirement could specify that if a student's test score is 70 or greater, the message "You passed the examination" should be displayed, while if the test score is less than 70, the message "You failed the examination" should be displayed.

To execute one set of instructions if a condition is true and another set of instructions if the condition is false, you can use the If . . . Then . . . Else statement. Figure 5-38 illustrates the syntax of the If . . . Then . . . Else statement.

```
16      If condition Then
17          Statement(s) executed if condition is true
18      Else
19          Statement(s) executed if condition is false
20      End If
```

FIGURE 5-38

If the condition tested by the If statement is true, the statement(s) between the Then keyword and the Else keyword will be executed. If the condition tested is false, the statement(s) between the Else keyword and the End If keywords will be executed.

The example in Figure 5-39 shows the use of the If . . . Then . . . Else statement to calculate student fees by testing the student's status.

statement is executed if
student is a graduate

```
27        If strStudentStatus = "Graduate" Then
28            decStudentFees = decGraduateFee * intNumberOfUnits
29        Else
30            decStudentFees = decUndergraduateFee * intNumberOfUnits
31        End If
```

statement is executed if
student is not a graduate

FIGURE 5-39

HEADS UP

A condition cannot be true and false at the same time, so statements for a true condition and statements for a false condition cannot both be executed based on a single comparison.

If the student is in graduate school, the student fees are calculated by multiplying the graduate fee by the number of units. If the student is not a graduate student, fees are calculated by multiplying the undergraduate fee by the number of units. Notice that a student cannot be both an undergraduate and a graduate student, so either the statement following the Then keyword will be executed or the statement following the Else keyword will be executed.

Compare to an Arithmetic Expression

An If statement can compare an arithmetic expression to a constant or other data type. For example, in Figure 5-40, the withdrawals from a bank account are compared to the value obtained by adding the current balance to deposits and then subtracting account charges.

```
41        If decWithdrawals > decCurrentBalance + decDeposits - decAccountCharges Then
42            lblAccountStatus.Text = "Overdrawn"
43        Else
44            lblAccountStatus.Text = "Balance is Positive"
45        End If
```

FIGURE 5-40

In Figure 5-40, if the value in the decWithdrawals variable is greater than the current balance plus the deposits minus the account charges, the Text property of the lblAccountStatus Label object is set to Overdrawn. If the value in decWithdrawals is less than or equal to the value from the arithmetic expression, the message Balance is Positive is placed in the Text property of the lblAccountStatus Label object. Notice that the arithmetic expression is evaluated prior to the comparison. If the condition is true, the statement between the Then and Else keywords is executed. If the condition is false, the statement between the Else and End If keywords is executed.

Use the If . . . Then . . . ElseIf Statement

Complex logic problems might require a more complex structure than the If . . . Then . . . Else logic structure. For example, consider the following logical problem that must be solved in a computer program:

An online store charges a shipping fee based on the dollar amount of the order being shipped. The rules are:

1. If the order amount is above $500, the shipping cost is $30.
2. If the order amount is more than $400 and not greater than $500, the shipping cost is $25.
3. If the order amount is more than $200 and not greater than $400, the shipping cost is $20.
4. If the order amount is equal to or less than $200, the shipping cost is $15.

When one of the conditions is found to be true, the rest of the conditions are not tested because the correct condition has been found. To solve this problem, you should think this way:

1. If the order amount is greater than $500.00, then the shipping cost is $30.00 and no more processing is needed to determine the shipping cost.
2. If, however, the order amount is not greater than $500.00, I must check further to see if it is greater than $400.00 (400.01 through 500.00). If so, the shipping cost is $25.00.
3. If the order amount is not greater than $400.00, the next step is to check whether it is greater than $200.00. In other words, check within the range of $201.00 to $400.00. If this is true, the shipping cost is $20.00.
4. If none of the above is true, then the order amount must be less than or equal to $200. In this case, the shipping cost is $15.00.

As you can see, a simple If . . . Then . . . Else statement could not solve this logic problem because the structure tests only a single condition and specifies the processing based on whether the condition is true or false. For a problem in which multiple conditions must be tested, the If . . . Then . . . ElseIf statement might be appropriate. The general format of the If . . . Then . . . ElseIf statement is shown in Figure 5-41.

```
105        If decOrderAmount > 500D Then
106            Statement(s) executed if condition is true
107        ElseIf decOrderAmount > 400D Then
108            Statement(s) executed if condition is true
109        ElseIf decOrderAmount > 200D Then
110            Statement(s) executed if condition is true
111        ElseIf decOrderAmount > 0D Then
112            Statement(s) executed if condition is true
113        End If
```

FIGURE 5-41

Once a condition is true in the code in Figure 5-41 on the previous page, Visual Basic bypasses the rest of the ElseIf statements. For example, assume the order amount is $455. The first condition tests whether the order amount is greater than 500. The first condition would test false because 455 is not greater than 500.

Next, the ElseIf entry will test whether 455 is greater than 400. Because the value 455 is greater than 400, the condition is true and the statement(s) on line 108 will be executed. The remaining ElseIf statements will not be evaluated because the true condition has been found.

Separate If . . . Then statements are not used in the example in Figure 5-41 because each condition would have to be tested even though a condition had already been found to be true. When using an If . . . Then . . . ElseIf statement, any remaining conditions are not tested after a condition is found to be true, making the process faster and more efficient.

Trailing Else Statements

You may want to include a trailing Else statement at the end of an If . . . Then . . . ElseIf conditional statement to handle a condition that does not meet any of the previous conditions tested. In the example in Figure 5-42, the code is determining whether the user is eligible for Social Security benefits. If the user's age is greater than or equal to 65, the user receives full benefits. If the user's age is between 0 and 65, the user is not eligible for benefits.

```
115        If intAge >= 65 Then
116            lblSocialSecurity.Text = "Full Benefits"
117        ElseIf intAge > 0 Then
118            lblSocialSecurity.Text = "Not Eligible for Benefits"
119        Else
120            lblSocialSecurity.Text = "Invalid Age"
121        End If
```

FIGURE 5-42

In Figure 5-42, the statement on line 120 that follows the trailing Else statement on line 119 is executed if the number in the intAge variable does not meet the conditions stated in the previous If statements. For example, if the intAge variable contains a negative value such as −12, the Text property of the lblSocialSecurity Label object will be set to "Invalid Age".

Nested If Statements

At times, more than one decision has to be made to determine what processing must occur. For example, if one condition is true, a second condition may need to be tested before the correct code is executed. To test a second condition only after determining that a first condition is true (or false), you must place an If statement within another If statement. When you place one If statement within another one, the inner If statement is said to be nested within the outer If Statement. The syntax of a nested If statement is shown in Figure 5-43.

nested If
statement –
(first inner
If statement)

```
123    If first condition Then
124        If second condition Then
125            Statement(s) executed if condition 1 is true and condition 2 is true
126        Else
127            Statement(s) executed if condition 1 is true and condition 2 is false
128        End If              end of first inner If statement
129    Else
130        If third condition Then
131            Statement(s) executed if condition 1 is false and condition 3 is true
132        Else
133            Statement(s) executed if condition 1 is false and condition 3 is false
134        End If              end of second inner If statement
135    End If
```

nested If
statement –
(second inner
If statement)

end of first If statement

FIGURE 5-43

In Figure 5-43, if the first condition tested is true, the statements following the keyword Then are executed. The statement to be executed when the first condition is true is another If statement (line 124) that tests the second condition. This second If statement is said to be a nested If statement or an inner If statement. If the second condition is true, the program executes the statement(s) on line 125 following the keyword Then for the first inner If statement. If the second condition is not true, the program executes the statement(s) on line 127 following the keyword Else for the first inner If statement. The End If entry (line 128) follows the first inner If statement, indicating the end of the effect of the first inner If statement.

If the first condition is not true, then the program executes the statements following the keyword Else on line 129 for the first If statement. The statement to be executed when the first condition is not true is an If statement that tests the third condition (line 130). If the third condition is true, the program executes the statement(s) on line 131 following the Then keyword of the second inner If statement. Finally, if the second inner If statement that tests the third condition is false, the statement(s) on line 133 are executed.

To illustrate a nested If statement, assume a college has the following admissions policy: If an applying student has a GPA (grade point average) greater than 3.5 and a score greater than 1000 on the SAT college entrance exam, then that student is granted admission. If an applying student has a GPA greater than 3.5 but an SAT score of 1000 or lower, the student is advised to retake the SAT exam. If an applying student has a GPA of 3.5 or lower but an SAT score greater than 1200, the student is granted probationary admission, which means she must achieve a 2.5 GPA in the first semester of college. If an applying student has a GPA lower than 3.5 and an SAT score of 1200 or lower, the student is denied admission. The nested If statement to process this admission policy is shown in Figure 5-44.

```
140        If decGPA > 3.5D Then
141            If intSatScore > 1000 Then
142                lblAdmissionStatus.Text = "You have earned admission"
143            Else
144                lblAdmissionStatus.Text = "Retake the SAT exam"
145            End If
146        Else
147            If intSatScore > 1200 Then
148                lblAdmissionStatus.Text = "You have earned probationary admission"
149            Else
150                lblAdmissionStatus.Text = "You have been denied admission"
151            End If
152        End If
```

FIGURE 5-44

Notice in Figure 5-44 that the test for greater than 1000 on the SAT (line 141) must take place only after the test for a GPA greater than 3.5 (line 140), because the test for greater than 1000 is required only after the program determines that the GPA is greater than 3.5. Therefore, a nested If statement is required. In addition, the test for greater than 1200 (line 147) should occur only after the program determines that the GPA is less than 3.5. As you can see, you should use a nested If statement when a condition must be tested only after another condition has been tested.

Other Nested If Configurations

You can use nested If statements in a variety of forms. Assume, for example, that a school's admissions policy is as follows: If an applying student has a GPA greater than 3.5 and an SAT score greater than 1100, then that student is granted admission. If an applying student has a GPA greater than 3.5 but an SAT score of 1100 or lower, the student is advised to retake the SAT exam. If an applying student has a GPA of 3.5 or lower, the student is denied admission. The nested If statement in Figure 5-45 solves this logic problem.

```
154        If decGPA > 3.5D Then
155            If intSatScore > 1100 Then
156                lblAdmissionStatus.Text = "You have earned admission"
157            Else
158                lblAdmissionStatus.Text = "Retake the SAT exam"
159            End If
160        Else
161            lblAdmissionStatus.Text = "You have been denied admission"
162        End If
```

FIGURE 5-45

In Figure 5-45, if the GPA is greater than 3.5, then the first inner If statement on line 155 is executed to determine if the SAT score is greater than 1100. If so, the person has earned admission. If not, the person is advised to retake the SAT exam. If the GPA is not greater than 3.5, the student is denied admission. Notice that an If statement does not follow the Else keyword on line 160. An inner If statement need not follow both the If and the Else keywords.

Sometimes, after a condition is found to be true, a statement must be executed before the inner If statement is executed. For example, assume that if a student's GPA is greater than 3.5, then the student should be informed that her GPA is acceptable for admission. The code in Figure 5-46 implements this condition.

```
164        If decGPA > 3.5D Then
165            lblGPAStatus.Text = "Your GPA is acceptable"
166            If intSatScore > 1100 Then
167                lblAdmissionStatus.Text = "You have earned admission"
168            Else
169                lblAdmissionStatus.Text = "Retake the SAT exam"
170            End If
171        Else
172            lblGPAStatus.Text = "Your GPA is not acceptable"
173            lblAdmissionStatus.Text = "You have been denied admission"
174        End If
```

FIGURE 5-46

On line 165 in Figure 5-46, the message "Your GPA is acceptable" is assigned to the Text property of the lblGPAStatus Label object before checking the SAT score. As you can see, after the first condition has been tested, one or more statements can be executed prior to executing the inner If statement. This holds true for the Else portion of the If statement as well.

Match If, Else, and End If Entries

When you write a nested If statement, the inner If statement must be fully contained within the outer If statement. To accomplish this, you must ensure that each Else entry has a corresponding If entry, and an inner If statement must be terminated with an End If entry before either the Else entry or the End If entry for the outer If statement. If you code the nested If statement incorrectly, one or more of its entries will be shown with a blue squiggly line, indicating an error in the structure of the statement.

You also must place the correct executing statements with the If and Else statements within the nested If statement. For example, in Figure 5-47, the code is incorrect because the statements following the Else statements have been switched.

```
164        If decGPA > 3.5D Then
165            lblGPAStatus.Text = "Your GPA is acceptable"
166            If intSatScore > 1100 Then
167                lblAdmissionStatus.Text = "You have earned admission"
168            Else
169                lblAdmissionStatus.Text = "You have been denied admission"
170            End If
171        Else
172            lblGPAStatus Text = "Your GPA is not acceptable"
173            lblAdmissionStatus.Text = "Retake the SAT exam"
174        End If
```

incorrect statements

FIGURE 5-47

You must be precise when placing the executing statements in the nested If statement. It is easy to miscode a nested If statement.

Nest Three or More Levels of If Statements

If statements are not limited to two levels of nesting. Three or more levels can be included in a nested If statement, although the statement can become difficult to understand and code. If more than two levels are required to solve a logic problem, great care must be taken to prevent errors such as the one shown in Figure 5-47.

Test the Status of a RadioButton Object in Code

In the Wood Cabinet Estimate application, the user selects one RadioButton in the GroupBox object to select the wood type. The code must check each RadioButton to determine if it has been selected by the user. When the user selects a radio button, its Checked property is changed from False to True. In addition, the Checked property for other RadioButton objects in the GroupBox object is set to False. This Checked property can be tested in an If statement to determine if the RadioButton object has been selected.

To test the status of the Checked property for the radPine RadioButton object, a programmer can write the general statement shown in Figure 5-48.

```
237        If radPine.Checked Then
238            Statement(s) to be executed if radio button is checked
239        End If
```

FIGURE 5-48

Notice in Figure 5-48 that the RadioButton property is not compared using a relational operator. Instead, when a program tests a property that can contain only True or False, only the property must be specified in the If statement. When the property contains True, then the If statement is considered true, and when the property contains False, the If statement is considered false.

Test RadioButtons with the If . . . Then . . . ElseIf Statement

When a program contains multiple RadioButton objects in a Panel object or a GroupBox object, only one of the radio buttons can be selected. The If . . . Then . . . ElseIf statement is used to check multiple radio buttons because once the checked radio button is detected, checking the remaining radio buttons is unnecessary.

In the Wood Cabinet Estimate application, the user taps or clicks one of three radio buttons (Pine, Oak, or Cherry) to select the type of wood used for cabinets. When using an If . . . Then . . . ElseIf statement to check the status of the radio buttons, the most likely choice should be checked first. Thus, the fewest number of tests are performed. Therefore, the first If statement should test the status of the Pine radio button (radPine). If the radPine button is checked, the Cost Per Foot should be set to the value in the decPineCost variable, which is 300.00. No further testing should be done (Figure 5-49).

```
31            If radPine.Checked Then
32                decCostPerFoot = decPineCost
33            ElseIf radOak.Checked Then
34                decCostPerFoot = decOakCost
35            ElseIf radCherry.Checked Then
36                decCostPerFoot = decCherryCost
37            End If
```

FIGURE 5-49

If the radPine button is not checked, then the radOak button should be tested. If it is checked, the Cost Per Foot should be set to the value in the decOakCost variable (500.00) and no further testing should be done. If the radOak button is not checked, then the radCherry button should be tested. If the other two buttons are not checked, then the radCherry button must be checked because one of the three must be checked. The Cost Per Foot will be set to the value in the decCherryCost variable (650.00).

As you learned earlier, during design time you can set the Checked property to True for the most frequently selected RadioButton to save the user from having to select it. In the Wood Cabinet Estimate application, after the Cost Per Foot has been determined and the Cost Estimate has been calculated, the user can tap or click the Clear button to clear the Linear Feet text box, clear the Cost Estimate, and reset the radio buttons so that the Pine button is selected. The code to reset the radio buttons is shown in Figure 5-50.

```
62        radPine.Checked = True
63        radOak.Checked = False
64        radCherry.Checked = False
```

FIGURE 5-50

© 2014 Cengage Learning

In Figure 5-50, the Checked property for the radPine RadioButton object is set to True using the same method you have seen in previous chapters for setting an object property. Similarly, the Checked property for the other two RadioButton objects is set to False. As a result of these statements, the Pine radio button will be selected in the user interface, and the Oak and Cherry radio buttons will not be selected.

Block-Level Scope

In Chapter 4 you learned that the scope of a variable is defined by where it is declared within a program. For example, if a variable is declared within an event handler, then only code within that event handler can reference the variable. Code in one event handler within a program cannot reference a variable declared in another event handler.

Within an event handler, an If . . . Then . . . Else statement is considered a block of code. To review, this statement is the code beginning with the If keyword and ending with the corresponding Else keyword, or the code beginning with the Else keyword and ending with the End If keywords. Variables can be declared within the block of code, but they can be referenced only within the block of code where they are declared. For example, variables defined within an If . . . Then block of code fall out of scope (cannot be referenced) outside that block of code. To illustrate this concept, the code in Figure 5-51 shows a variable named intYears declared within an If . . . Then block of code.

```
11          If intAge < 18 Then
12              Dim intYears As Integer
13              intYears = 18 - intAge
14              lblMessage.Text = "You can vote in " & intYears & " years(s)."
15          Else
16              lblMessage.Text = "You can vote!"
17          End If
```

FIGURE 5-51

On line 12 in Figure 5-51, the variable intYears is declared as an Integer variable. On line 13, the variable is used in an arithmetic statement to receive the result of the calculation 18 – intAge, which determines the number of years less than 18 that is stored in intAge. The result in intYears is concatenated with literals in the statement on line 14. The intYears variable can be referenced in any statement between the If keyword and the Else keyword. It cannot be referenced anywhere else in the program, not even in the Else portion of the If statement. When a statement referencing the intYears variable is written outside the area between the If keyword and the Else keyword, a compilation error will occur and the program will not compile and execute.

Although the scope of the intYears variable in Figure 5-51 is between the If keyword on line 11 and the Else keyword on line 15, you should realize that the variable itself perseveres during the execution of the event handler procedure. Therefore, if the If statement in Figure 5-51 is executed a second time, the value in the intYears variable will be the same as when the If statement was completed the first time. To avoid unexpected results when the If statement is executed the second time, you should initialize block variables at the beginning of the block. In Figure 5-51, the statement on line 13 sets the value in the intYears variable immediately after it is declared, which is good programming technique.

Use Logical Operators

The If statements you have seen thus far test a single condition. In many cases, more than one condition must be true or one of several conditions must be true to execute the statements in the Then portion of the If . . . Then . . . Else statement. When more than one condition is included in an If . . . Then . . . Else statement, the conditions are called a **compound condition**. For example, consider the following business traveling rule: "If the flight costs less than $300.00 and the hotel is less than $120.00 per night, the business trip is approved." In this case, both conditions — flight less than $300.00 *and* hotel less than $120.00 per night — must be true for the trip to be approved. If either condition is not true, then the business trip is not approved.

To create an If statement that processes the business traveling rule, you must use a **logical operator**. The most common set of logical operators are listed in Figure 5-52.

Logical Operator	Meaning
And	All conditions tested in the If statement must be true
Or	One condition tested in the If statement must be true
Not	Negates a condition

FIGURE 5-52

© 2014 Cengage Learning

For the business traveling rule, you should use the And logical operator.

Use the And Logical Operator

The **And logical operator** allows you to combine two or more conditions into a compound condition that can be tested with an If statement. If any of the conditions stated in the compound condition is false, the compound condition is considered false and the statements following the Else portion of the If statement will be executed. The code in Figure 5-53 uses the And logical operator to implement the business traveling rule.

```
137        If decFlightCost < 300D And decHotelCost < 120D Then
138            lblTripMessage.Text = "Your business trip is approved"
139        Else
140            lblTripMessage.Text = "Your business trip is denied"
141        End If
```

FIGURE 5-53

© 2014 Cengage Learning

In Figure 5-53, both conditions in the compound condition (flight cost less than 300 and hotel cost less than 120) must be true for the business trip to be approved. If one of the conditions is false, then the compound condition is considered false and the If statement would return a false indication. For example, if the flight cost is 300 or more, the trip will not be approved regardless of the hotel cost. Similarly, if the hotel cost is 120 or more, the trip will not be approved regardless of the flight cost. This process is illustrated in Figure 5-54.

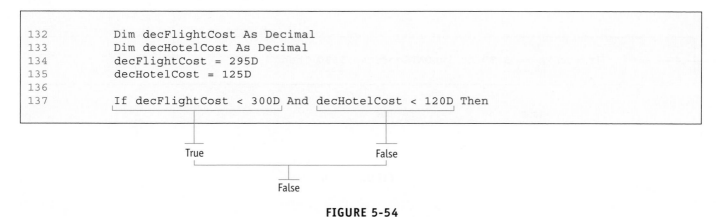

FIGURE 5-54

In Figure 5-54, the flight cost is 295, so it is less than 300 and the first part of the compound condition is true. Following the And logical operator, the hotel cost (125) is not less than 120. Therefore, the second part of the compound condition is false. When either condition is false with the And logical operator, the If statement considers the compound condition to be false. The result of the If statement in Figure 5-54 is that the compound condition is considered to be false.

Use the Or Logical Operator

When the **Or logical operator** is used to connect two or more conditions, the compound condition is true if any tested condition is true. Even if four conditional statements are included in the compound condition, only one conditional statement in the compound condition must be true for the entire statement to be considered true.

As an example, assume a college requires each student to have either at least a 3.5 GPA or at least a 1080 score on the SAT exam to be accepted for enrollment. If the student meets one or both conditions, the student is accepted. The If statement in Figure 5-55, which uses the Or logical operator, will solve this problem.

```
147        If decGPA >= 3.5D Or intSATScore >= 1080 Then
148            lblAcceptance.Text = "You have been accepted"
149        Else
150            lblAcceptance.Text = "You are not accepted"
151        End If
```

FIGURE 5-55

In Figure 5-55 on the previous page, if the decGPA is 3.2 but the intSATScore is 1130, the compound condition would be considered true because at least one of its conditions (intSATScore >= 1080) is true (Figure 5-56).

FIGURE 5-56

Use the Not Logical Operator

The **Not logical operator** allows you to state conditions that are best expressed in a negative way. In essence, the Not logical operator reverses the logical value of a condition on which it operates. For example, if a shoe store sells shoes under size 14 from its showroom but requires special orders for larger sizes, the code could use the Not logical operator shown in Figure 5-57 to negate the condition in the statement.

```
155        If Not decShoeSize >= 14 Then
156            lblOrderPolicy.Text = "Showroom shoe style available"
157        Else
158            lblOrderPolicy.Text = "Special order needed"
159        End If
```

FIGURE 5-57

The statement in Figure 5-57 works, but the use of the Not logical operator makes the If statement somewhat difficult to understand. Generally, a statement that avoids using the Not logical operator is more easily understood. For example, the code in Figure 5-58 accomplishes the same task as the code in Figure 5-57 and is easier to understand.

```
162        If decShoeSize < 14 Then
163            lblOrderPolicy.Text = "Showroom shoe style available"
164        Else
165            lblOrderPolicy.Text = "Special order needed"
166        End If
```

FIGURE 5-58

Other Logical Operators

The Visual Basic programming language provides three other logical operators, as shown in the table in Figure 5-59.

Logical Operator	Meaning
Xor	When one condition in the compound condition is true, but not both, the compound condition is true
AndAlso	As soon as a condition is found to be false, no further conditions are tested and the compound condition is false
OrElse	As soon as a condition is found to be true, no further conditions are tested and the compound condition is true

FIGURE 5-59

© 2014 Cengage Learning

Order of Operations for Logical Operators

You can combine more than one logical operator in the same If . . . Then statement. In an If statement, arithmetic operators are evaluated first, relational operators are evaluated next, and logical operators are evaluated last. The order of operations for logical operators is shown in Figure 5-60.

Logical Operator	Order
Not	Highest Precedence
And, AndAlso	Next Precedence
Or, OrElse, Xor	Last Precedence

FIGURE 5-60

© 2014 Cengage Learning

In most cases, if a developer uses multiple relational or logical operators in an If statement, the order of precedence should be established through the use of parentheses to clarify the sequence of evaluation. As in arithmetic expressions, conditional expressions within parentheses are evaluated before conditional expressions outside parentheses.

Select Case Statement

In some programming applications, different operations can occur based on the value in a single field. For example, in Figure 5-61, the user enters the number of the day in the week and the program displays the name of the day. The program must evaluate the number of the day value and display the name of the correct day.

user enters number

program displays corresponding day name

FIGURE 5-61

In Figure 5-61, if the number of the day is 1, then the value Monday should be displayed. If the number of the day is 2, then Tuesday should be displayed, and so on. If the number of the day is 6 or 7, then the value Weekend should be displayed. If the user does not enter a value of 1 through 7, the user should be prompted to do so.

To solve this problem, a series of If . . . Then . . . ElseIf statements could be used, but an easier and clearer way to solve the problem is to use the Select Case statement.

When using a Select Case statement, the value in a single field, such as the day number, is evaluated. Based on the value in the field, a distinct action is taken. In this case, the name of the day is displayed.

A general example of the Select Case statement is shown in Figure 5-62.

```
168        Select Case Test Expression
169            Case First Expression
170                Statement(s) for First Case
171            Case Second Expression
172                Statement(s) for Second Case
173            Case Third Expression
174                Statement(s) for Third Case
175            Case Else
176                Statement(s) for when the Case Conditions do not match the
177                    test expressions above
178        End Select
```

FIGURE 5-62

The code for the Determine Day of Week application is shown in Figure 5-63.

```
13          Select Case intDayNumber
14              Case 1
15                  lblDayOfWeek.Text = "Monday"
16              Case 2
17                  lblDayOfWeek.Text = "Tuesday"
18              Case 3
19                  lblDayOfWeek.Text = "Wednesday"
20              Case 4
21                  lblDayOfWeek.Text = "Thursday"
22              Case 5
23                  lblDayOfWeek.Text = "Friday"
24              Case 6
25                  lblDayOfWeek.Text = "Weekend"
26              Case 7
27                  lblDayOfWeek.Text = "Weekend"
28              Case Else
29                  lblDayOfWeek.Text = "Enter 1 through 7"
30          End Select
```

FIGURE 5-63

The Select Case statement begins with the Select Case command. The test expression specifies the value or variable to be tested in the Select Case statement. In Figure 5-63, the variable is intDayNumber. So, when the Select Case statement is executed, each of the cases will be compared to the value in the intDayNumber variable.

Each Case statement specifies the value for which the test expression is checked. For example, the first Case statement on line 14 in Figure 5-63 specifies the value 1. If the value in the variable intDayNumber is equal to 1, the program executes the statement following the first Case statement up to the second Case statement (line 16). In Figure 5-63, the assignment statement on line 15 that sets the Text property of lblDayOfWeek to Monday is executed if the value in intDayNumber is equal to 1. More than one statement can follow a Case statement.

If the expression following the first Case statement is not true, then the next Case statement is evaluated. In Figure 5-63, the Case statement on line 16 checks if the value in intDayNumber is equal to 2. If so, the Text property of lblDayOf-Week is set to Tuesday. This process continues through the remainder of the Case statements.

The Case Else statement on line 28 is an optional entry that includes all conditions not specifically tested in the other Case statements. In Figure 5-63, if the value in the intDayNumber variable is not equal to 1 through 7, then the statement following the Case Else statement is executed. While not required, good programming practice dictates that the Case Else statement should be used so that all cases are accounted for and the program performs a specific action regardless of the value found in the test expression.

The End Select statement is required to end the Select Case statement. When you enter the Select Case statement in Visual Studio 2012, IntelliSense automatically includes the End Select statement.

Select Case Test Expressions

The example in Figure 5-63 on the previous page used an integer as the test expression value, but a value of any data type can be used in the test expression. For example, the test expression in Figure 5-64 uses the Text property of the txtStudentMajor TextBox object as a string value.

```
217        Select Case txtStudentMajor.Text
218            Case "Accounting"
219                lblDepartment.Text = "Business"
220            Case "Marketing"
221                lblDepartment.Text = "Business"
222            Case "Electrical Engineering"
223                lblDepartment.Text = "Engineering"
224            Case "Biochemistry"
225                lblDepartment.Text = "Chemistry"
226            Case "Shakespearean Literature"
227                lblDepartment.Text = "English"
228            Case "Web Design and E-Commerce"
229                lblDepartment.Text = "CIS"
230            Case Else
231                lblDepartment.Text = "Other"
232        End Select
```

FIGURE 5-64

HEADS UP

If you forget to type the Is keyword in the Case Is statement, Visual Studio will insert it for you.

In Figure 5-64, the Select Case statement is used to test the value in the Text property of the txtStudentMajor TextBox object and move the corresponding department name to the Text property of the lblDepartment object. The Case statements specify the values to be tested in the text box. The use of a string for the Select Case statement works in the same manner as other data types.

Use Relational Operators in a Select Case Statement

You can use relational operators in a Select Case statement, but you must use the keyword Is with the relational operator. For example, in Figure 5-41 on page 309, an If . . . Then . . . ElseIf statement was used to determine the shipping cost. That same processing could be accomplished using a Select Case statement, as shown in Figure 5-65.

```
191        Select Case decOrderAmount
192            Case Is > 500D
193                decShippingCost = 30D
194            Case Is > 400D
195                decShippingCost = 25D
196            Case Is > 200D
197                decShippingCost = 20D
198            Case Is > 0D
199                decShippingCost = 15D
200            Case Else
201                decShippingCost = 0D
202        End Select
203
```

FIGURE 5-65

Use Ranges in Select Case Statements

Another way to specify values in a Select Case statement is to use ranges. In Figure 5-66, the Case statements illustrate testing for six different conditions.

```
224        Select Case intGradeLevel
225            Case 1 To 3
226                lblGradeLevelExam.Text = "Early elementary"
227            Case 4 To 6
228                lblGradeLevelExam.Text = "Late elementary"
229            Case 7 To 8
230                lblGradeLevelExam.Text = "Middle school"
231            Case 9 To 10
232                lblGradeLevelExam.Text = "Early high school"
233            Case 11
234                lblGradeLevelExam.Text = "Late high school"
235            Case 12
236                lblGradeLevelExam.Text = "Final exam"
237            Case Else
238                lblGradeLevelExam.Text = "Invalid grade level"
239        End Select
```

FIGURE 5-66

As you can see, a range of values is specified in a Case statement by stating the beginning value, the word To, and then the ending value in the range. The Case statements will test the value in the intGradeLevel variable and the appropriate statements will be executed.

You also can write Case statements so that more than one distinct value is tested. In Figure 5-67, the Case statement tests the individual values of 1, 3, 8, 11, and 17 against the value specified in the intDepartmentNumber variable.

```
230        Select Case intDepartmentNumber
231            Case 1, 3, 8, 11, 17
232
```

FIGURE 5-67

Notice in Figure 5-67 that each value in the Case statement is separated by a comma. The code in Figure 5-68 shows a combination of the two techniques, using both commas and a To statement.

```
234        Select Case intDepartmentNumber
235            Case 2, 4, 7, 12 To 16, 22
```

FIGURE 5-68

Select Which Decision Structure to Use

In some instances, you might need to determine if you should use the Select Case statement or the If . . . Then . . . ElseIf statement to solve a problem. Generally, the Select Case statement is most useful when more than two or three values must be tested for a given variable. For example, in Figure 5-64 on page 324, six different values are checked in the Text property of the txtStudentMajor TextBox object. This is a perfect example of when to use the Select Case statement.

The If . . . Then . . . ElseIf statement is more flexible because more than one variable can be used in the comparison. Programmers can also use compound conditions with the And, Or, and Not logical operators.

Use Code Snippets

Visual Basic includes a library of almost 500 pieces of code, called IntelliSense **code snippets**, that you can insert into an application. Each snippet consists of a complete programming task such as an If . . . Then . . . Else decision structure, sending an email message, or drawing a circle. Inserting these commonly used pieces of code is an effective way to enhance productivity. You also can create your own snippets and add them to the library.

In addition to inserting snippets in your program, you can display a code snippet to ensure you understand the syntax and requirements for a given type of statement. To insert and display a code snippet for the If . . . Then . . . Else statement, you can complete the following steps:

STEP 1   Press and hold or right-click the line in the code window where you want to insert the snippet.

Visual Studio displays a shortcut menu (Figure 5-69). It is important to press and hold or right-click the code window in the exact location where you want the code snippet to appear. If you press and hold or right-click outside this location, the shortcut menu might list customized choices for the wrong area of code. In addition, if you tap or click in the wrong place, the snippet will be positioned in the incorrect location in your program.

FIGURE 5-69

STEP 2   Tap or click Insert Snippet on the shortcut menu.

Visual Studio displays a menu of folders that contain snippets (Figure 5-70). The code snippets in each folder correspond to their folder titles.

FIGURE 5-70

STEP 3   Double-tap or double-click the folder named Code Patterns - If, For Each, Try Catch, Property, etc, which contains commonly used code such as the If . . . Then . . . Else statement.

Visual Studio displays a menu of folders for code patterns (Figure 5-71).

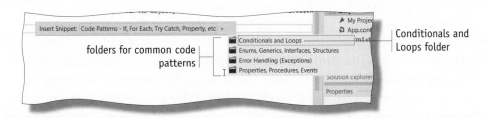

FIGURE 5-71

STEP 4   Double-tap or double-click the Conditionals and Loops folder because an If . . . Then . . . Else statement is a conditional statement.

Visual Studio displays the list of Conditionals and Loops code snippets (Figure 5-72). Some of these statements will be unfamiliar until you complete Chapter 6, but you can see that the list of code snippets includes several different types of If statements.

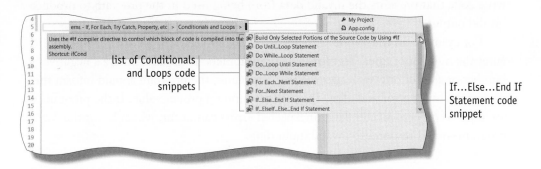

FIGURE 5-72

STEP 5   Double-tap or double-click the If . . . Else . . . End If Statement code snippet.

The If . . . Else . . . End If Statement code snippet is inserted into the code on the line selected in Step 1 (Figure 5-73). The highlighted text must be replaced by the condition(s) to be tested in the If statement. The programmer must add the code to be executed when the condition is true and the code to be executed when the condition is false.

FIGURE 5-73

You must modify the code snippet shown in Figure 5-73 for the code to work properly. You may find that modifying a complicated code snippet is more work than using IntelliSense to enter the statement.

Code snippets are also helpful for learning or reviewing the format and syntax of a statement. For example, if you want to review the syntax of an If . . . Then . . . ElseIf statement, you could insert the statement into the code window and examine it. You could then either tap or click the Undo button to remove the statement or you could comment out the snippet code and keep it for your review. In many cases when checking syntax, reviewing a snippet is faster and clearer than consulting Visual Basic help.

Validate Data

Since the first days of computers, the phrase "garbage in, garbage out" has described the fact that allowing incorrect input data into a program produces incorrect output. Developers should anticipate that users will enter invalid data. Therefore, they must write code that prevents the invalid data from being used in the program to produce invalid output.

For example, in the Wood Cabinet Estimate application, the user is asked to enter the number of linear feet for the wood cabinets. If the user enters a negative number or a letter or even leaves the text box blank, the program should inform the user of the input error and allow the user to reenter a proper value. If the program attempts to process invalid data, unexpected errors can occur, which is not the way a program should respond to invalid input data.

To properly check the linear feet value entered by the user, two tests must be performed. First, the program must check the value to ensure it is numeric. Second, the numeric value entered by the user must be checked to ensure it is greater than zero. These tests are explained in the following sections.

Test Input to Determine If the Value Is Numeric

In the Wood Cabinet Estimate application, if no check is performed on the input data and the user accidentally enters a nonnumeric character such as an "a" or does not enter a value at all, the program will fail when Visual Basic attempts to convert that value to a number. An exception (error) screen will open and the program will be terminated. Therefore, the program must check the value entered by the user to ensure it is numeric. In addition, if the user enters a nonnumeric value, the program should inform the user of the error and request a valid numeric value.

The Visual Basic **IsNumeric function** can check the input value to determine if it can be converted into a numeric value such as an Integer or Decimal data type. If so, it returns a True Boolean value. If the value is not recognized as a numeric value, the IsNumeric function returns a False Boolean value.

For example, the IsNumeric function can check the value in the Text property of the Linear Feet text box. If the user enters a letter such as "a" in the text box, the IsNumeric function will return a False Boolean value because the letter "a" is not numeric.

Because the IsNumeric function returns a Boolean value (True or False), it can be placed within an If statement as the condition to be tested. If the returned value is True, the condition in the If statement is considered true. If the returned value is False, the condition in the If statement is considered false. The code in Figure 5-74 uses an If statement to determine if the Text property of the txtLinearFeet TextBox object is numeric.

FIGURE 5-74

© 2014 Cengage Learning

In Figure 5-74, the If statement on line 27 calls the IsNumeric function. The Text property of the txtLinearFeet TextBox object is the argument for the IsNumeric function. As a result of this specification, the IsNumeric function will analyze the data in the Text property of the txtLinearFeet TextBox object. If the data can be converted to a numeric data type, then the function will return a Boolean value of True. If the data cannot be converted to a numeric data type, the function will return a Boolean value of False.

Once the function has returned a Boolean value, the If statement tests the Boolean value. If it is true, the value in the Text property of the txtLinearFeet Text-Box object is numeric, and the appropriate statements are executed. If the condition is false, meaning the value is not numeric, the statements on lines 51–55 are executed. The statement on line 52 displays a message box telling the user to enter the linear feet of the cabinet (see Figure 5-2 on page 285). The caption of the message box is "Input Error". The statement on line 53 clears the Text property. The statement on line 54 sets the focus on the text box so the user can reenter the value.

Check for a Positive Number

If the condition in Figure 5-74 on the previous page is true, the value in the Text property must be converted to a Decimal data type. Then, the program checks to ensure the entered value is greater than zero. These statements are shown in Figure 5-75.

```
27        If IsNumeric(txtLinearFeet.Text) Then
28            decLinearFeet = Convert.ToDecimal(txtLinearFeet.Text)
29
30            ' Is linear feet greater than zero
31            If decLinearFeet > 0 Then
⋮                Statement(s) executed when condition is true
33            Else
34                ' Display error message if user entered a negative value
35                MsgBox("You entered " & decLinearFeet.ToString() &
36                    ". Enter a Number Greater Than Zero.", , "Input Error")
37                txtLinearFeet.Text = ""
38                txtLinearFeet.Focus()
39            End If
40        Else
41            ' Display error message if user entered a nonnumeric value
42            MsgBox("Enter the Linear Feet of the Cabinets.", , "Input Error")
43            txtLinearFeet.Text = ""
44            txtLinearFeet.Focus()
45        End If
```

FIGURE 5-75

When the value in the Text property is numeric, it is converted to a Decimal value (line 28). On line 31, the Decimal value is compared to zero. If it is greater than zero, then the processing for a true statement is executed. If the value is not greater than zero, a message box is displayed to inform the user that an invalid entry was made (see Figure 5-29 on page 300). The user then can enter a valid value.

The process of validating input data is fundamental to programming when using a graphical user interface. A well-designed program must ensure the user enters valid data.

Is validating input only important for good design?
Creating a secure program that cannot be hacked starts with validating input. A program's first line of defense is to check every piece of entered data. If you can keep malicious data from entering a program, or at least keep it from being processed, your program becomes much harder to attack.

Program Design

As you have learned, the requirements document identifies the purpose of the program being developed, the application title, the procedures to be followed when using the program, any required equations and calculations, any conditions that must be tested, notes and restrictions that must be followed by the program, and any other comments that would be helpful to understanding the problem. The requirements document for the Wood Cabinet Estimate application is shown in Figure 5-76. The Use Case Definition document is shown in Figure 5-77 on the next page.

REQUIREMENTS DOCUMENT

Date Submitted: January 29, 2015

Application Title: Wood Cabinet Estimate

Purpose: This application calculates the estimated cost of wood cabinetry for a job bid.

Program Procedures: The user should enter the linear footage of cabinets needed and select the type of wood. The estimated cost for the cabinet job will be displayed.

Algorithms, Processing, and Conditions:
1. The user must be able to enter the number of linear feet of cabinetry.
2. The user must be able to select one of three wood types — pine, oak, or cherry.
3. The user can initiate the calculation and display the cost estimate for the wood cabinets.
4. The application computes the cost estimate of the cabinets based on the number of linear feet and the cost of the wood. Pine costs $300 per linear foot of cabinets, oak costs $500 per linear foot, and cherry costs $650 per linear foot.
5. The estimate calculation is linear feet x cost per linear foot.
6. The cost estimate is displayed in currency format.
7. The user should be able to clear the linear feet entered, reset the wood type to pine, and clear the cost estimate.

Notes and Restrictions:
1. If the user enters a nonnumeric value for the linear feet or leaves the TextBox object empty, the user should be advised and asked for a valid entry.
2. If the user enters a negative number for the linear feet, the user should be advised and asked for a valid entry.

Comments: The title of the Windows Form should be Wood Cabinet Estimate.

FIGURE 5-76

USE CASE DEFINITION

1. The window opens and displays the Wood Cabinet Estimate, a text box requesting the number of linear feet for the cabinets, radio buttons to select the wood type, and two buttons labeled Calculate and Clear.
2. The user enters the linear feet and selects one of the wood types.
3. The user clicks the Calculate button.
4. The user will be warned if a nonnumeric value is entered, the text box is left empty, or a negative number is entered.
5. The program displays the cost estimate for the cabinetry job.
6. The user clicks the Clear button to clear the Linear Feet text box, set the wood choice to Pine, and erase the cost estimate.
7. The user clicks the Close button to terminate the application.

FIGURE 5-77

© 2014 Cengage Learning

Event Planning Document

You will recall that the event planning document is a table that specifies which objects in the user interface will cause events, the action taken by the user to trigger each event, and the event processing that must occur. The event planning document for the Wood Cabinet Estimate application is shown in Figure 5-78.

EVENT PLANNING DOCUMENT

Program Name: Wood Cabinet Estimate	Developer: Corinne Hoisington	Object: frmWoodCabinets	Date: January 29, 2015
OBJECT	EVENT TRIGGER	EVENT PROCESSING	
btnCalculate	Click	Ensure data entered is numeric Display error message if data is not numeric or text box is empty Convert data entered to numeric Ensure data entered is greater than zero Display error message if data is not greater than zero Assign wood cost per foot based on type of wood selection Calculate cost (linear feet $\times$ cost per foot) Display cost	
btnClear	Click	Clear input text box Clear cost estimate Set the Pine radio button to checked Clear the Oak radio button Clear the Cherry radio button Set focus on input text box	
frmWoodCabinets	Load	Set focus on input text box Clear the placement zeros for cost	

FIGURE 5-78

© 2014 Cengage Learning

Design and Code the Program

After identifying the events and tasks within the events, the developer is ready to create the program. As you have learned, creating the program means designing the user interface and then entering Visual Basic statements to accomplish the tasks specified in the event planning document. As the developer enters the code, she also will implement the logic to carry out the required processing.

NOTE TO THE LEARNER

In the following activity, you should complete the tasks within the specified steps. Each of the tasks is accompanied by a Hint Screen. The purpose of the Hint Screen is to indicate where you should perform the activity in the Visual Studio window and to remind you which method to use. If you need further help completing a step, refer to the figure identified by *ref:*.

Guided Program Development

To design the user interface for the Wood Cabinet Estimate application and enter the code required to process each event in the program, complete the steps on the next page.

Guided Program Development

Phase 1: Design the Form

1

- **Create a Windows Application** Open Visual Studio using the Search charm (Windows 8) or the Start button on the Windows taskbar and the All Programs submenu (Windows 7). Create a new Visual Basic Windows Application project by completing the following: Tap or click the New Project button on the Standard toolbar; select and expand Windows in the left pane; select Windows Forms Application; name the project by entering Wood Cabinet Estimate in the Name text box; then tap or click the OK button in the New Project window.

HINT

Name: Wood Cabinet Estimate

- **Name the Form** In the Solution Explorer pane, press and hold or right-click Form1.vb and then tap or click Rename. Type frmWoodCabinets.vb, and then press the ENTER key. Tap or click the Yes button to automatically change the form (Name) in the Properties window.

HINT

Wood Cabinet Estimate
- My Project
- App.config
- frmWoodCabinets.vb

- **Change the Size Property** In the Properties window, change the Size property to 350, 500.

- **Change the BackColor Property** In the Properties window, change the BackColor property to Moccasin.

- **Change the Text on the Title Bar** To change the text on the title bar, tap or click the form, scroll down the Properties window until the Text property is displayed, double-tap or double-click the right column of the Text property, type Wood Cabinet Estimate, and then press the ENTER key.

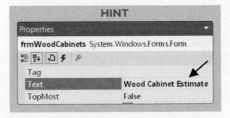

HINT

Properties

frmWoodCabinets System.Windows.Forms.Form

Tag
Text   Wood Cabinet Estimate
TopMost   False

- **Add a Heading Title** Drag a label onto the form and name the label lblHeading. Set the Text property for the Label object to Wood Cabinet Cost. Set the font to Goudy Old Style, Bold, 20 points. Position the label horizontally in the center of the form.

HINT

Wood Cabinet Esti...

Wood Cabinet Cost

- **Add a Label** Drag a second label onto the frmWoodCabinets Form object and name the label `lblLinearFeet`. Set the Text property of the Label object to `Linear Feet:`. Set the font to Goudy Old Style, Bold, 14 points. Position the label to resemble the one shown in Figure 5-79.

- **Add a TextBox Object** Drag a TextBox object onto the form. Using snap lines, align the top of the TextBox object with the top of the second Label object. Name the TextBox object `txtFeet`. Change the TextAlign property to Center. Change the font to Goudy Old Style, Bold, 14 points. Reduce the width of the TextBox object to closely resemble the one in Figure 5-79. Center the Label object and the TextBox object horizontally in the frmWoodCabinets Form object.

A title Label object is displayed on the first line of the form. A Label object and TextBox object occupy the second line of the frmWoodCabinets Form object (Figure 5-79). They are centered horizontally in the form.

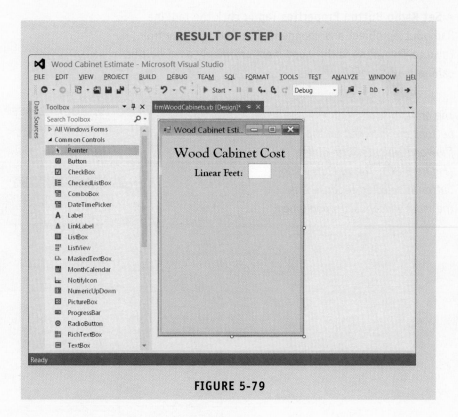

RESULT OF STEP 1

FIGURE 5-79

(continues)

• **Add a GroupBox** Drag a GroupBox object from the Container category of the Toolbox to the frmWoodCabinets Form object. Name the GroupBox grpWoodType. Change the Text property to Wood Type. Set the size of the GroupBox object to 160, 100. Change the BackColor of the GroupBox object to White. Center the GroupBox object horizontally in the frmWoodCabinets Form object, and change the font to Goudy Old Style, Regular, 12 points *(ref: Figure 5-4)*.

• **Add Radio Buttons** Place three RadioButton objects on the GroupBox object. Name the first RadioButton radPine and change its Text property to Pine. Name the second Radio-Button radOak and change its Text property to Oak. Name the third RadioButton radCherry and change its Text property to Cherry. If necessary, select the three Radio-Buttons and change the font to Goudy Old Style, Regular, 12 points *(ref: Figure 5-7)*.

• **Set Radio Button Properties** Tap or click the radPine RadioButton object and change its Checked property from False to True. Pine is the wood most commonly used by this cabinetmaker *(ref: Figure 5-11)*.

The group box and radio buttons are included on the frmWoodCabinets Form object (Figure 5-80). The radPine radio button is selected because it is the most widely used wood type.

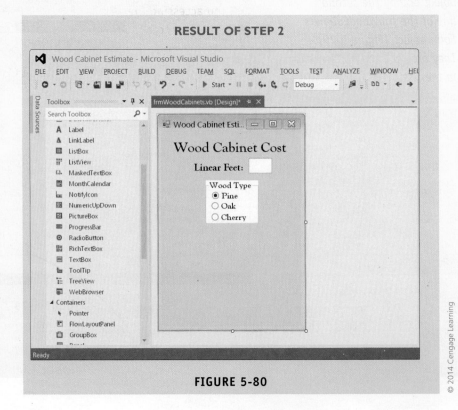

FIGURE 5-80

© 2014 Cengage Learning

3

- **Add Estimate and Cost Labels** Drag two more Label objects onto the form below the GroupBox object. Align these labels by their tops using snap lines. Name the first label `lblCost`, change its Text property to `Cost Estimate:`, and resize the Label object to view the text. Name the second label `lblCostEstimate` and set its Text property to `$0000.00`. These placement zeros allow you to view the Label object when it is not selected. The placement zeros will be cleared using code when the form is loaded. Change the font for both Label objects to Goudy Old Style, Bold, 14 points. Horizontally center the labels as a unit on the frmWoodCabinets Form object.

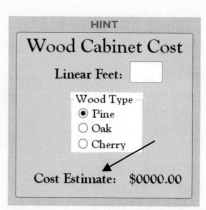

- **Add Calculate and Clear Buttons** Drag two Button objects onto the form. Align the tops of the Button objects using snap lines. Name the left Button object `btnCalculate` and change its Text property to `Calculate`. Name the right Button object `btnClear` and change its Text property to `Clear`. Change the font for these two buttons to Goudy Old Style, Regular, 12 points. Change the size of each button to `100, 30`. Change the BackColor property for each button to White.

- **Add a Picture to the Windows Form** Download the Cabinets.jpg picture by visiting CengageBrain.com and accessing the resources for this chapter. Drag a PictureBox object to the bottom of the Windows Form. Name the picture `picCabinets`. Change the Size property of the PictureBox object to `330, 115`. Change the SizeMode property to StretchImage.

The user interface is complete (Figure 5-81).

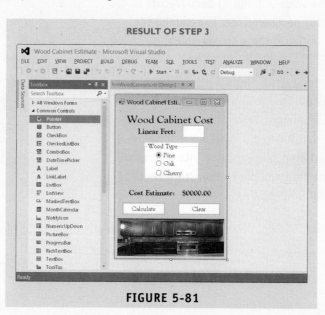

FIGURE 5-81

(continues)

Phase 2: Code the Application

4

- **Code the Comments** Double-tap or double-click the btnCalculate Button object on the frmWoodCabinets Form object to open the code window and create the btnCalculate_Click event handler. Close the Toolbox. Tap or click in front of the first words, Public Class frmWoodCabinets, and then press the ENTER key to create a blank line. Insert the first four standard comments. Insert the Option Strict On command at the beginning of the code to turn on strict type checking.

- **Add Comments to the btnCalculate_ Click Event Handler** Enter a comment to describe the purpose of the btnCalculate_ Click event.

- **Declare and Initialize the Variables** This application requires six Decimal variables: 1) decFeet: Holds the estimated linear footage of the cabinets; 2) decCostPerFoot: Holds the cost per linear foot based on the wood type; 3) decCost Estimate: Is assigned the calculated final estimated cost; 4) decPineCost: Is assigned the value 300.00; 5) decOakCost: Is assigned the value 500.00; 6) decCherryCost: Is assigned the value 650.00. Declare and initialize these six variables.

- **Write the If Statement to Test for Numeric Data** When the user clicks the Calculate button, the program must first ensure that the user entered a valid numeric value in the txtFeet TextBox object. If the user has entered a valid numeric value, the value must be converted from a string value into a Decimal data type. Write the If statement and conversion statement required for this process (ref: Figure 5-74).

- **Write the If Statement to Test for a Positive Number** If the value in the txtFeet TextBox object is numeric, then the converted numeric value must be checked to ensure it is a positive number. Write the If statement to check whether the converted numeric value is greater than zero *(ref: Figure 5-75)*.

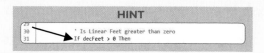

```
HINT
29
30          ' Is Linear Feet greater than zero
31          If decFeet > 0 Then
```

- **Write the If Statements to Determine the Cost Per Linear Foot** When the value is greater than zero, the cost per linear foot is determined by checking the status of the RadioButton objects and placing the appropriate cost per linear foot in the decCostPerFoot variable. Using the If . . . Then . . . ElseIf structure, write the statements to identify the checked radio button and place the appropriate cost in the decCostPerFoot variable *(ref: Figure 5-49)*.

```
HINT
32              ' Determine cost per foot of wood
33              If radPine.Checked Then
34                  decCostPerFoot = decPineCost
35              ElseIf radOak.Checked Then
36                  decCostPerFoot = decOakCost
37              ElseIf radCherry.Checked Then
38                  decCostPerFoot = decCherryCost
39              End If
```

- **Calculate and Display the Cost Estimate**
The next step is to calculate the cost estimate by multiplying the value in the decCostPerFoot variable by the linear feet. Next, display the cost estimate in the cost estimate label. Write the statements to calculate and display the cost estimate in the currency format.

```
HINT
41              ' Calculate and display the cost estimate
42              decCostEstimate = decFeet * decCostPerFoot
43              lblCostEstimate.Text = decCostEstimate.ToString("C")
```

- **Display a Message Box If the Value Entered Is Not Greater Than Zero**

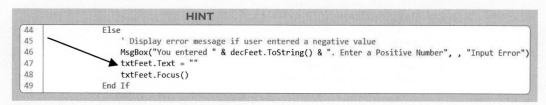

```
HINT
44          Else
45              ' Display error message if user entered a negative value
46              MsgBox("You entered " & decFeet.ToString() & ". Enter a Positive Number", , "Input Error")
47              txtFeet.Text = ""
48              txtFeet.Focus()
49          End If
```

After the processing is finished for the true portion of the If statements, the Else portion of the If statements must be written. Write the code to display the message box that contains the error message when the user enters a value that is not greater than zero *(ref: Figure 5-24)*.

- **Display an Error Message If the Value Entered Is Not Numeric** Write the Else portion of the If statement to display an error message if the value entered by the user is not numeric *(ref: Figure 5-24)*.

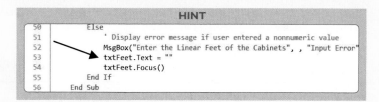

```
HINT
50          Else
51              ' Display error message if user entered a nonnumeric value
52              MsgBox("Enter the Linear Feet of the Cabinets", , "Input Error"
53              txtFeet.Text = ""
54              txtFeet.Focus()
55          End If
56      End Sub
```

(continues)

The code for the click event of the Calculate button is completed (Figure 5-82).

RESULT OF STEP 4

```vb
 1  ' Program Name:  Wood Cabinet Estimate
 2  ' Author:        Corinne Hoisington
 3  ' Date:          January 29, 2015
 4  ' Purpose:       This Windows application computes the estimated cost
 5  '                of wood cabinets based on the number of linear feet of
 6  '                cabinets and the following cost per linear foot:
 7  '                Pine - $300.00 per linear foot; Oak - $500.00 per
 8  '                linear foot; Cherry - $650.00 per linear foot.
 9
10  Option Strict On
11
12  Public Class frmWoodCabinets
13
14      Private Sub btnCalculate_Click(ByVal sender As System.Object, ByVal e As System.EventArgs) Handles btnCalculate.Click
15          ' The btnCalculate event handler calculates the estimated cost of
16          ' cabinets based on the linear feet and the wood type.
17
18          ' Declaration Section
19          Dim decFeet As Decimal
20          Dim decCostPerFoot As Decimal
21          Dim decCostEstimate As Decimal
22          Dim decPineCost As Decimal = 300D
23          Dim decOakCost As Decimal = 500D
24          Dim decCherryCost As Decimal = 650D
25
26          ' Did user enter a numeric value?
27          If IsNumeric(txtFeet.Text) Then
28              decFeet = Convert.ToDecimal(txtFeet.Text)
29
30              ' Is Linear Feet greater than zero
31              If decFeet > 0 Then
32                  ' Determine cost per foot of wood
33                  If radPine.Checked Then
34                      decCostPerFoot = decPineCost
35                  ElseIf radOak.Checked Then
36                      decCostPerFoot = decOakCost
37                  ElseIf radCherry.Checked Then
38                      decCostPerFoot = decCherryCost
39                  End If
40
41                  ' Calculate and display the cost estimate
42                  decCostEstimate = decFeet * decCostPerFoot
43                  lblCostEstimate.Text = decCostEstimate.ToString("C")
44              Else
45                  ' Display error message if user entered a negative value
46                  MsgBox("You entered " & decFeet.ToString() & ". Enter a Positive Number", , "Input Error")
47                  txtFeet.Text = ""
48                  txtFeet.Focus()
49              End If
50          Else
51              ' Display error message if user entered a nonnumeric value
52              MsgBox("Enter the Linear Feet of the Cabinets", , "Input Error")
53              txtFeet.Text = ""
54              txtFeet.Focus()
55          End If
56      End Sub
```

FIGURE 5-82

5

• **Create the Clear Button Click Event Handler** The Clear Button click event includes the following processing: 1) Clear the txtFeet Text property; 2) Clear the lblCostEstimate Text property; 3) Set the radPine Checked property to True; 4) Set the radOak and radCherry Checked properties to False; 5) Set the focus in the txtFeet text box. To enter this code, tap or click the frmWood-Cabinets.vb [Design] tab and then double-tap or double-click the Clear button. Using IntelliSense, enter the required code.

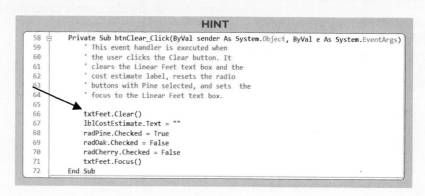

```
HINT
58    Private Sub btnClear_Click(ByVal sender As System.Object, ByVal e As System.EventArgs)
59        ' This event handler is executed when
60        ' the user clicks the Clear button. It
61        ' clears the Linear Feet text box and the
62        ' cost estimate label, resets the radio
63        ' buttons with Pine selected, and sets  the
64        ' focus to the Linear Feet text box.
65
66        txtFeet.Clear()
67        lblCostEstimate.Text = ""
68        radPine.Checked = True
69        radOak.Checked = False
70        radCherry.Checked = False
71        txtFeet.Focus()
72    End Sub
```

• **Create the Form Load Event Handler** When the frmWoodCabinets Form object loads, the following processing should occur: 1) The focus is in the txtFeet text box; 2) The lblCostEstimate Text property is set to null. Tap or click the frmWoodCabinets.vb [Design] tab to return to Design view and then double-tap or double-click the form. Enter the code for the form load event handler.

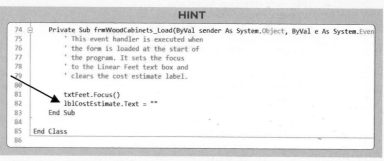

```
HINT
74    Private Sub frmWoodCabinets_Load(ByVal sender As System.Object, ByVal e As System.Even
75        ' This event handler is executed when
76        ' the form is loaded at the start of
77        ' the program. It sets the focus
78        ' to the Linear Feet text box and
79        ' clears the cost estimate label.
80
81        txtFeet.Focus()
82        lblCostEstimate.Text = ""
83    End Sub
84
85 End Class
86
```

6

• **Run the Application** After you have completed the code, you should run the application to ensure it works properly.

• **Test the Application** Test the application with the following data: 1) Linear feet 25, wood type Oak; 2) Linear feet 9, wood type Cherry; 3) Linear feet 100, wood type Pine; 4) Linear feet Fifteen (use this word), wood type Cherry; 5) Linear feet −21, wood type Oak; 6) Use other values to thoroughly test the program. After each test, tap or click the Clear button before entering new data.

• **Close the Program** After testing the application, close the window by tapping or clicking the Close button in the title bar of the window.

Code Listing

The complete code for the sample program is shown in Figure 5-83.

```vbnet
1   ' Program Name: Wood Cabinet Estimate
2   ' Author:        Corinne Hoisington
3   ' Date:          January 29, 2015
4   ' Purpose:       This Windows application computes the estimated cost
5   '                of wood cabinets based on the number of linear feet of
6   '                cabinets and the following cost per linear foot:
7   '                Pine - $300.00 per linear foot; Oak - $500.00 per
8   '                linear foot; Cherry - $650.00 per linear foot.
9
10  Option Strict On
11
12  Public Class frmWoodCabinets
13
14      Private Sub btnCalculate_Click(ByVal sender As System.Object, ByVal e As System.EventArgs) Handles btnCalculate.Click
15          ' The btnCalculate event handler calculates the estimated cost of
16          ' cabinets based on the linear feet and the wood type.
17
18          ' Declaration Section
19          Dim decFeet As Decimal
20          Dim decCostPerFoot As Decimal
21          Dim decCostEstimate As Decimal
22          Dim decPineCost As Decimal = 300D
23          Dim decOakCost As Decimal = 500D
24          Dim decCherryCost As Decimal = 650D
25
26          ' Did user enter a numeric value?
27          If IsNumeric(txtFeet.Text) Then
28              decFeet = Convert.ToDecimal(txtFeet.Text)
29
30              ' Is Linear Feet greater than zero
31              If decFeet > 0 Then
32                  ' Determine cost per foot of wood
33                  If radPine.Checked Then
34                      decCostPerFoot = decPineCost
35                  ElseIf radOak.Checked Then
36                      decCostPerFoot = decOakCost
37                  ElseIf radCherry.Checked Then
38                      decCostPerFoot = decCherryCost
39                  End If
40
41                  ' Calculate and display the cost estimate
42                  decCostEstimate = decFeet * decCostPerFoot
43                  lblCostEstimate.Text = decCostEstimate.ToString("C")
44              Else
45                  ' Display error message if user entered a negative value
46                  MsgBox("You entered " & decFeet.ToString() & ". Enter a Positive Number", , "Input Error")
47                  txtFeet.Text = ""
48                  txtFeet.Focus()
49              End If
50          Else
51              ' Display error message if user entered a nonnumeric value
52              MsgBox("Enter the Linear Feet of the Cabinets", , "Input Error")
53              txtFeet.Text = ""
54              txtFeet.Focus()
55          End If
56      End Sub
```

FIGURE 5-83 (continues)

```
58 ⊟    Private Sub btnClear_Click(ByVal sender As System.Object, ByVal e As System.EventArgs) Handles btnClear.Click
59             ' This event handler is executed when
60             ' the user clicks the Clear button. It
61             ' clears the Linear Feet text box and the
62             ' cost estimate label, resets the radio
63             ' buttons with Pine selected, and sets  the
64             ' focus to the Linear Feet text box.
65
66             txtFeet.Clear()
67             lblCostEstimate.Text = ""
68             radPine.Checked = True
69             radOak.Checked = False
70             radCherry.Checked = False
71             txtFeet.Focus()
72        End Sub
73
74 ⊟    Private Sub frmCabinetCost_Load(ByVal sender As System.Object, ByVal e As System.EventArgs) Handles MyBase.Load
75             ' This event handler is executed when
76             ' the form is loaded at the start of
77             ' the program. It sets the focus
78             ' to the Linear Feet text box and
79             ' clears the cost estimate label.
80
81             txtFeet.Focus()
82             lblCostEstimate.Text = ""
83        End Sub
84
85   End Class
```

FIGURE 5-83 (continued)

Summary

In this chapter you have learned to make decisions based on the user's input.

The items listed in the table in Figure 5-84 on the next page include all the new Visual Studio and Visual Basic skills you have learned in this chapter.

Visual Basic Skills

Skill	Figure Number	Video Number
Explore the Wood Cabinet Estimate Application	Figure 5-1	Video 5-1
Use a GroupBox Object	Figure 5-4	Video 5-2
Add RadioButton Objects	Figure 5-7	Video 5-3
Use Windows Application Container Objects	Figure 5-14	
Display a Message Box	Figure 5-16	Video 5-4
Concatenate Strings	Figure 5-29	
Code an If...Then Statement	Figure 5-31	
Turn on Pretty Listing for Indentation	Page 302	
Use Relational Operators	Figure 5-32	
Enter an If...Then Statement	Figure 5-34	Video 5-5
Compare Strings	Figure 5-37	
Code If...Then...Else Statements	Figure 5-38	
Compare Values Using an Arithmetic Expression	Figure 5-40	
Code an If...Then...ElseIf Statement	Figure 5-41	
Code a Nested If Statement	Figure 5-43	
Test the Status of a RadioButton Object in Code	Figure 5-48	
Understand Block-Level Scope	Figure 5-51	
Code Logical Operators	Figure 5-52	
Code Select Case Statements	Figure 5-62	
Insert Code Snippets	Figure 5-69	Video 5-6
Validate Input Data	Figure 5-74	

FIGURE 5-84

Learn Online

Reinforcement activities and resources are available at no additional cost on www.cengagebrain.com. Visit www .cengage.com/ct/studentdownload for detailed instructions about accessing the available resources at the Student Companion Site.

Knowledge Check

1. If a form opens and the first of three RadioButtons is checked within a GroupBox object, what happens to the first RadioButton object when you tap or click the second RadioButton object?

2. Name the six relational operators and state the purpose of each operator.

3. Write an If . . . Then statement that tests whether the value in the variable decMaleShoeSize is between 9.0 and 12.0. If the number is in that range, set the Text property for the lblResponse Label object to "Your size is in stock".

4. Write an If . . . Then . . . Else statement that assigns 65 to a variable named intSpeed if strHighway is equal to "I95". Otherwise, assign 45 to intSpeed.

5. List the three most common logical operators and explain their meaning.

6. Rewrite the following line of code without a Not logical operator, but keep the same logical processing:

   `If Not intHeight <= 75 Then`

7. The intent of the following statement is to check whether the radDormStudent RadioButton object is checked. What is the error in the statement? Rewrite the statement so it is correct.

   `If radDormStudent = Checked Then`

8. The intent of the following statement is to check whether the value in the intGrade variable is less than 0 or greater than 100. What is the error in the statement? Rewrite the statement so it is correct.

   `If intGrade < 0 And intGrade > 100 Then`

9. What is the most commonly used container object?

10. Fix this statement.

    `If decMinWage > 7.25 and < 15.25 Then`

11. Why do most developers indent the code within a decision structure?

12. Write a statement that creates the dialog box shown in Figure 5-85 in a Windows application. Use a single numerical value to create the button and picture icon.

13. What is the difference between a Panel object and a GroupBox object?

14. What is the difference between the Or logical operator and the Xor logical operator?

15. Write a data validation statement that would check to ensure the value in the intAge variable is between 1 and 120. If the age is not valid, display an error message box that states the age is invalid.

FIGURE 5-85

(continues)

16. How many radio buttons in a group can be selected at one time?

17. Using the concatenation operator (&), write a statement that would create the compound word "smartphone" from the following two strings: strTerm1 = "smart" and strTerm2= "phone". Assign the compound word to the strCompound string variable.

18. Write a statement that would clear the radio button named radSurfboard.

19. Write a Select Case statement using the fewest Case statements possible to display the number of days in each month. The user enters the number of the month, such as 8, which is converted to an integer and assigned to the intMonth variable. The Select Case statement should display a message box that states the number of days in the month, such as "31 Days".

20. Which logical operator has the highest precedence in the order of operations?

Debugging Exercises

1. Explain how the two statements shown in Figure 5-86 are evaluated.

```
If strAirline = "Jet Green" AndAlso strHotel = "Homeland Suites" Then

    If strAirline = "Jet Green" And strHotel = "Homeland Suites" Then
```

FIGURE 5-86

2. Identify the error in the code shown in Figure 5-87 and explain how to correct the code.

```
If dblCommission >= 2500 Then
    Dim intBonus As Integer
    intBonus = 500
Else
    intBonus = 0
End If
```

FIGURE 5-87

Debugging Exercises

3. The Select Case statement shown in Figure 5-88 contains one or more errors. Identify the error(s) and rewrite the statements correctly.

```
Select Case intNumberOfSeats
    Case > 5000
        strVenueType = "Stadium"
    Case > 2000
        strVenueType = "Amphitheater"
    Case > 1000
        strVenueType = "Auditorium"
    Case > 200
        strVenueType = "Theater"
    Case > 0
        strVenueType = "Club"
    Else Case
        strVenueType = "Error"
Select End
```

FIGURE 5-88

4. The Select Case statement shown in Figure 5-89 contains one or more errors. Identify the error(s) and rewrite the statements correctly.

```
Select Case charFlightCode
    Case 'F', 'A'
        lblFare.Text = 'First Class'
    Case 'B', 'Q'
        lblFare.Text = 'Business Class'
    Case 'Y', 'S', 'M'
        lblFare.Text = 'Full Fare Economy'
    Case 'K', 'C'
        lblFare.Text = 'Preferred Economy'
    Case 'U', 'J', 'P', 'G'
        lblFare.Text = 'Economy'
    Else
        lblFare.Text = 'Unknown'
End Select
```

FIGURE 5-89

(continues)

5. The If . . . Then . . . Else statement shown in Figure 5-90 contains one or more errors. Identify the error(s) and rewrite the statements correctly.

```
If strShippingMethod = "Overnite" Then
    If strDeliveryTime = "Morning"
        decDeliveryCost = 29.00D
    Else
        decDeliveryCost = 24.00D
Else
    If strShippingMethod = "Two Days" Then
        decDeliveryCost = 14.00D
    Else
        decDeliveryCost = 4.00D
End If
```

FIGURE 5-90

Program Analysis

1. Write an If . . . Then decision structure to compare the two numbers in the decDeveloperPay and decWebDesignerPay variables. Display a message box that states decDeveloperPay is greater than decWebDesignerPay.

2. Write an If statement that displays the message box "Sleet is possible" if the value in the variable decTemp is within the range from 30 to 35.

3. Write an If . . . Then . . . Else statement that checks the value in the variable chrGender for the value M (Male) or F (Female) and assigns the information shown in Figure 5-91 to lblCollegeExpectation.Text based on the gender. If the variable chrGender contains a value other than M or F, assign the message "Invalid Gender" to lblCollegeExpectation.Text.

Gender	College Expectation
Male	75% plan to graduate from college
Female	85% plan to graduate from college

FIGURE 5-91

Program Analysis *continued*

4. Write a Select Case statement that tests the user's age in a variable named intAge and assigns the generation name of that age group to the variable strGeneration, according to the information shown in Figure 5-92.

Age Group	Generation Name
50 and above	Baby Boomers
39–49	Generation X
18–38	Generation Y
Below 18	Millennials

FIGURE 5-92

5. Rewrite the Select Case statement shown in Figure 5-93 as an If . . . Then . . . Else statement.

```
Select Case chrDepartment
    Case "B", "b"
        strDept = "Baby / Infant Clothing"
    Case "T", "t"
        strDept = "Technology"
End Select
```

FIGURE 5-93

6. Rewrite the If . . . Then . . . Else statement shown in Figure 5-94 as a Select Case statement.

```
If intGrade >= 9 And intGrade <= 12 Then
    lblSchool.Text = "High School"
ElseIf intGrade >= 7 Then
    lblSchool.Text = "Middle School"
ElseIf intGrade >= 1 Then
    lblSchool.Text = "Elementary School"
Else
    lblSchool.Text = "Invalid Grade"
End If
```

FIGURE 5-94

(continues)

7. What is the output of the code shown in Figure 5-95 if the word Black is entered in the txtSkiSlope text box?

```
Select Case Me.txtSkiSlope.Text
    Case "Green"
        MsgBox("Beginner Slope")
    Case "Blue"
        MsgBox("Intermediate Slope")
    Case "Black"
        MsgBox("Expert Slope")
    Case Else
        MsgBox("Invalid Entry")
End Select
```

FIGURE 5-95

8. After the execution of the Select Case structure in Figure 5-96, what value will be found in the Text property of lblFemaleHeight if the user enters the number 74 into the txtEnterHeight text box? If the number 81 is entered? If the number 59 is entered?

```
Dim intHeightInches As Integer
intHeightInches = Convert.ToInt32(txtEnterHeight.Text)
Select Case intHeightInches
    Case Is < 61
        lblFemaleHeight.Text = "Petite"
    Case 61 To 69
        lblFemaleHeight.Text = "Average"
    Case 70 To 80
        lblFemaleHeight.Text = "Tall"
    Case 80 To 120
        lblFemaleHeight.Text = "Towering"
    Case Else
        lblFemaleHeight.Text = "Not Possible"
End Select
```

FIGURE 5-96

9. In each of the following examples, is the condition True or False?

a. "CVCC" >= "GRCC"

b. "G" >= "g"

c. "Nerdy" < "Nerd"

d. "Cool" < > "cool"

e. "50" >= "Fifty"

f. ("Paris" < "Barcelona") And ("Amsterdam" <= "Prague")

g. ("Ford" > "Chevrolet") Or ("Toyota" < "Honda")

h. $3 \wedge 2 <= 3 * 4$

i. Not ("CNN" >= "ABC")

j. Not ("Tim" > "Tom") And Not ("Great" < > "great")

Complete one or more of the following case programming assignments. Submit the program and materials you create to your instructor. The level of difficulty is indicated for each case programming assignment.

● = Easiest
●● = Intermediate
●●● = Challenging

1
●
POWER WASHER RENTAL

Design a Windows application and write the code that will execute according to the program requirements in Figure 5-97. Before writing the code, create a Use Case Definition, as shown in Figure 5-98 on the next page. Before writing the code, create an event planning document for each event in the program. The completed Form object and other objects in the user interface are shown in Figure 5-99 on the next page.

REQUIREMENTS DOCUMENT

Date Submitted:	May 6, 2015
Application Title:	Power Washer Rental Application
Purpose:	This Windows application calculates the cost of renting a power washer from a tool rental store.
Program Procedures:	The user selects the duration of time for renting the power washer from the tool rental store. The user then requests that the program calculate and display the cost of renting the power washer.
Algorithms, Processing, and Conditions:	1. The user selects the duration of rental time.
	2. The power washer can be rented for a half day ($24), full day ($35), or two full days ($50).
	3. The user must be able to initiate the calculation of the rental fee.
	4. The user should be able to clear the duration of the rental and the rental fee.
Notes and Restrictions:	n/a
Comments:	Obtain an image for this program from CengageBrain.com. The name of the image file is PowerWasher.

FIGURE 5-97

(continues)

Case Programming Assignments

Power Washer rental (continued)

USE CASE DEFINITION

1. The Windows application window opens.
2. The user selects the duration of time needed for the rental.
3. The user taps or clicks the Rental Fee button to display the cost of power washer rental.
4. The user clears the input and the result by tapping or clicking the Clear button.
5. If desired, the user repeats the process.

FIGURE 5-98

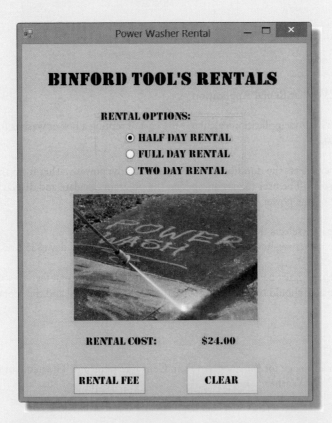

FIGURE 5-99

Case Programming Assignments

2

NEW YEAR'S EVE CELEBRATION TICKETS

Design a Windows application and write the code that will execute according to the program requirements in Figure 5-100 and the Use Case Definition in Figure 5-101 on the next page. Before writing the code, create an event planning document for each event in the program. The completed Form object and other objects in the user interface are shown in Figure 5-102 on the next page.

REQUIREMENTS DOCUMENT

Date Submitted: April 15, 2015

Application Title: New Year's Eve Celebration Tickets Application

Purpose: This Windows application calculates the cost of New Year's Eve celebration tickets.

Program Procedures: The user should enter the number of tickets for an exclusive New Year's Eve celebration. The event has three types of tickets. You cannot combine ticket types.

Algorithms, Processing, and Conditions:
1. The user enters the number of tickets to purchase.
2. The types of tickets include a full-evening dinner celebration for $125, an appetizers-only celebration for $75, and discounted entry with military ID (45% off the price of the full-evening dinner celebration). The user can only select one type of ticket for her entire party.
3. The user must be able to initiate the calculation and display the total cost of the tickets.
4. The user should be able to clear the number of tickets purchased, the type of ticket, and the total cost.

Notes and Restrictions:
1. If the user enters a negative number of tickets, the user should be advised and asked for a valid entry.
2. If the user enters a nonnumeric value for the number of tickets or does not enter a number, the user should be advised and asked for a valid entry.

Comments: Obtain an image for this program from CengageBrain.com. The name of the image file is NYE.

FIGURE 5-100

(continues)

Case Programming Assignments

New Year's Eve Celebration Tickets *(continued)*

USE CASE DEFINITION

1. The Windows application window opens.
2. The user enters the number of tickets and the ticket type needed for her party.
3. The user taps or clicks the Calculate button.
4. The program displays the total cost of the tickets, including any discount that applies.
5. A MsgBox appears and displays a warning if the user enters a negative number of tickets.
6. A MsgBox appears and displays a warning if the user enters a nonnumeric value for the number of tickets or does not enter a value.
7. The user can clear the input and the results by tapping or clicking the Clear button.

FIGURE 5-101

FIGURE 5-102

3

WINDOWS 8 ONLINE SHIPPING

Design a Windows application and write the code that will execute according to the program requirements in Figure 5-103 and the Use Case Definition in Figure 5-104 on the next page. Before writing the code, create an event planning document for each event in the program. The completed Form object and other objects in the user interface are shown in Figure 5-105 on the next page.

REQUIREMENTS DOCUMENT

Date Submitted:	May 11, 2015
Application Title:	Windows 8 Online Shipping Application
Purpose:	This Windows application computes the cost of shipping for an online Windows 8 accessories store.
Program Procedures:	The user enters the weight of the purchased item, the shipping destination, and the desired delivery time. The application computes the total shipping cost.
Algorithms, Processing, and Conditions:	1. A user must be able to enter the weight in pounds and select the destination and type of shipping. The user can select U.S. standard delivery or international delivery to Latin America or Canada.
	2. The user must be able to enter the weight of the purchased item. If the item weighs less than 5 pounds, the standard and international rates apply. If the item weighs more than 5 pounds, add a 25% surcharge to the standard or international shipping rate. The shipping rates are $6.00 for U.S. standard delivery and $8.00 for Latin American or Canadian standard delivery.
	3. If the customer requests overnight shipping, double the shipping cost.
	4. The user must be able to initiate the shipping calculation and the display of the total cost of shipping.
	5. The user must be able to clear the entries and results.
Notes and Restrictions:	1. If the user enters a nonnumeric value for the weight or does not enter a weight, the user should be advised and asked for a valid entry.
	2. If the user enters a negative weight, the user should be advised and asked for a valid entry.
	3. If the value entered is greater than 20 pounds, the user should be advised and asked for a valid entry.
	4. The default delivery rate is for the United States.
	5. The cost should be displayed in currency format.
Comments:	1. Use Case statements for the weight of the package.
	2. Obtain an image for this program from CengageBrain.com. The name of the image file is Shipping.

FIGURE 5-103

(continues)

Case Programming Assignments

Windows 8 Online Shipping (continued)

USE CASE DEFINITION

1. The Windows application window opens.
2. The user enters the weight of the package in pounds.
3. The user selects the destination.
4. The user selects whether overnight shipping is required.
5. The user taps or clicks the Shipping Fee button to display the online shipping cost.
6. The user clears the input and the result by tapping or clicking the Clear button.
7. If desired, the user repeats the process.

FIGURE 5-104

© 2014 Cengage Learning

FIGURE 5-105

© Ryan McVay/Photodisc/Getty Images

Case Programming Assignments

4 ●● PREMIUM GAMING SUBSCRIPTION

Design a Windows application and write the code that will execute according to the program requirements in Figure 5-106. Before designing the user interface, create a Use Case Definition. Before writing the code, create an event planning document for each event in the program.

REQUIREMENTS DOCUMENT

Date Submitted: April 22, 2015

Application Title: Premium Gaming Subscription Application

Purpose: This Windows application calculates the payment amount for a monthly membership to a cloud-based gaming subscription.

Program Procedures: The user should enter the name of the new member, the number of months the new member would like to prepay, and the type of membership. The gaming prepayment cost will be computed and displayed for the entered number of months. The monthly costs for the three types of membership are:
- Single Subscription: $12 per month
- Family Subscription (up to 5 members): $28 per month
- Game Developer Subscription: $7 per month

Algorithms, Processing, and Conditions:
1. The user must enter the name of the new member, the type of membership, and the number of months to prepay.
2. Based on the type of subscription, the prepayment cost is calculated using the following formula: number of prepaid months × cost per month.
3. The user must be able to initiate the calculation and display the prepaid amount for the gaming subscription, which covers the costs of unlimited gaming usage.
4. The user should be able to clear the name of the new member, the number of prepaid months, the type of membership, and the prepaid amount for the new member.

Notes and Restrictions:
1. If the user enters a nonnumeric value for the number of months, the user should be advised and asked for a valid entry.
2. If the user enters a negative number of months or does not enter a number, the user should be advised and asked for a valid entry.
3. If the user does not enter a member name, the user should be advised and asked for a valid entry.
4. The default subscription type is single membership.

Comments: n/a

FIGURE 5-106

5

WEIGHT ON THE MOON AND MARS

Design a Windows application and write the code that will execute according to the program requirements in Figure 5-107. Before designing the user interface, create a Use Case Definition. Before writing the code, create an event planning document for each event in the program.

REQUIREMENTS DOCUMENT

Date Submitted: May 6, 2015

Application Title: Weight on the Moon and Mars Application

Purpose: This Windows application calculates a user's weight in pounds and kilograms on the Moon or on Mars.

Program Procedures: The user enters her weight in pounds and selects either the Moon or Mars. The application will determine the user's weight on the Moon or Mars in pounds and kilograms.

Algorithms, Processing, and Conditions:
1. The user must be able to enter her weight in pounds and indicate that she wants to see her equivalent weight on the Moon or Mars.
2. One pound on the Moon is equivalent to 0.166 pounds. One pound on Mars is equivalent to 0.377 pounds.
3. One pound is equivalent to 0.454 kilograms.
4. The user must be able to initiate the calculation and the display of her weight on the Moon or Mars.
5. The user must be able to clear her input and the results.

Notes and Restrictions:
1. If the user's weight entry is blank or nonnumeric, the user should be advised and asked for a valid entry.
2. The results should be displayed one place past the decimal point.

Comments: n/a

FIGURE 5-107

6 ••
SECONDHAND STORE PAYROLL CALCULATOR

Design a Windows application and write the code that will execute according to the program requirements in Figure 5-108. Before designing the user interface, create a Use Case Definition. Before writing the code, create an event planning document for each event in the program.

REQUIREMENTS DOCUMENT

Date Submitted:	May 11, 2015
Application Title:	Secondhand Store Payroll Calculator Application
Purpose:	This application calculates the payroll for employees of a secondhand store.
Program Procedures:	In a Windows application, the user enters an employee's name, number of hours worked, and pay per hour. If the employee works more than 40 hours per week, the store pays time and a half for overtime. The tax rate can be a single rate (19%) or a family rate (16%). The application should compute and display the gross pay, the tax based on the single or family rate, and the net pay.
Algorithms, Processing, and Conditions:	1. The user must be able to enter the employee's name, hours worked, and pay per hour. 2. The user must be able to indicate whether the tax rate is the single rate (19%) or the family rate (16%). 3. The user must be able to initiate the calculation and display of the gross pay, the tax amount based on the single or family rate, and the net pay. 4. A Clear button will clear the user's input and final results.
Notes and Restrictions:	1. If the employee name, hours worked, or pay per hour is left blank, the user should be advised and asked for a valid entry. 2. If the hours worked or pay per hour is nonnumeric, the user should be advised and asked for a valid entry. 3. The minimum value for hours worked is 5. The maximum for hours worked is 60. If the user enters a value that is not within the valid range, the user should be advised and asked for a valid entry. 4. The minimum pay per hour is $8.00. The maximum pay per hour is $40.00. If the user enters a value that is not within the valid range, the user should be advised and asked for a valid entry. 5. The user must be able to clear the employee's name, the hours worked, the pay per hour, and the other pay information.
Comments:	n/a

FIGURE 5-108

7 ●●●
TECHNOLOGY CONFERENCE REGISTRATION

Based on the case project shown in Figure 5-109, create a requirements document and a Use Case Definition document and then design a Windows application. Before writing the code, create an event planning document for each event in the program.

It is important that developers update their skills by attending developers' conferences. The Dynamic International Management Consortium (DIMC) runs and manages the DSE (Developers Skill Enhancement) Conference two times per year. To encourage companies to send multiple employees to the conference, the cost per attendee is determined based on the number of attending developers from a given company. The following table specifies the cost per attendee.

Number of Conference Registrations per Company	Cost per Attendee
1	$895
2–4	$645
5–8	$480
9–16	$395

DIMC has asked you to develop a Windows application that can determine and display the total cost per company for developers attending the conference. DIMC has a policy that if any company member has attended a previous DIMC conference, the company receives a 15% discount for the total cost of the conference. The policy also states that no more than 16 people from a single company can attend the conference. DIMC has asked you to design the program so that the user must enter valid data.

FIGURE 5-109

8 ●●●
OFFICE 365 SUBSCRIPTION PLANS

Based on the case project shown in Figure 5-110, create a requirements document and a Use Case Definition document and then design a Windows application. Before writing the code, create an event planning document for each event in the program.

Your school has asked that you create a Windows application to determine how much it would cost a university student, an entire family, or a small business to use Microsoft Office 365 subscription plans over several months. The user can enter the number of months and a price comparison can be made. The user also can select one of three plan options; you can research the cost of these plans at *office365.com*. After the user selects a plan, its total cost for the entered amount of months is displayed to compare the prices of the plans. Do not accept negative numbers of months or nonnumeric values.

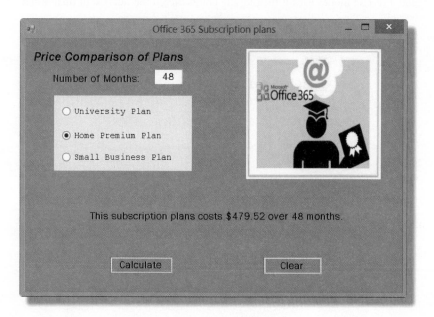

FIGURE 5-110

9 •••
HUMMUS RESTAURANT

Based on the case project shown in Figure 5-111, create a requirements document and a Use Case Definition document and then design a Windows application. Before writing the code, create an event planning document for each event in the program.

A local restaurant offers hummus platters made to order. The hummus restaurant has asked you to create a Windows application that allows customers to enter their orders on a flat-screen computer. Create an application that allows the user to select one of five hummus platters. Create and display a list of platters, along with a display of prices for each platter, three types of pita bread choices at no additional cost, and two toppings at no additional cost. The hummus restaurant has a loyalty program that deducts 5% of the total order cost for every 10 points a customer has earned. Allow users to enter their total number of loyalty points and compute the cost of their order. Customers cannot receive money back if their loyalty points exceed the full cost of their order.

FIGURE 5-111

CHAPTER 6

Loop Structures

OBJECTIVES

You will have mastered the material in this chapter when you can:

- Add a MenuStrip object
- Use the InputBox function
- Display data using the ListBox object
- Understand the use of counters and accumulators
- Understand the use of compound operators

- Repeat a process using a For… Next loop
- Repeat a process using a Do loop
- Avoid infinite loops
- Prime a loop
- Validate data
- Create a nested loop

- Select the best type of loop
- Debug using DataTips at breakpoints
- Publish a finished application using ClickOnce technology

Introduction

In Chapter 5, you learned about the decision structure, one of the major control structures used in computer programming. In this chapter you will learn another major structure called the **looping structure**, or the **iteration structure**.

A fundamental process in a computer program is to repeat a series of instructions either while a condition is true (or not true) or until a condition is true (or not true). For example, if a company is processing electronic paychecks for 5,000 employees, it can use the same set of instructions to post an electronic deposit for each employee, varying only the name of the employee and amount paid for each check. This process would continue until all checks are deposited. Unique check deposit instructions for each employee in the company are not required.

The process of repeating a set of instructions while a condition is true or until a condition is true is called **looping**. When the program is executing those instructions, it is said to be in a loop. Another term for looping is **iteration**.

The programming project in this chapter uses a loop to obtain input data and produce output information. A large company challenged groups of eight employees to form weight loss fitness teams. The Human Resource department requested a Windows application that determines the average weight loss for each team. This application, called the Fitness Challenge application, computes the average weight loss for up to eight team members that enter the total number of pounds they lost during their weight loss challenge. The application uses a loop to request and display the weight loss amounts of the team members. The application then displays the average weight loss by the fitness team (Figure 6-1).

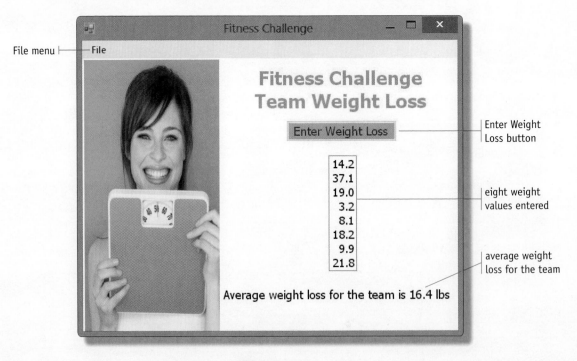

FIGURE 6-1
© Pando Hall/Photographer's Choice RF/Getty Images

Figure 6-1 shows eight values the user entered in a list. After the user enters the weight loss values, the application calculates the average weight loss of the entire team.

When the Fitness Challenge application begins, the main window shows no weight loss values (Figure 6-2).

FIGURE 6-2

© Pando Hall/Photographer's Choice RF/Getty Images

When the user taps or clicks the Enter Weight Loss button, the Weight Loss dialog box opens (Figure 6-3), allowing the user to enter the weight loss of the first team member. This dialog box is called an **input box**.

FIGURE 6-3

After entering the first weight loss value, the user taps or clicks the OK button in the Weight Loss dialog box. The application lists the weight loss value in the main window, and then displays the input box again, requesting the next team member's weight loss. This process repeats for up to eight team members, and is implemented using a loop in the program. When the user is entering weight loss values, the program is said to be in a loop. The loop is terminated when the user enters the weight loss for the eighth team member or taps or clicks the Cancel button in the Weight Loss dialog box. After the loop is terminated, the Fitness Challenge application displays the average weight loss for the team, as shown in Figure 6-1 on page 364.

The Fitness Challenge application has several other features. Figure 6-1 shows a menu bar containing the File menu at the top of the window. The File menu contains the Clear command, which clears the list and the average weight loss, and the Exit command, which closes the window and terminates the application. In this chapter, you will learn to design and code a menu.

In addition, the application contains input validation. For example, if a user enters a nonnumeric or negative value for the weight loss, the application requests the weight loss amount again, until the user enters a reasonable value.

Finally, the application displays the average weight loss to one decimal place, such as 9.2 lbs.

User Interface Design

The user interface for the Fitness Challenge application includes three new elements: a menu, an input box, and a list for the weight loss values. The menu and the list of team member weight loss values are objects placed on the Windows Form object. The input box is created through the use of a function call in the program code. Each of these items is explained in the following sections.

Insert a MenuStrip Object

A **menu bar** is a strip across the top of a window that contains one or more menu names. A **menu** is a group of commands, or items, presented in a list. In the sample program, a File menu is created in the application window (Figure 6-4).

FIGURE 6-4
© Pando Hall/Photographer's Choice RF/Getty Images

When the user taps or clicks File on the menu bar during program execution, a menu appears with two commands: Clear and Exit. The user taps or clicks the Clear menu command to clear the entered weight values and the results. Tapping or clicking the Exit menu command closes the application. An advantage of a menu is that it conserves space instead of cluttering the form with objects such as buttons.

Using Visual Studio 2012, you can place menus at the top of a Windows Form using the MenuStrip object. To place a MenuStrip object on a Windows Form, you can complete the following steps:

STEP 1   With a Windows Form object open in the Visual Studio window, scroll in the Toolbox to display the Menus & Toolbars category. If the category is not open, tap or click the expand icon (the right-pointing triangle) next to the Menus & Toolbars category name. Drag the MenuStrip .NET component to the Windows Form object.

The pointer changes when you place it over the Windows Form object (Figure 6-5).

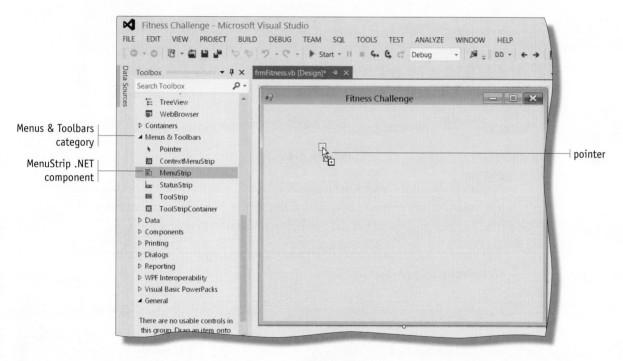

FIGURE 6-5

STEP 2 Release the object.

Visual Studio places the MenuStrip object at the top of the form regardless of where you released the object (Figure 6-6). The Component Tray, which is displayed below the form, organizes nongraphical Toolbox objects. It displays the MenuStrip1 object name.

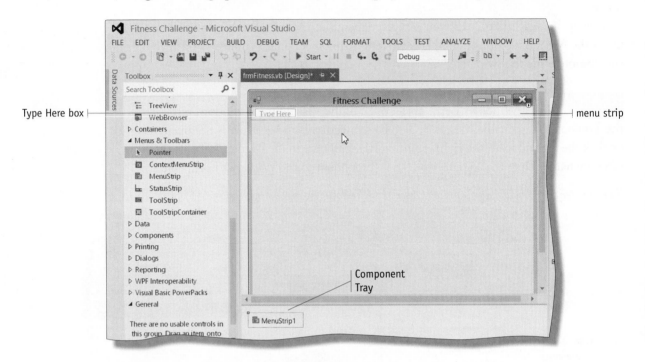

FIGURE 6-6

STEP 3 With the MenuStrip object selected, scroll in the Properties window until the (Name) property is visible. Change the MenuStrip object name to `mnuFitness`. (Note that the prefix for a MenuStrip object is mnu).

The name of the MenuStrip object is changed in the Properties window and in the Component Tray (Figure 6-7).

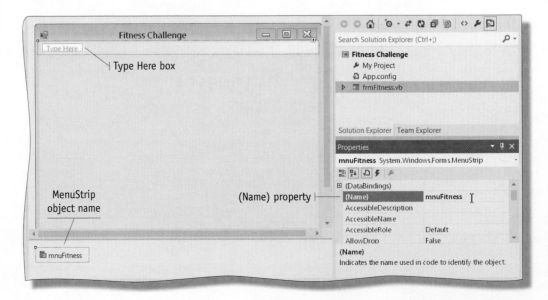

FIGURE 6-7

STEP 4 Tap or click the Type Here box on the menu bar. Type &File to identify the File menu, and then press the ENTER key.

The menu name File is displayed in the upper-left corner of the MenuStrip object and new Type Here boxes are available to create other menu items (Figure 6-8). The ampersand (&) you entered preceding the f indicates that F is a hot key. A hot key provides a keyboard shortcut for opening the menu. Instead of tapping or clicking File to open the menu, the user can press and hold the ALT key and then press the designated hot key, such as ALT+F. After you enter the menu name, the character following the ampersand is underlined to indicate it is the hot key.

File menu name

F is underlined

new Type Here boxes

FIGURE 6-8

STEP 5 Tap or click File in the MenuStrip object to select it, scroll in the Properties window to the (Name) property, and then change the name to mnuFile.

The name of the File menu is displayed in the (Name) property in the Properties window (Figure 6-9).

(Name) property

FIGURE 6-9

STEP 6   To add a menu item to the File menu, tap or click the Type Here box below the File menu name. Type &Clear and then press ENTER to create a new menu item named Clear with c as the hot key.

The Clear menu item is displayed below the File menu (Figure 6-10). After you press the ENTER key, the character following the ampersand is underlined to indicate it is the hot key.

Clear menu item

C is underlined

FIGURE 6-10

STEP 7   On the File menu, tap or click Clear to select it, scroll in the Properties window until the (Name) property is visible, and then change the name to mnuClear.

The mnuClear name is displayed in the (Name) property in the Properties window (Figure 6-11).

(Name) property

FIGURE 6-11

ONLINE REINFORCEMENT

To view a video of the process in the previous steps, visit CengageBrain.com and navigate to the resources for this title. Tap or click the link for Chapter 6 and then navigate to Video 6-2.

The letter representing a hot key appears underlined in the menu name, as shown in Figure 6-10. The first letter often is used for the hot key, but not always. For example, in the chapter project, the File menu includes the Exit item (see Figure 6-4 on page 366). The hot key typically used for the Exit item is the letter x. When entering the Exit menu item on the File menu, the developer can type E&xit, which assigns the letter following the & (x) as the hot key.

When assigning menu item hot keys, you should be aware that they are not case-sensitive. Therefore, you should not assign "T" to one menu item and "t" to another.

Event Handlers for Menu Items

Recall that the design of the user interface occurs before you write the code for event handlers. When you are ready to write code, however, you must write an event handler for each menu item because tapping or clicking it or using its hot key triggers an event. Writing a menu item event handler is the same as writing an event handler for a button tap or click.

To code the event handler for the Exit menu item, you can complete the following steps:

STEP 1 In Design view, double-tap or double-click the Exit menu item to open the code window.

The code window is displayed and the insertion point is located within the Exit item click event handler (Figure 6-12). When the user taps or clicks the Exit item on the File menu, the code in the event handler will be executed.

mnuExit event handler

FIGURE 6-12

STEP 2 Using IntelliSense, enter the Close procedure call to close the window and terminate the application.

When executed, the Close procedure will close the window and terminate the program (Figure 6-13).

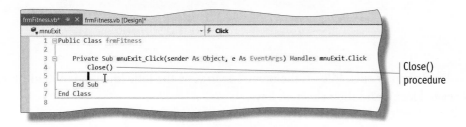

Close() procedure

FIGURE 6-13

Insert Standard Items for a Menu

Developers often customize the MenuStrip object for the specific needs of an application. In addition, Visual Basic 2012 contains an **Action Tag** that allows you to create a full standard menu bar commonly provided in Windows programs, with File, Edit, Tools, and Help menus. In Visual Basic 2012, an Action Tag (▶) appears in the upper-right corner of many objects, including a MenuStrip. Action Tags provide a way for you to specify a set of actions, called **smart actions**, for an object as you design a form. For example, to insert a full standard menu, you can complete the following steps:

STEP 1 With a new Windows Form object open, drag the MenuStrip .NET component onto the Windows Form object. Tap or click the Action Tag on the MenuStrip object.

The MenuStrip Tasks menu opens (Figure 6-14).

FIGURE 6-14

STEP 2 Tap or click Insert Standard Items on the MenuStrip Tasks menu.

The MenuStrip object contains four menu names: File, Edit, Tools, and Help (Figure 6-15). These are the standard menus found in many Windows applications. Each menu contains the items typically listed on the menus.

FIGURE 6-15

STEP 3 Tap or click File on the menu bar to view the individual menu items, their associated icons, and their shortcut keys.

The standard File menu items (New, Open, Save, Save As, Print, Print Preview, and Exit) are displayed with their associated icons and shortcut keys (Figure 6-16). The other menus also contain standard items. You can code an event handler for each menu item by double-tapping or double-clicking the item.

standard File menu

FIGURE 6-16

Use the InputBox Function

To calculate a team's weight loss, the Fitness Challenge application uses an InputBox object in which users enter the weight loss of each team member. The InputBox object is a dialog box that prompts the user to enter a value. You can use the InputBox function instead of a TextBox object to obtain input. Similar to coding a MessageBox object, you use the InputBox function to specify when the InputBox object appears. The InputBox function displays a dialog box that consists of a message asking for input, an input area, a title, an OK button, and a Cancel button (see Figure 6-3 on page 365). When the user enters the text and taps or clicks the OK button, the InputBox function returns the text as a string. If the user taps or clicks the Cancel button, the function returns a null string (""). Figure 6-17 shows the syntax of the InputBox function:

General Format: InputBox Function

```
strVariableName = InputBox("Question to Prompt User", "Title Bar")
```

FIGURE 6-17

For example, the code in Figure 6-18 creates a dialog box that requests the user's age for a driver's license application. The string returned by the InputBox function is assigned to the strAge variable.

```
5        Dim strAge As String
6
7        strAge = InputBox("Please enter your age", "Driver's License Agency")
```

FIGURE 6-18

When the application is executed, the InputBox object in Figure 6-19 opens, requesting that the user enter her age.

FIGURE 6-19

The InputBox object returns all data entered as a string, which then can be converted to the appropriate data type.

Display a Default Value in an InputBox Object

The InputBox object can be assigned a default value. For example, if a college application for admission requests the student's home state and the college or university is located in Virginia, the most likely state, Virginia, can be the default value in the InputBox, as shown in Figure 6-20.

FIGURE 6-20

The code to produce this input box is shown in Figure 6-21.

```
 9        Dim strState As String
10
11        strState = InputBox("Please enter the state in which you reside:", _
12            "College Application", "Virginia")
```

FIGURE 6-21

As you can see, the third argument for the InputBox function call is the default value that is placed in the input box. It must be a String value and follow the syntax shown in Figure 6-21.

Create the InputBox Object for Fitness Challenge Application

The Fitness Challenge application uses an InputBox object that requests the weight loss amounts of team members numbered 1–8, as shown in Figure 6-22.

FIGURE 6-22

The code for the Weight Loss InputBox is shown in Figure 6-23. Notice that the prompt message for the user is assigned to the strInputMessage variable, and the title bar text (Weight Loss) is assigned to the strInputHeading variable.

```
15        Dim strWeightLoss As String
16        Dim strInputMessage As String = "Enter the weight loss for team member #"
17        Dim strInputHeading As String = "Weight Loss"
18        Dim intNumberOfEntries As Integer = 1
19
20        strWeightLoss = InputBox(strInputMessage & intNumberOfEntries, strInputHeading, " ")
21
```

FIGURE 6-23

The variable intNumberOfEntries identifies the team member's number. It is included in the prompt message through the use of concatenation. The variable intNumberOfEntries is incremented later in the code so that it refers to the correct team member each time the InputBox function call is executed.

In Figure 6-23, the default value is specified as a space (" "). When the input box is displayed, a space will be selected in the input area. This space is required so that if a user taps or clicks the OK button without entering any data, the InputBox will not return a null character (""), which indicates the user tapped or clicked the Cancel button. This normally is a good programming practice.

When the user taps or clicks the Cancel button in an input box and the InputBox function returns a null character, the program can test for the null character to determine further processing.

Display Data Using the ListBox Object

In the Fitness Challenge application, the user enters weight loss values into the InputBox object, and the application displays the weight loss values in a list box (see Figure 6-1 on page 364). To create such a list, you use the ListBox object provided in the Visual Basic Toolbox. A ListBox object displays a group of values, called items, with one item per line. To add a ListBox object to a Windows Form object, you can complete the following steps:

STEP 1   Drag the ListBox object from the Toolbox to where you want to place the ListBox object on the Windows Form object. When the pointer is in the correct location, release the object.

The ListBox object is placed on the form (Figure 6-24).

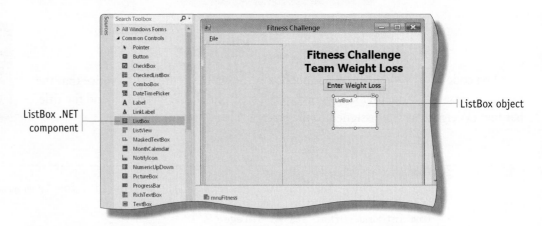

ListBox .NET component

ListBox object

FIGURE 6-24

STEP 2   With the ListBox object selected, scroll in the Properties window to the (Name) property. Name the ListBox object `lstWeightLoss`.

The name you entered is displayed in the (Name) property in the Properties window (Figure 6-25). Notice a ListBox object name begins with lst (be sure to use a lowercase letter l, not a one).

(Name) property

FIGURE 6-25

After placing a ListBox object on the Windows Form object, you can adjust the size by dragging the size handles (Figure 6-24). Be sure to resize the ListBox so that it is large enough to hold the application data. The ListBox object for the Fitness Challenge application is designed to be wide enough to hold three digits and a decimal point, and long enough to hold eight numbers (Figure 6-26).

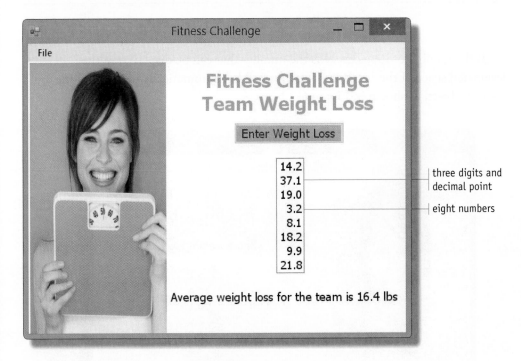

FIGURE 6-26

© Pando Hall/Photographer's Choice RF/Getty Images

To display the weight loss of each team member in the list box, you must write code to add each item to the ListBox object. After an item is added, it is displayed in the list box. The general format of the statement to add an item to a ListBox object is shown in Figure 6-27.

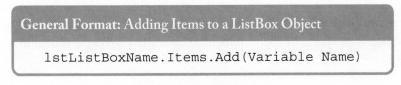

General Format: Adding Items to a ListBox Object

```
lstListBoxName.Items.Add(Variable Name)
```

FIGURE 6-27

© 2014 Cengage Learning

In Figure 6-27, the Add procedure will add the item contained in the variable identified by the Variable Name entry. The syntax for the statement must be followed precisely.

Figure 6-28 shows the code to add the team member weight loss values to the lstWeightLoss ListBox object and then display the weight loss of each team member (decWeightLoss) in the ListBox object.

```
45                    lstWeightLoss.Items.Add(decWeightLoss)
```

FIGURE 6-28

If the number of items exceeds the number that can be displayed in the designated space of the ListBox object, a scroll bar automatically is added to the ListBox object, as shown in Figure 6-29.

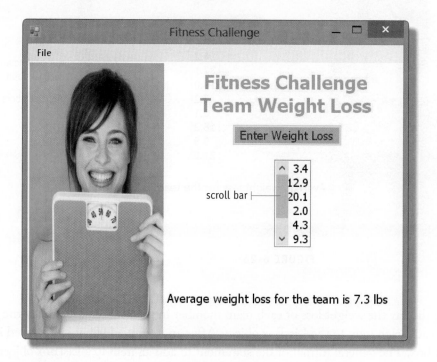

FIGURE 6-29

To clear the items in a ListBox object, the Clear method works as it does for the TextBox object. The syntax of the statement to clear the ListBox is shown in Figure 6-30.

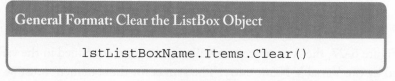

General Format: Clear the ListBox Object

```
lstListBoxName.Items.Clear()
```

FIGURE 6-30

In the Fitness Challenge application, the user can select the Clear menu item to clear the form. The code in Figure 6-31 removes the items from the lstWeightLoss ListBox.

```
81          lstWeightLoss.Items.Clear()
```

FIGURE 6-31

Can I control where the InputBox appears on the screen?
To control the position of the InputBox, you can add an optional X position and Y position representing the upper-left edge of the dialog box. The syntax of the InputBox with sample X and Y positions is:
myValue = InputBox(message, title, defaultValue, 150, 100)
The 150 pixels represents the X position (horizontal) and the 100 pixels represents the Y position (vertical).

Add ListBox Items During Design

The Fitness Challenge application allows the user to add items to the ListBox object during program execution, but you also can add items to a ListBox object while designing the form. Adding items to the ListBox object during the design phase allows the user to select an item from the ListBox object during execution. For example, in an application to select a favorite clothing store, you can add items to a ListBox object named lstStores during the form design by completing the following steps:

STEP 1   Assume the lstStores ListBox object already has been placed and named on the Windows Form object. Select the ListBox object on the Windows Form object and then tap or click the Items property in the Properties window.

The Items property in the Properties window is selected. An ellipsis button appears to the right of the (Collection) entry (Figure 6-32).

FIGURE 6-32

STEP 2　Tap or click the ellipsis button in the right column of the Items property.

The String Collection Editor window opens, allowing you to enter items that will be displayed in the lstStores ListBox object (Figure 6-33).

String Collection
Editor window

enter items to be
placed in the
ListBox object

FIGURE 6-33

STEP 3　Tap or click the String Collection Editor window. Type the following items to represent popular retail stores, and then press ENTER at the end of each line:

```
Abercrombie & Fitch
Aeropostale
American Eagle
Express
Hollister
```

The items representing favorite retail stores appear in the String Collection Editor window on separate lines (Figure 6-34).

items entered for
the ListBox object

OK button

FIGURE 6-34

STEP 4   Tap or click the OK button.

The Windows Form object displays the stores in the lstStores ListBox object (Figure 6-35).
The user can select one of the items in the ListBox object during execution.

items in the
ListBox object

FIGURE 6-35

Use the SelectedItem Property

The SelectedItem property identifies which item in the ListBox is selected. An
assignment statement assigns that property to a variable, as shown in Figure 6-36.

General Format: Assign the Selected Item in a ListBox Object
`strVariableName = lstListBoxName.SelectedItem`

FIGURE 6-36

© 2014 Cengage Learning

Figure 6-37 shows the code to display the user's selection of her favorite store
from the lstStores ListBox object in a message box.

```
5          MsgBox("Your favorite store is "_
6          &lstStores.SelectedItem & ".")
```

FIGURE 6-37

Use Accumulators, Counters, and Compound Operators

After the user enters the weight loss values of up to eight team members, the Fitness Challenge application calculates the average weight loss (see Figure 6-1 on page 364). The formula to calculate the average weight loss is: (total of all weight loss values entered) / (number of team members). For example, if the total of all the weight loss values entered is 145.2 and weight loss values were entered for eight team members, the average weight loss is 18.2 pounds.

To calculate the average, the program must add the weight loss of each team member to a variable. The variable that contains an accumulated value such as the total of all the weight loss values is called an **accumulator**.

To compute the average weight loss, the program also must keep track of how many weight loss values have been entered. The variable that keeps track of this value is called a **counter**. A counter always is incremented with a constant value. This value can be positive or negative. In the Fitness Challenge application, the counter is incremented by 1 each time the user enters a weight loss number for a team member. Only positive values that indicate how many pounds were lost are accepted; for example, 8.3 represents 8.3 pounds lost.

You can use one of two techniques to add a value to a variable and then update the value in the variable, as with an accumulator or a counter. The first technique is shown in Figure 6-38.

```
26        decTotalWeightLoss = decTotalWeightLoss + decWeightLoss
27        intNumberOfEntries = intNumberOfEntries + 1
```

FIGURE 6-38

On line 26 in Figure 6-38, the value in the decTotalWeightLoss variable is added to the value in the decWeightLoss variable and the result is stored in the decTotalWeightLoss variable. This statement accumulates the weight loss values in the decTotalWeightLoss accumulator. The statement in line 27 increments the number of entries counter by 1. The effect is that the value in the number of entries counter is increased by 1 each time the statement is executed.

A second method for accomplishing this task is to use a shortcut mathematical operator called a **compound operator** that allows you to add, subtract, multiply, divide, use modulus or exponents, or concatenate strings, storing the result in the same variable. An assignment statement that includes a compound operator begins with the variable that will contain the accumulated value, such as an accumulator or a counter, followed by the compound operator. A compound operator consists of an arithmetic operator and an equal sign. The last element in the assignment statement is the variable or literal containing the value to be used in the calculation.

An assignment statement using a compound operator such as:

```
intNumberOfEntries += 1
```

is the same as:

```
intNumberOfEntries = intNumberOfEntries + 1
```

The += compound operator adds the value of the right operand to the value of the left operand and stores the result in the left operand's variable. Similarly, the statement:

```
decTotalWeightLoss += decWeightLoss
```

is the same as:

```
decTotalWeightLoss = decTotalWeightLoss + decWeightLoss
```

The table in Figure 6-39 shows an example of compound operators used in code. Assume that intResult = 24, decResult = 24, and strSample = "tree".

Operation	Example with Single Operators	Example with Compound Operator	Result
Addition	intResult = intResult + 1	intResult += 1	intResult = 25
Subtraction	intResult = intResult − 3	intResult −= 3	intResult = 21
Multiplication	intResult = intResult * 2	intResult *= 2	intResult = 48
Decimal Division	decResult = decResult / 5	decResult /= 5	decResult = 4.8
Integer Division	intResult = intResult \ 5	intResult \ =5	intResult = 4
Exponents	intResult = intResult ^ 2	intResult ^= 2	intResult = 576
Concatenate	strSample = strSample & "house"	strSample &= "house"	strSample = "treehouse"

FIGURE 6-39

Developers often use compound operators in Visual Basic coding. The coding example in Figure 6-40 uses several compound operators and a MsgBox object. When the following code is executed, the result shown in the MsgBox object is "Final Result = 2".

```
30        Dim intTotal As Integer
31        intTotal = 7
32        intTotal += 6
33        intTotal *= 2
34        intTotal /= 13
35        MsgBox("Final Result = " & intTotal.ToString(), , "Compound Operators")
```

FIGURE 6-40

Compound operators also can be used to connect two strings with the concatenation operator (&). The code in Figure 6-41 creates the phrase "To err is human!" in a MsgBox object by using compound operators to concatenate the strPhrase variable. Each compound operator joins another word to the end of the phrase assigned to the strPhrase variable.

```
30        Dim strPhrase As String
31        strPhrase = "To err"
32        strPhrase &= " is "
33        strPhrase &= "human!"
34        MsgBox(strPhrase, , "Compound Operators")
```

FIGURE 6-41

Use Loops to Perform Repetitive Tasks

In the Fitness Challenge application, the user enters weight loss values in an InputBox for up to eight team members. The repetitive process of entering eight weight loss values can be coded within a loop to simplify the task with fewer lines of code. Unlike If…Then statements that execute only once, loops repeat multiple times. Each repetition of the loop is called an **iteration**. An iteration is a single execution of a set of instructions that are to be repeated.

Loops are powerful structures that repeat a section of code a certain number of times or until a particular condition is met. Visual Basic has two main types of loops: For…Next loops and Do loops.

Repeat a Process Using the For…Next Loop

You can use a For…Next loop when a section of code should be executed an exact number of times. The syntax of a For…Next loop is shown in Figure 6-42.

General Format: For…Next loop

```
For Control Variable = Beginning Numeric Value To Ending Numeric Value

    ' Body of the Loop

Next
```

FIGURE 6-42

In Figure 6-42, the For...Next loop begins with the keyword For. Following this keyword is the control variable, which is the numeric variable that keeps track of the number of iterations the loop completes. To begin the loop, the For statement places the beginning numeric value in the control variable. The program then executes the code between the For and Next statements, which is called the body of the loop.

Upon reaching the Next statement, the program returns to the For statement and increments the value of the control variable. This process continues until the value in the control variable is greater than the ending numeric value. The program then executes the statement(s) that follows the Next command.

Figure 6-43 shows a For...Next loop designed to execute four times. The control value is a variable named intNumber.

FIGURE 6-43

The first line in Figure 6-43 specifies that the control variable (intNumber) is assigned the value 1 because the literal 1 is the beginning value. Then the program executes the body of the loop. When the program encounters the Next statement, control returns to the For statement where, by default, the value 1 is added to the control variable. The code in the body of the loop is executed again. This process continues until the value in the control variable is greater than the ending value, which is 4 in this example. Then the program executes the statement(s) that follow the Next command. A loop never exits in the middle of the loop. The comparison is made to the upper limit of the For statement and when the value exceeds the upper limit, loop terminates. The table in Figure 6-44 illustrates the looping process.

Loop Iteration	Value of intNumber	Process
1	intNumber = 1	Executes the code inside the loop
2	intNumber = 2	Executes the code inside the loop
3	intNumber = 3	Executes the code inside the loop
4	intNumber = 4	Executes the code inside the loop
5 (exits the loop)	intNumber = 5	The control variable value exceeds the ending value, so the application exits the For...Next loop. This means the statement(s) following the Next command are executed.

FIGURE 6-44

Include a Step Value in a For...Next Loop

A Step value is the value in a For...Next loop that is added to or subtracted from the beginning value on each iteration of the loop. If you do not include a Step value in the For statement, as shown in Figure 6-45, by default the value in the control variable is incremented by 1 after each iteration of the loop.

In Figure 6-45, a Step value of 2 has been added to the For statement. The control variable intNumber is set to the initial value of 1, and the lines of code in the body of the loop are executed. After the first iteration of the loop, the Step value is added to the control variable, changing the value in the control variable to 3 (1 + 2 = 3). The For loop will continue until the value in intNumber is greater than 99.

```
49        For intNumber = 1 To 99 Step 2
50            ' Body of loop
51        Next
```

FIGURE 6-45

The Step value can be negative. If so, the value in the control variable is decreased on each iteration of the loop. To exit the loop, you must specify an ending value that is less than the beginning value, as shown in Figure 6-46.

```
55        For intCount = 25 To -10 Step -5
56            ' Body of loop
57        Next
```

FIGURE 6-46

In the first iteration of the For...Next loop in Figure 6-46, the control variable value is 25. The value in the intCount control variable is decreased by 5 each time the loop repeats. This repetition continues until the value in intCount is less than −10. Then the loop ends.

You also can assign decimal values to the control variable in a For...Next loop. For example, the For loop in Figure 6-47 has a starting value of 3.1. The loop ends when the value in the control variable is greater than 4.5. The Step value is 0.1, which means the value in decNumber increments by 0.1 on each pass through the loop.

decimal
Step value

```
61          For decNumber = 3.1 To 4.5 Step 0.1
62              ' Body of loop
63          Next
```

FIGURE 6-47

A For...Next loop also can include variables and mathematical expressions, as shown in Figure 6-48.

```
69          For intNumber = intBegin To (intEnd * 2) Step intIncrement
70              'Body of loop
71          Next
```

FIGURE 6-48

In Figure 6-48, the intNumber control variable is initialized with the value in the intBegin variable. Each time the Next statement is encountered and control is returned to the For statement, the value in intNumber is incremented by the value in the intIncrement variable. The loop continues until the value in intNumber is greater than the product of the value in intEnd times 2.

Use IntelliSense to Enter the For...Next Loop Code

Suppose an application is designed to have a list box that displays the population growth for Alaska during the next six years. Assume that the current population of Alaska is 675,000 people and is expected to grow at 5 percent per year for the next six years. The code in Figure 6-49 accomplishes this processing.

```
4         Dim intAlaskaPopulation As Integer = 675000
5         Dim intYears As Integer
6
7         For intYears = 1 To 6
8             intAlaskaPopulation += (intAlaskaPopulation * 0.05)
9             lstGrowth.Items.Add("Year " & intYears & " Population " & intAlaskaPopulation)
10
11        Next
```

FIGURE 6-49

To use IntelliSense to enter the code shown in Figure 6-49 on the previous page, you can complete the following steps, which assume a lstGrowth ListBox object has been defined on a Windows Form object.

STEP 1   In the code window, type `Dim intAlaskaPopulation As Integer = 675000` and then press the ENTER key. Type `Dim intYears As Integer` and then press the ENTER key two times. Type `for` and a space to open an IntelliSense list.

When you press the SPACEBAR, For is capitalized because it is a reserved word. The IntelliSense list shows all available entries (Figure 6-50).

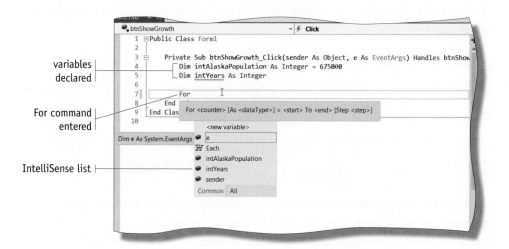

FIGURE 6-50

STEP 2   Type the first four letters of the intYears variable name (`intY`) to select intYears in the IntelliSense list. Type `= 1 to 6` and then press the ENTER key to specify the beginning value and ending value for the loop.

Visual Basic automatically inserts the Next statement in the code (Figure 6-51). For, To, and Next are blue to indicate they are keywords.

FIGURE 6-51

STEP 3 Use IntelliSense to select the appropriate variables. Enter the two new lines shown in Figure 6-52.

Each line of code automatically is indented between the For and Next statements (Figure 6-52).

statements in body of loop

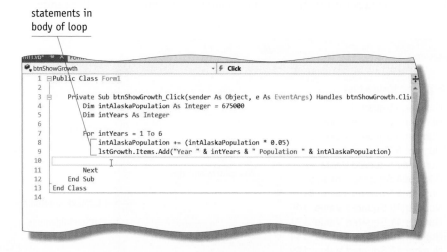

```
mrll.VD*  Form1
btnShowGrowth                              Click
1  Public Class Form1
2
3      Private Sub btnShowGrowth_Click(sender As Object, e As EventArgs) Handles btnShowGrowth.Cli
4          Dim intAlaskaPopulation As Integer = 675000
5          Dim intYears As Integer
6
7          For intYears = 1 To 6
8              intAlaskaPopulation += (intAlaskaPopulation * 0.05)
9              lstGrowth.Items.Add("Year " & intYears & " Population " & intAlaskaPopulation)
10
11         Next
12     End Sub
13 End Class
14
```

FIGURE 6-52

STEP 4 Run the program to see the results of the loop.

The loop calculates and displays the Alaskan population growth for six years based on 5 percent growth per year (Figure 6-53).

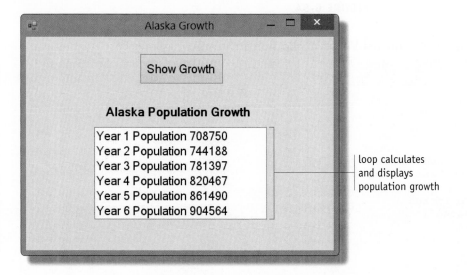

Alaska Growth

Show Growth

Alaska Population Growth

Year 1 Population 708750
Year 2 Population 744188
Year 3 Population 781397
Year 4 Population 820467
Year 5 Population 861490
Year 6 Population 904564

loop calculates and displays population growth

FIGURE 6-53

Handle User Input in a For...Next Loop

The beginning, ending, and Step values used in a For...Next loop can vary based on user input. For example, the Squared Values application shown in Figure 6-54 displays the squared values of a range of numbers the user enters. The user enters the beginning (minimum) and ending (maximum) range of values, and then taps or clicks the Calculate Values button to view the squares of the numbers in the range.

FIGURE 6-54

The code for the Squared Values application is shown in Figure 6-55.

```
5      Dim intCount As Integer
6      Dim intBegin As Integer
7      Dim intEnd As Integer
8
9      intBegin = Convert.ToInt32(txtMinimumNumber.Text)
10     intEnd = Convert.ToInt32(txtMaximumNumber.Text)
11
12     For intCount = intBegin To intEnd
13         lstSquaredValues.Items.Add("Number: " & intCount & " Squared Value: " & (intCount ^ 2))
14     Next
15
16     End Sub
```

FIGURE 6-55

On line 9 in Figure 6-55, the minimum value the user entered is converted to an integer and placed in the intBegin variable. Similarly, on line 10, the maximum value the user entered is converted to an integer and assigned to the intEnd variable.

On line 12, the value in intBegin is used as the beginning value in the For...Next loop, and the value in intEnd is used as the ending value. As you can see, the number of iterations for the loop is determined by values the user entered.

Within the loop, the value in intCount begins with the value in intBegin and is incremented by the default value of 1 each time through the loop. The application calculates the squared value from the number in intCount. As a result, the application calculates the squared values for all numbers beginning with the minimum number and ending with the maximum number.

Repeat a Process Using a Do Loop

You use a For...Next loop to repeat a process an exact number of times. In many applications, however, a loop should be repeated until a certain condition changes. For example, in the Fitness Challenge application, the user repeats the process of entering a weight loss value eight times, and then stops entering values by tapping or clicking the Cancel button. The loop in the Fitness Challenge application continues until one of two conditions becomes true: either the count of the weight loss values entered reaches 8 or the user taps or clicks the Cancel button on the InputBox object.

In a **Do loop**, the body of the loop is executed while or until a condition is true or false. The Do loop uses a condition similar to an If...Then decision structure to determine whether it should continue looping. In this way, you can use a Do loop to execute a body of statements an indefinite number of times. In the Fitness Challenge application, a Do loop can run an indefinite number of times because the user can end the loop at any time by tapping or clicking the Cancel button.

Visual Basic 2012 provides two types of Do loops: the Do While loop and the Do Until loop. Both Do loops execute statements repeatedly until a specified condition becomes true or false. Each loop examines a condition to determine whether the condition is true. The **Do While loop** executes as long as the condition is true. It is stated as, "Do the loop processing while the condition is true."

The **Do Until loop** executes until the condition becomes true. It is stated as, "Do the loop processing until a condition is true."

Do loops are either top-controlled or bottom-controlled, depending on whether the condition is tested before the loop begins or after the body of the loop has executed one time. A **top-controlled loop** is tested before the loop is entered. A top-controlled loop is also called a pre-test. The body of a top-controlled loop might not be executed at all because the condition being tested might be true before any processing in the loop occurs.

Bottom-controlled loops test the condition at the bottom of the loop, also called a post test, so the body of a bottom-controlled loop is executed at least once. Visual Basic provides top-controlled and bottom-controlled Do While and Do Until loops, meaning it can execute four types of Do loops.

Top-Controlled Do While Loops

You use a top-controlled Do While loop if you want the body of the loop to repeat as long as a condition remains true. Figure 6-56 shows the syntax of a top-controlled Do While loop.

General Format: Do While Loop (Top-Controlled)

```
Do While condition

    ' Body of loop

Loop
```

FIGURE 6-56

© 2014 Cengage Learning

A top-controlled Do While loop begins with the keywords Do While. Next, the condition is specified. The condition is expressed using the same relational operators that are available with the If statements that you learned in Chapter 5. Any condition that can be specified in an If statement can be specified in a Do While condition. The condition can compare numeric values or string values.

The body of the loop contains the instructions that are executed as long as the condition is true. The Loop keyword indicates the end of the loop. Visual Basic inserts it automatically when you enter the Do While keywords.

A statement within the body of the Do While loop must cause the condition to change at some point so the loop ends. For example, consider the following statement:

```
Do While strColor = "Red"
```

The loop continues to process as long as the value in the strColor variable remains Red. Based on the processing in the body of the loop, at some point the value in the strColor variable must be changed from Red. If not, the loop will not end. A loop that does not end is called an **infinite loop**.

The code in Figure 6-57 is an example of a top-controlled Do While loop. It continues to add 1 to the variable intScore while intScore is less than 5. It is considered a top-controlled loop because the condition is checked at the top of the loop.

```
17        Dim intScore As Integer = 0
18        Do While intScore < 5
19            intScore += 1
20        Loop
```

FIGURE 6-57

The loop in Figure 6-57 begins by testing whether intScore is less than 5. Because intScore starts with the value 0, the condition tested is true: 0 is less than 5. Next, the variable intScore is incremented by 1, and the loop repeats. The table in Figure 6-58 displays the values that are assigned to intScore each time the condition is checked in the code in Figure 6-57.

Loop Iteration	Value of intScore	Result of Condition Tested
1	intScore = 0	True
2	intScore = 1	True
3	intScore = 2	True
4	intScore = 3	True
5	intScore = 4	True
6	intScore = 5	False

FIGURE 6-58

The loop in Figure 6-57 is executed five times because intScore is less than 5 during five iterations of the loop. As shown in Figure 6-57, if the value in the variable intScore is 5 or greater when the Do While statement is first executed, the body of the loop never will be executed because the condition is not true prior to the first iteration of the loop.

Enter a Do Loop Using IntelliSense

To use IntelliSense to enter the Do While loop shown in Figure 6-57, you can complete the following steps:

STEP 1   In the code window, enter the intScore variable declaration and then press the ENTER key. Type Do While and a space to display an IntelliSense list. Type ints to highlight intScore in the list.

The words Do While appear in blue because they are Visual Basic keywords (Figure 6-59). The IntelliSense list contains the valid entries and the intScore variable name is highlighted.

FIGURE 6-59

STEP 2 Type < 5 and then press the ENTER key.

Visual Basic automatically inserts the intScore variable name and the characters you typed (Figure 6-60). The keyword Loop also is inserted and the insertion point is located inside the loop, ready to enter the body of the loop.

FIGURE 6-60

STEP 3 Type ints to highlight the intScore variable. Complete the statement by typing += 1 and then pressing the ENTER key. Press the DELETE key to delete the blank line.

The statement automatically is indented between the Do While and Loop statements (Figure 6-61). The intScore +=1 statement uses a compound operator to increment the intScore variable.

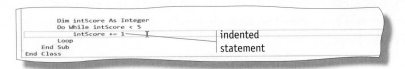

FIGURE 6-61

Bottom-Controlled Do While Loops

You can write a Do While loop in which the condition is tested at the bottom of the loop. A bottom-controlled loop works the same way as the top-controlled Do While loop except that the body of the loop is executed before the condition is checked the first time, guaranteeing that at least one iteration of a loop will be completed. The bottom-controlled Do While loop has the syntax shown in Figure 6-62.

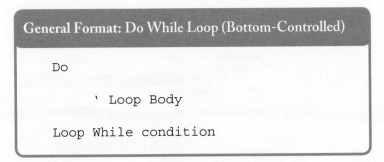

General Format: Do While Loop (Bottom-Controlled)

```
Do

        ' Loop Body

Loop While condition
```

FIGURE 6-62

In Figure 6-62, the word Do appears on its own line at the beginning of the loop. The loop body follows, and the Loop While statement is the last statement in the loop. The Loop While statement contains the condition that is tested to determine if the loop should be terminated. Because the While condition is in the last statement of the loop, the body of the loop is executed one time regardless of the status of the condition.

The code in Figure 6-63 is an example of a bottom-controlled Do While loop.

```
22          Dim intScore As Integer = 0
23          Do
24              intScore = intScore + 1
25          Loop While intScore < 5
```

FIGURE 6-63

The body of the Do loop in Figure 6-63 is executed one time before the condition in the Loop While statement is checked. The variable intScore begins with the initial value of 0 and is incremented in the body of the loop, changing the value to 1. The condition is then tested and found to be true because 1 < 5. The loop repeats and the value of intScore increases, as shown in Figure 6-64.

The body of the loop in Figure 6-63 is executed four times because intScore is less than 5 during five iterations of the loop.

Loop Iteration	Value of intScore at Start of the Loop	Value of intScore When Checked	Result of Condition Tested
1	intScore = 0	intScore = 1	True
2	intScore = 1	intScore = 2	True
3	intScore = 2	intScore = 3	True
4	intScore = 3	intScore = 4	True
5	intScore = 4	intScore = 5	False

FIGURE 6-64

© 2014 Cengage Learning

Use Do Until Loops

A loop similar to a Do While loop is called a Do Until loop. The Do Until loop allows you to specify that an action repeats until a condition becomes true. When the condition in a Do Until loop becomes true, the loop ends.

Top-Controlled Do Until Loops

A Do Until loop can be both top-controlled and bottom-controlled. The syntax of the top-controlled Do Until loop is shown in Figure 6-65.

General Format: Do Until Loop (Top-Controlled)

```
Do Until condition

        ' Loop Body

Loop
```

FIGURE 6-65

A top-controlled Do Until loop begins with the keywords Do Until. Next, as with the Do While top-controlled loop, the condition is specified. The condition is expressed using the same relational operators that are available with If statements. Any condition that can be specified in an If statement can be specified in a Do Until condition. The condition can compare numeric values or string values.

The Do Until loop example shown in Figure 6-66 displays a parking meter application that computes the number of minutes a user can purchase based on the cost of 25 cents for each 15 minutes of parking. If the user only has 88 cents in pocket change, for example, the application computes how many minutes of parking time 88 cents will purchase.

```
4        Dim decAmount As Decimal = 0.88
5        Dim intQuarters As Integer = 0
6        Dim intTime As Integer = 15
7        Dim intParkingTime As Integer
8
9        Do Until decAmount < 0.25
10           intQuarters += 1
11           decAmount -= 0.25
12       Loop
13       intParkingTime = intQuarters * intTime
14       lblParkingTime.Text = "Parking Time: " &
15                       intParkingTime.ToString() & " minutes"
```

FIGURE 6-66

In the code example in Figure 6-66, the application checks the Do Until loop condition before executing the body of the loop. The first time the condition is tested, the expression decAmount < 0.25 is false because the decAmount variable contains 0.88. The body of the loop is executed because the Do Until statement specifies that the loop continues until the value in decAmount is less than 0.25. When the body of the loop is executed, it adds 1 to intQuarters to count the number of quarters the user has for the parking meter, and then subtracts 0.25 from decAmount because a quarter is worth 25 cents. Because decAmount is first assigned the value 0.88, the loop executes three times (decAmount = 0.88, decAmount = 0.63, and decAmount = 0.38) and stops when decAmount becomes less than 0.25. The lblParkingTime Label object displays the text "Parking Time: 45 minutes".

Bottom-Controlled Do Until Loops

The last of the four Do loops is the bottom-controlled Do Until loop. This Do Until loop checks the condition after the body of the loop is executed. The loop continues until the condition becomes true. The syntax of the bottom-controlled Do Until loop is shown in Figure 6-67.

General Format: Do Until Loop (Bottom-Controlled)

```
Do

      ` Loop Body

Loop Until condition
```

FIGURE 6-67

In Figure 6-67, the bottom-controlled Do Until loop begins with the word Do. The body of the loop is executed one time regardless of the condition being tested. The Loop Until statement checks the condition. The loop will be repeated until the condition is true.

User Input Loops

Do loops often are written to end when the user enters a certain value or performs a certain action such as tapping or clicking the Cancel button in an input box. The developer determines the value or action. For example, the Do Until loop in Figure 6-68 accumulates the total of all the entered test scores until the user taps or clicks the Cancel button in the input box. If the user taps or clicks the Cancel button, the InputBox function returns a null string that is assigned to the strTestGrade variable. The Do Until statement tests the string. If it contains a null character, the loop is terminated.

```
40          Do Until strTestGrade = ""
41              strTestGrade = InputBox("Enter test grade", "Compute Average")
42              If IsNumeric(strTestGrade) Then
43                  decGrade = Convert.ToDecimal(strTestGrade)
44                  decTotal += decGrade
45              End If
46          Loop
```

FIGURE 6-68

Avoid Infinite Loops

Recall that an **infinite loop** is a loop that never ends. It happens when the condition specified to end the loop never occurs. If the loop does not end, it repeats until the program is interrupted. Figure 6-69 shows an example of an infinite loop.

```
22        Dim intProblem = 0
23        Do While intProblem <= 5
24           Box.Show("This loop will not end", "Infinite Loop")
25        Loop
```

FIGURE 6-69

The Do While loop in Figure 6-69 never ends because the value in the variable intProblem is never changed from its initial value of zero. Because the value in intProblem never exceeds 5, the condition in the Do While loop (intProblem <= 5) never becomes false. The processing in a loop eventually must change the condition being tested in the Do While loop so the loop will terminate. When working in Visual Basic 2012, you can interrupt an infinite loop by tapping or clicking the Stop Debugging button on the Standard toolbar.

CONSIDER THIS

How do I know which type of loop to use?
All loops have the same basic function of repeating certain lines of a program. Some loops are best suited under certain conditions. For example, if you want to check the condition before the loop is run, use a top-controlled loop. Often the type of loop you use is just programmer preference.

Prime the Loop

As you have learned, a top-controlled loop tests a condition prior to beginning the loop. In most cases, the value to test must be set before the condition is tested the first time in the Do While or Do Until statement. Starting a loop with a preset value in the variable(s) tested in the condition is called **priming the loop**. You have seen this in previous examples, such as in Figure 6-66 on page 396, where the value in decAmount is set before the condition is tested the first time.

In some applications, the loop is primed with a value the user enters or an action the user takes. For example, in the Fitness Challenge application, the user enters the weight loss value for each team member (up to eight values) or taps or clicks the Cancel button in the input box. Prior to executing the Do Until statement the first time in the Do Until loop that processes the data the user enters, the InputBox function must be executed to obtain an initial value. Then, the Do Until statement can test the action taken by the user (enter a value and tap or click the Cancel button). The coding to implement this processing is shown in Figure 6-70.

```
30          Dim strCancelClicked As String = ""
31          Dim intMaxNumberOfEntries As Integer = 8
32          Dim intNumberOfEntries As Integer = 1

38          strWeightLoss = InputBox(strInputMessage & intNumberOfEntries, strInputHeading, " ")
39
40          Do Until intNumberOfEntries > intMaxNumberOfEntries Or strWeightLoss = strCancelClicked

47                  intNumberOfEntries += 1

56              If intNumberOfEntries <= intMaxNumberOfEntries Then
57                  strWeightLoss = InputBox(strInputMessage & intNumberOfEntries, strInputHeading, " ")
58              End If
59
60          Loop
```

FIGURE 6-70

In the Do Until loop shown in Figure 6-70, the Do Until statement on line 40 tests two conditions: is the value in the intNumberOfEntries variable greater than the value in the intMaxNumberOfEntries variable, or is the value in the strWeight-Loss variable equal to the value in the strCancelClicked variable, which is a null character (see line 30)? If either condition is true, the body of the loop is not executed.

The Do Until loop must have two primed variables: the intNumberOfEntries variable and the strWeightLoss variable. The intNumberOfEntries variable is initialized to 1 on line 32. The strWeightLoss variable is initialized by the InputBox function call on line 38. In this function call, either the user entered a value or tapped or clicked the Cancel button. If the user tapped or clicked the Cancel button, the body of the loop should not be entered.

To continue the loop, the processing within the body of the loop eventually must change one of the conditions being tested in the Do Until statement or the loop never terminates. In the sample program, the conditions being tested are whether the user entered eight weight loss values or tapped or clicked the Cancel button. Therefore, within the loop, the variable containing intNumberOfEntries must be incremented when the user enters a valid weight loss value. The user then must be able to enter more weight loss values or tap or click the Cancel button. On line 47 in Figure 6-70, the value in intNumberOfEntries is incremented by 1 each time the user enters a valid weight loss value. In addition, the statement on line 57 displays an input box that allows the user to enter a new value or tap or click the Cancel button as long as the number of valid entries is not greater than the maximum number of entries.

Validate Data

As you learned in Chapter 5, you must test the data a user enters to ensure it is accurate and that its use in other programming statements, such as converting string data to numeric data, will not cause a program exception. When using an input box, the data should be checked using the IsNumeric function and If statements, as discussed in Chapter 5. If the data is not valid, the user must be notified of the error and an input box displayed to allow the user to enter valid data.

For example, if the user enters nonnumeric data, the input box in Figure 6-71 should be displayed.

FIGURE 6-71

Similarly, if the user enters a negative number, the message in Figure 6-72 should be displayed in an input box.

FIGURE 6-72

When error checking is performed within a loop and the user is asked to enter data in an input box, the body of the loop must be executed each time the user enters data, regardless of whether the data is valid or invalid. If the user enters valid data, then the data is processed according to the needs of the program.

If the user enters invalid data, an error message is displayed and the user is given the opportunity to enter valid data in the input box. The coding for the Fitness Challenge application that accomplishes these tasks is shown in Figure 6-73.

```
38          strWeightLoss = InputBox(strInputMessage & intNumberOfEntries, strInputHeading, " ")
39
40          Do Until intNumberOfEntries > intMaxNumberOfEntries Or strWeightLoss = strCancelClicked
41
42              If IsNumeric(strWeightLoss) Then
43                  decWeightLoss = Convert.ToDecimal(strWeightLoss)
44                  If decWeightLoss > 0 Then
45                      lstWeightLoss.Items.Add(decWeightLoss)
46                      decTotalWeightLoss += decWeightLoss
47                      intNumberOfEntries += 1
48                      strInputMessage = strNormalMessage
49                  Else
50                      strInputMessage = strNegativeError
51                  End If
52              Else
53                  strInputMessage = strNonNumericError
54              End If
55
56              If intNumberOfEntries <= intMaxNumberOfEntries Then
57                  strWeightLoss = InputBox(strInputMessage & intNumberOfEntries, strInputHeading, " ")
58              End If
59
60          Loop
```

FIGURE 6-73

In Figure 6-73, the loop is primed by the InputBox function call on line 38. The Do Until statement on line 40 checks the two conditions — if the value in the intNumberOfEntries counter is greater than the maximum number of entries, or if the user taps or clicks the Cancel button. In either case, the body of the loop is not executed.

When the body of the loop is executed, the application checks the data the user entered to verify it is numeric. If it is numeric, the value is converted to a Decimal data type and then is checked to ensure it is greater than zero (line 44). If it is greater than zero, it is added to the lstWeightLoss ListBox object, the decTotalWeightLoss accumulator is incremented by the weight loss value the user entered, the intNumberOfEntries counter is incremented by 1, and the normal message is moved to the strInputMessage variable. This variable contains the message that is displayed in the input box (see line 38).

If the value the user entered is not greater than zero, the statement following the Else statement on line 49 moves the value in the strNegativeError variable to the strInputMessage variable so that the next time the InputBox function is called, the message will indicate an error, as shown in Figure 6-72.

If the value the user entered was not numeric (as tested by the statement on line 42), the statement on line 53 moves the value in the strNonNumericError variable to the strInputMessage variable so that the next time the InputBox function is called, the message will indicate a nonnumeric error, as shown in Figure 6-71.

On lines 56 and 57, as long as the number of entries is not greater than the maximum number of entries, the InputBox function is called. The message that is displayed in the input box depends on whether an error occurred. The Do Until statement on line 40 is executed and the process begins again.

Create a Nested Loop

In the last chapter, you learned to nest If...Then...Else statements within each other. Loops also can be nested. You can place any type of loop within any other type of loop under the following conditions: interior loops must be completely contained inside the outer loop and must have a different control variable. The example in Figure 6-74 uses a nested For loop to display a list of the weeks in the first quarter of the year (13 weeks) along with the days in each week. The outer For...Next loop counts from 1 to 13 for the 13 weeks, and the inner For...Next loop counts from 1 to 7 for the days in each of the 13 weeks.

```
6        Dim intOuterCount As Integer ' Counts the first 13 weeks in a quarter
7        Dim intInnerCount As Integer ' Counts the 7 days in a week
8        For intOuterCount = 1 To 13 ' For weeks in the 1st quarter of the year
9            For intInnerCount = 1 To 7 ' For the 7 days in a week
10               lstDays.Items.Add("Week: " & intOuterCount.ToString() _
11                               & " Day: " & intInnerCount.ToString())
12           Next
13       Next
```

FIGURE 6-74

The code in Figure 6-74 displays the output shown in Figure 6-75.

FIGURE 6-75

Select the Best Loop

When writing a program, you might have to make a decision regarding which loop structure to use. For...Next loops are best when the number of repetitions is fixed. Do loops are best when the condition to enter or exit the loop needs to be re-evaluated continually. When deciding which loop to use, keep the following considerations in mind:

1. Use a Do loop if the number of repetitions is unknown and is based on a condition changing; a For...Next loop is best if the exact number of repetitions is fixed.
2. If a loop condition must be tested before the body of the loop is executed, use a top-controlled Do While or Do Until loop. If the instructions within a loop must be executed one time regardless of the status of a condition, use a bottom-controlled Do While or Do Until loop.
3. Use the keyword While if you want to continue execution of the loop while the condition is true. Use the keyword Until if you want to continue execution until the condition is true.

Use a DataTip with Breakpoints

As programs become longer and more complex, the likelihood of errors increases, and you need to carefully find and remove these errors. Resolving defects in code is called **debugging**. When you debug a program, you collect information and find out what is wrong with the code in the program. You then fix that code.

A good way to collect information is to pause the execution of the code where a possible error could occur. One way to pause execution is to use breakpoints. **Breakpoints** are stop points placed in the code to tell the Visual Studio 2012 debugger where and when to pause the execution of the application. During this pause, the program is in break mode. While in break mode, you can examine the values in all variables that are within the scope of execution through the use of **DataTips**. In the Fitness Challenge application, you can insert a breakpoint in the assignment statement that increments the decTotalWeightLoss accumulator to view its value after each iteration of the loop as the user enters each weight loss value. To set a breakpoint in your code and then check the data at the breakpoint using DataTips, you can complete the following steps:

STEP 1   With the Fitness Challenge application open in the code window, press and hold or right-click line 46, which contains the code where you want to set a breakpoint, and then point to Breakpoint on the shortcut menu.

A shortcut menu opens that contains the Breakpoint command (Figure 6-76). The Breakpoint submenu contains the Insert Breakpoint command. Setting a breakpoint on line 46 means that the program will pause at that line during execution so that the values in variables within the scope of execution can be examined.

FIGURE 6-76

STEP 2   Tap or click Insert Breakpoint on the submenu.

A breakpoint is set on line 46, which is the line in the Do Until loop that adds the weight loss value the user entered to the weight loss accumulator — decTotalWeightLoss (Figure 6-77). The breakpoint is identified by the bullet to the left of the line numbers and the highlight effect on the code.

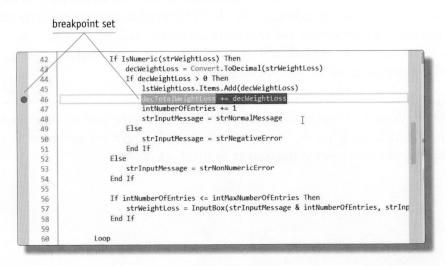

FIGURE 6-77

STEP 3   To run and test the program with the breakpoint, tap or click the Start Debugging button on the Standard toolbar.

The program starts and the Fitness Challenge window opens (Figure 6-78).

FIGURE 6-78
© Pando Hall/Photographer's Choice RF/Getty Images

STEP 4   Tap or click the Enter Weight Loss button. Type 3 . 4 as the weight loss amount of the first team member.

The Weight Loss input box contains 3.4 as the weight loss amount of the first team member (Figure 6-79).

3.4 entered in
Weight Loss
input box

FIGURE 6-79
© Pando Hall/Photographer's Choice RF/Getty Images

STEP 5 Tap or click the OK button in the input box.

The program executes the lines of code in the event handler until reaching the breakpoint, where it pauses execution on the accumulator line (Figure 6-80). The application is now in break mode. Notice the breakpoint line is highlighted in yellow.

program execution
paused at breakpoint

```
45          lstWeightLoss.Items.Add(decWeightLoss)
46          decTotalWeightLoss += decWeightLoss
47          intNumberOfEntries += 1
```

FIGURE 6-80

STEP 6 Point to the variable decWeightLoss on line 46.

A DataTip appears, displaying the value of the decWeightLoss variable when execution was paused (Figure 6-81). The value is 3.4 because the user entered this value in Step 4. It is a Decimal value (3.4D) because the statement in line 43 converted the value the user entered to a Decimal value.

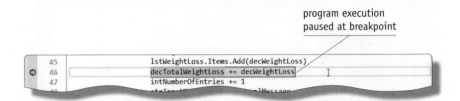

pointer on
decWeightLoss variable

DataTip displays the value
in the decWeightLoss
variable

```
42          If IsNumeric(strWeightLoss) Then
43              decWeightLoss = Convert.ToDecimal(strWeightLoss)
44              If decWeightLoss > 0 Then
45                  lstWeightLoss.Items.Add(decWeightLoss)
46                  decTotalWeightLoss += decWeightLoss
47                  intNumberOfEntries += 1          ● decWeightLoss 3.4D ▪
48                  strInputMessage = strNormalMessage
49              Else
50                  strInputMessage = strNegativeError
51              End If
```

FIGURE 6-81

STEP 7 You can view the value in any other variable within execution scope by pointing to that variable. To illustrate, point to the variable decTotalWeightLoss on line 46.

The value in the decTotalWeightLoss variable is displayed (Figure 6-82). The value is zero, which means the assignment statement on line 46 has not yet been executed. When a breakpoint is set, the program pauses before executing the statement that contains the breakpoint.

pointer on
decTotalWeightLoss
variable

DataTip displays the value
in the decTotalWeightLoss
variable

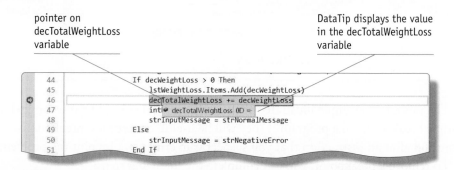

```
44          If decWeightLoss > 0 Then
45              lstWeightLoss.Items.Add(decWeightLoss)
46              decTotalWeightLoss += decWeightLoss
47              intl● decTotalWeightLoss 0D =
48              strInputMessage = strNormalMessage
49          Else
50              strInputMessage = strNegativeError
51          End If
```

FIGURE 6-82

STEP 8 Continue the program by tapping or clicking the Continue button on the Standard toolbar. Notice that the Continue button is the same as the Start Debugging button.

The program continues by opening the next InputBox function, where the user can enter the weight loss value for the next team member. The program runs until it again reaches the breakpoint, where it pauses so you can point to any variable to view its present value in a DataTip (Figure 6-83).

program execution
paused again

Continue button

FIGURE 6-83

STEP 9   Point to the decTotalWeightLoss variable.

The updated value in the decTotalWeightLoss variable is displayed (Figure 6-84). The value 3.4D is in the variable as a result of the processing in the first iteration of the loop. You also can examine the values in other variables by pointing to the variable name.

```
42          If IsNumeric(strWeightLoss) Then
43              decWeightLoss = Convert.ToDecimal(strWeightLoss)
44              If decWeightLoss > 0 Then
45                  lstWeightLoss.Items.Add(decWeightLoss)
46                  decTotalWeightLoss += decWeightLoss                              updated value
47                  intN  decTotalWeightLoss 3.4D                                      displayed
48                  strInputMessage = strNormalMessage
49              Else
```

FIGURE 6-84

The preceding example illustrated the use of one breakpoint, but you can include multiple breakpoints in a program if they will be useful. Sometimes, breakpoints before and after an instruction that you suspect is in error can pinpoint the problem.

To remove a breakpoint, you can complete the following steps:

STEP 1   Press and hold or right-click the statement containing the breakpoint, and then point to Breakpoint on the shortcut menu.

The shortcut menu is displayed, the pointer is located on the Breakpoint entry, and the Breakpoint submenu is displayed (Figure 6-85). You can press and hold or right-click the statement containing the breakpoint either when the program is running in Debugging mode or when the program is not running.

FIGURE 6-85

STEP 2   Tap or click Delete Breakpoint on the Breakpoint submenu.

If the program is running in Debugging mode, the breakpoint is removed when you tap or click the Continue button (Figure 6-86). If the program is not running, the breakpoint is removed immediately.

breakpoint is
removed, but variable
is highlighted

```
frmFitness.vb  ⊕ ✕   frmFitness.vb [Design]
🔵 btnWeightLoss                            ▼  ⚡ Click
    40        Do Until intNumberOfEntries > intMaxNumberOfEntries Or strWeightLoss = strCan┿
    41
    42            If IsNumeric(strWeightLoss) Then
    43                decWeightLoss = Convert.ToDecimal(strWeightLoss)
    44                If decWeightLoss > 0 Then
    45                    lstWeightLoss.Items.Add(decWeightLoss)
    46                    decTotalWeightLoss += decWeightLoss
    47                    intNumberOfEntries += 1
    48                    strInputMessage = strNormalMessage
    49                Else
    50                    strInputMessage = strNegativeError
    51                End If
    52            Else
    53                strInputMessage = strNonNumericError
    54            End If
    55
    56            If intNumberOfEntries <= intMaxNumberOfEntries Then
    57                strWeightLoss = InputBox(strInputMessage & intNumberOfEntries, strInp
    58            End If
    59
    60        Loop
    61
```

FIGURE 6-86

Using breakpoints and DataTips allows you to examine any variables during the execution of the program. By moving step by step through the program, normally you can identify any errors that might occur in the program.

Publish an Application with ClickOnce Deployment

After an application is completely debugged and working properly, you can deploy the project. Deploying a project means placing an executable version of the program on your hard disk (which then can be placed on CD, DVD, or in the cloud), on a Web server, or on a network server.

You probably have purchased software on a CD or DVD or downloaded software from a cloud-based site. To install the application on your computer, you insert the CD or DVD into your computer and then follow the setup instructions. The version of the program you receive on the CD or DVD is the deployed version of the program.

When programming using Visual Basic 2012, you can create a deployed program by using **ClickOnce Deployment**. The deployed version of the program you create can be installed and executed on any computer that has the .NET framework installed. The computer does not need Visual Studio 2012 installed to run the program.

To publish the Fitness Challenge application using ClickOnce Deployment, you can complete the following steps:

STEP 1   With the Fitness Challenge application open, tap or click BUILD on the menu bar.

The BUILD menu is displayed (Figure 6-87).

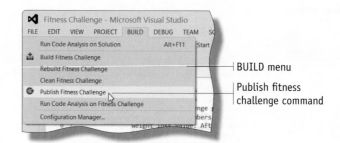

FIGURE 6-87

STEP 2   Tap or click Publish Fitness Challenge on the BUILD menu.

The Publish Wizard starts (Figure 6-88). The first Publish Wizard dialog box asks where you want to publish the application. The application can be published to a Web server, a network, or as a setup file on a hard disk or USB drive for burning on a CD or DVD. This dialog box includes publish\ as the default location, which you can change to a file location.

FIGURE 6-88

STEP 3 Change the default location from publish\ to a file location. To publish to a USB drive, type the drive letter. In this example, enter E: for a USB drive.

The Publish Wizard dialog box requests where you want to publish the application. The Fitness Challenge application will be saved to the USB drive, which is drive E: in this example (Figure 6-89).

location for publishing application

Next button

FIGURE 6-89

STEP 4 Tap or click the Next button. If necessary, tap or click the From a CD-ROM or DVD-ROM radio button.

Visual Basic displays a Publish Wizard dialog box that asks, "How will users install the application?" (Figure 6-90). When the user will install the application from a CD or DVD, such as when you purchase software, you should select the CD or DVD option.

From a CD-ROM or DVD-ROM selected

Next button

FIGURE 6-90

STEP 5   Tap or click the Next button. If necessary, tap or click the "The application will not check for updates" radio button.

The next Publish Wizard dialog box asks where the application will check for updates (Figure 6-91). You can select and enter a location or indicate that the application will not check for updates. Generally, when an application will be deployed to a CD or DVD, the application will not check for updates. If the application is deployed to a Web server or network server, then it might check for updates before being executed on the user's computer.

application will not
check for updates

Next button

FIGURE 6-91

STEP 6   Tap or click the Next button.

The Ready to Publish! window is displayed (Figure 6-92). Notice the message in this window — when the program is installed on the user's machine, a shortcut for the program will be added to the user's computer, and the program can be deleted using the Add/Remove Programs function in the Control Panel.

message describes
what happens when
application is installed

Finish button

FIGURE 6-92

STEP 7 Tap or click the Finish button.

The Visual Basic window displays several messages indicating that the application is being published. The last message is "Publish succeeded" (Figure 6-93).

Publish succeeded message

FIGURE 6-93

STEP 8 To view the finished result, minimize the Visual Studio window and then open the Search charm. Type `Computer` in the Search box. Double-tap or double-click the USB drive icon to view the published installation folder.

Installation files are placed on the USB drive (Figure 6-94). If all of these files are copied to a computer with the .NET framework, the user can double-tap or double-click the setup file to begin the installation.

installation files

double-tap or double-click setup to install the application

FIGURE 6-94

STEP 9 To install the application, double-tap or double-click the setup file.

After the user double-taps or double-clicks the setup file, the application is installed on the local computer. During installation, Windows might display the dialog box shown in Figure 6-95. This dialog box is intended to protect you from installing programs that might harm your computer. Because you know the source of this program, you can tap or click the Install button to continue installing the program.

Application Install – Security Warning dialog box

FIGURE 6-95

STEP 10 After installation, the program runs. To run the installed application again, open the Search charm, type `Fitness`, and then click the Fitness Challenge icon.

Program Design

As you have learned, the requirements document identifies the purpose of the program being developed, the application title, the procedures to be followed when using the program, any required equations and calculations, any conditions that must be tested, notes and restrictions that must be followed by the program, and any other comments that would be helpful to understanding the problem. The requirements document for the Fitness Challenge application is shown in Figure 6-96.

REQUIREMENTS DOCUMENT

Date Submitted:	September 30, 2016
Application Title:	Fitness Challenge Application
Purpose:	This application finds the average weight loss of a team of eight employees.
Program Procedures:	In a Windows application, the user enters the weight loss amounts of eight employees as positive numbers to compute the average weight loss for the entire team.
Algorithms, Processing, and Conditions:	1. The user must be able to enter each of eight weight loss values in pounds after tapping or clicking the Enter Weight Loss button.
	2. Each weight loss value is validated to confirm it is numeric and greater than zero.
	3. Each weight loss value is displayed in a ListBox object.
	4. After the user enters eight weight loss values or taps or clicks the Cancel button in an input box, the program calculates and displays the average weight loss for the team.
	5. A menu bar includes the File menu, which contains Clear and Exit items. The Clear menu item clears the result and the weight loss values. The Exit menu item closes the application.
Notes and Restrictions:	1. If a nonnumeric or negative value is entered for the weight loss, the program should display an error message and ask the user to re-enter the value.
	2. If the user taps or clicks the Cancel button before entering any weight loss values, a message should indicate no weight loss values were entered. An average is not calculated when no weight loss values are entered.
Comments:	1. The picture shown in the window can be found on CengageBrain.com. The name of the picture is Weight.
	2. The average weight loss should be formatted as a Decimal value with one decimal place.

FIGURE 6-96

The Use Case Definition shown in Figure 6-97 specifies the procedures the user will follow to use this application.

USE CASE DEFINITION

1. The Windows application opens, displaying the Fitness Challenge title, a ListBox object to hold the numeric entries, and a Button object that allows the user to begin entering up to eight weight loss values.
2. A menu bar displays the File menu, which has two menu items: Clear and Exit.
3. In an InputBox object, the user enters up to eight values representing the number of pounds lost, such as 3.2 pounds.
4. The program asks the user for the weight loss value again if a value is nonnumeric or negative.
5. The user terminates data entry by entering eight values or by tapping or clicking the Cancel button in the InputBox object.
6. The program calculates the average weight loss for the values the user entered.
7. In a Label object, the program displays the average weight loss as a Decimal value with one decimal place.
8. The user can clear the input and the results by tapping or clicking the Clear menu item, and can then repeat Steps 3 through 7.
9. The user taps or clicks Exit on the File menu to close the application.

FIGURE 6-97

© 2014 Cengage Learning

Event Planning Document

You will recall that the event planning document is a table that specifies which objects in the user interface will cause events, the action taken by the user to trigger each event, and the event processing that must occur. The event planning document for the Fitness Challenge application is shown in Figure 6-98.

EVENT PLANNING DOCUMENT

Program Name:	Developer:	Object:	Date:
Fitness Challenge Application	Corinne Hoisington	frmFitness	September 30, 2014

OBJECT	EVENT TRIGGER	EVENT PROCESSING
btnWeightLoss	Tap or click	Display an InputBox object to obtain each team member's weight loss up to eight times or until the user taps or clicks the Cancel button
		Check if strWeightLoss is numeric
		If the weight loss value is numeric, convert strWeightLoss to a Decimal value
		If strWeightLoss is numeric, check whether the value is positive
		If the weight loss value is positive: Display the value in lstWeightLoss Accumulate the total of the weight loss values in decTotalWeightLoss Update the number of entries Set the InputBox message to the normal message
		If the value entered is not numeric, display an error message in the input box
		If the value entered is not positive, display an error message in the input box
		After all weight loss values are entered, change the Visible property of lblAverageLoss to true
		If one or more weight loss values are entered: Calculate the average weight loss in decAverageLoss Display the average weight loss in lblAverageLoss
		If no values are entered: Display the text "No weight loss value entered"
		Disable the btnWeightLoss Button
mnuClear	Tap or click	Clear the lstWeightLoss ListBox
		Change the Visible property of lblAverageLoss to False
		Enable the btnWeightLoss Button
mnuExit	Tap or click	Exit the application

FIGURE 6-98

Design and Code the Program

Design and Code the Program

After identifying the events and tasks within the events, the developer is ready to create the program. As you have learned, creating the program means designing the user interface and then entering Visual Basic statements to accomplish the tasks specified in the event planning document. As the developer enters the code, she also will implement the logic to carry out the required processing.

Guided Program Development

To design the user interface for the Fitness Challenge application and enter the code required to process each event in the program, complete the steps on the following pages:

NOTE TO THE LEARNER

In the following activity, you should complete the tasks within the specified steps. Each of the tasks is accompanied by a Hint Screen. The purpose of the Hint Screen is to indicate where you should perform the activity in the Visual Studio window and to remind you which method to use. If you need further help completing a step, refer to the figure identified by *ref:*.

Guided Program Development

Phase 1: Design the Form

1

- **Create a Windows Application** Open Visual Studio and then close the Start page. Create a new Visual Basic Windows Forms Application project by tapping or clicking the New Project button on the Standard toolbar, selecting Windows as the project type, selecting Windows Forms Application as the template, naming the project Fitness Challenge in the Name text box, and then tapping or clicking the OK button in the New Project window.

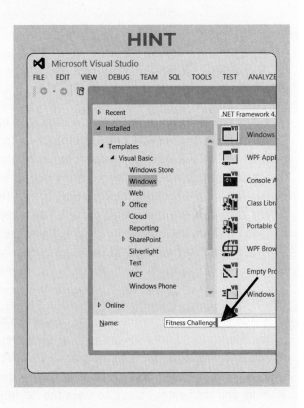

- **Display the Toolbox** Ensure that the Toolbox is displayed in the Visual Studio window and that the Common Controls are accessible.

- **Name the Windows Form Object** In the Solution Explorer window, press and hold or right-click Form1.vb, tap or click Rename, and then rename the form frmFitness.

- **Change the Text on the Title Bar for the Windows Form Object** Change the title bar text of the Windows Form object to Fitness Challenge.

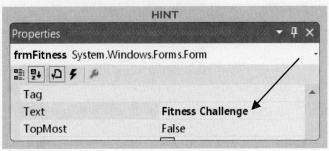

(continues)

Guided Program Development *continued*

- **Change the Size of the Form Object** Resize the
Form object by changing the Size property to 625, 500.

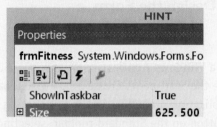

- **Add the MenuStrip Object** Drag a MenuStrip object from
the Menus & Toolbars category of the Toolbox to the Windows
Form object. The MenuStrip snaps into place below the title
bar. Name the MenuStrip object mnuFitness in the Properties window. Tap or click the Type Here box on the MenuStrip
object, type &File, and then press the ENTER key. The ampersand creates a hot key for the letter F. Name the File menu
item mnuFile (*ref: Figure 6-5*).

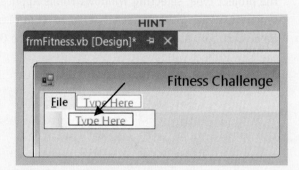

- **Add Menu Items** The next step is to add two menu items to
the File menu. Tap or click the Type Here box below the word
File, and then enter &Clear. Name the Clear menu item mnu-
Clear. Tap or click the Type Here box below the Clear menu
item, and then enter E&xit to make the "x" in Exit the hot
key. Name the Exit menu item mnuExit (*ref: Figure 6-10*).

- **Add a PictureBox Object** Drag a PictureBox .NET component
from the Toolbox to the left side of the Windows Form object.
Name the PictureBox object picFitness. Change the Size
property of the PictureBox object to 215, 450. Change the
Location property of the PictureBox object to 3, 30.

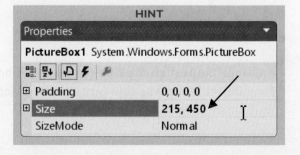

● **Add the Title Label Object** Drag a Label
.NET component onto the Windows Form
object. Name the label `lblTitle`. Enter
the text for this label as `Fitness
Challenge Team Weight Loss` on
two lines. (*Hint*: Tap or click the Text
property list arrow in the Properties window
to enter a label with multiple lines. Press
the ENTER key to move to a new line.) Choose
Tahoma as the font, Bold as the font style,
and 18 points as the size. Change the
TextAlign property to MiddleCenter by tapping or
clicking the TextAlign list arrow and then tapping
or clicking the Center block. Change the Location
property of the lblTitle Label object to `275, 40`.

● **Add the Enter Weight Loss Button Object**
Drag a Button object onto the Windows Form
object below the title label. Name the Button
`btnWeightLoss`. Change the text of the
button to `Enter Weight Loss`. Change the font to
11-point Tahoma. Resize the Button object to view the
complete text. Align the centers of the Button object with the
title Label object.

● **Add the ListBox Object for the Team Members' Weight
Loss** To add the ListBox object that displays the team
members' weight loss, drag a ListBox object onto the Windows
Form object below the Button object. Name the ListBox
`lstWeightLoss`. Change the font of the text in the ListBox
object to 11-point Tahoma. Resize the ListBox to the width of
four characters because the top weight loss of a team member
could reach an amount such as 46.3 pounds. Lengthen the
ListBox object to display eight numbers. The Size property for
the ListBox object in the sample program is `45, 180`. Change
the RightToLeft property to No to right-align the numeric
values. Align the centers of the ListBox object with the Button
object (*ref: Figure 6-24*).

(continues)

● **Add the Result Label** To add the label where the average weight loss message is displayed, drag a Label object onto the Windows Form object. Name the Label object `lblAverageLoss`. Change the text to `Average weight loss for the team is XX.X lbs`. Change the font to Tahoma 11-point. Align the centers of the Label object with the ListBox object.

The user interface mockup is complete (Figure 6-99).

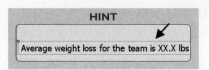

HINT

Average weight loss for the team is XX.X lbs

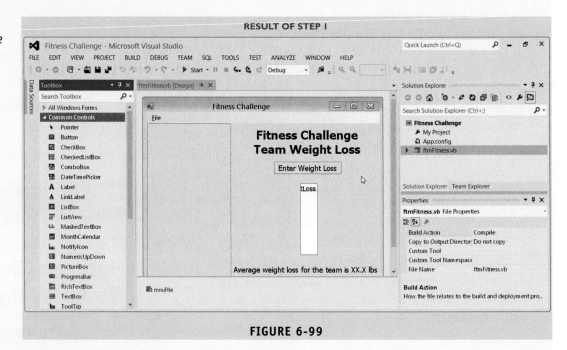

RESULT OF STEP I

FIGURE 6-99

Phase 2: Fine-Tune the User Interface

2

● **Change the BackColor Property of the Windows Form Object** Select the Windows Form object and then change its BackColor property to White on the Web tab.

HINT

● **Change the Color for the Title Label** Change
the ForeColor property for the lblTitle Label object
to DarkOrange on the Web tab.

● **Change the Button Color** Change the BackColor property
of the btnWeightLoss Button object to Orange.

● **Insert the Fitness Image into the PictureBox Object
and Size the Image** Make sure you have the data files for
this chapter (available on CengageBrain.com). Select the
picFitness PictureBox object. In the Properties window,
select the Image property and then tap or click the ellipsis
button in the right column. Import the Fitness image from
the location where you saved it. Tap or click the OK button
in the Select Resource dialog box. Select the SizeMode
property, tap or click the SizeMode arrow, and then tap or
click StretchImage.

(continues)

● **Change the Visible Property for the Average Weight Loss Label** Select the lblAverageLoss Label object and change its Visible property to False because the Label object is not displayed until the average weight loss is calculated.

● **Make the Enter Weight Loss Button the Accept Button** Tap or click the background of the Windows Form object to select it. In the Properties window, tap or click the AcceptButton list arrow to display the buttons in the user interface. Tap or click btnWeightLoss in the list. During program execution, when the user presses the ENTER key, the event handler for btnWeightLoss executes.

The user interface design is complete (Figure 6-100).

© Pando Hall/Photographer's Choice RF/Getty Images

FIGURE 6-100

Phase 3: Code the Program

3

● **Enter the Comments for the Enter Weight Loss Button Event Handler** Double-tap or double-click the btnWeightLoss Button object on the Windows Form object to open the button event handler. Insert the first four standard comments at the top of the code window. Insert the command Option Strict On at the beginning of the code to turn on strict type checking.

HINT

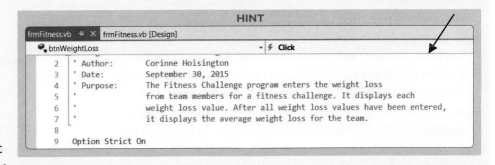

```
frmFitness.vb    frmFitness.vb [Design]
btnWeightLoss                                          Click
     2    ' Author:        Corinne Hoisington
     3    ' Date:          September 30, 2015
     4    ' Purpose:       The Fitness Challenge program enters the weight loss
     5    '                from team members for a fitness challenge. It displays each
     6    '                weight loss value. After all weight loss values have been entered,
     7    '                it displays the average weight loss for the team.
     8
     9    Option Strict On
```

● **Comment on the btnWeightLoss_Click Event Handler** Enter a comment to describe the purpose of the btnWeightLoss_Click event handler.

HINT

```
    11   Public Class frmFitness
    12       Private Sub btnWeightLoss_Click(sender As Object, e As EventArgs) Handles btnWeightL...
    13           ' The btnWeightLoss_Click event accepts and displays up to 8 weight loss values
    14           ' and then calculates and displays the average weight loss for the team
    15
    16       End Sub
```

● **Declare and Initialize the Variables to Calculate the Average Weight Loss** Four variables are used to calculate the average weight loss (besides the team member count). These variables are: 1) strWeightLoss: Is assigned the value from the InputBox function call; 2) decWeightLoss: Is assigned the converted team member weight loss; 3) decAverageLoss: Contains the calculated average weight loss; 4) decTotalWeightLoss: The accumulator used to collect the total weight loss values entered by a user. Declare and initialize these four variables.

HINT

```
    16           ' Declare and initialize variables
    17
    18           Dim strWeightLoss As String
    19           Dim decWeightLoss As Decimal
    20           Dim decAverageLoss As Decimal
    21           Dim decTotalWeightLoss As Decimal = 0D
```

(continues)

● **Declare and Initialize the Variables Used with the InputBox Function Call** Five variables contain messages used in the input box to obtain

HINT

```
22    Dim strInputMessage As String = "Enter the weight loss for team member #"
23    Dim strInputHeading As String = "Weight Loss"
24    Dim strNormalMessage As String = "Enter the weight loss for team member #"
25    Dim strNonNumericError As String = "Error - Enter a number for the weight loss of team member #"
26    Dim strNegativeError As String = "Error - Enter a positive number for the weight loss of team member #"
```

the team members' weight loss. These variables are: 1) strInputMessage: Is used in the function call to contain the message displayed in the input box; 2) strInputHeading: Contains the message displayed in the title bar of the input box; 3) strNormalMessage: The normal message that appears in the input box when no error has occurred; 4) strNonNumericError: The message that appears in the input box when the user has entered a nonnumeric value; 5) strNegativeError: The message that appears in the input box when the user has entered zero or a negative number. Declare and initialize these five variables.

● **Declare and Initialize Variables Used in the Loop Processing** Three variables are used for processing the loop in the program. These variables are: 1) strCancelClicked: This variable contains a null string and is used to determine if the user tapped or clicked the Cancel button in the input box; 2) intMaxNumberOfEntries: Contains the

HINT

```
28        'Declare and initialize loop variables
29
30        Dim strCancelClicked As String = ""
31        Dim intMaxNumberOfEntries As Integer = 8
32        Dim intNumberOfEntries As Integer = 1
```

maximum number of entries for team member weight losses (program requirements state the maximum number is eight); 3) intNumberOfEntries: The counter for the valid number of team member weight loss values entered by the user. This variable is used to determine when the maximum number of entries has been made and to act as the divisor when calculating the average weight loss per team member.

● **Write Comments for the Do Until Loop and Write the Priming InputBox Function Call** You often can use comments to document a loop or other set of major processing statements. The comments

HINT

```
34        ' This loop allows the user to enter the weight loss of up to 8 team members.
35        ' The loop terminates when the user has entered 8 weight loss values or the user
36        ' taps or clicks the Cancel button or the Close button in the InputBox
37
38        strWeightLoss = InputBox(strInputMessage & intNumberOfEntries, strInputHeading, " ")
39
```

here alert the reader to the role of the Do Until loop. The priming InputBox function call obtains the first team members' weight loss, or allows the user to tap or click the Cancel button. The normal message is displayed. The space at the end of the argument list places a space in the input box so if the user taps or clicks the OK button without entering any data, the command will not be treated the same as tapping or clicking the Cancel button *(ref: Figure 6-70)*.

● **Code the Do Until Loop**
Because the application
requests the weight loss values
of up to eight team members,

```
40          Do Until intNumberOfEntries > intMaxNumberOfEntries Or strWeightLoss = strCancelClicked
41
42          Loop
```

the Do Until loop should continue until eight weight losses
are entered or until the user taps or clicks the Cancel or
Close button in the input box. Enter the Do Until loop using
IntelliSense *(ref: Figure 6-65, Figure 6-70)*.

● **Validate That the Entry Is a Number** The first
process in the Do Until loop is to validate that
the team member weight loss entered by the user
is a numeric value. Enter the If...Then statement to
test if the value in the strWeightLoss variable is numeric.

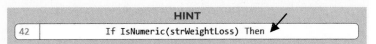

```
42          If IsNumeric(strWeightLoss) Then
```

● **Convert the Value Entered from a String
to the Decimal Data Type** If the user entered
a numeric value, the next step is to convert
the string value the user entered to a Decimal data type.
Using IntelliSense, enter the code to convert the value in the
strWeightLoss variable from the String to the Decimal data type
and place the result in the decWeightLoss variable.

```
43          decWeightLoss = Convert.ToDecimal(strWeightLoss)
```

● **Validate That the Entered Value Is a
Positive Number** After the value is converted,
the program must validate that the number is
positive. Write the If...Then statement to test whether the
value in the decWeightLoss variable is greater than zero.

```
44          If decWeightLoss > 0 Then
```

● **Perform the Processing When the User
Enters a Valid Weight Loss** After ensuring
the weight loss entered by the user is valid,
the next steps are to perform the processing
for valid weight loss. Four steps are required:

```
45          lstWeightLoss.Items.Add(decWeightLoss)
46          decTotalWeightLoss += decWeightLoss
47          intNumberOfEntries += 1
48          strInputMessage = strNormalMessage
```

1) Add the weight loss as an item to the lstWeightLoss ListBox
object *(ref: Figure 6-28)*; 2) Add the weight loss the user entered
to the decTotalWeightLoss accumulator *(ref: Figure 6-38)*. The
accumulated weight loss is used to calculate the average weight
loss; 3) Increment the intNumberOfEntries counter by 1 because
the user entered a valid weight loss *(ref: Figure 6-38)*. This value
is used as the divisor to determine the average weight loss, and
as one of the indicators that the loop should be terminated; 4)
Because the user entered a valid weight loss, the normal message
should appear the next time the input box is displayed. Therefore,
the normal message should be moved to the strInputMessage variable. Using IntelliSense, enter the code for these four activities.

(continues)

● **Assign an Error Message If the User Entered a Negative Weight Loss** If the user entered a negative weight loss, the next input box should display the negative number error message *(ref: Figure 6-73)*. Following the Else statement for the If statement that checks for a number greater than zero, enter the assignment statement that places the value in the strNegativeError variable in the strInputMessage variable.

	HINT
49	Else
50	strInputMessage = strNegativeError
51	End If

● **Assign an Error Message If the User Enters a Nonnumeric Weight Loss** If the user enters a nonnumeric weight loss, the next input box should show the nonnumeric error message *(ref: Figure 6-73)*. Following the Else Statement for the If statement that checks for numeric data, enter the assignment statement that places the value in the strNonNumericError variable in the strInputMessage variable.

	HINT
52	Else
53	strInputMessage = strNonNumericError
54	End If

● **Code the InputBox Function Call** The first InputBox function call was placed before the Do Until loop to prime the loop. To continue the process after the first value is entered, another InputBox function is needed as the last statement inside the loop to request subsequent values. This statement should be executed only if the maximum number of entries has not been exceeded. So, an If structure is required to determine if the maximum number of entries has been reached. If not, the InputBox function call is executed *(ref: Figure 6-73)*.

	HINT
56	If intNumberOfEntries <= intMaxNumberOfEntries Then
57	strWeightLoss = InputBox(strInputMessage & intNumberOfEntries, strInputHeading, " ")
58	End If

The coding for the variables and Do Until loop that processes the data in the program is complete (Figure 6-101). It is important that you examine the code in Figure 6-101 and understand the loop processing. The priming of the loop, both by setting the value in the intNumberOfEntries variable (line 32) and calling the InputBox function (line 38), is critical for proper execution of the loop. Increasing the loop counter when a valid entry is made (line 46) also is fundamental in the loop processing because testing this counter is one way the Do Until loop can be terminated. Also, using variables for messages instead of literals in the actual code demonstrates how professional programs are coded. You should follow these examples in your programming.

RESULT OF STEP 3

```
28          'Declare and initialize loop variables
29
30          Dim strCancelClicked As String = ""
31          Dim intMaxNumberOfEntries As Integer = 8
32          Dim intNumberOfEntries As Integer = 1
33
34          ' This loop allows the user to enter the weight loss of up to 8 team members.
35          ' The loop terminates when the user has entered 8 weight loss vales or the user
36          ' taps or clicks the Cancel button or the Close button in the InputBox
37
38          strWeightLoss = InputBox(strInputMessage & intNumberOfEntries, strInputHeading, " ")
39
40          Do Until intNumberOfEntries > intMaxNumberOfEntries Or strWeightLoss = strCancelClicked
41              If IsNumeric(strWeightLoss) Then
42                  decWeightLoss = Convert.ToDecimal(strWeightLoss)
43                  If decWeightLoss > 0 Then
44                      lstWeightLoss.Items.Add(decWeightLoss)
45                      decTotalWeightLoss += decWeightLoss
46                      intNumberOfEntries += 1
47                      strInputMessage = strNormalMessage
48                  Else
49                      strInputMessage = strNegativeError
50                  End If
51              Else
52                  strInputMessage = strNonNumericError
53              End If
54              If intNumberOfEntries <= intMaxNumberOfEntries Then
55                  strWeightLoss = InputBox(strInputMessage & intNumberOfEntries, strInputHeading, " ")
56              End If
57
58          Loop
```

FIGURE 6-101

(continues)

● **Set the Result Label's Visible Property** When you finish the Do Until loop, you

	HINT
62	'Calculates and displays average team weight loss
63	If intNumberOfEntries > 1 Then
64	lblAverageLoss.Visible = True

must complete three tasks to finish the Enter Weight Loss button click event handler: 1) Make the label that will contain the average weight loss visible; 2) Calculate and display the average weight loss; 3) Disable the Enter Weight Loss button. If at least one weight loss value has been entered using IntelliSense, write the code to create the If statement and make the lblAverageLoss label visible.

● **Calculate the Average Weight Loss** To calculate the average of the weight loss values the user entered, the value in the decTotalWeightLoss variable (accumulator) must be divided by the number of team members entered (counter). At the end

	HINT
65	decAverageLoss = decTotalWeightLoss / (intNumberOfEntries - 1)
66	lblAverageLoss.Text = "Average weight loss for the team is " & _
67	decAverageLoss.ToString("F1") & " lbs"
68	Else
69	MsgBox("No weight loss value entered")
70	End If

of the loop shown in Figure 6-101 on the previous page, the value in the intNumberOfEntries variable always will be one greater than the actual number of team members entered, so the total weight loss must be divided by the value in intNumberOfEntries minus 1. This calculation should occur only if one or more team member weight loss values were entered, so an If statement must be used to check whether the value in the intNumberOfEntries variable is greater than 1. If so, the average weight loss is calculated; if not, the "No weight loss value entered" message should be displayed using a MsgBox. Using IntelliSense, write the code to perform this processing.

● **Change the Enter Weight Loss Button Enabled Property to False** After the average weight loss is calculated and displayed, the Enabled property of the btnWeightLoss button is set to False to dim the button. Using IntelliSense, write the code to accomplish this processing.

	HINT
72	' Disables the Weight Loss button
73	btnWeightLoss.Enabled = False

The code for the btnWeightLoss button click event handler is completed (Figure 6-102).

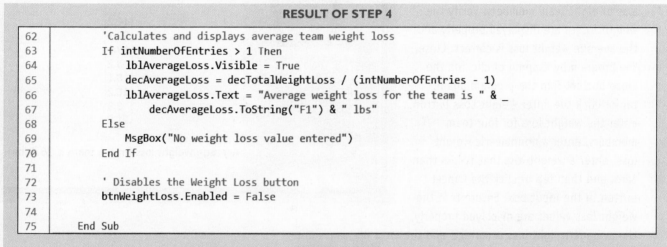

RESULT OF STEP 4

```
62      'Calculates and displays average team weight loss
63      If intNumberOfEntries > 1 Then
64          lblAverageLoss.Visible = True
65          decAverageLoss = decTotalWeightLoss / (intNumberOfEntries - 1)
66          lblAverageLoss.Text = "Average weight loss for the team is " & _
67              decAverageLoss.ToString("F1") & " lbs"
68      Else
69          MsgBox("No weight loss value entered")
70      End If
71
72      ' Disables the Weight Loss button
73      btnWeightLoss.Enabled = False
74
75  End Sub
```

FIGURE 6-102

(continues)

Guided Program Development *continued*

5

- **Run the Program** After coding a major section of the program, you should run the program to ensure it is working properly. Tap or click the Start Debugging button on the Standard toolbar to run the Fitness Challenge application. Tap or click the Enter Weight Loss button and then enter the weight loss of eight team members. Verify the weight losses are displayed properly and the average weight loss is correct. Close the program by tapping or clicking the Close button. Run the program again, tap or click the Enter Weight Loss button, enter the weight loss for four team members, enter a nonnumeric weight loss, enter a weight loss that is less than zero, and then tap or click the Cancel button in the input box. Ensure that the weight loss values are displayed properly, the average weight loss is correct, and the error messages are displayed properly in the input box. Close the program. Run the program again, tap or click the Enter Weight Loss button, and then tap or click the Cancel button in the input box. Ensure that the "No weight loss value entered" message is displayed. Close the program and then run it as many times as necessary to ensure the program is working properly. If the program does not run properly, consider setting a breakpoint and checking the values in the variables *(ref: Figure 6-76)*.

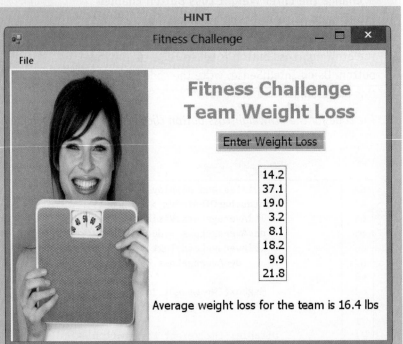

HINT

© Pando Hall/Photographer's Choice RF/Getty Images

6

- **Enter the Code for the Clear Menu Item Click Event** Tap or click the frmFitness.vb[Design]* tab in the code window to display the design window. Tap or click File on the MenuStrip object, and then double-tap or double-click the Clear menu item to open the Clear click event handler in the code window. The Clear click event handler must perform three tasks: 1) Clear the lstWeightLoss list box; 2) Hide the average weight loss Label object; 3) Enable the Enter Weight Loss Button object. Using IntelliSense, write the code for these three tasks.

HINT

```
76
77   Private Sub mnuClear_Click(sender As Object, e As EventArgs) Handles mnuClear.Click
78       ' The mnuClear click event clears the ListBox object and hides
79       ' the average weight loss label. It also enables the Weight Loss button
80
81       lstWeightLoss.Items.Clear()
82       lblAverageLoss.Visible = False
83       btnWeightLoss.Enabled = True
84
85   End Sub
```

● **Enter the Code for the Exit Menu Item Click Event** Return to the design window. Double-tap or double-click the Exit menu item. In the code window, enter a Close procedure call that will close the window and terminate the program.

HINT

```
Private Sub mnuExit_Click(sender As Object, e As EventArgs) Handles mnuExit.Click
    ' The mnuExit click event closes the window and exits the application
```

The code for the Clear menu item click event and the Exit menu item click event is completed (Figure 6-103). The code for the program is also completed.

RESULT OF STEP 6

```
77    Private Sub mnuClear_Click(sender As Object, e As EventArgs) Handles mnuClear.Click
78        ' The mnuClear click event clears the ListBox object and hides
79        ' the average weight loss label. It also enables the Weight Loss button
80
81        lstWeightLoss.Items.Clear()
82        lblAverageLoss.Visible = False
83        btnWeightLoss.Enabled = True
84
85    End Sub
86
87    Private Sub mnuExit_Click(sender As Object, e As EventArgs) Handles mnuExit.Click
88        ' The mnuExit click event closes the window and exits the application
89
90        Close()
91    End Sub
92 End Class
```

FIGURE 6-103

7

● **Publish the Fitness Challenge Application** After completing the program, you can publish it using ClickOnce deployment so it can be installed on multiple computers. To open the Publish Wizard and begin the deployment process, tap or click BUILD on the menu bar and then tap or click Publish Fitness Challenge on the BUILD menu *(ref: Figure 6-87)*.

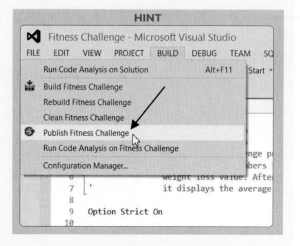

- **Select the Publish File Location** The Publish Wizard dialog box asks where you want to publish the application. Change the default location to the same file location that you used to save your Windows application by tapping or clicking the Browse button and then selecting the drive. For example, select the E: drive, a USB drive. After selecting the drive, tap or click the Next button in the Publish Wizard dialog box *(ref: Figure 6-88)*.

- **Select How Users Will Install the Application** In the next Publish Wizard dialog box, select the option that lets users install the application from a CD-ROM or DVD-ROM. Then, tap or click the Next button *(ref: Figure 6-90)*.

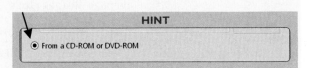

- **Indicate the Application Will Not Check for Updates** Tap or click the "The application will not check for updates" radio button to indicate no updates will be checked. This is the normal selection when programs are placed on CDs or DVDs. Then, tap or click the Next button in the Publish Wizard dialog box *(ref: Figure 6-91)*.

• **View the Summary Window** The Publish Wizard summary is displayed. Tap or click the Finish button to publish the application *(ref: Figure 6-92)*.

• **View the Installation Files** After the publishing succeeds, a folder is created with the installation files that could be placed on a CD, DVD, or other computer *(ref: Figure 6-94)*.

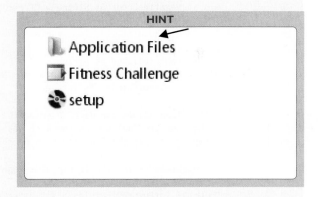

Code Listing

The complete code for the sample program is shown in Figure 6-104.

```vbnet
1  ' Program Name:  Fitness Challenge
2  ' Author:        Corinne Hoisington
3  ' Date:          September 30, 2015
4  ' Purpose:       The Fitness Challenge program enters the weight loss
5  '                from team members for a fitness challenge. It displays each
6  '                weight loss value. After all weight loss values have been entered,
7  '                it displays the average weight loss for the team.
8
9  Option Strict On
10
11 Public Class frmFitness
12     Private Sub btnWeightLoss_Click(sender As Object, e As EventArgs) Handles btnWeightLoss.Click
13         ' The btnWeightLoss_Click event accepts and displays up to 8 weight loss values
14         ' and then calculates and displays the average weight loss for the team
15
16         ' Declare and initialize variables
17
18         Dim strWeightLoss As String
19         Dim decWeightLoss As Decimal
20         Dim decAverageLoss As Decimal
21         Dim decTotalWeightLoss As Decimal = 0D
22         Dim strInputMessage As String = "Enter the weight loss for team member #"
23         Dim strInputHeading As String = "Weight Loss"
24         Dim strNormalMessage As String = "Enter the weight loss for team member #"
25         Dim strNonNumericError As String = "Error - Enter a number for the weight loss of team member #"
26         Dim strNegativeError As String = "Error - Enter a positive number for the weight loss of team member #"
27
28         'Declare and initialize loop variables
29
30         Dim strCancelClicked As String = ""
31         Dim intMaxNumberOfEntries As Integer = 8
32         Dim intNumberOfEntries As Integer = 1
33
34         ' This loop allows the user to enter the weight loss of up to 8 team members.
35         ' The loop terminates when the user has entered 8 weight loss values or the user
36         ' taps or clicks the Cancel button or the Close button in the InputBox
37
38         strWeightLoss = InputBox(strInputMessage & intNumberOfEntries, strInputHeading, " ")
39
40         Do Until intNumberOfEntries > intMaxNumberOfEntries Or strWeightLoss = strCancelClicked
41
42             If IsNumeric(strWeightLoss) Then
43                 decWeightLoss = Convert.ToDecimal(strWeightLoss)
44                 If decWeightLoss > 0 Then
45                     lstWeightLoss.Items.Add(decWeightLoss)
46                     decTotalWeightLoss += decWeightLoss
47                     intNumberOfEntries += 1
48                     strInputMessage = strNormalMessage
49                 Else
50                     strInputMessage = strNegativeError
51                 End If
52             Else
53                 strInputMessage = strNonNumericError
54             End If
55
56             If intNumberOfEntries <= intMaxNumberOfEntries Then
57                 strWeightLoss = InputBox(strInputMessage & intNumberOfEntries, strInputHeading, " ")
58             End If
59
```

FIGURE 6-104 (continues)

```
60          Loop
61
62          'Calculates and displays average team weight loss
63          If intNumberOfEntries > 1 Then
64              lblAverageLoss.Visible = True
65              decAverageLoss = decTotalWeightLoss / (intNumberOfEntries - 1)
66              lblAverageLoss.Text = "Average weight loss for the team is " & _
67                  decAverageLoss.ToString("F1") & " lbs"
68          Else
69              MsgBox("No weight loss value entered")
70          End If
71
72          ' Disables the Weight Loss button
73          btnWeightLoss.Enabled = False
74
75      End Sub
76
77      Private Sub mnuClear_Click(sender As Object, e As EventArgs) Handles mnuClear.Click
78          ' The mnuClear click event clears the ListBox object and hides
79          ' the average weight loss label. It also enables the Weight Loss button
80
81          lstWeightLoss.Items.Clear()
82          lblAverageLoss.Visible = False
83          btnWeightLoss.Enabled = True
84
85      End Sub
86
87      Private Sub mnuExit_Click(sender As Object, e As EventArgs) Handles mnuExit.Click
88          ' The mnuExit click event closes the window and exits the application
89
90          Close()
91      End Sub
92  End Class
93
```

FIGURE 6-104 (continued)

Summary

In this chapter you have learned to design and write code to implement loops and to create menus, list boxes, and an input box. The items listed in Figure 6-105 include all the new Visual Studio and Visual Basic skills you have learned in this chapter. Video 6-1 demonstrates the complete program execution.

Visual Basic Skills		
Skill	**Figure Number**	**Video Number**
Run the Completed Program	Figure 6-1	Video 6-1
Place a MenuStrip Object on the Windows Form Object	Figure 6-5	Video 6-2
Code the Exit Menu Item Event	Figure 6-12	Video 6-3
Insert a Full Standard Menu	Figure 6-14	Video 6-4
Code the InputBox Function	Figure 6-17	
Add a ListBox Object	Figure 6-24	Video 6-5
Add an Item to a ListBox Object	Figure 6-27	
Add Items to a ListBox Object During Design	Figure 6-32	Video 6-6
Assign a Selected Item from a ListBox Object	Figure 6-36	
Write Code using Compound Operators	Figure 6-39	
Write the Code for a For...Next Loop	Figure 6-42	
Use IntelliSense to Enter the Code for a For...Next Loop	Figure 6-50	Video 6-7
Write Code for a Top-controlled Do While Loop	Figure 6-56	
Use IntelliSense to Code a Do While Loop	Figure 6-59	Video 6-8
Write Code for a Bottom-Controlled Do While Loop	Figure 6-62	
Write Code for a Top-Controlled Do Until Loop	Figure 6-65	
Write Code for a Bottom-Controlled Do Until Loop	Figure 6-67	
Avoid Infinite Loops	Figure 6-69	
Prime a Loop	Figure 6-70	
Validate Data	Figure 6-73	
Create a Nested Loop	Figure 6-74	
Set a Breakpoint and Use a DataTip	Figure 6-76	Video 6-9
Publish an Application with ClickOnce Deployment	Figure 6-87	Video 6-10

FIGURE 6-105

Learn Online

Reinforcement activities and resources are available at no additional cost on *www.cengagebrain.com*. Visit *www.cengage.com/ct/studentdownload* for detailed instructions about accessing the resources available at the Student Companion Site.

Knowledge Check

1. Write a statement that displays the default value of 12 in the input box shown in Figure 6-106 and assigns the return value from the InputBox function to a variable named strMovieCount with the message Number of Instant Queue Movies with the title Hulu Plus.

FIGURE 6-106

2. Write compound operators for the following equations:

   a. intTouchdown = intTouchdown + 6

   b. dblSquare = dblSquare ^ 2

   c. strFast = strFast & "Comet"

3. Write For...Next loops that calculate the sum of the following ranges and assign their sum to a variable named intSum:

   a. The first 100 numbers starting with 1

   b. The even numbers beginning at 10 and ending with 50

   c. The numbers 20, 30, 40, 50, and 60

4. Find the errors in the following For...Next header statements:

   a. For intCounter = "1" To "19"

   b. For intNumber = 98 To 71 Step 2

   c. For intValue = 12 To 52 Step −4

   d. For strCount = −15 To 5 Step 5

(continues)

5. Explain the purpose of placing an ampersand before or within a MenuStrip item.

6. Write the command to clear a ListBox object named lstBaseballPlayers.

7. Write a command to add your favorite sports team to a ListBox object named lstFavoriteTeam.

8. Using a compound operator, write an assignment statement to increment the value in intAmount by 7.

9. Using a compound operator, write an assignment statement to decrease the value in intCounter by 4.5.

10. Using a compound operator, write an assignment statement to increment the value in intQuantity by 10.

11. Write a top-controlled Do Until loop with an empty body that would continue until intValue is greater than 19.

12. Write a bottom-controlled Do While loop with an empty body that continues while the user enters "Yes" into the strContinue variable.

13. Write a Do While loop to validate that the user enters a nonzero integer into an input box for a variable named intDenominator.

14. Is the For...Next loop top-controlled or bottom-controlled?

15. Write the code for an infinite Do Until loop with the variable intInfinite.

16. Which loop should be used if you know the required number of times the loop will be executed?

17. What is the fewest number of times a top-controlled Do Until loop is executed?

18. Write a data validation Do loop to check that the variable intAge entered from an input box is between 1 and 115.

19. A loop inside another loop is called a _____ _____.

20. When you insert standard items in a MenuStrip object, what File menu items are automatically created by default?

1. The loop shown in Figure 6-107 should repeat 10 times. If it will not repeat 10 times, change the code so it will.

```
7        For intRepeat = 20 To 10
8            MsgBox("The value is " & intRepeat.ToString("C0"))
9        Next
```

FIGURE 6-107

2. What output does the code shown in Figure 6-108 produce? How would you change the code to produce a list box containing the values 12–20?

```
15          intRate = 12
16          Do While intRate <= 10
17              lstDisplay.Items.Add(intRate)
18              intRate += 1
19          Loop
```

FIGURE 6-108

3. What is the output of the code shown in Figure 6-109?

```
5           Dim intAdd As Integer
6           Dim intOuterLoop As Integer
7           Dim intInnerLoop As Integer
8
9           intAdd = 0
10          For intOuterLoop = 1 To 8
11              For intInnerLoop = 3 To 7
12                  intAdd += 1
13              Next
14          Next
            MsgBox.Show("The final value is " & intAdd.ToString())
```

FIGURE 6-109

4. What is the output of the code shown in Figure 6-110?

```
33          Dim intValue As Integer
34
35          intValue = 2
36          Do While intValue <= 9
37              lstDisplay.Items.Add(intValue & " " & intValue ^ 3)
38              intValue += 2
39          Loop
```

FIGURE 6-110

(continues)

5. Fix the errors in the loop shown in Figure 6-111.

```
41          Dim intStart As Integer = 8
42
43          Loop
44          intStart = +4
45          Do While intStart < 24
```

FIGURE 6-111

6. What is the output of the code shown in Figure 6-112?

```
53          intCount = 40
54          Do Until intCount < 26
55              intCount -= 2
56              lstCount.Items.Add(intCount)
57          Loop
```

FIGURE 6-112

7. Fix the errors in the code shown in Figure 6-113.

```
5           Dim decCost As Decimal = 3.5D
6
7           Do Until decCost > 10.5D
8               MsgBox("The cost is now " & decCost.ToString("F1"))
9               decCost -= 0.5
10          Loop
```

FIGURE 6-113

8. In the example shown in Figure 6-114, you want the code to count the odd numbers from 1 to 99. What is missing?

```
66          Dim intOddNumber As Integer = 1
67
68          Do While intOddNumber <= 99
69              lstDisplay.Items.Add("Odd Numbers: " & intOddNumber.ToString())
70          Loop
```

FIGURE 6-114

Program Analysis

1. What is the value of lblResult after the code shown in Figure 6-115 is executed?

```
73          Dim intCounter As Integer = -20
74
75          Do While intCount < 25
76              intCount += 5
77              lblResult.Text &= intCount.ToString() & " "
78          Loop
```

FIGURE 6-115

2. What is the value of lblResult after the code shown in Figure 6-116 is executed?

```
80          Dim intCountIt As Integer
81
82          intCountIt = 6
83          Do
84              intCountIt += 3
85              lblResult.Text &= intCountIt.ToString() & " "
86          Loop Until intCountIt = 21
```

FIGURE 6-116

3. Rewrite the top-controlled Do While loop shown in Figure 6-117 as a top-controlled Do Until loop.

```
88          Dim intQuantity As Integer
89
90          intQuantity = -5
91          Do While intQuantity < 30
92              intQuantity += 5
93          Loop
```

FIGURE 6-117

4. Convert the Do loop shown in Figure 6-118 to a For...Next loop.

```
95          Dim intIncrease As Integer
96
97          intIncrease = 10
98          Do While intIncrease < 40
99              lstDisplay.Items.Add(intIncrease)
100             intIncrease += 2
101         Loop
```

FIGURE 6-118

(continues)

5. How many times will the inner statement inside the nested loop in Figure 6-119 be executed?

```
103          For intOuterLoop = 3 To 5
104              For intInnerLoop = 6 To 10
105                  lstDays.Items.Add("Value: " & intOuterLoop.ToString() & _
106                      " Count: " & intInnerLoop.ToString())
107              Next
108          Next
```

FIGURE 6-119

6. How many times will the loop in Figure 6-120 be executed?

```
110          Dim intQuantitySold As Integer
111          Dim decTax As Decimal
112
113          intQuantitySold = 1
114          Do Until intQuantitySold = 5
115              decTax = intQuantitySold * 0.07
116              lstDisplay.Items.Add("Tax Amount: " & decTax.ToString())
117              intQuantitySold += 1
118          Loop
```

FIGURE 6-120

7. Write a For...Next loop that adds the odd numbers 1 through 49 and assigns their sum to the variable intSum. The program should start with the lines shown in Figure 6-121 (use the variables shown in lines 120–123 in your code).

```
120          Dim intLoopValue As Integer
121          Dim intStartValue As Integer
122          Dim intEndValue As Integer
123          Dim intSum As Integer
124
125          intStartValue = 1
126          intEndValue = 49
127          intSum = 0
```

FIGURE 6-121

Case Programming Assignments

Complete one or more of the following case programming assignments. Submit the program and materials you create to your instructor. The level of difficulty is indicated for each case programming assignment.

●   = Easiest
●● = Intermediate
●●● = Challenging

1 ●

TOTAL SNOWFALL IN BUFFALO

Design a Windows application and write the code that will execute according to the program requirements shown in Figure 6-122. Before writing the code, create an event planning document for each event in the program. The Use Case Definition document is shown in Figure 6-123 on the following page. The completed user interface is shown in Figure 6-124 on the following page.

REQUIREMENTS DOCUMENT

Date Submitted:	March 17, 2015
Application Title:	Total Snowfall in Buffalo
Purpose:	This Windows application is written for the city of Buffalo to compute the total snowfall for the months of October through April.
Program Procedures:	In a Windows application, the user enters up to seven monthly snowfall amounts to compute the total snowfall for Buffalo.
Algorithms, Processing, and Conditions:	1. The user enters up to seven monthly snowfall totals in inches in an InputBox object.
	2. Each month's total snowfall is displayed in a ListBox object.
	3. After seven months of snowfall totals are entered, the total snowfall is calculated and displayed.
	4. A File menu contains a Clear and an Exit option. The Clear menu item clears the total snowfall and the seven values representing the monthly snowfall totals. The Exit menu item closes the application.
	5. If the user taps or clicks the Cancel button in the input box before entering seven values, compute the total for the number of months entered.
	6. If the user taps or clicks the Cancel button before entering any snowfall values, display a message indicating the user did not enter a value.
Notes and Restrictions:	1. Nonnumeric values should not be accepted.
	2. Negative values should not be accepted.
	3. The average total snowfall should be rounded to the nearest tenth of an inch.
Comments:	1. The application allows decimal entries.
	2. Obtain an image for this program from CengageBrain.com. The name of the image file is Snowfall.

FIGURE 6-122

(continues)

Case Programming Assignments

Total Snowfall in Buffalo (continued)

USE CASE DEFINITION

1. The Windows application opens with the heading "Buffalo Total Snowfall," a ListBox object that displays the monthly snowfall amounts, an image, and a Button object that allows the user to begin entering the monthly snowfall.
2. A menu bar displays the File menu, which has two menu items: Clear and Exit.
3. The user enters up to seven values in an InputBox object, with each value representing one month of snowfall in inches.
4. The program asks the user for the monthly snowfall again if the value is a negative number or the entry is a nonnumeric value.
5. The program displays the total monthly snowfall rounded to one decimal place.
6. The user can clear the input and the result by tapping or clicking the Clear menu item, and then can repeat Steps 3–5. If the user taps or clicks the Cancel button in the input box, the average for the values entered is calculated. If the user did not enter any values, the program displays an appropriate message.
7. The user taps or clicks the Exit menu item to close the application.

FIGURE 6-123

FIGURE 6-124

2 WHERE OUR STUDENTS LIVE

Design a Windows application and write the code that will execute according to the program requirements shown in Figure 6-125. Before writing the code, create an event planning document for each event in the program. The Use Case Definition document is shown in Figure 6-126 on the following page. The completed user interface is shown in Figure 6-127 on the following page.

REQUIREMENTS DOCUMENT

Date Submitted:	July 31, 2015
Application Title:	Where Our Students Live
Purpose:	This Windows application finds the average distance from a school to the homes of students from all over the world.
Program Procedures:	In a Windows application, 10 students enter the distance from their home to their school and the average distance is displayed.
Algorithms, Processing, and Conditions:	1. The user taps or clicks the Enter Mileage button to enter the distance that the student lives from the campus.
	2. Each distance in miles is displayed in a ListBox object.
	3. After 10 distances have been entered, the average is displayed.
	4. A File menu contains a Clear and an Exit option. The Clear menu item clears the average and the 10 individual distance values. The Exit menu item closes the application.
	5. If the user taps or clicks the Cancel button in the input box after entering one distance but before entering 10 distance values, use the distances the user entered for the calculations.
	6. If the user taps or clicks the Cancel button before entering any distance values, display an appropriate message.
Notes and Restrictions:	1. The result should include two places after the decimal point.
	2. Nonnumeric values should not be accepted.
	3. Negative numbers should not be accepted.
Comments:	1. The application allows decimal entries.
	2. Obtain an image for this program from CengageBrain.com. The name of the image file is World.`

FIGURE 6-125

(continues)

Where Our Students Live (continued)

USE CASE DEFINITION

1. The Windows application opens, displaying Where Our Students Live as the heading, a ListBox object that will display the distance in miles from students' homes to their schools, and a Button object that allows the user to enter the distance.
2. A menu bar displays the File menu, which has two menu items: Clear and Exit.
3. In an InputBox object, the user enters up to 10 distances in miles from students' homes to their schools.
4. The program asks the user for the distance again if the value is a negative or nonnumeric number.
5. The program displays the average distance to 2 decimal places.
6. The user taps or clicks the Clear menu item to clear the input and the result.
7. If the user taps or clicks the Cancel button in the input box before entering 10 distance values, the program uses the mileage entered for calculations. If the user entered no distance values, an appropriate message is displayed.
8. The user taps or clicks the Exit menu item to close the application.

FIGURE 6-126

© 2014 Cengage Learning

FIGURE 6-127

© Robert Churchill/the Agency Collection/Getty Images

3 BOWLING SCOREBOARD

Design a Windows application and write the code that will execute according to the program requirements shown in Figure 6-128. Before writing the code, create an event planning document for each event in the program. The Use Case Definition document is shown in Figure 6-129 on the following page. The completed user interface is shown in Figure 6-130 on the following page.

REQUIREMENTS DOCUMENT

Date Submitted: November 3, 2015

Application Title: Bowling Scoreboard

Purpose: This application calculates the score of each frame during a bowling game for one person.

Program Procedures: In a Windows application, the user enters the score of each frame to display the total on the scoreboard after 10 frames of bowling.

Algorithms, Processing, and Conditions:
1. The user taps or clicks the Enter Score button in an InputBox object to enter a score after each frame in a game.
2. The score for each frame and the running total is displayed in a ListBox.
3. After the user taps or clicks the Cancel button in the InputBox object to end the game scoring, the total final score is displayed.
4. A File menu contains a Clear and an Exit option. The Clear menu item clears the result and the frame scores. The Exit menu item closes the application.

Notes and Restrictions:
1. Nonnumeric values should not be accepted.
2. A negative value should not be accepted.

Comments: Obtain an image for this program from CengageBrain.com. The name of the image file is Bowling.

FIGURE 6-128

(continues)

Case Programming Assignments

Bowling Scoreboard (continued)

USE CASE DEFINITION

1. The Windows application opens with a heading, a Bowling Scoreboard subheading, a ListBox object that will display the frame scores throughout the game, and a Button object that allows the user to enter the scores.
2. A menu bar displays the File menu, which has two menu items: Clear and Exit.
3. In an InputBox object, the user enters points scored in each bowling frame.
4. The program asks the user for the score again if the value is a negative or nonnumeric number.
5. The program displays the running total score.
6. The program displays the final score when the user taps or clicks the Cancel button in the input box.
7. The user taps or clicks the Clear menu item to clear the input and the result.
8. The user taps or clicks the Exit menu item to close the application.

FIGURE 6-129

FIGURE 6-130

Case Programming Assignments

4 ●●
PENNY A DAY OR NICKEL A DAY

Design a Windows application and write the code that will execute according to the program requirements shown in Figure 6-131. Before writing the code, create an event planning document for each event in the program. Create a Use Case Definition document for the application.

REQUIREMENTS DOCUMENT

Date Submitted: June 21, 2014

Application Title: Penny a Day or Nickel a Day

Purpose: This Windows application finds the amount of your monthly pay if you are paid a penny or nickel for the first workday and the pay is doubled each subsequent workday. New employees are paid a penny for the first workday and experienced employees are paid a nickel for the first day.

Program Procedures: In a Windows application, the user enters the number of workdays in a monthly pay period and the pay for the first day. The program calculates and displays the amount of pay for the pay period.

Algorithms, Processing, and Conditions:
1. The user enters the number of days in the pay period.
2. The user selects a RadioButton object to indicate the pay amount for the first day: a penny or a nickel.
3. After the user enters the number of days and pay for the first day, the total amount earned is calculated and displayed.
4. A File menu contains a Clear and an Exit option. The Clear menu item clears the result and the RadioButton object. The Exit menu item closes the application.

Notes and Restrictions:
1. Nonnumeric values should not be accepted.
2. Negative values should not be accepted.
3. The minimum number of workdays in the pay period is 19 days for new employees and 16 days for experienced employees. The maximum number of workdays in a pay period is 22 days.

Comments: n/a

FIGURE 6-131

5 •• VACATION DISTANCE CALCULATOR

Design a Windows application and write the code that will execute according to the program requirements shown in Figure 6-132. Before writing the code, create an event planning document for each event in the program. Create a Use Case Definition document for the application.

REQUIREMENTS DOCUMENT

Date Submitted:	December 5, 2014
Application Title:	Vacation Distance Calculator
Purpose:	This application computes the number of miles traveled given the speed limit and the number of days traveled while driving cross country.
Program Procedures:	In a Windows application, enter the speed limit and the number of days you plan to travel across the country. You will enter the number of hours you would like to drive for each of the days, based on places you plan to visit and other factors. For example, the first day you plan to drive only four hours because you are driving after work. The application displays the distance that you are able to travel for the entire trip based on the speed limit and the hours driven.
Algorithms, Processing, and Conditions:	1. The application opens and displays a title. Enter the speed limit and the number of days you plan to drive.
	2. Tap or click the Distance button to enter the number of hours you plan to drive each day. The resulting total number of miles you plan to drive over the entire trip will be displayed.
	3. A File menu contains a Clear and an Exit option. The Clear menu item clears the result, the entered number of miles, and the time traveled. The Exit menu item closes the application.
Notes and Restrictions:	1. Nonnumeric values should not be accepted.
	2. The number of hours for one day of travel should not exceed 20 hours.
Comments:	The application allows decimal entries.

FIGURE 6-132

Case Programming Assignments

6 ••
NEXT DECADE PAY CALCULATOR

Design a Windows application and write the code that will execute according to the program requirements shown in Figure 6-133. Before writing the code, create an event planning document for each event in the program. Create a Use Case Definition document for the application.

REQUIREMENTS DOCUMENT

Date Submitted: August 23, 2014

Application Title: The Next Decade Pay Calculator

Purpose: This Windows application computes the amount of money an employee will earn over the next decade based on a raise, which is a percentage amount.

Program Procedures: In a Windows application, the user enters her present wage per hour and the raise percentage amount per year to compute her yearly pay over the next 10 years.

Algorithms, Processing, and Conditions:
1. The application opens, displaying a title and requesting the present amount of pay per hour and the expected raise percentage per year.
2. When the Compute Future Pay button is tapped or clicked, the program calculates the yearly pay based on 40 hours per week and 52 weeks per year. The raise increases each amount after the first year.
3. The yearly amount of pay earned is displayed for the next 10 years.
4. A File menu contains a Clear and an Exit option. The Clear menu item clears the result. The Exit menu item closes the application.

Notes and Restrictions:
1. Nonnumeric values should not be accepted.
2. Negative numbers should not be allowed.

Comments: The application allows decimal entries.

FIGURE 6-133

© 2014 Cengage Learning

7 • • •
FACTORIAL MATH

Create a requirements document and a Use Case Definition document and design a Windows application based on the case project shown in Figure 6-134:

Most calculators have an operation called a "factorial," which is shown on a calculator key as an exclamation point. For example, 5! (5 factorial) multiplies 5 * 4 * 3 * 2 * 1 to calculate the result of 120. Using loops to compute the factorial, display the following factorials in a ListBox object:

1! 1
2! 2
3! 6
4! 24
5! 120
6! 720
7! 5040
8! 40320
9! 362880

FIGURE 6-134

8 ●●● GALAXY HOTEL

Create a requirements document and a Use Case Definition document and design a Windows application based on the case project shown in Figure 6-135:

The Galaxy Hotel asks you to write a Windows application that computes the occupancy rate of the hotel. Occupancy rate is a percentage that is equal to the number of rooms sold divided by the total number of rooms available. The hotel has seven floors. The user should use an Input-Box function to respond to two questions about each floor: How many rooms are occupied on that floor? How many rooms on the floor are vacant? Display which floor you are asking about in each question. Display how many rooms are occupied and vacant on each floor in a ListBox object. After the user has entered all the information, display the following results: the total number of rooms at the hotel, the number of occupied rooms, and the number of vacant rooms. Also display the occupancy rate as a percentage, such as 61%. Nonnumeric values should not be accepted. Do not accept negative numbers. Publish the application after testing it.

FIGURE 6-135

9

● ● ●

BUYING A GAMING COMPUTER

Create a requirements document and a Use Case Definition document and design a Windows application based on the case project shown in Figure 6-136:

The newest gaming computer costs $5000 for a 31-inch screen, two 1 TB hard drives, a metallic case, and a blazing fast processor. Ten years ago, your grandmother gave you $2500. The money has been in a savings CD that earns compound interest of 7.5 percent annually. Write a Windows application that allows you to enter the amount of money in your savings account, the interest rate, and a number of years. Display a ListBox object for each year and the amount of money in the account at the end of that year. Determine whether you have saved enough money for the gaming computer. Nonnumeric and negative values should not be accepted. Debug and then publish the application. *Hint*: The formula for compound interest for one year is: Amount = Principal * (1 + Rate). For 10 years of compound interest, this formula should be executed 10 times with the principal increasing to the new amount each year.

FIGURE 6-136

APPENDIX A

Unicode

The 256 characters and symbols that are represented by ASCII and EBCDIC codes are sufficient for English and western European languages (see Figure A-1 on the next page), but do not provide enough characters for Asian and other languages that use different alphabets. Further compounding the problem is that many of these languages use symbols, called ideograms, to represent multiple words and ideas. One solution to the problem of accommodating universal alphabets is Unicode. Unicode is a 16-bit coding scheme that can represent all the world's current, classic, and historical languages in more than 65,000 characters and symbols. In Unicode, 30,000 codes are reserved for future use, such as ancient languages, and 6,000 codes are reserved for private use. Existing ASCII coded data is fully compatible with Unicode because the first 256 codes are the same. Unicode is implemented in several operating systems, including Windows 7, Windows Vista, Windows XP, Mac OS X, and Linux. To view a complete Unicode chart, see www.unicode.org.

UNICODE KEYBOARD CHARACTERS

Decimal	Hexadecimal	Octal	Binary	Character
32	20	040	00100000	
33	21	041	00100001	!
34	22	042	00100010	"
35	23	043	00100010	#
36	24	044	00100100	$
37	25	045	00100101	%
38	26	046	00100110	&
39	27	047	00100111	'
40	28	050	00101000	(
41	29	051	00101001	)
42	2A	052	00101010	*
43	2B	053	00101011	+
44	2C	054	00101100	,
45	2D	055	00101101	-
46	2E	056	00101110	.
47	2F	057	00101111	/
48	30	060	00110000	0
49	31	061	00110001	1
50	32	062	00110010	2
51	33	063	00110011	3
52	34	064	00110100	4
53	35	065	00110101	5
54	36	066	00110110	6
55	37	067	00110111	7
56	38	070	00111000	8
57	39	071	00111001	9
58	3A	072	00111010	:

FIGURE A-1 (continued)

Decimal	Hexadecimal	Octal	Binary	Character
59	3B	073	00111011	;
60	3C	074	00111100	<
61	3D	075	00111101	=
62	3E	076	00111110	>
63	3F	077	00111111	?
64	40	100	01000000	@
65	41	101	01000001	A
66	42	102	01000010	B
67	43	103	01000011	C
68	44	104	01000100	D
69	45	105	01000101	E
70	46	106	01000110	F
71	47	107	01000111	G
72	48	110	01001000	H
73	49	111	01001001	I
74	4A	112	01001010	J
75	4B	113	01001011	K
76	4C	114	01001100	L
77	4D	115	01001101	M
78	4E	116	01001110	N
79	4F	117	01001111	O
80	50	120	01010000	P
81	51	121	01010001	Q
82	52	122	01010010	R
83	53	123	01010011	S
84	54	124	01010100	T
85	55	125	01010101	U
86	56	126	01010110	V

FIGURE A-1 (continued)

Decimal	Hexadecimal	Octal	Binary	Character
87	57	127	01010111	W
88	58	130	01011000	X
89	59	131	01011001	Y
90	5A	132	01011010	Z
91	5B	133	01011011	[
92	5C	134	01011100	\
93	5D	135	01011101	]
94	5E	136	01011110	^
95	5F	137	01011111	]
96	60	140	01100000	,
97	61	141	01100001	a
98	62	142	01100010	b
99	63	143	01100011	c
100	64	144	01100100	d
101	65	145	01100101	e
102	66	146	01100110	f
103	67	147	01100111	g
104	68	150	01101000	h
105	69	151	01101001	i
106	6A	152	01101010	j
107	6B	153	01101011	k
108	6C	154	01101100	l
109	6D	155	01101101	m
110	6E	156	01101110	n
111	6F	157	01101111	o
112	70	160	01110000	p
113	71	161	01110001	q

FIGURE A-1 (continued)

Decimal	Hexadecimal	Octal	Binary	Character
114	72	162	01110010	r
115	73	163	01110011	s
116	74	164	01110100	t
117	75	165	01110101	u
118	76	166	01110110	v
119	77	167	01110111	w
120	78	170	01111000	x
121	79	171	01111001	y
122	7A	172	01111010	z
123	7B	173	01111011	{
124	7C	174	01111100	|
125	7D	175	01111101	}
126	7E	176	01111110	~
127	7F	177	01111111	DEL

FIGURE A-1 (continued)

The My Namespace

Rapid application development (RAD) uses a number of tools to help build graphical user interfaces that would normally take a large development effort. One of the Visual Basic RAD tool innovations introduced in the 2005 version and continued with the 2012 version is the **My** namespace. The My namespace provides a shortcut to several categories of information and functionality and is organized so that you can use IntelliSense to find code elements you use often. Microsoft created the My namespace to make it easier to execute common code patterns that you use when developing .NET applications. By providing a shortcut to the most commonly used .NET Framework Class Library classes and methods, the My namespace helps you retrieve settings and resources that your application requires.

The My namespace feature provides rapid access to the classes and methods through the My classes shown in the table in Figure B-1.

Object	Allows Access to
My.Application	The application information and its services such as name, version, log, and current directory.
My.Computer	The host computer and its resources, and services. My.Computer provides access to a number of very important resources including My.Computer.Network, My.Computer.FileSystem, and My.Computer.Printers.
My.Forms	All the forms in the current project.
My.Request	The current Web request.
My.Resources	The resource elements.
My.Response	The current Web response.
My.Settings	The configuration settings of the user and application level. This object enables great personalization without writing many lines of code.

FIGURE B-1 (continues)

Object	Allows Access to
My.User	The security context of the current authenticated user. The My.User object analyzes the user at runtime, which assists security issues.
My.WebServices	The XML Web services referenced by the current project. Consuming Web services is a necessary ability for modern Web applications.

FIGURE B-1 (continued)

Coding Examples

My is a wrapper that makes accessing the advanced features of .NET easier. For example, you can use the class **My.Application** to determine the version of the current application by using the line of code shown in Figure B-2. Figure B-3 shows the dialog box that displays the version number. You often need to know the latest version of the application to determine whether the application is in final form.

```
MsgBox(My.Application.Info.Version.ToString())
```

FIGURE B-2

FIGURE B-3

The **My.Application** class also can be used to display the current setting of the culture of a computer. Figure B-4 shows the code you can use to display the culture, which is the language that the computer has been assigned in the language settings. In Figure B-5, the culture is set to English – United States.

```
MsgBox(My.Application.Culture.ToString())
```

FIGURE B-4

FIGURE B-5

Another class called **My.Computer** can return information about the computer on which the application is deployed, as determined at run time. The My.Computer class provides properties for manipulating computer components such as audio, the clock, the keyboard, and the file system. The My.Computer class can play .wav files and system sounds using the Audio object. You can use the My.Computer.Audio.Play and My.Computer.Audio.PlaySystemSound methods to play .wav sound files and system sounds. The code shown in Figure B-6 plays a .wav file named beachmusic.wav.

```
My.Computer.Audio.Play("C:\beachmusic.wav")
```

FIGURE B-6

A .wav file also can be played in the background when a file named AudioPlayMode.Background is specified, as shown in Figure B-7.

```
My.Computer.Audio.Play("C:\blues.wav", _
            AudioPlayMode.Background)
```

FIGURE B-7

The My.Computer class can access the Clipboard and show what is temporarily stored in the system buffer. For example, if you copied the phrase, "Examples of the My.Computer Class", the phrase would be stored in the Clipboard system buffer of the computer. Use the code shown in Figure B-8 to display the contents of the Clipboard in a dialog box as shown in Figure B-9.

```
MsgBox(My.Computer.Clipboard.GetText())
```

FIGURE B-8

FIGURE B-9

The My.Computer class can access an object that provides properties for displaying the current local date and time according to the system clock by entering the code shown in B-10. Figure B-11 on the next page shows the dialog box that displays the system date and time.

```
MsgBox(My.Computer.Clock.LocalTime.ToString())
```

FIGURE B-10

FIGURE B-11

Another My.Computer class determines the current state of the keyboard, such as which keys are pressed, including the CAPS LOCK or NUM LOCK key. The code shown in Figure B-12 provides a true result if the CAPS LOCK key has been pressed. Figure B-13 shows the dialog box that displays the result.

```
MsgBox(My.Computer.Keyboard.CapsLock.ToString())
```

FIGURE B-12

FIGURE B-13

The My.Computer.Mouse class allows you to determine the state and hardware characteristics of the attached mouse, such as the number of buttons or whether the mouse has a wheel. The code shown in Figure B-14 determines if the mouse has a wheel, and Figure B-15 shows the dialog box that displays the result.

```
MsgBox(My.Computer.Mouse.WheelExists.ToString())
```

FIGURE B-14

FIGURE B-15

The My.Computer.Network class interacts with the network to which the computer is connected. For example, if the code in Figure B-16 is entered in the code window, the result would be true, as shown in Figure B-17, if the computer is connected to an intranet or Internet network.

```
MsgBox(My.Computer.Network.IsAvailable.ToString())
```

FIGURE B-16

FIGURE B-17

You can use the My.Computer.Network class to ping another computer. Ping is a basic network function that allows you to verify a particular IP address exists and can accept requests. Ping is used diagnostically to ensure that a host computer you are trying to reach is operating. The code shown in Figure B-18 determines if the IP address is active, and the dialog box shown in Figure B-19 displays the result.

```
MsgBox(My.Computer.Network.Ping("71.2.41.1"))
```

FIGURE B-18

FIGURE B-19

The My.Computer.Screen object can be used to determine many properties of the screen connected to the computer system. You can determine the properties of each monitor attached to the computer system, including the name, the brightness of the screen, and the working area size. The number of bits per pixel can be determined by the code shown in Figure B-20. In a digitized image, the number of bits used to represent the brightness contained in each pixel is called bits per pixel. Bits per pixel is a term that represents the brightness of the screen resolution. Figure B-21 shows the result of the code.

```
MsgBox(My.Computer.Screen.BitsPerPixel.ToString())
```

FIGURE B-20

FIGURE B-21

The My.Computer.Screen class also can display the current resolution of the user screen, as shown in Figures B-22 and B-23 on the next page.

```
MsgBox(My.Computer.Screen.Bounds.Size.ToString())
```

FIGURE B-22

FIGURE B-23

Another class called **My.User** allows you to gather information about the current user. The code example in Figure B-24 shows how to use the **My.User.Name** property to view the user's login name. An application uses Windows authentication by default, so **My.User** returns the Windows information about the user who started the application, as shown in Figure B-25.

```
MsgBox(My.User.Name)
```

FIGURE B-24

FIGURE B-25

The My namespace also provides a simpler way of opening multiple forms in the same project by using the My.Forms object. If the project includes more than one form, the code shown in Figure B-26 opens a second form named Form2.

```
My.Forms.Form2.Show()
```

FIGURE B-26

Naming Conventions

The table in Figure C-1 displays the common data types used in Visual Basic 2012 with the recommended naming convention for the three-character prefix preceding variable names of the data type.

Data Type	Sample Value	Memory	Range of Values	Prefix
Integer	48	4 bytes	−2,147,483,648 to +2,147,483,647	int
Double	5.3452307	8 bytes	−1.79769313486232E308 to +1.79769313486232E308	dbl
Decimal	3.14519	16 bytes	Decimal values that may have up to 29 significant digits	dec
Char	'?' or 'C'	2 bytes	Single character	chr
String	"The Dow is up .03%"	Depends on number of characters	Letters, numbers, symbols	str
Boolean	True or False	Typically 2 bytes; depends on implementing platform	True or False	bln

FIGURE C-1

The table in Figure C-2 displays the less common data types used in Visual Basic 2012 with the recommended naming convention for the three-character prefix preceding variable names of the data type.

Data Type	Sample Value	Memory	Range of Values	Prefix
Byte	7	1 byte	0 to 255	byt
Date	April 22, 2014	8 bytes	0:00:00 (midnight) on January 1, 0001 through 11:59:59 PM on December 31, 9999	dtm
Long	345,234,567	8 bytes	$-9,223,372,036,854,775,808$ to $+9,223,372,036,854,775,807$	lng
Object	Holds a reference	4 bytes (32-bit) 8 bytes (64-bit)	A memory address	obj
Short	16,567	2 bytes	$-32,768$ to $32,767$	shr
Single	234,654.1246	4 bytes	$-3.4028235E+38$ to $-1.401298E-45$ for negative values and $1.401298E-45$ to $3.4028235E+38$ for positive values	sng

FIGURE C-2

Form Object Naming Conventions

The table in Figure C-3 displays the prefix naming conventions for Form objects. The three-letter prefixes used before variables names especially are helpful when you use IntelliSense.

Object Type	Prefix	Object Type	Prefix
Button	btn	ListBox	lst
Calendar	cld	MenuStrip	mnu
CheckBox	chk	NumericUpDown	nud
ComboBox	cbo	PictureBox	pic
CompareValidator	cmv	RadioButton	rad
DataGrid	dgd	RangeValidator	rgv
DateTimePicker	dtp	RegularExpressionValidator	rev
DropDownList	ddl	RequiredFieldValidator	rfv
Form	frm	TextBox	txt
GroupBox	grp	ValidationSummary	vsm
Label	lbl		

FIGURE C-3

INDEX

Note: **Boldface** page numbers indicate key terms.

A

AbortRetryIgnore message button type, 298
Accept button, 205–206
    Calculate Cost button as, 257
AcceptButton property, 205–206, 257
Account Balance label, 7, 9
Account Number text box, 7
accumulators, **382**
actions
    repeating until condition true, 395–397
    undoing and redoing, 57
Action Tags, 199, 201, **372**
ActiveX Data Objects (ADO), 23
addition arithmetic operator (+), 228, **229**–230
addition compound operator (+=), 383
Add procedure, 377
ADO. *See* ActiveX Data Objects (ADO)
ADO.NET 4.5, 23–24
Airline Snack Selection program, 108, 186
Align command, 64
alignment, **63**–65
Align submenu, 64–65, 88, 90
All Programs command, 34
All Programs submenu, 34, 83, 248, 334
American Standard for Information Interchange (ASCII),
    APP 1
AndAlso logical operator, 321
And logical operator, **318**–319, 326
applications, **5**
    current version, APP 8
    types, 27
apps, **2,** 3
arguments, **224**
arithmetic expressions
    comparing to constant or data type, 308–309
    literals, 229–230
    variables, 223
arithmetic operations, 10–11, 190, 226–245
    answer use, 230

arithmetic operators, **228**–233
    assignment statements, 227
    Digital Downloads program, 226–227
    forcing order of operations with
        parentheses (), 234
    hierarchy, 233–234
    multiple in assignment statements, 233
arithmetic operators, **228**–233
    addition arithmetic operator (+), 228, **229**–230
    division arithmetic operator (/), 228, 231
    exponentiation arithmetic operator (^), 228, 232–233
    integer division arithmetic operator (\), 228, 231–232
    MOD arithmetic operator (modulus), 228, 231, 232
    multiplication arithmetic operator (*), 228, 231
    subtraction arithmetic operator (-), 228, **230**
ARROW key, 137
ASCII. *See* American Standard for
    Information Interchange
As keyword, 208, 210
ASP.NET 4.5
    classes, 24
    Web designer interface, 25
assignment statements, **133, 209**–214, 215
    addition, 229–230
    arithmetic operations, 227
    assigning null length string ("") to Text property, 238
    automatically converting data types, 226
    compound operators, 382–384
    division, 231–232
    equal sign (=) and, 209
    exponentiation, 232–233
    integer value substituted in procedure, 225
    literals, **219**–220
    multiple arithmetic operations, 233
    multiplication, 231
    subtraction, 230
    using variables before declaring, 222
Audio object, APP 9
AudioPlayMode.Background file, APP 9
Auto Hide button, **40,** 83
AutoSize option, 123